THINK COLLEGE!

Postsecondary Education Options
for Students with Intellectual Disabilities

Postsecondary Education Options
for Students with Intellectual Disabilities

by

Meg Grigal, Ph.D.
Senior Research Associate
TransCen, Inc.
Rockville, Maryland

Debra Hart, M.Ed.
Education Coordinator
Institute for Community Inclusion
University of Massachusetts
Boston, Massachusetts

with invited contributors

·P·A·U·L·H·
BROOKES
PUBLISHING CO. ®

Baltimore • London • Sydney

Paul H. Brookes Publishing Co.
Post Office Box 10624
Baltimore, Maryland 21285-0624
USA

www.brookespublishing.com

Typeset by Matrix Publishing Services, York, Pennsylvania.
Manufactured in the United States of America by
Sheridan Books, Inc., Ann Arbor, Michigan.

The majority of individuals described in this book are composites of real people whose situations have been masked and are based on the authors' experiences. Names and identifying details have been changed to protect confidentiality.

The vignettes and examples in this book that were provided by parents/guardian are used by permission of the individuals described and/or their parents/guardians.

Library of Congress Cataloging-in-Publication Data

Think college! : postsecondary education options for students with intellectual
disabilities / by Meg Grigal, Debra Hart.
    p.   cm.
 Includes bibliographical references and index.
 ISBN-13: 978-1-55766-917-9 (pbk.)
 ISBN-10: 1-55766-917-1 (pbk.)
 1. People with disabilities—Education (Higher)—United States. 2. Learning
disabled—Education (Higher)—United States. I. Grigal, Meg. II. Hart, Debra,
1951–III. Title.

 LC4813.T55 2010
 371.9'0474—dc22

                                        2009034140

British Library Cataloguing in Publication data are available from the British Library.

2013   2012   2011   2010   2009

10   9   8   7   6   5   4   3   2   1

Contents

About the Authors

Meg Grigal, Ph.D., is a Senior Research Associate at TransCen Inc., where she is currently the Director and Principal Investigator of the Postsecondary Education Research Center (PERC) Project and the Co-Principal Investigator of the Center on Postsecondary Education for Students with Intellectual Disabilities. She has worked with students with disabilities, their families, and the professionals and advocates who support them in the transition process for over 20 years. For the past 10 years she has focused on the topic of postsecondary education and students with intellectual disabilities. Through this work, Dr. Grigal has provided consultation to families, school systems, and states across the country on the planning, implementation, and evaluation of services in postsecondary settings for students with intellectual disabilities. As part of the PERC Project, Dr. Grigal provides technical assistance and conducts research on exemplary practices for supporting students with intellectual disabilities ages 18–21 in postsecondary settings. Prior to her work at TransCen, Inc., Dr. Grigal served as the Co-Principal Investigator and Director of On-Campus Outreach at the University of Maryland in the Department of Special Education. She is a co-author of the book *Transition Services for Students with Significant Disabilities in College and Community Settings: Strategies for Planning, Implementation, and Evaluation* and has conducted and published research in the areas of transition planning, postsecondary access, self-determination, inclusion, and the use of person centered planning techniques.

Debra Hart, M.Ed., is Director of the Education and Transition Team for the Institute for Community Inclusion at the University of Massachusetts, Boston. She has over 25 years of experience working with youth and adults with disabilities, their families, faculty, and professionals that support youth in becoming contributing valued members of their community via participation in inclusive secondary and postsecondary education and competitive employment. Over the past 12 years, Ms. Hart has directed five federal grants designed to create access to postsecondary education for youth with disabilities—including youth with intellectual disabilities. Currently, she is the Principal Investigator for two national postsecondary education grants funded by the National Institute on Disability and Rehabilitation Research (NIDRR) and the Administration on Developmental Disabilities (ADD). Together, these projects will conduct research to better understand characteristics and outcomes of postsecondary education options for youth with intellectual/developmental disabilities, provide training and technical assistance to enhance existing initiatives, and grow the choice of a postsecondary education for youth with intellectual/developmental disabilities and their families nationwide.

About the Contributors

Amy Dwyre, M.S., a Senior Associate at TransCen, Inc., is the Project Coordinator on the Postsecondary Education Research Center (PERC) project funded by the Office of Special Education Programs (OSEP) to set up technical assistance centers and collect data on college-based transition programs for students with intellectual disabilities (ID). In addition, Ms. Dwyre is working on the Center for Postsecondary Education for Individuals with Intellectual Disabilities, in partnership with the Institute on Community Inclusion at the University of Massachusetts in Boston. The Center will conduct research and disseminate information on promising practices that support individuals with intellectual disabilities so that they can gain access to and be successful in inclusive postsecondary education. Formerly, she coordinated the Baltimore Transition Connection, a 5-year federally funded transition project for students with ID on 2- and 4-year colleges and universities in Baltimore, integrating the local school system, adult service providers, the colleges and universities, and the community. Ms. Dwyre is a national trainer for TransCen in the areas of transition, marketing and job development, special education, community classroom models, and self-determination. She has a master's in rehabilitation counseling with a focus on transition and supported employment from the University of Illinois at Urbana-Champaign.

Laura T. Eisenman, Ph.D., is an Associate Professor in the School of Education at the University of Delaware. Through the University's Center for Disabilities Studies (CDS), Dr. Eisenman also coordinates the interdisciplinary Disabilities Studies Minor. Since 2000, she has been faculty liaison to a campus program for young adults with significant disabilities, a collaborative effort of CDS and local school districts. Dr. Eisenman's research centers on the transition to adult life for students with disabilities. She is currently studying the experiences of young adults and teachers in an inclusive technical high school. Her interests include understanding how schools can foster students' self-determination and the social and community experiences of young adults with significant disabilities. She is on the editorial boards of *Career Development for Exceptional Individuals* and *Review of Disability Studies*. She received her Ph.D. in Special Education from Vanderbilt University and her master's in rehabilitation counseling from University of South Florida-Tampa.

Janice Fialka, LMSW, ACSW, is a nationally recognized speaker, author, and social worker with expertise in adolescent health, parent–professional partnerships, inclusion, and disability. Ms. Fialka has directed several teen health centers in Michigan, including the Taylor Teen Health Center, which she co-founded. Currently she is the Special Projects Trainer Michigan's Part C (of IDEA) Training and Technical Assistance. Ms. Fialka speaks and writes from her dual perspectives as a seasoned social worker and as a mother of two adult children, Micah and Emma, both of whom also present and write on disability issues from their unique perspectives. Micah, who has cognitive disabilities, is a strong advocate and has been fully included in general education and his community. Ms. Fialka and her husband co-produced the award winning DVD, *Through the Same Door: Inclusion Includes College*, which documents Micah's experiences as a college

student. She has authored three books, various articles, a CD, and several po-
ems. Ms. Fialka's website www.danceofpartnership.com is a highly regarded comprehensive resource for parents and professionals. She was awarded *Social Worker
of 2007* by the Michigan chapter of the National Association of Social Workers.
In 2009, Ms. Fialka and her family received the *Family Voices Lifetime Achievement
Award* in Washington, D.C.

Stephanie Smith Lee, a Senior Policy Advisor for National Down Syndrome Society (NDSS), National Policy Center, provides technical assistance to parents, educators, and institutes of higher education on developing and implementing high
quality services for students with disabilities. Ms. Lee is project leader for a systems change project in South Carolina that is funding new model programs at
two universities. She speaks at state and national conferences and with the media. Ms. Lee also coordinates an expert group that provides advice to Congress on
this topic of providing high quality services for students with disabilities at institutes of higher education. Ms. Lee previously served as the Director of the Office
of Special Education Programs (OSEP) in the U.S. Department of Education.

Richard G. Luecking, Ed.D., is the President of TransCen, Inc., a non-profit
organization based in Rockville, Maryland, that is dedicated to improving education and employment outcomes for people with disabilities. Dr. Luecking has
held this position since 1987, when he was charged by the Board of Directors as
the organization's first employee to create improved linkages between schools,
employment service providers, government, business, and families so that youth
with disabilities experience improved post-school employment outcomes. During his tenure with the organization, he and his TransCen colleagues have been
responsible for the design and implementation of numerous model demonstration and research projects related to school-to-work transition and employment
of people with disabilities. He is the author of a range of publications on related
topics, including the book, *The Way to Work: How to Facilitate Work Experiences for
Youth in Transition* (Paul H. Brookes Publishing Co., 2009).

Karen Doneker Mancini, M.Ed., is the Director of the Disability Support Services Office at the University of Delaware. Ms. Mancini is responsible for ensuring the University's compliance to the Americans with Disabilities Act (ADA).
She has worked in this area since the institution of ADA in 1992 and has been
on multiple taskforces to consider the effective implementation of ADA on college campuses. Ms. Mancini works with students, employees, and families to assist with identifying and implementing accommodations. In addition, she provides support to build self-awareness and self-advocacy for students and staff with
disabilities. Ms. Mancini is currently studying the factors influencing the transition from high school into higher education. Her interest areas extend to understanding family support when working with students with physical and psychological disabilities and the use of technology to enhance access to higher
education. Ms. Mancini is currently completing her Ph.D. in human development and family studies at the University of Delaware. She received her master's
of education from the University of Delaware.

Maria Paiewonsky, Ed.D., is a Transition Specialist at the Institute for Community Inclusion at the University of Massachusetts, Boston. Dr. Paiewonsky has
supported numerous school districts to develop transition services that include
inclusive postsecondary education options for transition-age youth with intellectual disabilities. Through this work, Dr. Paiewonsky has assisted school districts
to create partnerships through use of local and regional student support teams,

train teachers to prepare students with an individual transition support model, and prepare families for the transition to adult supports and services. In addition to this work, Dr. Paiewonsky has coordinated two initiatives that are focused on preparing Massachusetts educators, administrators, and guidance counselors to develop a transition specialty through a series of online graduate level courses. She has also concentrated her efforts on gathering the voice and feedback of youth about their perceptions of the transition process and their inclusive college experiences using participatory action research methods coupled with multimedia tools.

Jerri Roach Ostergard is the district wide Transition Specialist for the Worcester Public Schools. She has been working in the school system for the past 10 years, initially as a high school special education teacher. While working in a self-contained classroom with students with significant disabilities, Ms. Ostergard began to focus on supporting youth in more inclusive educational experiences. For the past 8 years, she has supported transition-age youth with intellectual disabilities using an individual support model to create access to inclusive postsecondary education and employment options. In particular, Ms. Ostergard has used her skills in person centered planning with youth to drive the development of the individual services and supports that they need to be successful in inclusive community-based opportunities. She has combined her background in special education with her knowledge of adult services to enable a smoother transition for youth as they move from high school to adulthood.

Madeleine Will is the Director of the National Down Syndrome Society (NDSS) National Policy Center. Ms. Will chairs the NDSS Transition and Postsecondary Education Initiative for individuals with intellectual disabilities (ID). Technical assistance from NDSS is provided to parents, educators, and institutions of higher education in developing and implementing high-quality services. NDSS systems change efforts include funding the development of model demonstration projects for students with intellectual disabilities in New Jersey and South Carolina. Ms. Will is the former Chairperson of the President's Committee for People with Intellectual Disabilities (PCPID) and the former Assistant Secretary of the Office of Special Education and Rehabilitation Services in the U.S. Department of Education.

Foreword

The emergence of postsecondary education for students with intellectual disabilities is a cause for celebration. There is no question that the concept has captured the imagination of individuals with intellectual disabilities, their families, and institutions of higher education. This is due in part to the fact that the concept is based on the shared and deeply held belief that these students should have access to postsecondary education—and the resulting employment and independent living opportunities—just as their non-disabled peers do. In 2009, the 150 post secondary programs that exist in 31 states represent the dawn of an exciting new era of progress and achievement for people with disabilities.

The successes and advances achieved in our society during the past thirty years in public attitudes, education, pedagogy, technology, and medicine have made this postsecondary innovation possible. At the individual level, these successes spring from the patience, love, and courage of parents and families working every day to nurture and prepare their youngsters to function in a complex world. These successes also spring from the doggedness, creativity, and courage of professionals, teachers, researchers, physicians, and therapists, working day after day to understand, to heal, and to teach.

This postsecondary education innovation, emerging as it has at the beginning of the 21st century, is extremely well timed. New ideas will indeed be necessary to complete the social revolution for people with disabilities that began in the 20th century. Students who benefit from a postsecondary education can look forward to a future (research indicates that even taking one course in a post secondary education setting leads to better outcomes) that refutes the negative statistics that comprise the current reality. Data reveal that 90% of adults with intellectual disabilities were not employed; fewer than 15% participated in postsecondary education; and over 700,000 people with intellectual disabilities lived with parents aged 60 or over.

A major contributing factor explaining the lack of progress in employment among people with intellectual disabilities is the failure to understand the competence of these individuals by the majority of our countrymen. Surveys of public attitudes toward people with intellectual disabilities in our country indicate that Americans are tolerant and want to support persons with disabilities, but that there is a presumption of incompetence about people with intellectual disabilities. The rampant use of the "R" word only makes matters worse; it is not only emotionally hurtful but reinforces the presumption of incompetence and creates significant obstacles to employment—diminishing people with intellectual disabilities in the eyes of many with one hurled stigma.

Another factor contributing to unemployment and lack of independence for persons with intellectual disabilities lies in the flawed social contract that exists between our society and people with disabilities. The common understanding of this contract is that a person with a disability who needs support should receive public assistance. But in exchange for public assistance, the person with a disability must be contented with a life of enforced poverty and an absence of freedom; a crucially important requirement for the receipt of specific public benefits is that the beneficiary not have more than $2,000 in assets. As the 2004 report of the President's Committee for People with Intellectual Disabilities stated to the President, "This is a deal that fails all parties to the arrangement: the people with intellectual disabilities, their families, and the American people."

For many reasons postsecondary education is a most important key to shaping a new reality for people with disabilities. It has the exciting potential to create a future based *not* on low expectations, the can'ts and shouldn'ts, but on the high expectations of productivity and personal and economic freedom. It has the exciting potential to drive improvements in the way we prepare young students for employment and systematize skill development into curriculum, instruction, job training, and experience. It has the potential to demand change from the adult service providers so that young students are guided and seamlessly supported across programs into employment and independence. Lastly, postsecondary education has the potential to fundamentally alter perceptions of people with intellectual disabilities as the competent, capable, and productive citizens we know them to be.

Madeleine Will
Director of the National Down Syndrome Society
(NDSS) National Policy Center

Preface

WHAT'S THE POINT?

Recently, I was asked to serve as an "expert" on postsecondary education (PSE) options for student's intellectual disabilities (ID) at a national event. I met with various groups of individuals and answered their questions regarding how to implement or improve postsecondary education access for students with intellectual disabilities in their states. One man said to me, "*Yeah, I understand why students might want to take weight training or aerobics. But what is a kid like this gonna get out of taking an art history class? Why should we waste our time setting that up?*"

This is not an unusual question. . . . Actually, it's probably one of the best places to start when having a conversation about the reason for offering students with intellectual disabilities the opportunity to access postsecondary education. What's the point? Most students with intellectual disabilities will not be going to college to get a degree. Many, if not most, will not have received a high school diploma. So then why would we "waste our time" giving students like this a chance to attend a college course—especially on a topic as esoteric as art history?

The answer to this question is that the purpose of providing students with intellectual disabilities access to PSE is not limited to simply getting a student into a class, or the student learning the content of the course. While these elements are both important, the bigger picture has less to do with the classes students take and more to do the outcomes that are possible when students with ID are afforded the opportunity to access college experiences. And by college experiences, I am not referring solely to taking classes at a college. The college experience is comprised of a wide array of possible experiences; some social, some academic, and some employment. These experiences will likewise be unique for every individual who attends college. There is not one right way to do it. A student's experience will reflect their personal needs and goals. Some students will take many classes, while others choose to go part-time. Some students seek skills that will lead to employment; others may want to explore a new area of personal interest. It is in this aspect that college environments provide an array of experiences that most students with intellectual disabilities are not afforded during their tenure in public school; the chance to explore, define, and redefine personal goals related to adult learning, employment, and social connections.

Students with and without disabilities go through their primary and secondary school years taking a prescribed course of study. High school provides a few limited opportunities for students to choose a course or an elective, but even those elective classes are designed for the young adult learner—where the student is a passive respondent. Students with intellectual disabilities will likely have even fewer choices in their course options than their peers without or with other disabilities. They may be included in a variety of general education courses, but may not have much choice in which ones they can attend. They might be limited to the life skills or functional academic courses that are provided to students with significant support needs in their school district. Regardless of the type of courses they attend, all of these high school options come with a strict set of guidelines. They are provided in a high school setting; a bell will signal you when to go to class and when to leave class. The teacher provides a set of expected outcomes, and in most cases, will make all necessary modification or accommodations without any input or requests from a student. This is how high school students with intellectual disabilities are expected to learn.

The employment experiences of students with intellectual disabilities are often just as teacher directed. Most students participate in job tryouts or training experiences that they rotate through that are not connected with the student's coursework, interests, skills, or—most importantly—to a paid job that they are trying to obtain. These employment preparation experiences prepare students for adult employment experiences about as well as their high school preparation experiences prepare them to go to college. The traditional transition experiences of students with intellectual disabilities have not been demonstrated to produce great outcomes for students in adulthood. But given the opportunity, access, and support—students with ID who receive transition services in college settings can have great outcomes. Using the college campus as the platform for their education, students can learn how to access education as an adult, learn how to connect this education to a paid job, and learn how to navigate between jobs like all other adults. The option of postsecondary education for students with intellectual disabilities is ultimately just good transition planning. It allows students to engage in adult learning and working environments within a context of support and guidance. It also lays the groundwork for students to obtain the skills necessary for them to continue to access learning throughout their adult lives.

In today's public special education system, students with intellectual disabilities (and their families) are not provided with the expectation that students should continue to access adult learning after they leave high school. In most cases, students with ID have not been introduced to the possibility of attending college, or any kind of postsecondary education—academic, continuing education, or otherwise. The staff person in high school who is generally the gatekeeper to college is most often a guidance counselor. However, students with ID seldom have access to a guidance counselor. As a result, it is unlikely for students with ID to be presented with information about potential postsecondary education opportunities in their community.

Instead, the transition component of the IEP under postsecondary education goals will likely say "not applicable." The student with ID and their family will be referred to the state vocational rehabilitation center, and perhaps the state developmental disabilities agency. If the student is lucky, he or she will be assigned to an adult service provider who will find them a job in the community. But as the latest statistics on transition outcomes for youth with ID will indicate, most of these youth will remain unemployed or under employed. And most will not engage in any kind of adult learning, whether at a college or in other community adult education settings.

In our current system of education, people with intellectual disabilities are expected to stop learning in any formal way at the ripe old age of 21. Imagine, if you will, if you had stopped learning after high school. No classes at college, no professional development days, no workshops or conferences. We often lament the poor post-school outcomes of students with intellectual disabilities. However, we never seem to make the connection that the system does not support students with intellectual disabilities to learn *anything* after they leave high school.

How successful would the general population be if all learning ended after high school? The current rate of unemployment for individuals who graduated from high school is twice that of those who graduated from college. Going to college is and always has been connected to greater rates of employment and higher wages. It is likely given the opportunity, and the means to document the outcomes, that students with intellectual disabilities would mirror these trends.

The purpose of exposing students with intellectual disabilities to PSE is to provide them, for perhaps the first time in their lives, the expectation that they CAN learn after leaving high school and the opportunity to CHOOSE to learn. Due to the nature and structure of high school, students with ID are seldom provided the chance to choose what they want to learn about. Nor are they given guidance about how to access knowledge as an adult. Choosing to learn about something is a process that takes some skills. First, a person must identify what it feels like to want to learn about something and know that there are places that that knowledge can be found. College is a great place to find out what interests you and the types of classes that are available on various topics. But it is not enough to know what is out there; you need to know how to access it.

How do you gain access to adult learning environments? Are they all the same? Is the process of registering for a basic math class at a community college the same as signing up to take a water aerobics class through your local park and recreation department? The flexible nature of a college setting allows students with intellectual disabilities the opportunity to learn about the various types of adult education and means through which each can be accessed. Students with ID can register for courses at the college for audit or for credit, or take a continuing education course, or sign up for one of the many adult classes that are available in the community through county or city programs or in local home improvement stores such as Home Depot or Michaels Arts and Crafts. It is important to recognize that students who participate in programs located on college campuses are *not* limited to taking classes at that college.

Finally, it is important to apply the learning in your life. Were the skills gained from a class useful to you on your job? Will they help you get a better job? Are you learning to be a better listener, writer, or thinker as a result of your class? Or perhaps the class was to explore a new area of interest. Are you still interested in the topic? Do you want to find out more? What other opportunities exist to do this? I think it's especially important not to assign judgment to the type of education that someone desires. If you want to learn how to speak French, great. If you want to learn how to tile your bathroom floor, great. Do you know where to learn these skills and can you apply them in your life? That is the measure of a successful learner. Many might respond with "Well, what if they fail?" or "Students with intellectual disabilities aren't going to do well in college classes." And it some cases this may in fact be true. Some students will fail. And yet when do we learn more about ourselves than when we fail? I can guarantee that every person reading this book right now has failed at something. Maybe at a number of things. But you managed to rally, hopefully apply the lessons learned, and move on. As Oscar Wilde says, *"Experience is simply the name we give our mistakes."* And I'm sure we all have a number of college "experiences" that served to teach us a thing or two.

And so we revisit our friend's question, "what's the point?" The point is to give students with intellectual disabilities who have the desire to learn, the skills and the expectations to do so, and continue doing so throughout their lifetime. The term lifelong learner is bandied about pretty frequently. But what does that mean? To be a lifelong learner? It means that you know how to access desired knowledge about a topic. In order to support students with intellectual disabilities to become lifelong learners we must arm them with the skills to access desired knowledge. We must also provide them with the experiences to practice these skills so that when they are 25, 30, 35, or 40 years old, and determine that they want to learn something that they know what to do. We set PSE as an expectation early on for the student and their family. We talk about the prospect of college and other forms of adult education and determine what kinds of opportunities might be available to them.

So why should we waste our time getting a young person with intellectual disabilities into an art history class? Let's review just some of the information that would be needed for a young woman with intellectual disabilities to take an art history class:

Where in the community do they offer art history?
How does she register for classes?
What is a bursar?
Are there prerequisites?
What is the schedule?
Does it work with her work schedule?
How will she get to and from class?
What kind of help will she need in the class to be successful?

Yet the lessons learned are not limited to what is needed to access a class. Being enrolled in an art history class will also give this young woman a chance to set goals, to advocate for herself with a professor and possibly an employer. She will be immersed in a class that she finds personally fulfilling. She will meet others who are also interested in the topic, and will make acquaintances—if not friends—with a mutual interest. She will determine not only if the content of the course is right for her, but if the method in which the course is taught works for her. This knowledge may influence the type of courses she takes in the future. She will be exposed to the ebb and flow of the college workload, the rhythm of a college class lecture, and get a feel for when it's ok to ask questions, when and how to take notes, or how to ask a friend or a professor for a copy of the notes. All of these skills will ultimately allow her to be more successful in other realms of her life—in her job, with her friends, as she makes her way in the community.

There are a great deal of skills required to access adult learning opportunities. And there are very few chances for students with intellectual disabilities to learn those skills in high school or as adults. Transition services has for many years been defined almost primarily around employment and the transition from school to work. And this is a vital aspect of transition. We all believe in the power of integrated community employment as a hugely successful outcome for students. But none of us expect a student to exit school with a paid job with benefits if that student has never had a job tryout, some training, and some experiences in the world of work. So how can we expect a student with intellectual disabilities to know how to access any kind of adult learning option, if we have not given him or her opportunity to sample what adult learning is about?

Students with ID need to be given the chance to experience adult learning while we are still in the position of providing support and guidance. Our transition outcomes do not have to be limited to "does this student have a job?" and "Are they connected with an adult service provider?" Our goals can also include "Can this student, if he or she wants to, access the adult learning options in their community?" Just as we teach them the process of obtaining and keeping a job and the necessary process of changing jobs, we must teach them that their learning needs and desires may change as they mature. And that the skills to access learning are ones that they can use for a lifetime. I think that college doesn't give anything special to students with ID, instead I think it gives them something that everyone else that goes to college gets; the opportunity to learn about yourself, get a better job, and quite possible grow up a little bit.

Who knew an art history class had so much to offer?

Acknowledgments

This book is the culmination of knowledge gained over many years and many projects; it is the product of contributions both intellectual and inspirational from many people. To my friend and colleague on the PERC Project, Amy Dwyre, your contributions to this book and the work it represents are enormously appreciated. I would like to thank Micah Fialka-Feldman for his friendship, his willingness to share his experiences, and for his leadership in boldly pushing himself and others to go that extra mile. And of course, I owe Micah an additional debt of gratitude as he is how I met his mom, Janice, whose positive spirit, and gentle strength, remind me why all of this is worth the effort. Janice's words of encouragement and kind feedback were always a constant source of inspiration.

I am indebted to my colleagues at TransCen Inc., who provide me with the guidance, support, and friendship and make this rewarding work possible—George Tilson, Christy Stuart, Kelli Crane, Maggie Leedy, Lisa Stern, Jose Diaz, Susie Farrington, Monica Simonsen, LaVerne Buchanan, Becca Smith, and Marion Vessels. I also thank Barbara Van Dyke for taking on the many challenges associated with getting a manuscript ready, and for always helping out with a smile on her face. And of course, my heartfelt thanks go to Richard Luecking, President of TransCen, Inc., who gave freely of his time, expertise, and support to this project.

To the wonderful education professionals in Maryland who have worked tirelessly to advance the college programs for students with ID in our state. We began this journey in 1998 with our first OCO Forum and it is because of your continued support that we are able to continue it. In particular I would like to thank Ann Lindsey, Kathy Kolan, Joy Camp, Mary Jo Bastacky, Helen Brunetta, Susan Overbey, Frank Schneider, and Donna MacDonald in Montgomery County Public Schools. Your commitment to high quality transition services serves as a model for our state. To my colleagues in Connecticut, thank you for your willingness to set the bar higher and again for your hard work and dedication in reaching it. Your contributions to this book are enormous—Rich Emmett, Joyce Emmett, and Jennifer Perri. Also, I am grateful to colleagues Karen Halliday (formerly of the Connecticut Department of Education); Karen Stigliano, Consultant, State Education Resource Center (SERC); and Pat Anderson, Transition Specialist, CT State Department of Education, who have been committed to improving postsecondary education services and outcomes for the students with ID in their state.

Finally, I am grateful to my mother, Eileen Bransfield, whose constant belief in me has helped me to pursue my passions. And, most of all, I would like to thank my husband Marc Meklir, whose support for my work never falters, and to our two children, Sarah and Sean, who help me remember when it's time to stop working and start playing.

—Meg Grigal

On my behalf, a great deal of credit for this book should go to the dedicated professionals on the Education and Transition Team at the Institute for Community Inclusion (ICI) who have worked tirelessly with Institutes of Higher Education and school districts to create access to a postsecondary education for youth with intellectual disabilities. These colleagues are Maria Paiewonsky, Nancy Hurley, Stel Gragoudas, Cate Weir, and Molly Boyle. I would also like to recognize three past team members for all of their hard work in making postsecondary education a possibility for youth with intellectual disabilities. These include Karen Zimbrich at Leslie College, Kirsten Behling at Suffolk University, and Cynthia Zafft at World Education.

Additionally, I would like to thank Bill Kiernan, Director of the ICI, for his leadership and support of postsecondary education options for youth with intellectual disabilities.

I would like to also extend acknowledgment to a number of other professionals with whom I have worked and whose efforts have grown the option of postsecondary education for youth with intellectual disabilities statewide. These colleagues include Jerri Roach, Worcester Public Schools; Julia Landau, Massachusetts Advocates for Children; Tom Sannicandro, State Representative; and Madeline Levine, Department of Elementary and Secondary Education. Further, I would like to thank all of the professionals, students, and families across six Inclusive Concurrent Enrollment partnerships comprised of institutes of higher education and school districts statewide for all of their respective efforts in further developing postsecondary education options. A special thanks to my colleague and friend, Paula Sotnik, Director of the National Service Inclusion Project, at the Inclusion for Community Inclusion, whose contribution on the relationship of national service and postsecondary education for students with intellectual disabilities is a noteworthy addition to this publication.

I would be remiss if I did not acknowledge how indebted I am to my parents, Irene Goldstein and Michael Hart, who have always encouraged me to dream and to pursue that which does not seem obtainable at the moment. Without that type of spirit and guidance, I would have not ever ventured into this area.

Finally, I am most grateful for the inspiration and ongoing support that two young people and their respective moms have provided as I began my work to identify strategies for creating access to postsecondary education for students with intellectual disabilities. So, Katie and Paulette Apostolides and Micah Fialka Feldman and Janice Fialka—an enormous thank you!

—Debra Hart

We would like to offer our sincere appreciation and gratitude to the contributing authors, who offered their knowledge, experience and time so graciously and without whose efforts this book would not have been possible. Our work relies upon the vision and leadership of others, and foremost among the many is Madeleine Will, Director of the Policy Center at the National Down Syndrome Society. Madeleine's visionary leadership has set the stage for this movement to unfold. Her brilliant understanding of how to guide and influence systems change has provided us with so many of the current opportunities we have to expand postsecondary education for people with intellectual disabilities. Another sincere debt of gratitude goes to Stephanie Smith Lee, Senior Policy Advisor at the National Down Syndrome Society, who set into motion much of the current research on postsecondary education options through her leadership at OSEP. Her advocacy efforts on the national forefront help to ensure that all of this work will culminate in better outcomes for students with ID. We would also like to offer our gratitude to our esteemed former Project Officer at the Office of Special Education Programs, Debra Price-Ellingstad, who provided steadfast support of our work and our mission around this area. We also wish to honor the work of Sherril Moon and Debra Neubert at the University of Maryland. Both of these women recognized early on that college was the next step for students with intellectual disabilities, and their contributions to the field have been vital. We want to also acknowledge and thank our colleagues nationwide who have also worked to expand support for and access to postsecondary education for students with intellectual disabilities.

We want to thank David Temelini, of the Institute for Community Inclusion, for his talent in producing the Think College! logo that has been used on the cover for this book.

A special thanks to Rebecca Lazo, our editor extraordinaire, for her unyielding support, genuine interest, and endless patience as she helped to navigate us through this process.

—Meg Grigal and Debra Hart

To Team Meklir—Marc, Sarah, Sean—for your constant support, love, and most of all, the joy and laughter that you bring me every day. —MG

To youth with intellectual disabilities and their families who have had, or who will have, the choice of a postsecondary education. —DH

Postsecondary Education: The Next Frontier for Individuals with Intellectual Disabilities

Meg Grigal, Debra Hart, and Maria Paiewonsky

This chapter provides readers with a description of the students and postsecondary education (PSE) services that this book focuses on, a historical and philosophical basis for why students with intellectual disabilities (ID) desire postsecondary opportunities, and changes that have occurred in special education that have led to this desire. Some of the relevant advances in research and practice are also discussed.

THE ISSUE OF DEFINITION

When discussing PSE options for students with ID, it is vital to clearly define not only the student population to which we are referring, but also the PSE experience, services, and supports to which these students will have access. Initially when PSE services for this group of students were being implemented, professionals in the field used the terms *severe*, *cognitive*, and *significant* to describe these students' disabilities. These terms often led to some confusion, as the definitions were somewhat nebulous and could be used to describe students with very different kinds of abilities.

The Rehabilitation Act of 1973 (PL 93-112) defines *significant disabilities* as follows:

> Rehabilitation Act Section 7(21) Individual with a significant disability
>
> (A) In general except as provided in subparagraph (B) or (C), the term "individual with a significant disability" means an individual with a disability—
>
> (i) who has a severe physical or mental impairment which seriously limits one or more functional capacities (such as mobility, communication, self-care, self-direction, interpersonal skills, work tolerance, or work skills) in terms of an employment outcome;
>
> (ii) whose vocational rehabilitation can be expected to require multiple vocational rehabilitation services over an extended period of time; and
>
> (iii) who has one or more physical or mental disabilities resulting from amputation, arthritis, autism, blindness, burn injury, cancer, cerebral palsy, cystic fibrosis, deafness, head injury, heart disease, hemiplegia, hemophilia, respiratory or pulmonary dysfunction, mental retardation, mental illness, multiple sclerosis, muscular dystrophy, musculo-skeletal disorders, neuro-

1

logical disorders (including stroke and epilepsy), paraplegia, quadriplegia, and other spinal cord conditions, sickle cell anemia, specific learning disability, end-stage renal disease, or another disability or combination of disabilities determined on the basis of an assessment for determining eligibility and vocational rehabilitation needs described in subparagraphs (A) and (B) of paragraph (2) to cause comparable substantial functional limitation.

This definition, by necessity, is very broad and includes, among others, students with specific learning disabilities. Students who have been labeled as having learning disabilities may often require accommodations to access and succeed in college settings, but they likely would be able to gain access to college through standard application and admission procedures. On the other hand, students who have been labeled as having mental retardation or an intellectual disability often need alternative pathways to postsecondary education. Use of the term *significant disabilities* has begun to wane in the literature. Similarly, the term mental retardation is also becoming less prevalent and the term *intellectual disabilities* is being used more frequently. For example, the American Association of Mental Retardation has recently changed its name to the American Association on Intellectual and Developmental Disabilities (AAIDD) in order to reflect this change in terminology. The AAIDD defines *intellectual disability* as follows:

Intellectual disability is a disability characterized by significant limitations both in intellectual functioning and in adaptive behavior as expressed in conceptual, social, and practical adaptive skills. This disability originates before the age of 18.
    The term *intellectual disability* covers the same population of individuals who were diagnosed previously with mental retardation in number, kind, level, type, and duration of the disability and the need of people with this disability for individualized services and supports. Furthermore, every individual who is or was eligible for a diagnosis of mental retardation is eligible for a diagnosis of intellectual disability. (AAIDD, 2009)

The term *intellectual disability* has also been used in a variety of federal grant priorities related to research and training. The Office of Special Education Programs (2004) and the National Institute on Disability Rehabilitation Research (2008), both under the Office of Special Education and Rehabilitative Services, in the U.S. Department of Education have included the term in a variety of research priorities and calls for grant proposals.

The most recent and perhaps the most significant use of the term *intellectual disabilities* seen thus far was in the reauthorization of the Higher Education Opportunity Act (HEOA) of 2008 (PL 110-315). This act, signed into law by President George W. Bush on August 14, 2008, includes amendments that expand PSE opportunities for students with ID. These amendments allow students with ID who are attending higher education programs designed for them to be eligible for the first time for Pell grants, Supplemental Educational Opportunity grants, and the Federal Work-Study Program. In addition, it authorizes the development and expansion of high-quality, inclusive model, comprehensive transition, and postsecondary programs. Finally, these amendments provide for the establishment of a coordinating center for the new model demonstration programs. This center will provide technical assistance, evaluation, and development of recommendations for model accreditation standards, as well as outreach and dissemination to postsecondary programs, families, and prospective students. (For a comprehensive discussion of the HEOA Amendments of 2008, see Chapter 2.)

In the HEOA of 2008, students with an ID are defined as follows:

> (2) STUDENT WITH AN INTELLECTUAL DISABILITY— The term "student with an intellectual disability" means a student—
> (A) with mental retardation or a cognitive impairment, characterized by significant limitations in—
> (i) intellectual and cognitive functioning; and
> (ii) adaptive behavior as expressed in conceptual, social, and practical adaptive skills; and
> (B) who is currently, or was formerly, eligible for a free appropriate public education under the Individuals with Disabilities Education Act.

Although this definition is much more specific, it may be open to interpretation and become a challenge for students who have various other disability labels. This definition is subject to a negotiated rulemaking process that commenced in the spring of 2009 to further refine and describe the student population it represents. Clarification on this definition will be very important and could have an impact on its application to students with various disability labels such as those students who are on the autism spectrum, and in some cases, students with forms of significant learning disabilities who may also seek alternative pathways to college.

Further confounding the issue of definition of the target student population for this publication are individuals labeled with developmental disabilities. By definition, the term *developmental disability* (DD) also includes individuals with intellectual disabilities, who comprise the largest portion of the population labeled with DD. This can sometimes lead to confusion, as the terms are often, whether correctly or incorrectly, used interchangeably. The lack of consistency in definitions across different laws and organizations that are targeting the same population highlights how complex it is to clearly define whom we mean when we use the term *intellectual disability*. It also highlights the need to have a common definition that all laws align with.

In working with families, professionals, and others, it is often useful to step away from the legal definitions and provide a functional definition that describes the experiences or other characteristics of such students. The following functional definition has been developed since the 1990s, with the help of parents and professionals involved in supporting the development or implementation of PSE services for students with ID.

Students with ID

- Would qualify to receive services under the Individuals with Disabilities Education Improvement Act (IDEA) of 2004 (PL 108-446) until they are 21 years old, in most states (26 years old in Michigan)
- Would likely, but not always, take the state's alternative assessment in high school
- Would in many states exit secondary education with an alternative diploma, such as an individualized education program (IEP) diploma or a certificate of attendance, instead of a typical high school diploma

- Would not access the PSE system in a typical manner, but would require significant planning and collaboration to gain access

Given this definition, professionals and family members are provided with an array of characteristics about students and can winnow their point of reference down to a smaller group of students. Students with ID have not typically been seen as having the potential to go to college and are seldom provided with knowledge about the supports they would need to access PSE or adult learning options after high school.

For the purposes of this book, we define PSE to include all learning options available to students following high school. This includes credit and noncredit or continuing education courses in community colleges and 4-year colleges and institutions, vocational-technical colleges, and other forms of adult education. Defined in this manner, the range of educational options also includes adult classes offered in the community through local, regional, and state park and recreation departments; local community programs such as the YMCA; adult basic education programs offered through state departments of education; personal learning clinics and workshops offered through retail establishments and national chains such as Home Depot and Michaels; personal development classes offered at fitness or wellness centers; and all other learning opportunities available to adults.

This broad definition of PSE provides students with ID and their families the widest array of options and demonstrates that PSE does not necessarily mean going to college. It can and should mean having the opportunity to access the adult learning options available in the community that meet a student's personal or professional goals.

Another term that merits discussion is *dual enrollment*. Hart, Mele-McCarthy, Pasternack, Zimbich, and Parker (2004) referred to supporting students with ID through a "dual-enrollment" approach, meaning that students are simultaneously enrolled in high school and at a PSE institution. These students are most often in the 18- to 21-year-old age bracket and are receiving their final 3 years of transition services in special education in a PSE setting. The term was originally used to describe students without disabilities who are taking college classes as they complete their junior or senior year of high school. Traditional dual-enrollment programs have been associated with positive outcomes for high school graduation and college enrollment rates, college grade point averages, and progress toward college completion (Karp, Calcagno, Hughes, Jeong, & Bailey, 2007). Dual enrollment for students with ID has been evident in research reports and briefs (Dolyniuk et al., 2002; Grigal, Dwyre, & Davis, 2006; Neubert, Moon, Grigal, 2004; Neubert & Redd, 2008), program descriptions (Dolyniuk, Kamens, Corman, DiNardo, Totaro, & Rockoff, 2002; Eskow & Fisher, 2004, Grigal, Neubert, & Moon, 2001; Hall, Kleinert, & Kearns, 2000; Hamill, 2003); and, most recently, amendments to the HEOA. However, no proven link has been established between participation in a dual-enrollment program and improved outcomes for students with ID.

A GROWING NEED EMERGES

There are greater numbers than ever of students with ID who receive special education services in the United States. These services are provided until students with ID graduate with a diploma or "age out" with a certificate of attendance at the age of 21 (or 26 in Michigan). A total of 69,532 students with the label of "mental retardation" between the ages of 18 and 21 years received special education services in 2006 under Part B of IDEA (U.S. Department of Education, 2007a). Of these students, 17,005 graduated in 2006 with a diploma and 16,453 exited the school system with a high school certificate (U.S. Department of Education, 2007b).

Since the 1970s secondary students with ID have participated in functional or life skills programs and community-based instruction in employment, community mobility, recreation, and daily living (Billingsley & Albertson, 1999). Beginning in the mid-1980s, these programs were expanded to include inclusive academic and social activities during the secondary (14–17) and transition (18–21) years (Agran, Snow, & Swaner, 1999; Tashie, Malloy, & Lichtenstein, 1998). Despite these programmatic changes at the secondary level, students with ID often exit public school with alternative diplomas (Johnson & Thurlow, 2003) and encounter waiting lists from agencies that support adults with ID.

The outcomes of students with ID have historically been poor among disability groups. Researchers analyzing the National Longitudinal Transition Survey-2 found that a low percentage of youth with ID transitioning from public education to adult life have jobs upon exiting school (Wagner, Newman, Cameto, Garza, & Levine, 2005). In many cases, students with ID exiting school receive no vocational services, and few are provided with independent living options (Noyes & Sax, 2004). Students with ID who did have work were the only disability group that did not experience an increase in wages. Furthermore, youth with ID are among those least likely to attend postsecondary school and are the least likely to be expected to do so.

A national survey of day and employment services for people with developmental disabilities indicated that only 22% are participating in integrated employment and 57% are receiving services in facility-based settings (Winsor & Butterworth, 2007). As for community living, as of June 2006, nearly 85,000 individuals with ID/DD across the country were on a waiting list for residential services (Bruininks et al., 2007).

Poor employment and community living outcomes for individuals with ID, in conjunction with an increasing level of dissatisfaction with the existing range of services in high school for students aged 18 or older (Grigal et al., 2001; Stodden, Jones, & Chang, 2005) and expansion and success of inclusive K–12 education opportunities, have led to increased expectations for what is possible after high school for students with ID. Growing numbers of parents, researchers, and practitioners have questioned whether the practice of serving students with ID in high school settings alongside peers as young as 14 is age appropriate and have advocated that these students receive instruction in settings similar to those experienced by their same-age peers without disabilities (Fisher & Sax, 1999; Moon & Inge, 2000; Smith & Puccini, 1995; Tashie et al., 1998).

Parents of students with ID are increasingly expecting their children to continue education beyond high school. In a study of parents of students with disabilities (including students with ID), college was found to be the *most* desired outcome, regardless of the student's disability (Grigal & Neubert, 2004); 57% of parents of students with low-incidence disabilities chose a two- or four-year college as their desired outcome. Students themselves are expressing the desire to go to college just like their siblings and peers without disabilities.

The need for different education and transition services for students with ID between the ages of 18 and 21 has also been highlighted in reports and position papers (National Council on Disability, 2000; Schmidt, 2005; Smith & Puccini, 1995). The President's Committee for People with Intellectual Disabilities recommended support for the "new emerging opportunities for students with ID to become involved in various transitional programs located at two-year colleges or four-year universities, or to participate in vocational education and training programs in inclusive community-based settings" (2004, p. 25).

Recently, a growing number of students with ID have sought access to various forms of PSE (Getzel & Wehman, 2005; Hart, Grigal, Sax, Martinez, & Will, 2006). Students with ID, who had previously not been offered opportunities to access PSE, are now taking part in a variety of PSE options that allow them to experience college and other adult learning options firsthand. Self-advocates, parents, and disability advocates have partnered with secondary and postsecondary educators to create increased diversity in and access to PSE options for youth and young adults with ID, which may include community colleges, four-year colleges and institutes of higher education, vocational-technical colleges, and other various forms of adult education (Hart & Grigal, 2008). This national trend is fueled by research that demonstrates that PSE experiences generally lead to better outcomes, such as increased employment opportunities and higher wages (Migliore, Butterworth, & Hart, 2009).

The numbers of students referenced earlier represent only about one fourth of the emerging need for PSE options; another 280,470 students with intellectual disabilities between the ages of 12 and 17 were served in 2006, and these students and their families are likely to seek access to PSE in much greater numbers. Institutes of higher education, school systems, and adult service providers across the nation have begun to respond to these higher expectations by creating opportunities for these youth to reap the potential benefits of a PSE. This has resulted in a growing national trend to develop dual enrollment and/or adult PSE options for youth with ID so that they may have the same choices as their peers without disabilities.

THE IMPETUS FOR CHANGE

The motivation for creating access to PSE for students with ID stems from a variety of factors. A major reason for seeking access to PSE relates to the amount of time students with ID spend in high school. Many students with ID who are supported through the special education system remain in high school until they are 21 years old; in Michigan this may extend until the age of 26. The age discrepancy with their peers without disabilities, along with the frustration felt by students and their families of having to stay in high school for seven years, was likely the major impetus for creating access to alternative education environments. Thomas Edison said, "Restlessness and discontent are the first necessities of progress"; many of the earliest programs in postsecondary settings were the result of grassroots efforts on the part of family members or teachers looking to create alternatives to seven-year high school careers (Neubert, Moon, & Grigal, 2002).

Another impetus for change arose as an unexpected outcome of the inclusion movement, as a generation of students with ID, who had been educated with their same-age peers throughout elementary, middle, and high school, wished to remain with their peers as they went off to college. Students with ID may be influenced by their desire for continued social experiences that are like those of their counterparts without disabilities. Parents of students with ID have also reported a desire for their sons or daughters with ID to attend college (Grigal & Neubert, 2004) and are increasingly asking school systems to consider the provision of transition services to students with ID in college and community settings (Moon, Grigal, & Neubert, 2001).

Finally, there are a number of factors motivating school districts to develop new transition and PSE options for students with ID, including federal mandates that require "results-oriented" transition planning, new accountability for transition and postsecondary outcomes, transition-related litigation, and the need to prepare youth for the 21st-century workforce.

Federal Mandates for Transition

Federal mandates support goal-oriented transition and continued PSE for students with disabilities. The No Child Left Behind (NCLB) Act of 2001 (PL 107-110) holds schools accountable for adequately educating and assessing the academic achievement of all students, including those with disabilities. IDEA 2004 specifically implies that children with disabilities are educated not only for future employment and independent community living, but also for the prospect of continued, life-long learning that is results-oriented and delineated in measurable terms [20 U.S.C. A, §§ 601(d)(1)(A)]. Furthermore, the Americans with Disabilities Act of 1990 (PL 101-336) and Section 504 of the Rehabilitation Act of 1973 (PL 93-112) mandate the protection of the civil rights of people with disabilities by promoting equal access to continued learning and PSE. To support access to postsecondary options, among other life areas, legislation such as the Assistive Technology Act of 1998 (PL 105-394) can provide federal resources to states in order to address the assistive technology needs of citizens with disabilities, who can use these resources to purchase devices or services. (Additional laws and initiatives are discussed in Chapter 2.)

Transition and Postschool Outcome Accountability

In conjunction with the reauthorization of IDEA in 2004, the U.S. Department of Education, through the Office of Special Education Programs, requires states to develop state performance plans based on 20 indicators, on which data are to be reported annually (National Secondary Transition Technical Assistance Center, 2007). Among those indicators are two that directly relate to transition. Indicator 13 requires data specifically on "the percent of youth aged 16 and above with an Individualized Education Program with goals and transition services that will reasonably enable the student to meet the post-secondary goals" [20 U.S.C. 1416(a)(3)(B)]. These data should reflect how the team is addressing a student's course of study, employment experiences, and independent living needs to achieve his or her postschool goals and whether adult services representatives are involved in this plan (National Secondary Transition Technical Assistance Center, 2006). Indicator 14 requires data on the percentage of youth who have been through IEPs, are no longer in secondary school (graduated or aged out), and have been competitively employed, enrolled in some type of postsecondary school, or both, within 1 year of leaving high school [20 U.S.C. 1416(a)(3)(B)]. The impetus for some school systems to create or expand their dual-enrollment programs may be a response to these new requirements.

Transition-Related Litigation

Another factor leading to the creation of new programs and services is the increase in litigation brought on by dissatisfied parents specifically concerned about the lack of transition planning and services that support the achievement of their child's postschool goals. In an analysis of 36 published decisions from administrative hearings, district courts, and appellate courts concerning transition, Etscheidt (2006) outlined five key transition issues brought to the courts. They include:

1. The extent to which districts are making an effort to invite agencies that may provide or pay for transition services
2. How effectively teams are soliciting students' preferences and interests and the extent to which they are obliged to endorse them
3. The efforts of districts to individualize transition services based on students' needs
4. The obligation school districts have to provide appropriate and genuine transition supports and services
5. The appropriateness of the transition plan itself

Transition mandates are complex, but parents are increasingly frustrated with schools that do not prioritize transition and only minimally adhere to the mandated process.

Preparation for the 21st-Century Workforce

Another motivation for schools to develop PSE options for all students, including students with ID, stems from growing evidence that more needs to be done to merge secondary and postsecondary policies so that young adults are prepared to pursue meaningful work in the 21st-century workplace (Kirst & Venezia, 2004). Studies indicate that current secondary practices are not sufficient to prepare students for work success, especially those from historically underserved communities (Cassner-Lotto & Barrington, 2006; National Center on Education and the Economy, 2006). In addition to basic academic skills, employers need workers with strong applied work skills, such as teamwork, critical thinking, and communication. They want young people who are able to work comfortably with people from other cultures, solve problems creatively, and write and speak well. Employers also need workers to be punctual, dependable, and industrious. Without these skills, young adults are likely to linger in low-skill, low-wage jobs (*Education Week*, 2007; Partnership for 21st Century Skills, 2006). For young adults with disabilities who face incredible employment challenges (National Organization on Disability, 2004), the stakes are even higher for the development of academic and work skills through a coordinated set of transition activities. By bridging the gap between high school and college (also referred to as the K–16 initiative), meaningful partnerships between schools and institutes of higher education can lead to creative and successful transition pathways to work (Grigal, Neubert, & Moon, 2005; Hart, Zafft, & Zimbrich, 2001; Kirst & Venezia, 2004; Partnership for 21st Century Skills, 2006).

HOW ACCESS TO POSTSECONDARY EDUCATION HAS CHANGED

While providing access to PSE to students with ID is still in many instances looked upon as a new idea, there has been evidence of this emerging practice in the literature for over 30 years (Baxter, 1972; Bilovsky & Matson, 1974; Caparosa, 1985; Corcoran, 1979; Dahms, Ackler, & Aandahl, 1977; Daily, 1982; Doyle, 1997; Duran, 1986; Frank & Uditsky, 1988; Goldstein, 1993; Hall, Kleinert, & Kearns, 2000; Jones, & Moe, 1980; McAfee, & Sheeler, 1987). Neubert, Moon, Grigal, and Redd (2001) summarized the available literature from previous decades in a comprehensive review. These authors indicated that the programs in the 1970s appeared to develop as a response to various movements (e.g., normalization and deinstitutionalization), were primarily focused on adults (not students), and instruction was generally provided in segregated settings.

As the focus of special education shifted toward transition and employment in the 1980s, so did the literature on PSE, shifting from community integration to compliance with Section 504 of the Rehabilitation Act of 1973. Few program descriptions were available in the 1980s, and Neubert et al. (2001) contended that this may have resulted from public school provision of educational and transitional services for students with disabilities until age 22, in compliance with the Education for All Handicapped Children Act of 1975 (PL 94-142) and the Education of the Handicapped Act Amendments of 1983 (PL 98-199).

A shift occurred in the literature in the 1990s, when program descriptions and position papers began to look more at students instead of adults with ID (Neubert et al., 2001). In 1995, the Division on Mental Retardation and Developmental Disabilities of the Council for Exceptional Children issued a position statement recommending that students who required educational services beyond the age of 18 be allowed to graduate with their peers and then continue their education until the age of 22 in age-appropriate settings, such as college campuses, and that federal funds should follow the student to the postsecondary setting (Smith & Puccini, 1995).

Indeed, there was a flurry of program development in the 1990s, as shown by Gaumer, Morningstar, and Clark (2004), who established a national database of community-based transition programs (available at the Transition Coalition web site at the University of Kansas). These researchers identified 101 programs in 29 states, including 48 at postsecondary institutions, 27 at business locations, 13 at apartments or houses, and 13 non–site-based or individual support models. These researchers described the disability of the population served (mild/moderate, moderate/significant), the funding sources, and the operational calendar that was followed. Gaumer et al. (2004) found that 82% of the programs had been developed after the 1990s.

The Current Status of Postsecondary Education for Students with Intellectual Disabilities

Much has changed since the 1990s in regard to the available literature on PSE for students with ID. Two national databases have attempted to gather and share information about available programs in the United States (Gaumer et al., 2004; Hart, 2008). There has been an array of program descriptions (Bergin & Zafft, 2000; Dolyniuk et al., 2002; Gaumer et al., 2004; Hart & Grigal, 2008; Hart et al., 2004), additional qualitative studies (Casale-Giannola & Kamens, 2006; Page & Chadsey-Rusch, 1995; Hamill, 2003; Hughson, Moodie & Uditsky, 2006; Mosoff, Greenholtz, Hurtado, & Jo, 2007; Redd, 2004), and a smattering of quantitative studies conducted (Grigal et. al., 2001; Neubert et al., 2004; Zafft, Hart, & Zimbrich, 2004). The following provides a brief summary of the research that has been conducted thus far on postsecondary options for students with ID and highlights two of the most current research projects on this topic.

The current base of knowledge about PSE services for students with disabilities is most often focused on students with learning disabilities, including physical or sensory impairments, who comprise the largest percentage of college students with disabilities. (National Longitudinal Transition Study-2, 2006). Much less is known about the various types of PSE programs, and associated activities and outcomes, for students with ID, as these students have not typically been supported in their efforts to seek out college. In addition, many recent national education studies provide little if any information on students with ID. This is unfortunate, as such an effort would allow for meaningful comparisons between disability groups. In a recent report, *Parents' Expectations and Planning for College* (released by the Institute on Educational Sciences, National Center for Education Statistics [NCES], 2008), there was only a cursory mention of students with any disability and no mention of students with ID. The student characteristics used as independent variables included age, sex, race, and grades, but not disability. The absence of this one variable makes the results of this important study difficult to apply to any student with ID.

Even previous research efforts specifically targeting the topic of PSE for students with disabilities have largely failed to include students with ID. This issue is reflected in other national studies on PSE, in which students with ID are either omitted entirely, as is the case in the *Beginning Postsecondary Students Longitudinal Study* (NCES, 2007), or combined with students with other disability labels, making it difficult to discern meaning from the findings, as in the report *Student with Disabilities in Postsecondary Education: A Profile in Preparation, Participation, and Outcomes* (NCES, 1999).

The existing research on PSE for students with ID has provided descriptions of the characteristics, activities, and/or outcomes of students in programs at the state level (Grigal et al., 2001; Neubert et al., 2004) and at the national level (Gaumer et al., 2004; Hart & Grigal, 2008; Hart et al., 2004; Zafft, Hart, & Zimbrich, 2004). These studies have provided the field with a glimpse of the potential that PSE programs have to increase access to integrated employment and social activities, and to improve collaboration between local education agencies and adult service providers. Yet the limited information currently available does not reflect the vast variation in the array of services provided, nor does it allow researchers or practitioners to determine whether student outcomes vary with participation in particular types of PSE programs.

Gaumer et al. (2004) referred to these PSE programs as community-based transition programs, which they define as alternative special education opportunities, specifically for students 18–21 years old, developed by public school systems, located in age-appropriate settings such as postsecondary institutions (e.g., universities, community colleges, and vocational-technical schools) and in other community settings (e.g., apartments, houses, offices, and businesses). Gaumer et al. (2004) discussed the difficulty of locating community-based transition programs and the issues associated with a lack of standard reporting systems to document the existence of such programs. Other terms that have been used to describe various types of programs are *substantially separate programs*, *mixed programs*, and *inclusive individualized services* (Hart et al., 2004; Neubert, Moon, & Grigal, 2002; Stodden & Whelley, 2004).

The most recent national survey identified approximately 130 PSE programs for students with ID across 31 states. Of these 130 programs, 75 responded to a follow-up telephone survey that was designed to collect basic information about services and supports offered, how long the program had been in existence, who funded the program, and the students they support (Hart & Grigal, 2008). Since the completion of this survey, another 120 programs have self-identified on the ThinkCollege web site, bringing the total to 250 programs. Although the program structures varied immensely, this survey's analysis revealed that they fell within three overall models—mixed or hybrid, substantially separate, and totally inclusive using individualized supports. There was a great degree of variability within models, each of which included a wide range of services (see Chapter 3 for greater detail).

Quantitative Research

Surveys have been used to describe the characteristics, activities, or outcomes of students in mixed programs at the state level (Grigal et al., 2001; Neubert et al., 2004) and in separate, mixed, or inclusive models at the national level (Gaumer et al., 2004; Hart et al., 2004). These studies provide the first documentation of the number of programs that serve 18- to 22-year-old students with ID at college or community sites.

Grigal et al. (2001) used a survey to interview 13 teachers of the mixed model dual-enrollment programs in one state to provide an overview of characteristics, funding patterns, program components, and challenges to program development and implementation. Nine programs were located at community colleges, two at universities, and two in the community. Students were referred to the programs through their high school teachers and had to meet certain criteria to be admitted (e.g., participation in travel training, previous unpaid work experiences). All programs incorporated a separate class at the postsecondary site that focused on functional skills, self-determination skills, and/or career planning. Key characteristics of the programs included community-based instruction, job training, participation in college classes, interagency linkages, and parental involvement. Identified challenges included the need for more inclusive opportunities on college campuses, ability to access classroom and office space at the colleges, the need for flexible teacher schedules, transportation to and from the postsecondary sites, scheduling differences between local school and college campuses, and procedures for dispensing medication, handling disciplinary actions, and conducting IEP meetings (Grigal et al., 2001).

A similar survey was conducted by Neubert et al. (2004), who collected information from teachers in mixed programs in one state through a written survey. The 13 programs served a total of 163 students with ID who were 18–21 years of age and who exited the school system with a certificate rather than a diploma. Program teachers reported data on students' access to college courses, inclusion in campus and community activities, participation in employment training and jobs, linkages with state and local adult services, and follow-up activities for a specific school year.

Only one published study has been able to link PSE experiences with employment outcomes. In a preliminary study of the correlation between college participation and postschool outcomes, Zafft, Hart, and Zimbrich (2004) compared the outcomes of 20 students with ID who took at least one college class with the outcomes of 20 students who did not take a college class. Among their findings was that participation in postsecondary education correlated positively with two employment variables: competitive employment and independent employment.

This previous work provides a foundation for researchers to identify a more comprehensive and descriptive system for classifying the types of programs and services that are currently being used to support students with ID in postsecondary environments. It also demonstrates that there is little known about the long term outcomes that can be associated with accessing PSE during or after the transition experience.

Qualitative Research

Although there are descriptions of these service models in the literature, there are few research studies that document the impact and effectiveness of such programs. A number of qualitative studies have been conducted (Casale-Giannola & Kamens, 2006; Hughson, Moodie, & Uditsky, 2006; Mosoff et al., 2007; Page & Chadsey-Rusch, 1995; Redd, 2004) in the past 15 years. The results of these studies provide additional information that can inform future research on this topic.

Page and Chadsey-Rusch (1995) compared the experiences of four young men attending a community college: two who had disabilities (ID) and two who did not. These researchers found that the expectation to go to college was affected by others' perceptions and the availability of supports. For students without ID, there was a belief that a college education could expand their employment opportunities; however, the relationship between college coursework and specific career goals was not present for students with ID. All four students reported that attending the community college had a positive effect on their social and interpersonal relationships.

Page and Chadsey-Rusch (1995) described how supports were provided to the two students with ID by the local school system as they attended classes on a community college campus and worked in the community. The authors pointed out that attending a community college does not necessarily lead to a career but recognized other potential benefits. They called for additional research to document outcomes of students with significant disabilities who attend postsecondary programs.

Redd (2004) examined a mixed program in a community college setting in terms of practices and characteristics, activities, and outcomes for students with ID, as well as student and parent satisfaction. Three students had individual paid jobs, and 13 other students chose between enclave work in a landscape mobile crew or a uniform cleaning company. Although inclusive experiences on campus and in employment were somewhat limited, students and parents indicated satisfaction with the program and staff.

Hughson et al. (2006) employed participatory action research methods to look at inclusive postsecondary education. This study was designed to capture the reflections and experiences of students with developmental disabilities attending college, including an analysis of the models and daily operations. The results were descriptive and reflected various stakeholder groups, including students, families, facilitators, and mentors. A significant finding was that for students with developmental disabilities who had graduated from inclusive PSE, 70% were employed either part time (often in more than one part-time position) or full time in a wide range of job opportunities.

Finally, Mosoff et al. (2007) conducted a qualitative study to identify a range of factors considered to be important to the success of inclusive PSE. Using a grounded theory approach, they conducted 27 interviews with five different stakeholder groups: students, faculty, inclusion facilitators, campus staff, and parents. Five critical elements of inclusive PSE were identified by at least three of the stakeholder groups: student engagement, impact on the classroom or institution, individualized paths and autonomy, higher aspirations and confidence, and authenticity and coherence.

CURRENT AND ONGOING RESEARCH ON POSTSECONDARY EDUCATION FOR STUDENTS WITH INTELLECTUAL DISABILITIES

In 2004, the Office of Special Education Programs funded two research and innovation projects related to PSE access for students with ID. Both projects were funded for 5 years and were aimed at demonstrating and researching exemplary practices supporting 18- to 21-year-old students with ID in postsecondary settings.

One of these projects, the Postsecondary Education Research Center (PERC) Project, was awarded to TransCen in Rockville, Maryland. The other, the College Career Connection (C^3) Project, was awarded to the Institute for Community Inclusion at the University of Massachusetts at Boston. These two projects have gathered the most recent data regarding the activities and outcomes of students with ID receiving services in PSE settings.

The PERC Project partnered with established dual-enrollment programs in Maryland and Connecticut to evaluate the efficacy and outcomes of serving 18- to 21-year-old students with ID in two- and four-year colleges. At each site, PERC staff conducted an intensive program evaluation using the PERC Postsecondary Program Evaluation Tool: A Self-Assessment for College and Community-Based

Services (see Figure 1.1) with each level of program staff, including the director of special education or a similar administrator, the program coordinator, and all support staff (instructional assistants and job coaches). This tool asks users to rate services in 10 key areas (program planning, staffing, administration, student planning, college course access, employment, self-determination, interagency

 PERC POSTSECONDARY PROGRAM EVALUATION TOOL

This tool provides a snapshot of the quality of existing services and provides users with a concise evaluation report. It also provides users with an itemized action plan that can be used to address areas in need of improvement.

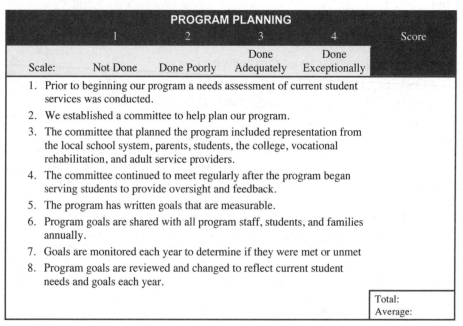

PROGRAM PROFILE
Name of Program:
Name of School System:
Year program started:
Current School Year:
Number of students this year:
Fill in the number of program staff:
Teacher(s)/Coordinator(s):
Paraprofessionals/Job Coaches/Education Coaches:
Administrator(s):
Other: fill in blank and number
Name of person completing assessment:
Position of person completing assessment:
Date of assessment:

PROGRAM PLANNING				
	1	2	3	4	Score
Scale:	Not Done	Done Poorly	Done Adequately	Done Exceptionally	

1. Prior to beginning our program a needs assessment of current student services was conducted.
2. We established a committee to help plan our program.
3. The committee that planned the program included representation from the local school system, parents, students, the college, vocational rehabilitation, and adult service providers.
4. The committee continued to meet regularly after the program began serving students to provide oversight and feedback.
5. The program has written goals that are measurable.
6. Program goals are shared with all program staff, students, and families annually.
7. Goals are monitored each year to determine if they were met or unmet
8. Program goals are reviewed and changed to reflect current student needs and goals each year.

Total:
Average:

Figure 1.1. PERC postsecondary program evaluation tool. (From the PERC Project. Available online at http://www.transitiontocollege.net/percpubs/perc_eval_tool.pdf; reprinted by permission.)

STAFFING					
	1	2	3	4	Score
Scale:	Not Done	Done Poorly	Done Adequately	Done Exceptionally	

1. Our program provides adequate staffing for student support to be properly individualized.
2. Our program teacher/coordinator has training and experience in transition (i.e., employment support, community-based instruction, and facilitating social networks for students).
3. Our program support staff (paraprofessionals, job coaches, education coaches) are trained and experienced in transition (employment support, community-based instruction, and facilitating social networks for students).
4. Our staffing hours are flexible so that students are supported to access activities and employment after school hours.
5. Our program staff meets regularly to discuss students' needs.
6. Our program staff meets regularly to discuss staffing needs.

Total:
Average:

ADMINISTRATION					
	1	2	3	4	Score
Scale:	Not Done	Done Poorly	Done Adequately	Done Exceptionally	

1. Our school system administrator understands and supports the mission of our program.
2. Our school system administrator provides oversight and leadership to our program.
3. Our school system administrator meets with the program teacher/staff on a regular basis.
4. The staff receives training on relevant issues (transition, adult services, employment, self-determination) on a regular basis.
5. Our program has a memorandum of understanding regarding our collaboration with the college or community organization.
6. The program teacher/coordinator has a copy of the memorandum of understanding.
7. The school system has written guidelines for referring students to the program.
8. Referring teachers effectively use the referral guidelines to refer students who will be successful to the program.

Total:
Average:

© 2007 The Postsecondary Education Research Center (PERC) Project, TransCen Inc.
www.transitiontocollege.net
www.transcen.org

(continued)

Figure 1.1. (*continued*)

STUDENT PLANNING					
	1	2	3	4	Score
Scale:	Not Done	Done Poorly	Done Adequately	Done Exceptionally	

1. Before a student is referred to the program, the student and their family are provided with a tour/site visit of the program.
2. Students and their families are provided with a clear overview of the expectations of the program including increased level of student responsibility and independence.
3. Students referred to the program are prepared with the skills they need to succeed (e.g., paid and unpaid employment, self-advocacy and social skills, academic and functional skills).
4. Person-centered planning is used to identify and address student goals, concerns, and support needs prior to the student entering the program.
5. Students' schedules are individualized based upon their personal goals and needs.
6. Students interested in attending college classes can choose from a wide array of courses.
7. Students are involved in the process of course selection, registration, payment, accessing accommodations in college classes.
8. Students can choose from a range of employment opportunities that match their interests and preferences.
9. Students develop and follow a personal daily or weekly schedule.
10. Students go to and from classes and work independently.

Total:
Average:

STUDENT ACTIVITIES

ACCESSING COLLEGE OR CONTINUING EDUCATION COURSES

If none of your students attend college course, skip this section.

1. What percentage of their day do students spend with other students with disabilities receiving instruction in a separate classroom? 0/20/40/60/80/100
2. What percentage of their day do students spend in college classes? 0/20/40/60/80/100
3. How many students are auditing college classes? (...)
4. How many students are taking college classes for credit? (...)
5. How many students received a grade in their college course? (...)
6. How many students are pursuing a certification or degree at the college? (...)
7. How many students do you anticipate will enroll in some form of college or continuing education course after exiting the program? (...)

EMPLOYMENT OPPORTUNITIES

If none of your students are employed, skip this section.

1. How many students are in **individual paid jobs** (minimum wage or above) in the community or on campus?   (…)
2. How many of the students in your program are in **individual unpaid** job training sites?   (…)
3. How many students are in paid positions in the community, but are also in unpaid job training positions in another employment site?   (…)
4. How many students are in paid enclave sites supported by the school system or an adult service provider?   (…)
5. How many students are in unpaid enclave sites supported by the school system or an adult service provider?   (…)
6. How many students receive benefits from an employer?   (…)
7. How many students have evening or weekend jobs and do not require job support from the program?   (…)
8. How many students do you anticipate will exit the school system and retain their paid job?   (…)
9. How many students do you anticipate will exit the school system without paid jobs?   (…)

EMPLOYMENT DATA

The following worksheet can be used to calculate your students' average salaries/hours in paid positions.

Student's Initials	Rate of Pay $ per hour	Hours per week

(continued)

Figure 1.1. (*continued*)

SELF-DETERMINATION				
	1	2	3	4	Score
Scale:	Not Done	Done Poorly	Done Adequately	Done Exceptionally	

1. Students are provided with direct instruction on self-determination skills (i.e., decision making, problem solving, goal setting).
2. Students review their IEPs with staff prior to their IEP meetings.
3. Students are provided with the opportunity to add goals to their IEPs.
4. Students monitor their progress on IEP goals throughout the year.
5. Students attend all of their IEP meetings.
6. Students participate in their IEP meeting by presenting their accomplishments or future goals.
7. Students receive instruction to help them understand and explain their disability.
8. Students receive instruction on the types of accommodations they require to be successful in college or continuing education classes.
9. Students receive instruction on the types of accommodations they require to be successful at their jobs.
10. Students receive practice asking professors or employers for appropriate accommodations.
11. Students receive instruction and practice regarding the types of questions to ask adult service providers about future services.

Total:
Average:

INTERAGENCY COLLABORATION				
	1	2	3	4	Score
Scale:	Not Done	Done Poorly	Done Adequately	Done Exceptionally	

1. Students and families are supported by our program to apply for services from the state developmental disabilities agency.
2. Students and families are supported to apply for services from the state vocational rehabilitation agency.
3. Students and families are connected with our local one-stop center.
4. Our program makes arrangements for students and families to meet with local adult service agency personnel to ask questions about future services and options.
5. Students and families are supported to apply for services from the Social Security Administration for Supplemental Security Income (SSI) benefits.

Total:
Average:

MONITORING					
	1	2	3	4	Score
Scale:	Not Done	Done Poorly	Done Adequately	Done Exceptionally	

1. We maintain an up-to-date log of all employers including name, organization, e-mail, phone number and address.
2. We maintain an up-to-date log of all professors teaching our students including name, department, course name, phone, e-mail, and office.
3. We maintain a log of all community recreation facilities accessed by students including name of facility, phone number, web site, contact person, if applicable, and address.
4. We maintain an account of each student's job history including student name, job title and employment location, start date, rate of pay, number of hours worked, frequency and type of support provided, benefits received, means of transportation and end date/reason for leaving.
5. We maintain a log of all students attending college courses including the student's name, semesters of course, name of course, instructor, credit or audit, method of payment, class schedule, grade received, and frequency and type of support provided.

Total:
Average:

EVALUATION					
	1	2	3	4	Score
Scale:	Not Done	Done Poorly	Done Adequately	Done Exceptionally	

1. We conduct satisfaction surveys about our program with students each year.
2. We conduct satisfaction surveys about our program with parents each year.
3. We conduct satisfaction surveys about our program with employers each year.
4. We conduct satisfaction surveys about our program with college instructors each year.
5. We collect exit data when a student leaves the program including contact info for student and their family (phone numbers, addresses, e-mail addresses), age at exit, employment information, adult service agency chosen, current living situation, continuing education, and community activities.
6. We conduct follow-up on former students every year to determine their employment and independent living outcomes.
7. We compile our evaluation data to review at the end of the year.
8. We review all monitoring and evaluation data annually to identify changes needed in the program.
9. We revise the program goals, services, and supports annually, based upon evaluation feedback, if needed.
10. We share findings from our evaluations and plans for program improvement with interested parties annually (students, parents, employers, administrators).
11. We request additional staff positions based upon program evaluation data, if needed.
12. We have expanded our program based upon our program evaluation data.

Total:
Average:

(continued)

Figure 1.1. (*continued*)

<table>
<tr><td colspan="2">**PROGRAM PROFILE**</td></tr>
</table>

Name of Program
Name of School System
Current school year

Students served in the (2   /2   ) school year: .... ( )
Staffing for the (2   /2   ) school year: .... ( )
Number of Teacher(s)/Coordinator(s): .... ( )
Number of Paraprofessionals/Job Coaches/Education Coaches: .... ( )
Number of Administrator(s): .... ( )
Number of Other: *fill in blank and number* .... ( )
Name of person completing assessment:
Position of person completing assessment:
Date of assessment:

Scores
Program Planning Score: .... ( )
Staffing Score: .... ( )
Administration Score: .... ( )
Student Planning Score: .... ( )
Self-Determination Score: .... ( )
Interagency Collaboration Score: .... ( )
Monitoring Score: .... ( )
Evaluation Score: .... ( )
Highest Score was in the area of:
Lowest score was in the area of:
Student Activities Summary:

College Courses
Percentage of the day students spend with other students with disabilities .... (%)
Percentage of the day students spend in college classes .... (%)
Percentage of students are auditing college classes .... (%)
Percentage of students are taking college classes for credit... (%)
Percentage of students will receive a grade in their college course.............................. (%)
Percentage of students are pursuing a certification or degree at the college................. (%)

Employment
Average wage earned by students:.. ($)
Range of student salaries:.. ($-$)
Average number of hours worked by students: .... (   )
Range of hours worked by students: .... (   )
Percentage of students are in individual paid jobs .... (%)
Percentage of students are in individual unpaid job training sites ....(%)
Percentage of students are in both paid and unpaid positions in community .....(%)
Percentage of students are in paid enclave sites..(%)
Percentage of students are in unpaid enclave sites ....(%)
Percentage of students receive benefits ....(%)
Percentage of students have evening or weekend jobs ....(%)
Percentage of students will exit the school system with a paid job....................(%)
Percentage of students will exit the school system without a paid job.............(%)

collaboration, monitoring, and evaluation) and provides a summary of each program's strengths and weaknesses. Based upon the outcomes of the evaluation, action plans for each PERC site were created to improve student services, which guided the direction of technical assistance activities conducted during the project.

For example, in one PERC site, the Western Connection Program at Western Connecticut State University in Danbury, Connecticut, a noted strength of the program was student access to college courses, as every student was taking a different course in the fall and spring semesters. The variety of these courses was vast, from history and theater to psychology and English. An area of need was student employment—there were no participating students in paid, competitive employment. The program evaluation tool helped staff to determine that the employment goals and corresponding services were not adequately defined. In addition, program staff needed technical assistance and training on job development and training techniques. Over the course of the first year of the project, the Western Connection staff changed their focus from developing "job training sites" to establishing real paid work in the community. This new focus necessitated the hiring of a dedicated job developer, who received training from PERC staff on job development techniques. One of the most striking outcomes of conducting the program evaluation was that the percentage of students exiting the program with a paid job increased from 0% to 90% in one school year.

During the 2006–2007 school year, 92% (or 12 of 13 students) had paid, competitive jobs. The one student who was not in paid work was involved in two work training sites and received a stipend in preparation for paid competitive work. On average, the working students were paid $7.50 an hour and worked in retail clothing and grocery stores, with animals, and in restaurants in their communities. In addition to these off-campus jobs, five of the 13 students had on-campus internships where they received stipends, in the areas of child care, office work, library work, and food service.

To date, this project has collected data on employment and college course access on 75 dually enrolled students from 35 high schools in eight school systems in Connecticut and Maryland served in five program sites on college campuses (four community colleges and one four-year university). Student self-determination, exit, and follow-up data are currently being analyzed to gauge the impact on student outcomes. The project's activities and resources are documented on its web site, www.transitiontocollege.net.

Although the PERC project will not be completed until 2010, the preliminary findings indicate that students who participate have very positive outcomes. In a recent report, Grigal (2008) documented that in the five dual-enrollment programs studied by the project in 2007, 94% of 42 supported students with ID were employed in paid jobs earning on average $7.86/hour and working an average of 15.5 hours per week. Of these students, 72% had also taken a college course in a wide array of offerings, including American History, Europe Ancient & Medieval, Acting 1—Sight, Sound & Motion, Habits of Writing, Intro to Psychology, Basic Writing Skills, Interpersonal Communication, Middle Eastern Culture, Social Psychology, Written Communications, Health Promotion and Maintenance, Introduction to Fiction, Criminal Justice, Sociology, Video Production, and American Perspectives.

The Institute for Community Inclusion's College Career Connection (C^3) project is an inclusive individual support model that was originally funded as a model demonstration project by the Department of Education, Office of Special Education Programs, from 1998 to 2003. A current grant, funded by the Office of Special Education Program under the Research and Innovation Projects, has partnered with the Massachusetts Inclusive Concurrent/dual-enrollment partnerships to evaluate the efficacy and outcomes of serving students ages 18–21 with ID in two- and four-year colleges. Project staff provided training and technical assistance to personnel within each partnership as needed, in support of students with ID in inclusive college courses, for all aspects of college life.

The primary purpose behind C^3 is to improve adult outcomes for students with ID by improving access to PSE options that are currently unavailable to them. Mirroring many of the evidence-based quality indicators outlined by the National Alliance for Secondary Education and Transition (2005) and the Transition Guideposts developed by the National Collaborative on Workforce Disability for Youth (2005), the model uses a student-centered framework to identify strengths and preferences (Butterworth et al., 1993; National Center for the Study of Postsecondary Educational Supports–Hawai'i, 2003); a collaborative, interagency team (Ginsberg et al., 1997; Stodden, Brown, & Galloway, 2005) to develop individual PSE services for students who want them; and a resource-mapping strategy (Crane & Skinner, 2003; Ferber, Pittman, & Marshall, 2002) to identify service gaps or duplication. Individual supports are determined by analysis of student interests and needs and may be provided by educators, family members, adult service personnel, and educational coaches (Hart et al., 2001; National Center for the Study of Postsecondary Educational Supports-Hawai'i, 2003; Rammler & Wood, 1999).

C^3 is one of the few existing PSE approaches that is fully inclusive and addresses the needs of the widest range of students with disabilities, including students with ID (Hart et al., 2004). This model takes into account unique aspects of each student, such as aspirations, family wishes, and cultural background. It is based on several guiding principles: individual student vision sets the direction and controls decision making; all options are inclusive and occur in settings that reflect natural proportions of students with and without disabilities; there are no special programs or specially designated classes; supports are individualized; and interagency collaboration is essential.

The C^3 model includes the following key features: interagency collaboration, resource mapping, person-centered planning, work-based learning, educational coaching, self-determination, and universal course design. Currently, this model is being implemented across six Institutes of Higher Education and 26 partnering school districts with approximately 98 students statewide. Each partnership is unique and reflects the culture of the IHE but adheres to the aforementioned guiding principles. This initiative is supported via a line item in the state budget (for additional detail, see Chapters 2, 3, and 10).

SUMMARY

Over the past 30 years, there have been significant changes regarding the purpose and outcomes of students with ID who gain access to PSE. New terms such as *intellectual disabilities* and *dual enrollment* reflect the evolution of these changing practices in our field. As we evolve, so does the language we use to reflect our beliefs, our practices, and people whom we support. The increase in newly developed programs and services across the country, as well as the increased focus on researching the activities and outcomes of students with ID served in PSE settings, demonstrates that this new level of service provision is one that has staying power. When we describe PSE as the next frontier for the individual with ID, this is not mere hyperbole; we really are in uncharted territory. We know little about the impact that PSE can have on the lives of these individuals. We have yet to determine the effect increasing such services will have on secondary education, higher education, and adult developmental disabilities and vocational rehabilitation systems. Yet, these unknowns demonstrate that we are making great progress in the education of students with ID. Kahlil Gibran said, "Progress lies not in enhancing what is, but in advancing toward what will be." In 1975, this country legislated access to public school for students with disabilities, including students with ID. Today, a law supports increased access, which heretofore would have been thought impossible, to higher education for those same students. We are making progress.

REFERENCES

Agran, M., Snow, K., & Swaner, J. (1999). Teacher perceptions of self-determination: Benefits, characteristics, strategies. *Education and Training in Mental Retardation and Developmental Disabilities, 34*, 293–301.

American Association on Intellectual and Developmental Disabilities. (2009). *FAQ on intellectual disability.* Available online at http://www.aaidd.org/content_104.cfm?navID=22

Americans with Disabilities Act of 1990, PL 101-336, 42 U.S.C. §§ 12101 *et seq.*

Assistive Technology Act of 1998, PL 105-394, 29 U.S.C. §§ 3001 *et seq.*

Baxter, J.M. (1972). Clerical training for the mentally retarded on a college campus. *Education and Training of the Mentally Retarded, 7*, 135–140.

Behling, K., & Hart, D. (2008). Universal course design: A model for professional development. In S.E. Burgstahler & R.C. Cory (Eds.), *Universal design in higher education* (pp. 109–125). Cambridge, MA: Harvard Education Press.

Billingsley, F.F., & Albertson, L.R. (1999). Finding a future for functional skills. *Journal of The Association for Persons with Severe Handicaps, 24*, 298–302.

Bilovsky, D., & Matson, J. (1974). The mentally retarded: A new challenge. *Community and Junior College Journal, 44*, 16–18.

Briel, L.W., & Getzel, E.E. (2001). Internships in higher education: Promoting success for students with disabilities. *Disability Studies Quarterly, 21*(1), 38–48.

Bruininks, R., Soo-Yung, B., Alba, K., Lakin, K.C., Larson, S., Prouty, R., et al. (2007). Residential services for persons with developmental disabilities: Status and trends through 2006. In R.W. Prouty, G. Smith, & K.C. Lakin (Eds.), *Residential services for persons with developmental disabilities: Status and trends through 2006.* Minneapolis: University of Minnesota, Research and Training Center on Community Living, Institute on Community Integration.

Butterworth, J., Hagner, D., Heikkinen, B., Faris, S., DeMello, S., & McDonough, K. (1993). *Whole life planning: A guide for organizers and facilitators.* St. Augustine, FL: Training Resource Network.

Caparosa, C. (1985). Community colleges: A resource for postsecondary opportunities for the handicapped. *Rehabilitation World, 16–17*, 43–46.

Casale-Giannola, D., & Kamens, M.W. (2006). Inclusion at a university: Experiences of a young woman with Down syndrome. *Mental Retardation, 44*(5), 344–352.

Cassner-Lotto, J., & Barrington, L. (2006). *Are they really ready to work? Employers' perspectives on the basic knowledge and applied skills of new entrants to the 21st century U.S. workforce.* New York: Conference Board, Society for Human Resource Management (U.S.), Corporate Voices for Working Families, Partnership for 21st Century Skills.

Chadsey, J., Leach, L., & Shelden, D. (2001). *Including youth with disabilities in education reform: Lessons learned from school-to-work states.* Champaign: University of Illinois at Urbana-Champaign, Transition Research Institute.

Corcoran, E.L. (1979). Campus life for retarded citizens. *Education Unlimited, 1,* 22–24.

Crane, K., & Skinner, B. (2003). *Community resource mapping: A strategy for promoting successful transition for youth with disabilities* (Information Brief, 2[1]). Minneapolis: University of Minnesota, National Center on Secondary Education and Transition.

Dahms, A.M., Ackler, E.J., Jr., & Aandahl, V.S. (1977). Scarecrows as students at Colorado's college for living. *Phi Delta Kappan, 59,* 11–12, 17.

Daily, A.L. (1982). The community college as a resource for retarded adults: A working model. *Lifelong Learning: The Adult Years, 6,* 10–11, 31.

Dolyniuk, C.A., Kamens, M.W., Corman, H., DiNardo, P.O., Totaro, R.M., & Rockoff, J.C. (2002). Students with developmental disabilities go to college: Description of a collaborative transition project. *Focus on Autism and Other Developmental Disabilities, 17*(4), 236–241.

Doyle, M.B. (1997). College life: The new frontier. *Impact, 10,* 16–17.

Duran, E. (1986). A university program provides services to young adults with severe handicaps and limited English proficiency. *College Student Journal, 20,* 43–46.

Education for All Handicapped Children Act of 1975, PL 94-142, 20 U.S.C. §§ 1400 *et seq.*

Education for the Handicapped Act Amendments of 1983, PL 98-199, 20 U.S.C. §§ 1400 *et seq.*

Etscheidt, S. (2006). Issues in transition planning: Legal decisions. *Career Development for Exceptional Individuals, 29,* 28–47.

Everson, J., & Guillory, J. (1998). Building statewide transition services through collaborative interagency teamwork. In F. Rusch & J. Chadsey (Eds.), *Beyond high school: Transition from school to work.* Belmont, CA: Wadsworth.

Everson, J.M., & Zhang, D. (2000). Person-centered planning: Characters, inhibitors, and supports. *Education and Training in Mental Retardation and Developmental Disabilities, 35,* 36–43.

Ferber, T., Pittman, K., & Marshall, T. (2002). *State youth policy: Helping all youth to grow up fully prepared and fully engaged.* Takoma Park, MD: The Forum for Youth. Retrieved June 17, 2008 from http://www.forumforyouthinvestment.org/node/106

Fisher, D., & Sax, C. (1999). Noticing differences between secondary and post-secondary education: Extending Agran, Snow, and Swaner's discussion. *Journal of The Association for Persons with Severe Disabilities, 24,* 303–305.

Frank, S., & Uditsky, B. (1988). On campus: Integration at a university. *Entourage, 3,* 33–40.

Gaumer, A.S., Morningstar, M.E., & Clark, G.M. (2004). Status of community-based transition programs: A national database. Division on Career Development and Transition, Council for Exceptional Children. *Career Development of Exceptional Individuals, 27*(2), 131–149.

Getzel, E.E., & Wehman, P.H. (2005). *Going to college: Expanding opportunities for people with disabilities.* Baltimore: Paul H. Brookes Publishing Co.

Goldstein, M.T. (1993). LINK: A campus-based transition program for non-college bound youth with mild disabilities. *Career Development for Exceptional Individuals, 16*(1), 75–84.

Gramlich, M., Crane, K., Peterson, K., & Stenhjem, P. (2003). Work-based learning and future employment for youth: A guide for parents and guardians. *Information Brief, 2*(2). Minneapolis: University of Minnesota, National Center on Secondary Education and Transition.

Grigal, M. (2008). *The Postsecondary Education Research Center Project.* Rockville, MD: TransCen, Inc.

Grigal, M., Dwyre, A., & Davis, H. (2006). *Transition service for students aged 19-21 with intellectual disabilities in college and community settings: Models and implications for success.* Minneapolis: University of Minnesota, National Center on Secondary Education and Transition.

Grigal, M., & Neubert, D. (2004). Parents' in-school values and post-school expectations for transition-aged youth with disabilities. *Career Development for Exceptional Individuals, 27*(1), 65–86.

Grigal, M., Neubert, D.A., & Moon, M.S. (2001). Public school programs for students with severe disabilities in post-secondary settings. *Education and Training in Mental Retardation and Developmental Disabilities, 36*(3), 244–254.

Grigal, M., Neubert, D.A., & Moon, M.S. (2002). Postsecondary options for students with significant disabilities. *Teaching Exceptional Children, 35*(2), 68–73.

Grigal, M., Neubert, D.A., & Moon, M.S. (2005). *Transition services for students with severe disabilities in college and community settings: Strategies for planning, implementation and evaluation.* Austin, TX: PRO-ED.

Hall, M., Kleinert, H.L., & Kearns, J.F. (2000). Going to college! Postsecondary programs for students with moderate and severe disabilities. *Teaching Exceptional Children, 32*(3), 58–65.

Hamill, L.B. (2003). Going to college: The experiences of a young woman with Down syndrome. *Mental Retardation, 41*(5), 340–353.

Hart, D. (2008). *National survey of postsecondary education programs that support students with intellectual disabilities.* Unpublished raw data.

Hart, D., & Grigal, M. (2004). Individual support to increase access to an inclusive college experience for students with intellectual disabilities. In *Online training modules from the University of Maryland On-Campus Outreach.* Retrieved June 17, 2008, from http://www.education.umd.edu/oco/training/oco_training_modules/IndividualSupports/start.html

Hart, D., & Grigal, M. (2008, March). New frontier: Postsecondary education for youth with intellectual disabilities. *Section 504 Compliance Handbook,* 10–11.

Hart, D., Grigal, M., Sax, C., Martinez, D., & Will, M. (2006). Postsecondary education options for students with intellectual disabilities. *Research to Practice, 45,* 1–4.

Hart, D., Mele-McCarthy, J., Pasternack, R.H., Zimbich, K., & Parker, D.R. (2004). Community college: A pathway to success for youth with learning, cognitive, and intellectual disabilities in secondary settings. *Education and Training in Developmental Disabilities, 1*(1), 54–66.

Hart, D., Zafft, C., & Zimbrich, K. (2001). Creating access to college for all students. *The Journal for Vocational Special Needs Education, 23*(2), 19–31.

Higher Education Opportunity Act of 2008, PL 110-315, 122 Stat. 3078.

Hughson, E.A., Moodie, S., & Uditsky, B. (2006). *The story of inclusive post-secondary education in Alberta: A research report.* Retrieved June 18, 2008, from http://stepsforward.homestead.com/The_Story_of_Inclusive_Post_Secondary_Education_in_Alberta.pdf

Individuals with Disabilities Education Improvement Act of 2004, PL 108-446, 20 U.S.C. §§ 1400 *et seq.*

Jacobson, L. (2008, October 30). Pilot projects to aim at workforce projects. *Education Week.* Retrieved November 8, 2008, from http://www.edweek.org/login.html?source=http://www.edweek.org/ew/articles/2008/10/29/11workforce.h28.html&destination=http://www.edweek.org/ew/articles/2008/10/29/11workforce.h28.html&levelId=2100

Johnson, D.R., Sharp, M., & Stodden, R. (2001). *The transition to postsecondary education for students with disabilities.* Minneapolis: University of Minnesota, Institute on Community Integration.

Johnson, D.R., & Thurlow, M.L. (2003). *A national study on graduation requirements and diploma options for youth with disabilities* (Technical Report 36). Minneapolis: University of Minnesota, National Center on Educational Outcomes. Retrieved January 24, 2004, from http://education.umn.edu/NCEO/OnlinePubs/Technical36.htm

Jones, L.A., & Moe, R. (1980). College education for mentally retarded adults. *Mental Retardation, 18*(2), 59–62.

Karp, M., Calcagno, J., Hughes, K., Jeong, D.W., & Bailey, T. (2007). *The postsecondary achievement of participants in dual enrollment: An analysis of student outcomes in two states.* New York: Community College Research Center, Institute on Education and the Economy, Teachers College, Columbia University. Retrieved November 27, 2007, from http://www.ecs.org/html/IssueSection.asp

Kirst, M.W., & Venezia, A. (Eds.). (2004). *From high school to college: Improving opportunities for success in postsecondary education.* San Francisco: Jossey-Bass.

Learning for the 21st Century. (2002). *Partnership for 21st century schools.* Washington, DC: Author.

McAfee, J.K., & Sheeler, M.C. (1987). Accommodation of adults who are mentally retarded in community colleges: A national study. *Education and Training in Mental Retardation, 22*(4), 262–267.

Migliore, A., Butterworth, J., & Hart, D. (2009). *Fast facts: Postsecondary education and employment outcomes for youth with intellectual disabilities* (No. 1). Boston: Institute for Community Inclusion.

Moon, M.S., Grigal, M., & Neubert, D. (2001). High school and beyond: Students with significant disabilities complete high school through alternative programs in postsecondary settings. *Exceptional Parent, 31*(7), 52–57.

Moon, M.S., & Inge, K.V. (2000). Vocational preparation and transition. In M. Snell & F. Brown (Eds.), *Instruction of students with severe disabilities* (5th ed., pp. 591–628). Upper Saddle River, NJ: Merrill.

Mosoff, J.M., Greenholtz, J., Hurtado, T., & Jo, J. (2007). *Models of inclusive post-secondary education for young adults with developmental disabilities (1st year of 3 year research project).* Retrieved June 18, 2008, from http://www.steps-forward.org/Research.html

National Alliance for Secondary Education and Transition. (2005). *National standards and quality indicators: Transition toolkit for systems improvement.* Minneapolis: University of Minnesota, National Center on Secondary Education and Transition.

National Center for the Study of Postsecondary Educational Supports. (1999). *Postsecondary education and employment for students with disabilities: Focus group discussion on supports and barriers in lifelong learning.* Honolulu, HI: Author.

National Center for the Study of Postsecondary Educational Supports. (2003). *Students with intellectual disabilities and postsecondary education: Discussions of development in practice and policy* (Capacity Building Institute Proceedings). Honolulu, HI: Author.

National Center on Education and the Economy. (2006). *Tough choices or tough times: The report of the new commission on the skills of the American workforce.* Retrieved October 15, 2008, from http://www.ncee.org/index.jsp?setProtocol=true

National Collaborative on Workforce and Disability for Youth. (2005). *Guideposts for success.* Retrieved November 16, 2005, from http://www.ncwdyouth.info/resources&Publications/guideposts/guidepostsprint.html

National Council on Disability. (2000). *Transition and post-school outcomes for youth with disabilities: Closing the gaps to postsecondary education and employment.* Washington, DC: Author.

National Longitudinal Transition Study-2. (2006). *NLTS2 Home and News.* Retrieved July 27, 2006, from http://www.nlts2.org/gindex.html.

National Organization on Disability. (2004). *Harris Survey of Americans with Disabilities.* Washington, DC: Author.

National Secondary Transition Technical Assistance Center (NSTTAC). (2006). *NSTTAC Indicator 13 Checklist: Form B (Enhanced for Professional Development).* Retrieved October 15, 2008, from http://www.nsttac.org/tm_materials/Default.aspx

National Secondary Transition Technical Assistance Center (NSTTAC). (2007). *What is Indicator 13?* Retrieved October 15, 2008, from http://www.nsttac.org/indicator13/indicator13.aspx

Neubert, D.A., Moon, M.S., & Grigal, M. (2002). Post-secondary education and transition services for students ages 18–21 with significant disabilities. *Focus on Exceptional Children, 34*(8), 1–11.

Neubert, D.A., Moon, M.S., & Grigal, M. (2004). Activities of students with significant disabilities receiving services in postsecondary settings. *Education and Training in Developmental Disabilities, 39*(1), 16–25.

Neubert, D.A., Moon, M.S., Grigal, M., & Redd, V. (2001). Postsecondary educational practices for individuals with mental retardation and other significant disabilities: A review of the literature. *Journal of Vocational Rehabilitation, 16*(3/4), 155–168.

No Child Left Behind Act of 2001, PL 107-110, 115 Stat. 1425, 20 U.S.C. §§ 6301 *et seq.*

Noyes, D., & Sax, C. (2004). Changing systems for transition: Students, families, and professionals working together. *Education and Training in Mental Retardation and Developmental Disabilities, 39*(1), 35–44.

Page, B., & Chadsey-Rusch, J. (1995). The community college experience for students with and without disabilities: A viable transition outcome? *Career Development for Exceptional Individuals, 18*, 85–95.

Partnership for 21st Century Skills. (2006). *Results that matter: 21st century skills and high school reform.* Retrieved October 15, 2008, from http://www.21stcenturyskills.org/index.php?option=com_content&task=view&id=204&Itemid=185

Powers, L.E., Singer, G.H.S., & Sowers, J. (1996). *On the road to autonomy: Promoting self competence in children and youth with disabilities.* Baltimore: Paul H. Brookes Publishing Co.

President's Committee for People with Intellectual Disabilities. (2004). *A charge we have to keep: A road map to personal and economic freedom for persons with intellectual disabilities in the 21st century.* Washington, DC: Author.

Rammler, L., & Wood, R. (1999). *College lifestyle for all!* Middleford, CT: Rammler & Wood Consultants.

Redd, V. (2004). *A public school-sponsored program for students ages 18 to 21 with significant disabilities located on a community college campus: A case study.* Unpublished doctoral dissertation, University of Maryland, College Park.

Rehabilitation Act of 1973, PL 93-112, 29 U.S.C. §§ 701 *et seq.*

Rose, D.H., & Meyer, A. (2002). *Teaching every student in the digital age: universal design for learning.* Alexandria, VA: Association for Supervisors of Curriculum Development. Available online at http://www.cast.org/teachingeverystudent/

Schmidt, P. (2005). From special ed to higher ed: Students with mental retardation are knocking on college doors, and colleges are responding. *Chronicle of Higher Education, 51*(24), A–36.

Smith, T.E.C., & Puccini, I.K. (1995). Position statement: Secondary curricula and policy issues for students with MR. *Education and Training in Mental Retardation and Developmental Disabilities, 30*, 275–282.

Stodden, R.A., Brown, S.E., Galloway, L.M., Mrazek, S. & Noy, L. (2005). *Essential tools: Interagency transition team development and facilitation.* Minneapolis: National Center on Secondary Education and Transition.

Stodden, R.A., Jones, M., & Chang, K. (2005, February 25). *Services, supports and accommodations for individuals with disabilities: An analysis across secondary education, postsecondary education and employment.* (Capacity Building Institute White Paper.) Unpublished manuscript, Honolulu, HI.

Stodden, R.A., & Whelley, T. (2004). Postsecondary education and persons with intellectual disabilities: An introduction. *Education and Training in Developmental Disabilities, 39*(1), 6–15.

Tashie, C., Malloy, J.M., & Lichtenstein, S.J. (1998). Transition or graduation? Supporting all students to plan for the future. In C.J. Jorgensen (Ed.), *Restructuring high schools for all students: Taking students to the next level* (pp. 234–259). Baltimore: Paul H. Brookes Publishing Co.

U.S. Department of Education, Office of Special Education and Rehabilitative Services, National Institute on Disability and Rehabilitation Research. (2008). *FY 2008 application package for new grants under Disability Rehabilitation Research Projects (DRRP): A Center on Postsecondary Education for Students with Intellectual Disabilities.* Washington, DC: Author.

U.S. Department of Education, Office of Special Education and Rehabilitative Services, Office of Special Education Programs. (2004). *Fiscal Year 2004 Application for New Grants Under the Individuals with Disabilities Education Act (IDEA) Research and Innovation to Improve Services and Results for Children with Disabilities (CFDA 84.324) program—Research and innovation.* Washington, DC: Author.

U.S. Department of Education, Office of Special Education Programs. (2007a). *IDEA Part B trend data: Table B2A—Number, percent of population, and disability distribution, by disability and age group (6–21, 6–11, 12–17, and 18–21):1993 through 2006* [Data file]. Available from Individuals with Disabilities Education (IDEA) data web site, https://www.ideadata.org/PartBTrendDataFiles.asp

U.S. Department of Education, Office of Special Education Programs. (2007b). *IDEA Part B trend data: Table B5A—Number of diplomas, certificates of completion, and dropouts, and as a percentage of special education students (ages 14–21) exiting school, by disability: 1992–93 through 2005–06* [Data file]. Available from Individuals with Disabilities Education (IDEA) data web site, https://www.ideadata.org/PartBTrendDataFiles.asp

U.S. Department of Health & Human Services, Administration for Children and Families. (2008). *Funding opportunity: National training initiatives on critical and emerging needs.* Washington, DC: Author.

Wagner, M., Newman, L., Cameto, R., Garza, N., & Levine, P. (2005). *After high school: A first look at the postschool experiences of youth with disabilities. A report of findings from the National Longitudinal Transition Study-2 (NLTS2)* (SRI Project P11182). Available from the SRI International web site, http://www.nlts2.org/reports/2005_04/nlts2_report_2005_04_complete.pdf

Wehman, P. (1996). *Life beyond the classroom: Transition strategies for young people with disabilities* (2nd ed.). Baltimore: Paul H. Brookes Publishing Co.

Whelley, T. (2002). *Introduction to significant cognitive disabilities and postsecondary education.* Paper presented at the Second Summit of the Coalition for the Support of Individuals with Significant Disabilities in Postsecondary Education, Boston.

Winsor, J., & Butterworth, J. (2007). *National day and employment service trends in MR/DD agencies* [Data Note Series, Data Note XII]. Boston: Institute for Community Inclusion.

Zafft, C., Hart, D., & Zimbrich, K. (2004). College career connection: A study of youth with intellectual disabilities and the impact of postsecondary education. *Education and Training in Developmental Disabilities, 1*(1), 45–54.

The Role of Legislation, Advocacy, and Systems Change in Promoting Postsecondary Opportunities for Students with Intellectual Disabilities

Stephanie Lee and Madeleine Will

A child with significant disabilities born in the United States in 2007 has little chance of escaping poverty, despite advances in educational practices and policies, health care, and technology (National Council on Disability, 2008). A contributing factor to this condition is limited access to postsecondary education (PSE) and its benefits. Of all disability groups, youth with intellectual disabilities (ID) have the lowest rates of engagement in PSE, work, or preparation for work after high school (Wagner, Newman, Cameto, Garza, & Levine, 2005).

To advance PSE opportunities for students with ID, it is important for individuals to have knowledge of existing legislation and policies, and systems-change strategies, that directly and indirectly affect K–12, higher education, and adult services for people with ID. For the most part, the majority of these legislative acts and initiatives have been underutilized in supporting access to PSE for students with ID. To this end, this chapter provides the reader with a description of the most relevant current federal legislation and initiatives that support or have the potential to support access to PSE for individuals with ID and, it is hoped, promote greater utilization of these options. Next, systems-change efforts in New Jersey, South Carolina, and Massachusetts are discussed. Finally, we make recommendations for policy, practices, and systems change.

Federal legislation, policies, and/or initiatives that are covered include:

- Individuals with Disabilities Education Improvement Act (IDEA) of 2004 (PL 108-446)
- Higher Education Opportunity Act (HEOA) of 2008 (PL 110-315)
- Developmental Disabilities Act of 2000 (PL 106-402)
- Americans with Disabilities Act (ADA) of 1990 (PL 101-336)
- Workforce Investment Act (WIA) of 1998 (PL 105-220), Title I—Youth
- WIA, Title IV: Rehabilitation Act of 1973 (including Sections 504 & 508)
- Carl D. Perkins Career and Technical Education Improvement Act of 2006
- National and Community Service Trust Act of 1993 (PL 103-82)
- Assistive Technology Act of 2004 (PL 108-364)
- Social Security Administration (SSA) Work Incentives

FEDERAL ROLE IN SUPPORTING THE DEVELOPMENT OF POSTSECONDARY EDUCATION

It is important that the federal government support research, model demonstration programs, technical assistance, outreach, and dissemination. Funding is

needed for institutions of higher education (IHEs) for the development and expansion of programs and services for students with ID. Information about
evidence-based best practice, cost-sharing and collaboration strategies could
guide future planning and implementation efforts. Support for universal course
design and training for faculty who have students with ID in their courses is
also critically important. Increased public awareness and media coverage; advocacy by individuals with disabilities and their families and organizations representing them, such as the National Down Syndrome Society (NDSS); and successful model program development are all contributing to new federal support
for research and program development and improved legislation. Key champi-
ons such as Eunice Kennedy Shriver also play an important role. Mrs. Shriver,
a life-long advocate for individuals with intellectual disabilities, became an important champion and "behind the scenes supporter" after visiting PSE programs
for students with ID.

University Centers of Excellence in Developmental Disabilities Education
(UCEDDs) and the Developmental Disability Councils (DD Councils) have been
increasingly important in the development of high-quality, inclusive postsecondary opportunities. UCEDDs and DD Councils receive funding from the Administration on Developmental Disabilities (ADD). The ADD convened a stakeholder group in February 2008, which included individuals with developmental
disabilities and family members. The group was consulted to help identify the
unmet needs of individuals with DD and their families that should be prioritized
for National Training Initiatives funding. The group identified the need to enhance PSE opportunities for individuals with DD as a very important priority
area. This resulted in funding of a National Consortium of University Centers for
Excellence in Developmental Disabilities to Enhance Postsecondary Education for
Individuals with DD. This project was awarded to the Institute for Community
Inclusion at the University of Massachusetts, Boston, in collaboration with seven
UCEDDs (Delaware, Minnesota, Hawaii, South Carolina, Tennessee [Vanderbilt],
Ohio, California) and the Association of University Centers on Disabilities. The
Consortium will conduct research, provide training and technical assistance, and
disseminate information on evidence-based promising practices that support in-
dividuals with DD to increase their independence, productivity, and inclusion
through access to PSE, resulting in improved long-term independent living and
employment outcomes.

The U.S Department of Education, National Institute of Rehabilitation Research, also funded a National Center on Postsecondary Education to the Institute for Community Inclusion in partnership with TransCen, Inc. The major focus of the center is research on postsecondary education for students with ID (for
more information on both projects, see Chapter 10).

HIGHER EDUCATION ACT REAUTHORIZATION

The Higher Education Opportunity Act (HEOA) (PL 110-315) was enacted on
August 14, 2008; it reauthorizes the Higher Education Act (HEA) of 1965, as
amended. This law contains a number of important new provisions that will improve PSE for students with disabilities and professional development for spe-

cial and general education teacher candidates who will teach students with disabilities in the future. Of particular note are several provisions that address affordability issues and create a new model demonstration program and coordinating center for students with ID.

NEW ELIGIBILITY FOR FINANCIAL AID

HEOA allows for students with ID to be eligible for the first time for Pell Grants, Supplemental Educational Opportunity Grants, and the Federal Work-Study Program. Such students are usually not eligible for financial aid because they do not meet two criteria. A student with an ID typically does not receive a regular diploma or a General Educational Development equivalency test or pass an "ability to benefit" test. He or she is also not usually accepted for enrollment in a degree or accredited certificate program.

The HEOA requires the Secretary of Education to promulgate regulations that will waive these requirements for students with ID who are accepted for enrollment or are enrolled in comprehensive transition and PSE programs, and specify how these students will qualify for eligibility. These regulations are part of Title IV of the Act, which will be subject to a "negotiated rule-making process" conducted by the U.S. Department of Education with representatives of the constituencies who will be significantly affected by the regulations. The department has conducted public hearings, accepted written comments on the regulations, appointed negotiators and began negotiations in March 2009. Once the negotiations are concluded, the Department will publish a Notice of Proposed Rulemaking (NPRM), accept public comments on the NPRM, and then publish final regulations in the *Federal Register*. Students with ID will not be able to receive grants or work-study jobs until the regulations are finalized. Following is more detailed information from the new law regarding these provisions and recommendations for the regulations submitted by a number of disability organizations during the public comment period. These recommendations were developed by a group of experts who provided ongoing advice to Congress during the legislative process, under the leadership of the NDSS Policy Center.

The following are three general recommendations that were submitted to the Department:

- The HEOA-negotiated rulemaking team should include individuals with expertise in higher education programs for students with ID, including family members and persons with ID who have experience with such programs, or organizations that represent them.
- The process for application for financial aid should be as similar as possible to that used by students not enrolled in, or accepted for enrollment in, comprehensive transition and PSE programs for students with ID, and as streamlined as possible.
- Dual or concurrent enrollment and financial support from other agencies should not preclude any student from having access to eligible financial aid they would otherwise be qualified to receive.

LAW: BASIC REQUIREMENTS AND WAIVER AUTHORITY

The Conference Report accompanying H.R. 4137 (the bill passed by Congress) contains the requirement for the Secretary to promulgate regulations to waive certain sections of the law. In Title IV, Part G, Section 485(a)(8)(s), it also requires that the student

> (A) be enrolled or accepted for enrollment in a comprehensive transition and postsecondary program for students with intellectual disabilities at an institution of higher education; (and) (B) be maintaining satisfactory progress in the program as determined by the institution, in accordance with standards established by the institution;

Therefore, in order to qualify for grants and work assistance, a student must meet the definition of "a student with an intellectual disability" and be currently enrolled in or accepted for enrollment in "a comprehensive transition and postsecondary program" that is offered by an institution of higher education (IHE). The IHE must set standards for what constitutes "maintaining satisfactory progress" in the program, and the student must maintain satisfactory progress in order to be eligible.

In developing these regulations, it will be necessary for a number of requirements to be waived, including but not limited to the following:

- Certain requirements related to student eligibility
- Accreditation standards for the programs
- State licensing of such programs (in states that license individual postsecondary programs)
- The rule that gainful employment must lead to a specific recognized occupation listed in a U.S. Department of Labor publication
- The IHE should determine whether students maintain satisfactory progress based on standards the IHE sets.

LAW: THE DEFINITION OF A PROGRAM

In Title VII, Part D, Section 760, *program* and *student* are further defined as follows:

> (1) COMPREHENSIVE TRANSITION AND POSTSECONDARY PROGRAM FOR STUDENTS WITH INTELLECTUAL DISABILITIES.—The term "comprehensive transition and postsecondary program for students with intellectual disabilities" means a degree, certificate, or nondegree program that is—
> (A) offered by an institution of higher education;
> (B) designed to support students with intellectual disabilities who are seeking to continue academic, career and technical, and independent living instruction at an institution of higher education in order to prepare for gainful employment;
> (C) includes an advising and curriculum structure; and
> (D) requires students with intellectual disabilities to participate on not less than a half-time basis, as determined by the institution, with such participation focusing on academic components and occurring through one or more of the following activities:

     (i)   Regular enrollment in credit-bearing courses with nondisabled students offered by the institution.

    (ii)   Auditing or participating in courses with nondisabled students offered by the institution for which the student does not receive regular academic credit.

   (iii)   Enrollment in noncredit-bearing, nondegree courses with nondisabled students.

   (iv)   Participation in internships or work-based training in settings with nondisabled individuals.

In developing the regulations regarding programs, rather than a complex application process, IHEs should provide "assurances" that they offer a program that meets the criteria of a "comprehensive transition and postsecondary program for students with intellectual disabilities," and this process should be as streamlined as possible. According to *The Guide to Federal Student Aid*, a resource published by the U.S. Department of Education, IHEs are responsible for determining that a program is eligible.

As a point of clarification, if an IHE desired to design a "program" around a single student with an intellectual disability, this should be allowable as long as the program meets the criteria of a "comprehensive transition and postsecondary program for students with intellectual disabilities." With respect to the definition of a "comprehensive transition and postsecondary program for students with intellectual disabilities," language from the statute should be used, with further clarification that the "advising and curriculum structure" may be the same advising and curriculum (or program of study) structure used by students not enrolled in the program.

The IHE should determine whether the students maintain satisfactory progress based on standards the IHE sets. The regulations should further clarify that "participating on not less than a half time basis, as determined by the institution," means that the amount of time the student participates (that represents at least half time) should be similar to the clock hours and credit hours for matriculating students enrolled in typical courses at the IHE. However, the participation of the students with ID focuses on academic components occurring through the activities outlined in the statute, with the intent (noted in the conference report) that Congress encourages such programs "to integrate students with intellectual disabilities into inclusive activities, coursework and campus settings with nondisabled postsecondary students."

LAW: THE DEFINITION OF A STUDENT WITH AN INTELLECTUAL DISABILITY

   (2)   STUDENT WITH AN INTELLECTUAL DISABILITY.—The term "student with an intellectual disability" means a student—

       (A)   with mental retardation or a cognitive impairment, characterized by significant limitations in—

           (i)   intellectual and cognitive functioning; and

          (ii)   adaptive behavior as expressed in conceptual, social, and practical adaptive skills; and

       (B)   who is currently, or was formerly, eligible for a free appropriate public education under the Individuals with Disabilities Education Act.

The process for identifying whether an individual meets the definition of a "student with an intellectual disability" should be determined by the admitting IHE and should be minimally burdensome for students, families, and the IHE. Whenever possible, existing documentation should be utilized from school records or sources such as previous evaluations conducted for public agencies to determine eligibility for disability benefits.

According to congressional intent as highlighted in the conference report,

> Some students with disabilities who are eligible for a free and appropriate public education may not enroll in public schools, nor choose to receive special education services under the Individuals with Disabilities Education Act. The Conferees intend to include such students in the definition of students with intellectual disabilities under this Act, if such students can otherwise meet the eligibility criteria.

The regulations should specifically state that such students, including students who are or were schooled at home or in private schools, are included in this definition. The definition in the statute also states that the student "is currently, or was formerly, eligible for a free appropriate public education (FAPE) under the Individuals with Disabilities Education Act." The regulations should use the statutory word *eligible* for FAPE instead of "receiving" FAPE to include students who may be eligible but chose not to receive special education services under IDEA and were educated in settings such as home school or private school. The regulations should also reflect the congressional intent that the student is either currently eligible for FAPE or was formerly eligible for FAPE but is no longer eligible because he or she has completed school or "aged out" of services.

MODEL DEMONSTRATION PROGRAMS AND COORDINATING CENTER

HEOA also authorizes the development and expansion of high-quality, inclusive model comprehensive transition and postsecondary programs to meet the rising interest and demand for this type of educational experience among students with ID and their families. In addition, the reauthorization includes the establishment of a coordinating center for technical assistance, evaluation, and development of recommendations for model accreditation standards. This center will address model accreditation criteria, standards, and procedures for such programs, analyze possible funding streams, and develop model memoranda of agreement between institutions of higher education and agencies providing funding for such programs. Appropriations for the model demonstration programs and coordinating center are necessary.

This reauthorization of the HEA will make it possible for many more students with ID who do not currently have the economic means to benefit from a PSE experience to do so through access to Pell Grants, Supplemental Educational Opportunity Grants, and the Federal Work-Study Program. The model demonstration programs and the coordinating center will provide models of best practice and practical information to families and institutions of higher education.

Another important part of the reauthorization is the inclusion for the first time of a good definition of universal design for learning (UDL) in a federal law and requirements for the use of UDL in teacher training programs and other aspects of the law. Appropriate regulations for the financial aid provisions, funding for the model demonstration projects and coordinating center, and implementation of the UDL provisions are critical for the long-term success of students with ID in PSE.

Policy Recommendations

Specific recommendations for the regulations are specified above. In addition, appropriations are needed for the model demonstration programs and coordinating center.

AFFORDABILITY AND FUNDING ISSUES

Despite the challenges, students with ID have made significant progress under the IDEA and the No Child Left Behind Act (NCLB) of 2001 (PL 107-110) and are completing secondary education better prepared than ever before. As described elsewhere in this book, a growing number of IHE are now including students with ID in educational, independent living, and vocational opportunities and are seeking to meet their needs. Affordability, however, is an ongoing issue for students and their families. Although the work-study jobs and federal grants described above will provide important support to students who meet the financial eligibility criteria to receive them, much more needs to be done.

Some school districts are providing financial support for students with ID who are still eligible for special education under IDEA. This support is provided to students who have not yet received a regular diploma or "aged out" of receiving services (which typically happens at age 21 or 22). One way financial support is provided by school districts is through "dual enrollment" (also called "concurrent enrollment") programs with agreements between the postsecondary institution and the school district. These agreements take a variety of forms, with school districts paying all of the expenses in some cases, and in others the family or an adult disability organization (such as vocational rehabilitation) pays part of the expenses. The Massachusetts Inclusive Concurrent Enrollment initiative is a good example of collaboration between school districts and IHEs. In that case, funding is also provided by the state department of elementary and secondary education through grants to the IHEs. School districts may also "place" a student with an ID in a postsecondary program through the Individualized Education Program (IEP) process. The district then pays for tuition and other services, such as transportation, that are determined to be necessary by the IEP team. For example, a number of students at The College of New Jersey have been placed through the IEP team, and the student's tuition is paid by their school district. If the student is "placed" through the IEP process, then the educational services are provided at no cost to the student and his or her family.

After IDEA was reauthorized in 2004, an NPRM was published in the *Federal Register* with proposed regulations to implement the newly revised law. Over 3,000 parents and members of the public submitted public comments in support of the NDSS comments on the NPRM. One of the recommendations was a request that the regulations clarify that IDEA Part B funds may be used to support students with ID who are still eligible for IDEA in postsecondary programs or in community-based settings. Instead of including that clarification in the final regulations, the preamble to the regulations stated the following on page 46668:

> *Comment:* A few commenters recommended that the regulations clarify that schools can use funds provided under Part B of the Act to support children in transitional programs on college campuses and in community-based settings.
> *Discussion:* We do not believe that the clarification requested by the commenters is necessary to add to the regulations because, as with all special education and related services, it is up to each child's IEP Team to determine the special education and related services that are needed to meet each child's unique needs in order for the child to receive FAPE. Therefore, if a child's IEP Team determines that a child's needs can best be met through participation in transitional programs on college campuses or in community based settings, and includes such services on the child's IEP, funds provided under Part B of the Act may be used for this purpose.
> *Changes:* None.

Policy Recommendations

The preamble of a final regulation includes a summary of the comments received, the department's response to the comments, and an explanation of any changes made to the regulations that differ from the proposed regulations. Despite this preamble language, confusion apparently exists. In the short term, policy guidance should be issued, and in the long term the law must be revised to include the preamble language and clearly state that the least restrictive environment provisions apply to students who are finished with secondary school and are still eligible for IDEA services.

If a student is "parentally placed" in PSE, the family must pay the tuition or find other non-IDEA funds for tuition. However, the student *may* receive some services directly from a school district through a Service Plan. Such services might include an educational coach, transportation, job coach, language therapy, and so forth and are provided directly to the student, with no funds going to the IHE. Although there is not an individual entitlement for services for parentally placed children, a "proportionate share" of the federal funds the district receives must be spent on services for such students. For more information, see the U.S. Department of Education web site at http://idea.ed.gov/explore/home.

In the short term, policy guidance should be issued and in the long term, the IDEA statute must be amended to clearly state that students with disabilities who are still eligible for IDEA services and are placed in private or public postsecondary programs by their parents are eligible for services through a Service Plan for parentally placed children.

Other Funding Sources for Individual Students

Funding may also be available through the vocational rehabilitation system, developmental disability state agencies, the Social Security system, and Department of Labor programs, although trying to access those funds can be daunting. Although there is nothing in the Vocational Rehabilitation Act or regulations preventing students with ID from utilizing vocational rehabilitation (VR) funds for tuition assistance, often funding requests for these students are rejected. There are other ways that the VR system could and should provide services directly to students with ID in postsecondary settings, such as providing job coaches and extended situational assessments, as well as blending and braiding funding with other agencies.

The largest source of funds is the students' parents, who are already stretched thin financially. This is particularly true of students who are over the age of 21 and are no longer eligible for IDEA funding. These parents are not able to make use of 529 college savings accounts and other sources typically available to parents of students who are not disabled. In the 109th Congress, Rep. Ander Crenshaw (R-FL) introduced legislation to create savings accounts for Americans with disabilities. In the 110th, he introduced H.R. 2370, the Financial Security Accounts for Individuals with Disabilities, with strong bipartisan support. At that time, U.S. Senators Bob Casey (D-PA) and Orrin Hatch (R-Utah) introduced S. 2743, a bipartisan bill (with the same name) in the Senate. Senator Christopher J. Dodd (D-CT) also introduced a savings bill, S. 2741, the Disability Savings Act of 2008. These bills would allow individuals with disabilities and their families to create tax-exempt savings accounts similar to Individual Retirement Accounts and 529 College Savings accounts and to save for specific needs without jeopardizing benefits. As this book goes to press at the beginning of the 111th Congress, Representative Crenshaw continues to promote his legislation in the House and the sponsors of the two Senate bills are working together to develop and jointly introduce a savings bill. (See the section on the HEOA for information on new opportunities for these students to qualify for work-study jobs and federal grants.)

Students, parents, school districts, and IHEs have found creative ways to fund postsecondary opportunities. For example, NDSS provides grants of up to $1,000, through the Joshua O'Neill and Zeshan Tabani Enrichment Fund, to young adults with Down syndrome who are 18 years old or older and wish to participate in postsecondary programs or are taking enrichment classes that will help them to enrich life through employment or independent living skills. Some IHEs seek scholarship funds from nonprofit organizations, individuals, and foundations to provide financial support to students. In some states, agencies for developmental disabilities provide funds. In California, regional centers may fund participation. Although creative options are available, finding the financial resources to participate can be daunting.

Policy Recommendations

- The Vocational Rehabilitation Act is overdue for reauthorization and needs to be amended to clearly state that tuition assistance and other services may be provided to students with ID. In the short term, policy guidance should be issued.
- The Financial Security Accounts for Individuals with Disabilities needs to be passed and signed by the president.

- The Developmental Disabilities Act (DD Act) is currently up for reauthorization and this provides an excellent opportunity to provide more of a focus on PSE for students with ID and DD. The laws described above could and should provide supports to individual students. The DD Act has the potential to promote systems change and to fund support for the creation and expansion of high quality programs and services. The Act should be amended to include postsecondary education as a "priority area" for DD Councils and as an "area of emphasis" for UCEDDs.

OTHER FEDERAL LEGISLATION AND POLICY ISSUES

The following laws are not currently aligned with each other or with other federal laws and in many cases do not address PSE for individuals with ID. Each of these statutes should be amended to be aligned, enable improvements, and ensure that barriers to participation are eliminated.

The Americans with Disabilities Act

The Americans with Disabilities Act (ADA) of 1990 (PL 101-336) is one of the main acts that applies directly to IHEs. It prohibits discrimination on the basis of disability in employment, state and local government, public accommodations, commercial facilities, transportation, and telecommunications. The ADA also applies to the U.S. Congress. To be protected by the ADA, one must have a disability. An individual with a disability is defined by the ADA as a person who has a physical or mental disability that substantially limits one or more major life activities, a person who has a history or record of such a disability, or a person who is perceived by others as having such a disability. The ADA does not specifically name all of the disabilities that are covered.

The Office of Civil Rights in the U.S. Department of Education enforces Title II of the ADA (Title II), which prohibits discrimination on the basis of disability. Almost every school district and IHE in the United States is subject to this law. The responsibilities of IHEs are significantly different from those of school districts. Furthermore, students have responsibilities as a postsecondary education student that they do not have as a high school student. Students must know their responsibilities and those of IHEs under ADA Title II. Every IHE must have a person, often called the ADA Coordinator, or Disability Services Coordinator, who coordinates the school's compliance with Title II of the law. Title II protects elementary, secondary, and postsecondary education students from discrimination.

To receive an academic adjustment, the student must self-identify as having a disability. The student must also have documentation of his or her disability that is not more than 3 years old. Furthermore, students must let IHE personnel know about their disability if they want to ensure that they are provided accessible facilities. The appropriate academic adjustment must be determined based on the student's disability and individual needs. Academic adjustments may include auxiliary aids and changes to academic requirements as are necessary to ensure equal educational opportunity. Examples of such adjustments are arranging for priority registration; reducing a course load; substituting one course for another; providing note takers; recording devices; sign language interpreters; extended time for testing; alterations in setting; and, if telephones are provided in dorm rooms, a teletypewriter in the dorm room, and equipping school computers with screen-reading, voice recognition, or other adaptive software or hardware.

In providing an academic adjustment, the IHE is not required to lower or effect substantial modifications to essential requirements. For example, although an IHE may be required to provide extended testing time, it is not required to change the substantive content of the test. In addition, the IHE does not have to make alterations that would fundamentally alter the nature of a service, program, or activity or would result in undue financial or administrative burdens. Furthermore, the IHE does not have to provide personal attendants, individually prescribed devices, readers for personal use or study, or other devices or services of a personal nature, such as tutoring and typing.

Workforce Investment Act Title IV: Rehabilitation Act of 1973 as Amended by PL 105-220 (Including Sections 504 and 508)

The Rehabilitation Act prohibits discrimination on the basis of disability in programs conducted by federal agencies, in programs receiving federal financial assistance, in federal employment, and in the employment practices of federal contractors. Services are provided to individuals with disabilities based on an Individualized Plan for Employment. In accordance with a state plan approved by the federal government, VR (vocational rehabilitation) services are provided through local offices of state agencies and through community-based organizations (often referred to as community rehabilitation programs), under contractual arrangements with the state agencies. Transition services are an allowable activity and are often provided through cooperative agreements between state systems (e.g., vocational rehabilitation agency), local schools, and college districts. Comparable benefits and services must be explored prior to the provision of VR services.

An individual must have a physical or mental disability that results in a substantial impediment to employment; be able to benefit from receiving VR services; and require VR services to prepare for, secure, retain, or regain employment. There is no age requirement, but regulations encourage agencies to work with students as early as possible.

VR may provide resources and supports for students to attend college as a means of securing employment. When support from VR agencies is requested, it is imperative to link individual employment goals with participation in PSE. (See the section called Other Funding Sources for Individual Students regarding difficulties for students with ID in accessing services and supports and policy recommendations.)

Section 504

Section 504 states that "no qualified individual with a disability in the United States shall be excluded from, denied the benefits of, or be subjected to discrimination under" any program or activity that either receives federal financial assistance or is conducted by any executive agency or the United States Postal Service. The Office for Civil Rights in the U.S. Department of Education enforces Section 504. Section 504 protects elementary, secondary, and postsecondary education students from discrimination.

Requirements common to these regulations include reasonable accommodation for employees with disabilities; program accessibility; effective communication with people who have hearing or vision disabilities; and accessible new construction and alterations. Each agency is responsible for enforcing its own regulations. There are no age requirements. Section 504 requires PSE institutions to provide reasonable accommodations to students with disabilities. Students must know their responsibilities and those of IHEs under Section 504.

Several of the requirements that apply through high school are different from the requirements that apply beyond high school. For instance, Section 504 requires a school district to provide free and appropriate public education (FAPE) to each child with a disability in the district's jurisdiction. Whatever the disability, a school district must identify an individual's education needs and provide any regular or special education and related aids and services necessary to meet those needs as well as it is meeting the needs of students without disabilities.

Under Section 504 IHEs are not required to provide FAPE but are required to provide appropriate academic adjustments as necessary to ensure that it does not discriminate on the basis of disability. Additionally, if an IHE provides housing to students without disabilities, it must provide comparable, convenient, and accessible housing to students with disabilities at the same cost. The IHE may require students to follow reasonable procedures to request an academic adjustment. Students are responsible for knowing and following these procedures. IHEs usually include, in their publications providing general information, information on the procedures and contacts for requesting an academic adjustment. These materials may include recruitment materials, catalogs, and student handbooks, and are often available on school web sites.

Section 508

Section 508 establishes requirements for electronic and information technology developed, maintained, procured, or used by the federal government. Section 508 requires federal electronic and information technology to be accessible to people with disabilities, including employees and members of the public.

An accessible information technology system is one that can be operated in a variety of ways and does not rely on a single sense or ability of the user. For example, a system that provides output only in visual format may not be accessible to people with visual impairments, and a system that provides output only in audio format may not be accessible to people who are deaf or hard of hearing. Some individuals with disabilities may need accessibility-related software or peripheral devices to use systems that comply with Section 508. There is no age requirement. Section 508 requires PSE institutions to provide electronic and information technology that is accessible to students with disabilities.

Table 2.1 describes other federal laws and initiatives that have relevance to postsecondary education and students with ID.

SYSTEMS CHANGE: THE NATIONAL DOWN SYNDROME SOCIETY

In 2002, the NDSS began creating a strategic plan to promote transition and PSE opportunities. This effort was spurred by pressure from parents who always identified transition and PSE as a critical priority. This NDSS Transition and Postsecondary Initiative has grown organically and now represents a comprehensive approach to educational advancement that addresses barriers and promotes improved public policy and systems change at the federal and state levels; promotes research, model demonstration projects, technical assistance, and outreach and dissemination efforts; promotes public awareness and improved public attitudes; and provides technical assistance and scholarship funds.

New Jersey Initiatives

The development of PSE initiatives in a state was identified as a key element of this plan, whether it is funded by private or public sources. Fortunately, NDSS received a generous grant from Steve and Laura Riggio to develop inclusive postsecondary education models for students with ID in New Jersey. The first step, in the spring of 2004, was to establish a steering committee with broad-based expertise, including experts in higher education, general and special education, parents, self-advocates, and state agency leaders. The steering committee reviewed the practices and procedures of PSE efforts across the nation. By learning from the varied initiatives that existed across the country, the committee sought to expand on the successes of these other efforts and develop a model that could be replicated nationwide. Other key objectives included development of an affordable model, identification of desired outcomes for students, and development of a request for proposals (RFP) based on the desired outcomes, including academic enrichment, socialization, independent living skills, and competitive employment.

In February 2005, the RFP was distributed to all two- and four-year public and private IHEs in New Jersey. The RFP provided for IHEs to receive funds for a planning year (August 2005 through August 2006). Upon successful completion of the planning year, the IHE would be eligible for additional funding for the first and second operational years of the program, with the understanding that after the second operational year the program must be self-sustaining. Upon review of the applications received, the Committee selected Mercer County Community College and The College of New Jersey.

Although each college followed the guidelines established by the steering committee in the RFP, each initiative has developed in a manner appropriate to its respective cultural milieu. The first year of classes began in August/September 2006, and the 3-year grant ended in August 2008. Both the College of New Jersey and Mercer County Community College are still serving students with intellectual disabilities on their campuses.

South Carolina Initiatives

Not unlike many other PSE initiatives nationally, systems change in South Carolina (SC) began with the vision of a parent, Donald Bailey, who formed the Col-

Table 2.1. Acts/initiatives and their relationship to PSE for students with intellectual disabilities

Act/initiative	Overview	Relationship to PSE
Workforce Investment Act of 1998 Title I—Youth	WIA Title I offers: tutoring, study skills training, and instruction leading to completion of secondary school and alternative secondary school services. Programs vary greatly among local areas and among providers of programs. Preparation for employment is an integral part of WIA youth programs. WIA also supports summer employment, paid and unpaid internships, work experiences, and occupational skills training. Supportive services are specifically authorized. Leadership development opportunities and adult mentoring are also offered.	Postschool supports thorough structured arrangements in postsecondary institutions and adult service agencies Employment supports
Assistive Technology Act 2004	Administered through Office of Special Education and Rehabilitative Services, Rehabilitation Services Administration. States receive grants through federal appropriations for • A state finance program to increase access to and funding for assistive technology devices and assistive technology services • A device utilization program that provides for the exchange, repair, recycling, or other reutilization of assistive technology devices • A device loan program that provides for short-term loans of assistive technology devices • Device demonstrations • Training and technical assistance • Public awareness	Resources to support acquisition of assistive technology needed for successful participation in PSE
Carl D. Perkins Career and Technical Education Improvement Act of 2006	Assists students in meeting academic achievement standards, especially in preparation for high-demand occupations in emerging or established professions Supports student achievement in core academic subjects, as defined by the No Child Left Behind Act of 2001, and emphasizes math and science education that incorporates the use of technology. Ensures access to career and technical education for special populations, including students with disabilities. Supports innovative programs and activities that contribute to the development of a statewide system of high-quality career and technical education pathways, including enhancement of services to special populations that include students with disabilities	Potential pathway to PSE opportunities that include high-quality career and technical education

	Enhances coordination between secondary and postsecondary programs and establishes a new provision for state development of model sequences of courses for vocational and technical programs: Funds: • career and technical education • tech-prep	
The National and Community Service Trust Act of 1993	The Corporation for National and Community Service administers grants that provide service opportunities, training, a living allowance, and educational awards to persons participating in service. For more information see: http://www.americorps.org/for_individuals/benefits/benefits_ed_award.asp The new Heroes Earnings Assistance and Relief Tax (HEART) Act of 2008 (PL 110-245), effective August 18, 2008, directs the Social Security Administration to ignore an individual's receipt of AmeriCorps benefits (living allowance, health insurance, child care, and the education award) for purposes of SSI eligibility AmeriCorps is open to U.S. citizens, U.S. nationals, and lawful permanent resident aliens age 17 and older. Members serve full time or part time over a 9- to 12-month period, or during summer	Upon completion, members receive an Education Award, $4,725 for a year of full-time or prorated for part-time service, to pay education costs at qualified institutions of higher education. Seventy-eight IHEs match the Education Award.
Social Security Administration Work Incentives	Social Security has several programs that reduce the impact of work on disability benefits. These work incentives allow individuals to subtract certain work-related expenses from their income in order to maintain SSI/SSDI eligibility and/or reduce the amount of money taken out of their benefit check. The two main programs are: 1. Impairment-Related Work Expenses (IRWE): a work incentive that can be used to help reduce the impact of earnings on Social Security disability benefits. IRWEs include the reasonable cost of items and services (e.g., attendant care, medical or prosthetic devices, drugs and medical services, residential modifications, special transportation) that, because of a disability, a person needs and uses in order to work. 2. Plan for Achieving Self-Support (PASS): a work incentive that allows an individual with a disability to set aside income and/or resources toward a work goal for a specified period of time (e.g., a person could set aside money for education, vocational training, or business start-up expenses). A PASS can be used to help reduce the amount that the Social Security Administration (SSA) deducts from an SSI check because of a person's earned income. SSA must approve PASS plans. For further information and/or updates on any changes, contact the Social Security Administration and/or the local Work Incentives Planning and Assistance program. Resources can be found at http://www.ssa.gov/redbook/ or http://www.ssa.gov/disabilityresearch/wi/generalinfo.htm	Can be used to support students in PSE as long as it relates to an employment goal

lege Transition Connection (CTC), an organization of families and professionals with the goal of creating PSE opportunities for individuals with ID. To further its efforts, CTC then established a partnership with NDSS and the Center for Disability Resources (CDR), the UCEDD in SC. Additionally, CTC established a Task Force to conduct research on PSE nationally, including site visits to various PSE programs. State leaders, including IHEs, were then invited to attend a Roundtable meeting (funded by NDSS, CTC, CDR, and the SC Developmental Disability Council), to hear about PSE options and outcomes from national experts. The Roundtable meeting also provided the Task Force with the opportunity to distribute a RFP to state IHEs to establish PSE options for students with ID. It was a tipping point in developing interest and collaboration among state agencies and IHEs.

CTC raised over $300,000 and convinced the SC General Assembly to provide $300,000 per year for the project (for the past 2 years). The state DD council funded national experts to provide technical assistance at Task Force meetings and the VR agency is piloting funding for tuition support. The project goal is to develop inclusive, replicable PSE options for students with ID. Grants have been awarded to University of South Carolina, Columbia (Fall 2008); Clemson University (January 2009); and Coastal Carolina University (Fall 2009).

Tennessee Initiatives

Another successful NDSS collaboration was with the state of Tennessee. A training session was held with Tennessee affiliates to form a Governmental Affairs Committee (GAC); assist them in identifying key priorities; and provide advocacy training. Then NDSS supported the new GAC in developing relationships with key state agencies to achieve access to PSE for students with ID. An invitation-only conference was organized and sponsored by NDSS affiliates, the Tennessee Council on DD, and the Vanderbilt Kennedy Center for Excellence in Developmental Disabilities (a UCEDD) and was attended by a number of colleges and representatives of all relevant state agencies. The result of the conference was an agreement among those present to form a task force to work toward establishing PSE options for students with ID in Tennessee. Representatives of the Task Force visited several other PSE models in other states. Subsequently, the Tennessee Council on DD awarded $525,000 over 3 years to the Vanderbilt UCEDD to develop model initiatives in the state. Again, motivated parent organizations, the DD Council, and a UCEDD all played important roles in this systems change effort.

Technical assistance has been particularly effective in states where NDSS has GACs. For instance, the NDSS GAC in Ohio has been instrumental in promoting a statewide task force and organizing a statewide conference on PSE. Based on the successes and lessons learned in New Jersey, South Carolina, and Tennessee, NDSS has found that the following recommendations and strategies have been helpful in creating state-level systems change in developing postsecondary programs:

- Start with committed parent and disability advocacy organization(s) in the state.
- Develop a task force of key stakeholders who will work together to identify possible funding sources, promote interest and collaboration, and support the development of postsecondary opportunities on an ongoing basis.

- Identify funds for start-up expenses for the first few years and include the task force in creating an RFP. Funds may come from donations, organizations, state agencies, the Developmental Disability Council, the UCEDD, or other sources.
- Hold a roundtable/conference and invite experts, representatives of key state agencies, IHEs, and others to learn about PSE opportunities and the RFP.
- Fund at least one model.
- Utilize a task force to collaborate with parent and self-advocacy organizations and key state agencies to address needed policy and practice changes as well as funding sources to support individual students, program development, and sustainability. Agencies should include, at a minimum: the state department of education, a UCEDD, the DD Council, Parent Training Centers, the state higher education commission, Vocational Rehabilitation, and the state developmental disability agency.
- Ensure that the RFP requires an evaluation component.
- Follow up with regular communication, networking opportunities, and technical assistance.
- Ensure that there is rigorous qualitative and quantitative evaluation of student outcomes and overall satisfaction of all involved.

MASSACHUSETTS SYSTEMS CHANGE EFFORTS

The Institute for Community Inclusion, a UCEDD at the University of Massachusetts, has had work in postsecondary education for students with intellectual disabilities via three federally funded projects, two model research and innovation projects funded by the Office of Special Education Programs (OSEP) since 1997, and a research project funded by a Rehabilitation Research Training Center (RRTC) grant on postsecondary education for students with disabilities at the University of Hawaii from 1998 to 2003. Based on the results of these projects, the Massachusetts Advocates for Children (MAC), in 2005, through the Massachusetts DD Council–funded Transition Committee, crafted a line item for the state budget that would support establishment of an Inclusive Concurrent Enrollment (ICE) initiative for students with severe disabilities who are 18 to 22 years old and still enrolled in their school district under the IDEA. MAC also enlisted a state representative to broker the line item through the state budgeting process. These efforts proved to be successful, and the ICE initiative has been operational since January of 2007, when it was funded at $2,000,000 ($1,575,000 in 2008; approximately $1,360,000 in 2009). The decrease in funding is a reflection of the fiscal crisis within the state but also demonstrates the legislature's and governor's commitment to the initiative, inasmuch as the cuts in the line item were modest. The state Department of Elementary and Secondary Education (DESE), in collaboration with the Department of Higher Education (DHE), administers the grant. Moreover, a leadership team composed of key stakeholders (e.g., DESE, DHE, Parent Training and Information Center, all state disability agencies, workforce development agency, advocacy organizations) guides all grant activities.

There are six partnerships statewide, each of which is led by at least one IHE with several participating school districts (see Figure 2.1). As the initiative has

Inclusive Concurrent Enrollment

Mount Wachusett Community College
- Ashburnham-Westminster Reg. School District
- Fitchburg Public Schools
- Gardner Public Schools
- Leominster Public Schools
- Narragansett Regional Public Schools
- Ralph C. Mahar Regional Schools

UMass Boston/Bunker Hill Community College/Roxbury Community College
- Boston Public Schools (Madison Park, Academy of Public Service, Noonan Business Academy, Charlestown High School)
- Quincy Public Schools

Bristol Community College
- Fall River Public Schools
- Old Rochester Public Schools
- Somerset Public Schools
- Seekonk Public Schools
- Taunton Public Schools

Holyoke Community College
- Agawam Public Schools
- Belchertown Public Schools
- Monson Public Schools
- Northampton Public Schools
- South Hadley Public Schools
- Ware Public Schools
- Westfield Public Schools

Quinsigamond Community College
- Berlin–Boylston Public Schools
- Leicester Public Schools
- Millbury Public Schools
- West Boylston Public Schools
- Worcester Public Schools

MassBay Community College (Wellesley Hills Campus)
- Boston Public Schools
- Needham Public Schools
- Newton Public Schools

Figure 2.1. Partnerships for PSE in Massachusetts. (Created by Debra Hart and the Institute for Community Inclusion.)

grown, so have the number of participating school districts and the number of students. There are 26 school districts and close to 100 students with intellectual disabilities participating in inclusive PSE options, including academic courses and overall campus life. Each partnership is unique and responsive to the cultural context of the IHE (for more information on this initiative, see Chapter 3).

Over the last decade, more decisions and power have devolved to states. It is our view that to be successful over the long term, the field must do more than promote the development of programs and services at individual IHEs. Rather, to create sustained progress a systems change approach must be utilized, bringing together and encouraging collaboration among and funding from state agencies. Along with networking opportunities and collaboration among IHEs in the state, this will promote long-lasting change and financial support for PSE initiatives and individual students.

POLICY AND PROMISING PRACTICE RECOMMENDATIONS

1. Secure Department of Education "Dear Colleague" letter to State Departments/Boards of Higher Education, informing them that the reauthorization of the Higher Education Act supports access to PSE options for students with ID and asking them to support the development or enhancement of such options and services. Policy guidance recommendations provided previously in

the chapter related to IDEA and VR should be included in this "Dear Colleague" letter.

2. Ensure that State Performance Plans and monitoring indicators 13 and 14 required under IDEA include PSE options and track outcomes for students with ID.

3. Modify and align existing legislation to support increased access to PSE for students with ID (e.g., IDEA, HEA, NCLB, WIA, SSA, Transportation Act, DD Act, Medicaid, *Olmstead v. L. C.* supreme court decision).

4. States should examine the use of developmental disability funds to ensure that such funds may be used to financially support these students.

5. States and IHEs should develop/modify existing policies to help students with ID gain access to campus housing.

6. Ensure that students with ID are included in generic college admissions advising, awareness, experience, and materials development efforts (e.g., helping students apply to college through application and essay assistance, college visits, college selection assistance, and accessible technological infrastructure).

7. Ensure that students with ID are included in activities designed to develop college aspirations for students without disabilities no later than the eighth grade and include practices such as information dissemination through required information courses for students, information workshops, parental and peer involvement, adequate counseling resources, and well-structured mentoring programs.

SUMMARY

This is just the beginning. There is need to continue federal and state efforts to create increased access to PSE options for individuals with ID nationwide. Grass roots efforts coupled with state and federal systems change initiatives need to be magnified to continue to expand the choice of PSE for individuals with ID and their families, so that the option is available regardless of where they live. Further efforts should benefit from lessons learned from current initiatives, evidenced-based practices, and research and evaluation to determine the efficacy of different models, related practices, and subsequent student outcomes. Finally, all federal legislation must be aligned with the HEOA to maximize all initiatives.

REFERENCES

Americans with Disabilities Act of 1990, PL 101-336, 42 U.S.C. §§ 12101 *et seq.*

Assistive Technology Act of 1998, PL 105-394, 29 U.S.C. §§ 3001 *et seq.*

Carl D. Perkins Career and Technical Education Improvement Act of 2006, Stat. 2435, 20 U.S.C. §§ 2301 *et seq.*

College Access and Opportunity Act of 2005, H.R. 609, 109th Cong. (2005).

Developmental Disabilities Assistance and Bill of Rights Act of 2000, 42 U.S.C. §§ 15001 *et seq.*

Heroes Earnings Assistance and Relief Tax Act of 2008, PL 110-245, U.S.C. §§ 302.

Higher Education Opportunity Act of 2008, PL 110-315, 122 Stat. 3078.

Individuals with Disabilities Education Improvement Act of 2004, PL 108-446, 20 U.S.C. §§ 1400 *et seq.*

National and Community Service Trust Act of 1993, 42 U.S.C. §§ 12501 *et seq.*

National Council on Disability. (2008). *The state of 21st century financial incentives for Americans with disabilities.* Washington, DC: Author.

No Child Left Behind Act of 2001, PL 107-110, 115 Stat. 1425, 20 U.S.C. §§ 6301 *et seq.*

Rehabilitation Act of 1973, PL 93-112, 29 U.S.C. §§ 701 *et seq.*

Ticket to Work and Work Incentives Improvement Act of 1999, PL 106-170, 42 U.S.C. §§ 3141 *et seq.*

Wagner, M., Newman, L., Cameto, R., Garza, N., & Levine, P. (2005). *After high school: A first look at the postschool experiences of youth with disabilities* (National Longitudinal Transition Study 2). Menlo Park, CA: SRI International.

Workforce Investment Act of 1998, 29 U.S.C. §§ 2801 *et seq.*

The Spectrum of Options: Current Practices

Debra Hart and Meg Grigal

An important aspect to keep in mind when thinking about creating postsecondary education (PSE) options for students with intellectual disabilities (ID) is that there is no one way to do it. Each option is different and often depends upon the philosophical underpinnings of the program design, the governance structure and mission of the college, the community in which the student and the college are located, and the range and intensity of resources that are available to support the initiative. It would be great to be able to say, "This is the best way to do this; follow this formula, and it will result in the ideal program or array of individualized services." Currently that is not possible for a number of reasons. First, all of the iterations of existing PSE programs are not yet known, especially efforts of individual students and their families in creating access to a PSE. Second, there are minimal data on the known PSE options, making it difficult to contrast and compare them in any statistically meaningful way. Finally, most PSE options that have been in existence long enough to produce graduates have not been subjected to systematic follow-up to identify student outcomes. As a result, it is not possible to identify the PSE option that might produce the best student outcomes. However, lessons have been learned and robust data have been gathered on promising practices used to support students with ID as they make the transition to adult life and to adult service systems, along with some preliminary data on existing PSE practices, that can be used to guide the development of new services and supports for students with ID seeking to access PSE.

Given the need for a greater understanding of PSE options for students with ID, in this chapter we discuss the model frameworks of PSE options and service delivery models that are currently being used to serve students with ID in PSE. In addition, to illustrate the different models, we provide profiles of several PSE programs as each model is discussed. We also examine when or how these models are initiated and the benefits and challenges of the different PSE models. This includes policies and practices that create barriers to inclusive PSE, such as entrance criteria, placement and ability to benefit tests, financial aid, and "otherwise qualified" issues. Results from a national survey on PSE options for students with ID are examined in detail. The chapter concludes with a presentation of suggested promising practices that have been drafted to guide the development or enhancement of PSE services for students with ID.

CURRENT MODELS AND SERVICE DELIVERY OPTIONS

Model Frameworks

The following information provides detail on the model frameworks for service delivery, followed by profiles of the different types of programs as each is discussed. The model frameworks vary immensely, but an examination reveals that they fall within three broad designs. The models are categorized based on the degree to which the program supported student participation in typical inclusive college courses, in addition to all other aspects of college life. This unit of analysis was chosen to reflect the reality that one of the primary reasons individuals without disabilities choose PSE is to pursue a course of study that relates to a career goal; this should not be different for individuals with ID. Lessons learned from K–12 school and adult service systems indicate that the more inclusive an approach is to supporting individuals with disabilities, whatever the context (e.g., general education, employment, community living), the better the outcome.

However, we recognize and want to emphasize that these broad categories are *descriptive* and not *prescriptive*. We are not suggesting that to create access to PSE for students with ID, one must first *pick* one of these model structures. Planning at any level should always begin with a student's needs. These categories, however limited they may be, do provide the field with an initial framework through which to view current services used to help students with ID access college courses. Part of the challenge now is to broaden the scope of defining the services provided within these models and to further understand how the range of services within each model affects student outcomes. Simultaneously, it will be important to identify and understand the theories and assumptions that underlie these postsecondary education models.

The three PSE models are mixed or hybrid, substantially separate, and inclusive individual supports. There is a great degree of variability within each model; each provides a wide range of supports and services across all aspects of college and community life. As previously mentioned, there has been minimal research on the effectiveness of each model. The models are described in the order of prevalence.

Mixed/Hybrid Model

In the mixed/hybrid model, students with ID participate in academic classes (audit, credit, or noncredit) and social activities with students without disabilities. The level of integration of students with ID in typical college courses ranges from supporting one student in one class to supporting any number of students taking typical college courses across the range of offerings of the institute of higher education (IHE). Often students may also participate in classes designed particularly for students with disabilities (sometimes referred to as "life skills" or "transition" classes). Aside from access to courses, this model typically provides students with a wide range of activities, including employment experience on or off campus, acquisition of life skills (e.g., independent living, financial literacy), and participation in student clubs and organizations on campus. There is a broad range of employment options. Some students are rotated across different unpaid or paid employment experiences that have been preestablished in different work sites, such as fast food restaurants, convenience stores, maintenance jobs, landscaping, and office work, and some students are provided a more customized job experience based on their personal career goal.

There is usually a base where the program staff's offices are housed and, in some cases, a place where students can meet for individual or small-group counseling or instruction. Again, it is important to note that there is an immense variability in the type of services and the degree of inclusion in the college community for this type of program. A major challenge that this type of program faces is working with the IHE to find dedicated space, because it is in high demand and short supply. Depending on the overall design of the mixed/hybrid model and the level of inclusion of the students, additional challenges the program may face include low expectations of all involved, including the student; a lack of student preparation; alternative pathways that circumvent placement tests, entrance criteria, "otherwise qualified" requirements, and prerequisite requirements; and funding for tuition and the development and enhancement of services. But these challenges are not insurmountable. There are a number of IHEs and/or school systems that are working to address these challenges and are providing students with ID access to a PSE. Many students use these experiences to gain greater independence and employment and to access future PSE options on their own. There are a number of articles that describe a mixed/hybrid approach in greater detail, with descriptions of the activities, funding structures, and other aspects of the model (Casale-Giannola & Wilson Kamens, 2006; Grigal, Dwyre, & Davis, 2006; Grigal, Neubert, & Moon, 2001; Hall, Kleinert, & Kearns, 2000; Hamill, 2003). Program Profiles 1-3 show three examples of the mixed/hybrid model.

Program Profile 1

The Western Connection
Western Connecticut State University
Danbury, Connecticut

Type of program: dual enrollment

Funding source(s): IDEA/tuition

Model: Mixed/hybrid

Goal: The Western Connection Program helps a diverse population of students with disabilities in an integrated college setting to gain the skills and experience needed to achieve success during adult life in the areas of employment, self-determination, and PSE.

Eligibility criteria: Students with disabilities who
- Are 18–21 years old
- Have met the high school academic requirements but are still enrolled in high school
- Have demonstrated interest/motivation to attend the program at the college
- Are able to perform with appropriate support in a college setting
- Have successfully completed one or two community work experiences
- Are able to obtain and maintain competitive or supported employment in the community

(continued)

Student population: Students with ID, learning and behavior disorders, and pervasive developmental disabilities (such as autism or Asperger syndrome).

Overview: Currently, the program serves 10 students who are enrolled in several different school systems within southwestern Connecticut. The program is funded by tuition, which is determined by the costs involved for the number of students enrolled, divided by that number of students, and then shared by all of the sending school districts. Western Connecticut State University (WCSU) provides, at no cost, office space on campus, along with access to copiers, telephones, fax machines, and campus facilities (including college ID cards, food areas, gyms, libraries, computer labs, and the career center).

The program opened in September 2003, and staffing includes the program coordinator, an instructional assistant, and a job developer. There are also strong partnerships with college student mentors, college administrative personnel, and professors, all of whom provide support either directly to the students or to the overall program.

The focus of Western Connection is to increase student skills and experiences in the areas of employment, self-determination, and PSE. This is achieved through several components. All students participate in person-centered planning activities upon entering the program to determine the focus and expected outcomes of services. All Western Connection students audit college classes on campus each semester. When courses are not available (during intercessions) students participate in employability skills workshops taught by WCSU professors. Job-seeking skills are taught by the special educator as needed, along with travel training, social and personal skills, and self-determination skills. Students are supported in the creation of personal goals and encouraged to share these during IEP meetings each year. Career development and awareness are nurtured through such activities as job interviewing practice, filling out job applications, and visits by students to the college career development center on campus. Students are provided with job training experiences as needed to identify or refine their career objectives. By the spring semester of the student's first year, students work with staff to obtain integrated community-based paid employment. Once a student acquires a paid position, the program coordinator and job coach provide follow-along support to the student and the employers.

Constant collaboration occurs with the Dean of Professional Studies and the Dean of Graduate Studies at WCSU to maintain satisfaction levels for all parties and to brainstorm for new ideas for access and integration. Collaboration also occurs with professors who are teaching classes that Western Connection students are auditing. Students are involved in campus activities, clubs, and organizations that are of interest to them.

The program has developed a partnership with college student mentors. These college students spend 3 hours a week with Western Connection students for both social and academic support. The mentors are paid $9.00 an hour by the Danbury Public Schools and have monthly staff meetings with the teacher to share assessment information. The instructor has a strong collaborative relationship with the Bureau of Rehabilitation Services, meeting monthly to review individual student cases.

Data collection & outcomes:
For the 2006–2007 school year
- 92% of students were in paid work (clothing retail, humane society, restaurants, grocery stores) and worked an average of 8.3 hours per week for an average of $7.50 per hour.
- 100% of students audited classes at the college (history, theater, psychology, English courses)

Program Profile 2

Pathway at UCLA Extension
UCLA Campus/Westwood
10995 Le Conte Ave, Room 413
Los Angeles, CA 90024
310.794.1235
www.uclaextension.edu/pathway

Type of program: Postschool (adult)

Funding source(s): Student/family, adult services (via reimbursement to student/family), scholarship fund

Model: Mixed/hybrid

Goals:
1. To provide life skill training and an opportunity to live independently in an inclusive residential setting
2. To provide inclusive learning experiences through participation in the social, recreational, and cultural activities of the UCLA campus
3. To provide learning opportunities for career development through coursework and work experience
4. To provide opportunities for employment on the UCLA campus and engagement with UCLA students
5. To assist participants' transition from Pathway to independent living and meaningful employment

Eligibility criteria: Potential Pathway students should meet the following criteria:
- Age 18–25 when starting Pathway
- Have completed a high school program with a diploma, certificate of completion, or equivalent from a certified secondary school
- Be able to safely get around campus during class transitions, meal times, and recreational activities after initial orientation training
- Be able to actively participate in completing Pathway application forms and personal interview process
- Have basic safety skills in unsupervised settings
- Have practical reading and writing skills
- Have family support and a personal desire to gain skills necessary for employment and independent living
- Have academic, vocational, and social experiences that contribute to successful independent living

Student population served: Intellectual and developmental disabilities

Average number of students served annually: 35–40 (17–20 per 2-year cohort)

Overview of program: Pathway at UCLA Extension is a 2-year, certificated educational program for young adults with developmental disabilities. Through a combination of educational, vocational, social, and residential experiences, the program helps participants develop skills required for personal success at work, at home, and in the community, while providing opportunities for continuing educational growth. Pathway's goal is to prepare young adults with DD for independent living, employment, and lifelong learning.

(continued)

Staffing includes: teacher, faculty, residential coordinator, resident assistants, vocational coordinator, transition coordinator, tutors

As with other UCLA Extension programs, instructors are hired on a part-time per class basis.

Student's day includes

Employment	Course access	College campus & community involvement
Internship (8–10 hrs/wk) during year 2. These are individually driven and are based on student interests/ skills.	Students take 66 units (three to four classes per quarter) of Pathway-specific courses over 2 years covering • General education (15 units) • Academic courses (24 units) • Life skills (8 units) • Career (19 units) Students must also take 12 units of electives outside of Pathway offerings through - UCLA Extension - UCLA - UCLA recreation - Other postsecondary	• UCLA recreation membership • UCLA student mentorship for social/academics • Service learning incorporated into course work • Teamworks—Pathway students receive leadership training and then organize community volunteers in engagement activities. Spring 2008—Tree planting and beach clean-up.

Data collection & outcomes: The first cohort has just finished its first year, and outcome data have not been analyzed yet. Data are being gathered on the seven outcomes listed below, and the program will continue to gather information from graduates for a number of years after leaving.

1. Enhanced academic skills: to set a foundation for lifelong learning
2. Career development: identifying *career goals* and participating in activities that support future employment
3. Independence: achieving an increased level of *independence* and participating in community activities
4. Social competence: by developing personal social and work relationships
5. Self-advocacy: practicing skills in academic and daily living
6. Healthy living: assessing one's own *health needs* and engaging in a healthy lifestyle
7. Self-enrichment: Pursuing *self-enrichment* activities that match personal goal

---

Program Profile 3

Edgewood College
Cutting-Edge Program
1000 Edgewood College
Madison, WI 53711

Type of program: Postschool (adult)

Funding source(s): Tuition-driven and development of an endowment

Model: Mixed / hybrid

Goals:
1. Extend the college experience to individuals with disabilities who have traditionally been denied admittance to college.
2. Provide students with skills to succeed as lifelong learners in PSE.
3. Provide on/off campus internships for students to gain employment.
4. Provide students with opportunities to interact with peers in academic and student-life activities.
5. Provide students the opportunity to increase their independence through integrated on-campus student housing.
6. Provide undergraduate and graduate students the opportunity to learn from individuals with disabilities in inclusive academic and social settings.
7. Provide graduate students in the College Special Education Teacher Training Program the opportunity to teach adults with disabilities study skills, social skills, community health and safety, and interpersonal communication.
8. Provide graduate students in the College Special Education Teacher Training Program with opportunity to learn to evaluate, adapt and prioritize curriculum in regular education classrooms in order to meet the needs of individuals with disabilities.

Eligibility Criteria: There is no disability-specific criteria or academic requirements. Candidates are screened for their desire to attend college, and identified based on their potential to serve as good ambassadors of the program.

Average number of students served annually: 7-25 per year.

Overview of program: The *Cutting-Edge* is an individualized approach to inclusion in college for adult learners with significant disabilities. Based on best practices on inclusion in postsecondary education, Edgewood College is the first four-year college in Wisconsin to open their doors to adult learners with more significant disabilities. These are individuals who have either traditionally not been able to meet the standard admissions criteria for college or require additional supports in order to be successful in college.

The primary objective of the *Cutting-Edge* is to serve individuals with disabilities on a college campus with peers without disabilities, giving them the opportunity to experience college life. The program strives to give students a complete college experience, both academic and social inclusion, to the greatest degree possible. The program strives to fit the individual needs of each student, rather than having the students try to fit into a predetermined mold.

The *Cutting-Edge* has a set of core credit courses (a total of 5 credits each semester) that are required for students. In addition, the students are encouraged to take 1 to 4 inclusive college courses a semester. The inclusive college courses can be taken either for credit or audit.

(continued)

Student participation is facilitated by the Director of the *Cutting-Edge*, a Program Coordinator, and through peer mentor relationships where *Cutting-Edge* students are paired with undergraduate and graduate students in academic and social settings. This program is designed to meet multiple objectives for both students with and without disabilities. Students who serve as peer mentors gain firsthand knowledge about people with disabilities on campus as part of their course requirements. Peers and classmates learn how the campus community serves as a microcosm for the community at large, with individuals with disabilities being woven into the fabric of our college culture.

In addition, three faculty members in the School of Education have incorporated a practicum experience as part of their course requirements. Faculty requires the students to complete their practicum by serving as peer mentors. Students who are seeking teaching certification are able to earn practicum hours and gain hands-on experience with inclusion in college. This program ties the practicum experience to students majoring in Education, Psychology, Child Life, and Art Therapy.

Staffing includes: The program is designed to maximize the use of natural supports to facilitate inclusion. The full-time Director of the *Cutting-Edge* and the Program Coordinator work closely with 25 undergraduate and 10 graduate students who have been recruited to serve as peer mentors to the *Cutting-Edge* students in classes, in study skills, and socially. Students are paired with *Cutting-Edge* students to help ensure successful integration into the college community. Students who have successfully managed to meet academic requirements of college appear to be especially adept at helping *Cutting-Edge* students understand requirements for success in the classroom. Peer mentors are vital in teaching higher level skills such as time management skills, group dynamics in class projects, and interpersonal communication. Some peer mentors go beyond core requirements of their practicum to developing genuine friendships with *Cutting-Edge* students.

Course participation

The program implements a core content of pre-college level courses specifically designed to meet the educational needs of the students with developmental disabilities. The courses are team-taught by graduate students who are seeking their teaching certification in special education. These include seven 2 and 3 credit courses: Resource Seminar; Safety in the Community; Friends, Dating, and Your Place in a Diverse Community; Internships; Human Issues in the Community; Independent Living Seminar (required for students living on campus); and Career Exploration.

Students typically enter Edgewood College as non-degree seeking students. In addition to taking a core set of courses through the *Cutting-Edge* program, students take between 1 to 4 regular education courses. Students have the option of taking the inclusive college courses either for credit or audit. Some students may choose to become degree-seeking students, who are then required to take courses for credit. Non-degree seeking students who audit courses have the option of completing the course again for credit.

This is a list of regular education courses completed by students during the 2007-08 and 2008-09 school years. The *Cutting-Edge* program is also open to supporting inclusion of *Cutting-Edge* students in courses that are not yet on this list.

Course Title	Course #	Credit or Audit
Acting I	Th265	Credit
Basic Writing Skills	Eng99	Audit
Career and Majors	IC205	Credit
College Writing	Eng110	Credit
Computer Graphics	Art150	Audit
Creative Writing	Eng205	Credit
Digital Photography	Art204	Audit
East Asian History	Hist111	Credit
Exceptional Child	Ed310	Audit
First-Semester Spanish	Span101	Audit
Infancy and Childhood	Psych210	Audit
Instructional Resources and Media	Ed250	Audit
Introduction to Earth Science	Geo102	Credit
Introduction to Interpersonal Communications	Comm240	Audit
Introduction to Literature and Drama	Th136	Audit
Introduction to the Natural World	Nat106	Audit
Introduction to the Natural World for Elementary Educators	Nat104	Audit
Literature for Adolescents & Middle School	Ed382	Audit
Modern China	Hist117	Credit
Multicultural Art in USA	Eth264	Audit
Painting I	Art205	Audit
Painting II	Art305	Audit
Palestine & Israel	HI404	Audit
Photography I	Art207	Audit
ProSeminar in Historian Research	Hist295	Credit
Roots N Shoots	Envs305	Audit
Second-Semester Spanish	Span102	Audit
Speech	Comm101	Audit
Survey of American Music	Mus154	Credit
The Helping Relationship	Ed334	Audit
Topics in Early Childhood	Ed337	Audit
Video	Art120	Audit
Women's Choir	Mus130	Audit

Substantially Separate Model

In the substantially separate model, students participate *only* in classes with other students with disabilities and do not have access to typical college classes. In some cases these specially designed classes may already exist at the college, are being offered through their continuing education department to any community member with a disability, and are not specifically created for a particular group of students enrolled in a program. For example, Palomar College, in its 2008–2009 course catalog, offers 14 classes that are listed as designed for students with developmental disabilities. Topics range from very student-centered courses such as Personal Adjustment and Growth, and Educational Assessment and Guidance, to broader topics such as Pre-Algebra Support, Composition, and Adapted Computer Skills. The catalog states that there are no credits associated with these classes and that students may take certain classes repeatedly.

Another version of this program model is one that is created in partnership with community service providers. For example, at Maryland's Montgomery College Graduate Transition Programs (GTP), the college partners with two adult service providers, Target Community and Educational Services and Potomac Community Resources, to create a community program for students with disabilities exiting high school. GTP is a 2-year, tuition-based, credit-free certificate program. The college supports student access to classes through their Workforce Development and Continuing Education Department and collaborates with these two outside agencies to address students' employment and recreation needs. The overall objective is to enable students to transition to greater independent living through functional education, residential, vocational, and life-skills services. Although these programs do not create access to typical college courses, they are potentially able to address some of the initial needs a student with ID may have after leaving the high school setting. In addition, exposure to such learning experiences may provide students with the opportunity to build their skills as adult learners and enable them to be better prepared to access typical college classes in the future.

Another iteration of the substantially separate program model is one in which the initiators of a new program at the college create new coursework designed specifically for students with ID in that program. Often in these programs, the college will engage graduate students or instructors to teach the classes. For example, the Mason LIFE Program at George Mason University (GMU) is a 4-year curriculum-based tuition program for incoming students between the ages of 18 and 23. In this program the instructors are master's students enrolled at GMU who are majoring in special education. The specially designed courses available to students in the Mason LIFE Program include Astronomy, Blackboard Support, Citizenship, Community Access, Employment Opportunities, Exploratory Mathematics Time & Measurement, Featured Writing—Short Stories with a Moral, Fitness & Well-Being, Horticulture, Independent Living—Nutrition, Medical & Self-Care Management, Multi-Media Analysis I, Non-Fiction I—Folklore and Fables, Self-Advocacy & Leadership, Theatre Arts II, Virginia History, Visual Arts, and Yearbook. Classes follow the GMU academic calendar schedule, but students may participate in classes only between the hours of 9 a.m. and 3 p.m.

Students who enroll in substantially separate programs may have the opportunity to participate in generic social activities on campus and may be offered work-based learning experiences, which may range from vocational training in preestablished sites to internships and job placements on or off campus. Typically these programs have a separate curriculum designed by program personnel; sometimes they use a commercially available life skills curriculum, such as Council for Exceptional Children's Life Centered Career Education, to teach these skills in the classroom. Although instruction is limited to courses designed specifically for students with ID, participating students may have the opportunity to participate in other social clubs and organizations on campus. In some cases, these experiences may be facilitated by use of on-campus groups such as Best Buddies. In other cases, staff provide students with calendars of upcoming campus events and cultural activities.

A major challenge for segregated programs, just like with the mixed/hybrid model, is securing space on an IHE campus from which to operationalize the program. Once the program has created a series of separate courses, it may preclude student participation in typical courses at the college. Program Profile 4 illustrates a substantially separate model.

Inclusive Individual Support Model

The inclusive individual support model provides students with individualized services (e.g., educational coaching, tutoring, technology, natural supports) to facilitate access to and participation in college courses, certificate programs, and/or degree programs (audit, noncredit, or credit). The individual student's vision and career goals drive services. There is no program base on campus or anywhere else, because these students participate in the campus community—academically and socially—just like any other college student. The focus is on establishing a student-identified career goal that directs the course of study and employment experiences (e.g., time-limited internships, apprenticeships, work-based learning), ultimately culminating in competitive employment.

Overall, the individual support model is initially more difficult to operationalize because of the individualized nature of student schedules and the level of inclusion of the students in academics and all other aspects of college life. This brings up the need to address how students will access courses by an alternative path that will likely differ from the traditional entrance criteria for matriculating students. The Institute for Community Inclusion's College Career Connection (C[3]) project illustrates how this model can be used in collaboration with school systems and IHEs.

The primary purpose of the C[3] Project is to improve adult outcomes for students with ID by creating access to PSE and employment options that are typically unavailable to them. Mirroring many of the evidence-based quality indicators outlined by the National Alliance for Secondary Education and Transition (2005) and the Transition Guideposts developed by the National Collaborative for Workforce Development—Youth (2005), the model uses a student-centered framework to identify individual strengths and preferences (Butterworth et al., 1993; NCSPES–Hawai'i, 2003) and a collaborative interagency team (Ginsberg, Johnson, Moffett, & Association for Supervision and Curriculum Development, 1997; Stodden, Brown, Galloway, Mrazek, & Noy, 2005) to develop customized PSE services for students who want them. Individual supports are determined by analysis of student interests, needs, and career goals and may be provided by educators, adult service personnel, and education/transition coaches (Hart, Zafft, & Zimbrich, 2001; NCSPES–Hawai'i, 2003; Rammler & Wood, 1999). Additionally,

---

Program Profile 4

REACH–Realizing Educational and Career Hopes
The University of Iowa College of Education
N297 Lindquist Center
Iowa City, IA 52242-1529
Phone: 319-384-2127
E-mail: reach@uiowa.edu

Type of program: College sponsored

Funding source(s): Private payment of tuition. The REACH Program at the University of Iowa does not qualify for federal financial aid at this time. Need-based scholarships are available through the REACH Program.

Model: Substantially separate

Goals:
REACH is a 2-year comprehensive program that allows students to earn a certificate of completion with a career emphasis that prepares the student for independent living and pursuit of a job in their selected field of study. Students receive a summary of their growth and development in the four core areas as documented in their personal development plan (PDP).
Areas of focus include academic coursework, career internship, student activities, and enrichment.

Eligibility criteria: Applicants
• Are typically between 18 and 25 years old
• Have completed a high school program or received a certificate of attendance
• Possess a well-rounded background in education, life-skills training, and some work experience
• Have other qualities, including strong social and adaptive skills, enthusiasm for learning and the college experience, a desire to live independently of their family, and a family that supports that desire and the goals of the REACH Program. To ensure a good match, REACH participants are selected through an application and interview process.

Average number of students served annually: 20–25 students

Overview: The REACH experience integrates the areas of academic enhancement, career development, university life, and community life to create a dynamic collegiate opportunity for students. REACH is committed to excellence in all areas of student education.

Academic enhancement: Students complete a variety of courses to enhance their knowledge in literature, writing, math, problem solving, personal finances, and career courses. Elective courses allow students to gain a liberal arts education and take classes related to their career area of emphasis. Classes are taught by REACH instructors who are trained to meet the unique learning needs of students. REACH advisors work with each student to develop a PDP to set and track goals in the areas of academics, career development, independent living, and life skills. Students receive grades in each class and assessments on their progress in the different areas of their PDP. Students are expected to participate in class and complete assignments. Passing grades and effort toward achieving goals are part of the graduation requirements.

Career development: The first year of career development in the REACH Program includes instruction in a classroom setting, opportunities to practice studied skills, and exploration of careers through real-world experiences. This year includes exploring job interests through tours, informational interviews, job shadows, job try-outs, and an internship. During the second year, students identify an area of interest for work (focus) through internships in either volunteer or paid positions on campus or in the community. Students learn how to organize a job search by developing a resume; practicing interviewing skills; networking; locating job opportunities; and learning about workplace expectations, policies, and benefits. An employment advisory board offers guidance to the REACH Program regarding internships, classroom instruction topics, community awareness, and fund-raising.

Community life: REACH students discover the communities of Iowa City and Coralville as they develop their social and life skills, which helps graduates to live independently and contribute to their community through employment, leisure, and service. Students gain self-confidence, interpersonal skills, knowledge of community resources, and an awareness of personal safety as they explore the city for work, service, and leisure activities. Community experiences provide students with the opportunity to use in real-life situations the skills and knowledge they get in course instruction. Students manage their weekly schedule and learn to balance work, personal, and leisure activities responsibly.

Staffing includes: Directors (interim and founding); department assistant; coordinators of career development, student life, academic life, and community life; student and career life instructors; personal relationships and sexuality course instructor; tutor coordinator; computer and technology course instructor; science and civics course instructor; human services seminar instructor; and office and resident assistants

Student's day includes

Employment	Course access	College campus & community involvement
• Career exploration • Job shadowing • Short-term job explorations • Three internships • Creation of an Eportfolio™	• Students must participate in REACH classes developed by REACH program instructors. • Small group study sessions • Personal tutoring • Some examples of coursework include: Literature, Personal Finance, Healthy Lifestyles, Communication, Critical Thinking, and Current Events.	• Numerous activities and learning opportunities are offered, and attendance at most activities is expected of students. • Training is offered in skills needed to live and work independently, including healthy lifestyles, personal care and safety, civic responsibilities, safety awareness, time management, and self-advocacy.

Data collection & outcomes: None noted

Adapted from the REACH web site: www.education.uiowa.edu/reach.

this model takes full advantage of natural supports that exist within the context of the IHE (e.g., students without disabilities). Figure 3.1 highlights the key elements that comprise the C^3 model.

All options are fully inclusive and address the needs of the widest range of students with disabilities, including students with ID (Hart, Mele-McCarthy, Parker, Pasternack, & Zimbrich, 2004). This model takes into account unique aspects of each student, such as aspirations, family wishes, and cultural background. It is based on several guiding principles: individual student vision sets the direction and controls decision making; all options are inclusive and occur in settings that reflect a natural proportion of students with and without disabilities; there are no special programs or specially designated classes; supports are individualized, not "one size fits all"; and interagency collaboration is essential to the effectiveness of the approach. Vignettes 1 and 2 are two examples of the inclusive individual support model.

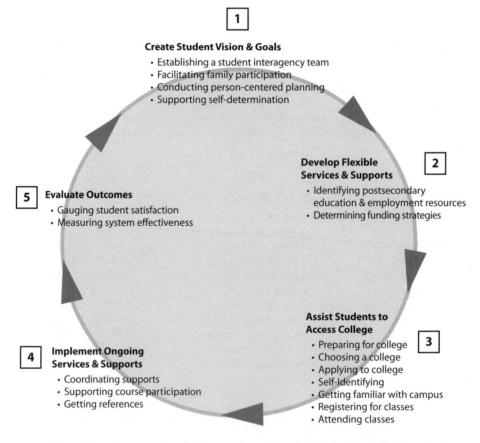

Figure 3.1. Key elements of C^3. (From Hart, D., Zimbrich, K., & Parker, D.R. [2006]. Dual enrollment as a postsecondary education option for students with intellectual disabilities. In E.E. Getzel & P. Wehman [Eds.], *Going to college: Expanding opportunities for people with disabilities.* [p. 260]. Baltimore: Paul H. Brookes Publishing Co.; reprinted by permission)

Vignette 1 (Katie)

As Katie was finishing high school and preparing for adult life, there was no question that she would be going on to college. All of her friends were going to college and she had the same goal for herself. She had been included in general education classes since kindergarten all the way through high school, so why would she and her family have any different expectation? Katie's passage into postsecondary education, unfortunately, wasn't going to be easy for she is a young woman with Down syndrome and at the time she began to seek admission to college there were very few Institutes of Higher Education that were supporting students with intellectual disabilities in an inclusive course of study. There were some substantially separate programs but that wasn't what Katie wanted. It quickly became apparent to Katie and her parents that going to college would require much more effort than they originally anticipated simply because she was a young adult with an intellectual disability. After much research, she and her mother were able to identify Becker College in Worcester, Massachusetts. They had two courses of study (education and physical therapy) which were in Katie's area of interest at the time and the college had experience supporting a few other students who had an intellectual disability. The then Vice-President of Student Recruitment indicated that they were open to supporting Katie in accessing college, as the mission of the college was to embrace and support a diverse student body of varying talents, but Katie would have to take the same path as any other student. This meant a visit to campus for an orientation and tour, an interview, taking SATs, completing the application process, and then the anxiety of waiting to hear if she were accepted — not unlike any other student.

Katie was accepted and began Becker College in September 2004. First semester was simultaneously very exciting and challenging. There was getting used to living in a dormitory with a roommate, balancing a full course load with wanting to socialize with classmates, making friends, navigating campus, being away from home, and learning how to advocate for needed accommodations to name a few. For the most part, Katie's experience was very similar to any other freshman beginning college. During her two years at Becker, Katie took a wide range of courses including:

- English Composition I
- Computers
- Psychology
- Introduction to Psychology
- Developmental Child Psychology
- Literature for Children
- Principles of Education
- Art
- Foundations of Science
- Public Speaking
- Effective Communication

(continued)

While at Becker, Katie assisted a fellow classmate who happened to have a hearing disability and required additional support in a psychology class they both attended. During the semester, Katie was inspired by their ability to communicate through American Sign Language. This experience compelled Katie to follow her passion of working with individuals who were deaf and studying ASL. It was a difficult decision for Katie, but in late 2006 she left Becker College to pursue her studies in deaf education.

In September of 2007 Katie entered her second college, Mt. Aloysius, as a transfer student to study in their Deaf Education and Interpreting program. Her advisor at Mount Aloysius College comments, "From the moment I met this exceptional young lady, I was impressed with her eagerness to learn immediately. Any request I make of Katie is quickly accepted, completed, and well done. Katie is a motivated student of numerous talents and considerable self-discipline."

A sample of courses taken at Mount Aloysius include:
- Rhetoric 1
- Computers (2 classes)
- Anatomy
- American Sign Language 1 and 2
- Cultural Literacy
- Psychology/Social Issues of Deafness
- American National Government
- Old Testament

In order for Katie to participate and be successful in college, she needs a wide range of accommodations and these include:
- Enlarged print: 18pt. font minimum
- Print double spaced or more, pages of material not condensed
- Note taker
- Limited handwriting
- Use of computer rather than handwriting for class work
- Peer tutors
- Study guides given one week minimum ahead of tests
- All quizzes, if not oral, extended time
- Oral tests – untimed
- Assistive technology – continually updated
- Kurtzweil Reader
- Federation for Blind and Dyslexic (RFBD) – Books on CD
- Specialized computer software used on personal computer (i.e., Inspiration, Visual Thesaurus)

Katie's outside interests include music, dancing, and spending time with her friends and family. Beyond making new friends, Katie's college experience allowed her to learn about different lifestyles and how to make her individual choices. For example, drinking, men in girls' rooms, students who elected not to study, staying up all night, learning to live without parental rules, learning to live on her own, time management, and most important for Katie has been managing her own emotions. Katie had a tendency to overwhelm students with giving too much attention to her friends. She made great strides this year with the help of the Mount Aloysius Director of Disability Services and a counselor. Katie is now maintaining space for herself and her friends. Her roommates now come home with her on the weekend, they go to basketball games at college, enjoy movies together, and other social activities.

Katie plans to graduate from Mount Aloysius in May of 2009. She will have an Associates of Science, General Studies Degree with an emphasis on Deaf Education. Katie's long-term goal is to return to Boston and work in a hospital or educational setting with individuals who are deaf, where she could use her love of sign language to communicate and assist them in getting their needs met.

Vignette 2 (Sara)

Sara is 21 years old and leads a very active life in the community. When she was 19, she expressed during her IEP transition meeting a desire to attend college. Not sure what opportunities were available, Sara's mom contacted VCU-RRTC to inquire about the possibility of Sara attending college. VCU-RRTC staff members held a series of meetings with Sara and her family, and with the high school's transition team. It was decided that Sara would participate in a PATH plan to further determine the next steps in her transition process. As a result of the PATH plan, the high school transition coordinator and employment specialist established a series of on-site work experiences for Sara in a hospital setting. Sara expressed an interest in working in a hospital, and it was agreed that she needed further exposure to this setting to identify her skills and interests. Additionally, Sara was working part time as a hostess in a local department store's café.

VCU-RRTC staff members began working with a local community college to implement the C^3 model with Sara. A meeting was held with the Disability Support Services Office, where Sara, her family, and VCU-RRTC staff discussed the model and Sara's interest in attending the community college. Sara applied to the community college and enrolled in the fall to audit "College Success Skills," a class required for all incoming freshmen. An educational coach was recruited through a faculty member at the community college. Sara audited the class and worked with her family and the educational coach to complete the course. In the spring, Sara enrolled to audit "Principles of Public Speaking," which is part of the college's Speech and Drama school. She has a high interest in public speaking, so she was excited about taking this class. Sara worked with a new educational coach recruited from the class, and VCU-RRTC met with the coach to discuss her roles and responsibilities, and with the course instructor. Sara developed, with assistance from her coach and family, a series of presentations for the class. She was able to bring in pictures or other visual cues to help her remember the presentation she prepared.

(continued)

VCU-RRTC staff provided suggestions to each of Sara's educational coaches and instructors to enhance Sara's learning experience. Examples provided include:
- Highlighting and reviewing key information points discussed in class
- Using more visuals when teaching (flash cards, magazines, etc.)
- Using demonstrations as much as possible to reinforce materials
- Explaining concepts in a variety of ways
- Simplifying directions
- Breaking tasks down into specific steps
- Providing opportunities to participate
- Using course tests as a take-home learning experience

Types of PSE Options

Next we present overviews of the three ways that PSE options for students with ID are initiated; they could work with any of the three models already discussed.

Dual Enrollment

Dual-enrollment programs are collaborative efforts between high schools and colleges in which high school students (usually juniors and seniors) are permitted to enroll in college courses (Karp, Calcagno, Hughes, Jeong, & Bailey, 2007). This model has been adapted to provide similar access to 18- to 21-year-old students with ID who are still receiving education and transition services from their school system under the Individuals with Disabilities Education Improvement Act (IDEA) of 2004 (PL 108-446). These dual-enrollment options are initiated when local school systems partner with 2- and 4-year public and private colleges to offer students the opportunity to complete their final 2 to 3 years of public education in a college setting. Students participate in a wide range of college activities related to their transition goals, including participation in academic courses, job shadowing, time-limited internships, competitive employment, learning self-determination skills, learning how to take public transportation or paratransit, and other skills needed for adult living. Other programs are structured so that students may be on campus only 2 or 3 days a week and spend the remainder of their time working.

Parents and local school systems typically initiate development of dual-enrollment options, and local school system personnel coordinate student services as indicated in the student's Individualized Education Plan (IEP). Services typically end when the student with ID ages out of public school, most often at age 21 or 22. In the most ideal dual-enrollment program, students with ID will exit public school into competitive employment with a strong system of supports from adult service systems such as the Departments of Development Disabilities or Mental Retardation and/or Vocational Rehabilitation.

There are significant benefits derived from implementing a dual-enrollment program for school districts, families, and students when it is linked to research-based transition practices. The opportunity to have the choice of a PSE option for students with ID who are transitioning out of high school provides support personnel with an incredibly rich transition curriculum in which to teach students the skills they will need as adults, in the environment that they will use them in, making the likelihood of skill acquisition greater. Moreover, dual enrollment provides an environment of natural supports, such as students without disabilities who can serve as same-age peer role models, which would not be available to students who remain on a high school campus. In addition, the school district will better meet the requirements of IDEA 2004 by educating students in the least restrictive environment, especially if the PSE option is inclusive across academic and other aspects of campus life.

Finally, dual enrollment in PSE provides students and their families with choices that previously have not been offered to them. Students with ID now have the same choice as their siblings and peers without disabilities. The positive impact on their self-esteem and self-image is immeasurable and is frequently cited by families as one of the most noticeable gains in their child. Although the dual-enrollment model was initially derived from one that focused on advanced high school students with impressive credentials, the benefits of such programs have led some to argue that many types of students could benefit from participation in a dual-enrollment program. Karp et al. (2007) published a long list of positive outcomes for all participating youth, including increasing the academic rigor of the high school curriculum; helping low-achieving students meet high academic standards; providing more academic opportunities and electives in cash-strapped, small, or rural schools; reducing high school dropout rates and increasing student aspirations; helping students acclimate to college life; and reducing the cost of college for students. Each of these benefits could also be applied to and reaped by students with ID. Program Profiles 5 and 6 illustrate two dual enrollment programs that use the inclusive individual supports model.

Program Profile 5

Massachusetts Bay Community College
50 Oakland Street
Wellesley Hills, MA 02481-5399

Type of Program: Dual enrollment

Funding Source(s): IDEA, State (e.g., line item in State budget)

Model: Inclusive individual supports

Goals:
1. Assist students with ID in establishing a career path and taking courses (audit, noncredit, credit) related to career goal.
2. Provide students with work-related experiences (e.g., job shadowing, national service, internships, apprenticeships) that culminate in competitive employment related to their career goal.
3. Increase self-determination skills and self-esteem.

Eligibility criteria:
- Has an interest in attending college
- Severe disability
- Age 18–22
- Unable to achieve the Competency Determination necessary for high school graduation (by passing the Massachusetts Comprehensive Assessment System exam)
- Will remain in high school until age 22

(continued)

Average number of students served annually: 5–20 students with severe disabilities

Overview: Massachusetts Bay Community College (MBCC) is committed to providing all students with the opportunity to be active members of the college community, to assisting them in meeting their future goals, and to helping them become contributing members of their communities. Faculty and learning specialists have been trained in Universal Course Design, and they have integrated this strategy into their courses to ensure access to course content by a diverse array of students. In addition, MassBay's education coaches work closely with each student to support his or her experience and meet individual needs.

In December 2006, MassBay, as part of the Inclusive Concurrent Enrollment initiative, entered into a partnership with the Newton Public Schools to help high school students with ID access inclusive academic courses and other aspects of college life, using the same supports as any other student, the difference being that they are provided these supports with a greater intensity, as needed. This partnership has expanded to include two additional school districts (Boston and Needham) and has gone from supporting an average of 5 students to close to 20.

Overall, students are aged 18–22, are still in high school, and are dually enrolled in MBCC; occasionally students choose to continue to take courses even after they graduate from high school. The overarching goal of this initiative is to provide students with ID typical inclusive academic, social, and paid employment experiences that students without disabilities participate in and that lead to competitive employment when or as they are leaving school.

Initially students participate in person-centered planning to assist them in identifying a career path and other transition-related goals. They are then supported in enrolling in courses of their choosing as they relate to their career goal and in taking part in all aspects of college life (e.g., use of fitness center, lunch in student union, signing up for tutoring services). The six students with ID who participated in the spring semester (2007) all completed their courses and demonstrated an increase in self-determination skills and overall self-esteem. All students learned to independently take public transportation from their home to the Wellesley campus. Students collected a portfolio of their work and created reflections of their college experiences to share with peers and future employers. Students participate in job shadowing, internships, and community service, and eventually enter paid employment in a job related to their career goal (e.g., massage therapist, office manager).

Staffing Includes: IHE coordinator, education coaches, faculty, disability services

Student's day includes

Employment	*Course access*	*College & community involvement*
• Job shadowing • Time-limited internships • Community Service • Part-time employment • Full-time employment	Access to all courses including: • Computers & technology • Career development • Physiology • Writing • Anatomy • Therapeutic message • Intro to sociology	• Total access to college community (e.g., gym/athletic center, student center, student clubs, library) • Training on use of public & para-transportation

Data collection & outcomes: In process
- Student Pre-/posttest
- Parent survey
- Case study

Program Profile 6

Holyoke Community College
303 Homestead Avenue
Holyoke, MA 01040

Type of Program: Dual enrollment

Funding Sources: IDEA, state (e.g. line item in state budget)

Model: Inclusive individual supports

Goals:

1. Assist students with ID in establishing a career path and taking courses (audit, noncredit, credit, continuing ed) related to career goal
2. Provide students with work-related experiences (e.g., job shadowing, national service, internships, apprenticeships) that culminate in competitive employment related to their career goal
3. Increase self-determination skills and self-esteem

Eligibility criteria:

- Has an interest in attending college
- Severe disability
- Age 18–22
- Unable to achieve the Competency Determination necessary for high school graduation (by passing the Massachusetts Comprehensive Assessment System exam)
- Will remain in high school until age 22
- Documentation of disability

Student population served: Students with intellectual and severe disabilities

Overview: Holyoke Community College (HCC), in December 2006, as part of the Inclusive Concurrent Enrollment initiative, formed a partnership with eight high schools. The partnership provides a range of services and supports to a maximum of 25 students with severe disabilities to ensure that students have full access to all HCC courses and campus life. All students have the same privileges as any other HCC student (e.g., HCC student ID, use of library, career center, Bartley Athletics and Recreation Center). HCC requires that an assistive technology assessment and a person-centered plan be completed for every student prior to his or her enrollment. HCC then develops an individualized schedule of courses, campus activities, and a support plan (e.g., accommodations, education coaches) with each student. Students actively participate in this planning to give them the opportunity to learn about the type of supports and accommodations that they need to be successful.

Students also complete a career portfolio as part of their course work. Students are trained to use the inclusive HCC student "MyHCC" web-based portal and are coached to utilize the system weekly at a minimum. The system includes access to student e-mail, accounts, class schedules, the online library catalogue, and other resources.

To ensure ongoing communication, the HCC staff submits weekly updates to all partners via e-mail and conducts monthly partnership meetings. In addition, each semester HCC convenes an interagency team with key stakeholders, including the Department of Mental Retardation, the Massachusetts Rehabilitation Commission, one-stop career centers, and family members. HCC uses the interagency team to conduct resource mapping and to develop an action plan on how prioritized transition-related service needs will be addressed. The interagency team is also used to discuss individual student needs and general service referrals, and students are invited to present their career goals and learn about the different services and supports that are available to assist them in achieving their goals.

(continued)

HCC connects students with the College Career Center and with local one-stop career centers in their home communities. HCC facilitates job-shadowing opportunities on campus and in the community and assists students in securing employment.

Student's day includes

Employment options	Course access	College & community involvement
• Job shadowing • Internships • Community Service • Part-time employment	Access to all courses, including: • English • Career development • Music • Psychology • Sociology • Communication • Business • Health/fitness • Art • Earth science	• Total access to college community (e.g., gym/athletic center, student center, student clubs, library) • Training on use of public & para-transportation

Data collection & outcomes: In process
• Pre-/posttest
• Parent survey
• Case study

Sponsored Programs and Services for Adults with ID

PSE experiences can also be initiated by adult service agencies or organizations that partner with an IHE to create a PSE option for adults with ID. These programs offer the same range and diversity of services as the dual/concurrent enrollment options. The major difference between dual enrollment and adult PSE options is that in the latter case the local education system no longer participates in providing student supports or services. Most often if these programs or services are initiated by a college, they are tuition based and require families to cover costs of supports and services provided to students. The Pathways UCLA program provides an example of the college-sponsored program that supports adult students with ID. In other cases, the student and family may seek support for PSE through federal and state initiatives, such as an education award through the Americorp service (Segal AmeriCorp Education Award, n.d.), Plans for Achieving Self-Support (PASS) through Social Security Work Incentives, or the state vocational rehabilitation agency, which may support participation in PSE if it is related to the student's career goal (see Chapter 2 for a more detailed listing of possible funding options). Some of the programs for adults with ID also serve students who are dually enrolled and continue to support them as adults.

Student- and Family-Initiated Experiences

It is not necessary to have a program in order for a person with ID to engage in a PSE experience. Individual students and their families may approach an IHE to seek access and support for just one student. There is much less known about these individual family efforts, because most go unreported or undocumented. There has been little research done on these practices, because there has not been an effective mechanism for identifying those who have chosen this route. Most efforts are haphazard and are often dependent upon whom the family knows and how facile they are with web-based searches for information. There are a variety of ways that families create access to PSE for their child. Some go through the standard admission process, whereas others approach an individual instructor to gain permission for the student to take a course. Still others may seek a sympathetic champion on campus to broker access. And there are those who work with disability services personnel to identify courses in which the student has an interest and attempt to match them with a willing instructor who is known to be supportive of students with diverse learning styles. Families and students may use any combination or all of the aforementioned strategies. Unfortunately, families who create PSE options for their child all too often are left to do so without the benefit of knowing about the resources that exist to help them. Table 3.1 provides a comparison between postsecondary education service options and models of instruction.

GOALS AND OUTCOMES OF PSE EXPERIENCES FOR STUDENTS WITH ID

Overall, the goals and desired outcomes for students with ID who participate in PSE are not different from the goals of students without disabilities. Student goals relate to a variety of outcomes, such as achieving competitive employment, learning about a topic of personal interest, acquiring enhanced self-determination or self-advocacy skills, or gaining a better understanding of how to access learning opportunities as an adult. The benefits of accessing PSE for students with ID can be measured in their growth in a number of areas, including academic and personal skill building, competitive employment, self-advocacy, and self-confidence (Uditsky & Hughson, 2008; Zafft, Hart, & Zimbrich, 2004). Being part of campus life, taking classes, and learning to navigate a world of high expectations lead to the development of skills needed for successful adult life.

Supports and Services that Lead to Success

Overall, services and supports are going to depend on the needs of the individual student. Students need to know how they learn best and the types of accommodations that help them learn, so that they can take the lead on acquiring those supports. To begin with, it is critical that the student have documentation of their disability that is not more than 3 years old. The student should first check with the college to find out what type of documentation is required, because it varies across IHEs. Many colleges have an office charged with determining eligibility for and then providing needed accommodations to students with disabilities. The name of this office may vary at different colleges, but it is most often some variation on the Disability Service Office (DSO). If a student is deemed to be eligible for accommodation services from the DSO, then there is no cost associated

Table 3.1. The nexus between postsecondary education service options (the how) and models of instruction (the what).

Models of Postsecondary Education Instruction	Postsecondary Education Service Options		
	Dual / Concurrent Enrollment Serves students ages 18-21 transitioning to adult life and services are typically coordinated by the public school system or in partnership with an IHE.	**Programs & Services for Adults with ID** Serves adults no longer receiving services under IDEA and services are coordinated by the college or an adult service organization — some serve both dually enrolled and adult students.	**Individuals Accessing College without Formal Supports** Can be implemented by students 18+ and services are coordinated by a variety of entities including families.
Mixed / Hybrid Model: Students access campus facilities and organizations, and are supported to participate in some regular college courses, but also receive some specialized individual or group instruction with only students with disabilities.	Either a school system or an IHE operates a college-based transition program where students attend typical college courses, but are also provided with additional specialized instruction.	A college creates a program, with or without a partnership with an adult service agency, in which adults with ID are provided the opportunity to take some typical college courses, but are also provided with specialized instruction.	An individual with ID may enroll in college classes during or after high school — these courses may consist of typical courses, courses that are specifically designed for students with disabilities, or both.
Substantially Separate Model: Students may access facilities and activities on campus, but all instruction is specialized and only for students with disabilities. Students do not access typical college courses.	A school system or an IHE operates a transition program at a college location but students do not participate in typical college courses — only specialized courses for students with disabilities	A college creates a program on campus that supports adults to access facilities and organizations on campus, but does not provide access to and supports in typical college courses.	An individual with ID may enroll in specialized courses for people with disabilities.
Inclusive Individual Support Model: All instruction and supports are individualized— There is no program home base and the student, their family, or an outside agency or person coordinates services.	A school system or an IHE supports access to typical college courses and the entire college community for individual students as part of their transition experience.	A college creates access to courses, services, and supports for individuals with ID via their existing systems.	An individual participates in college courses without the support of a school system or a particular college program.

with those services. Typical accommodations include note takers, extended time for taking tests, and assistive technology. In addition to the standard accommodations that DSOs typically offer, there is a wide range of additional services and supports that can be used to create access to and success in PSE for students with ID, such as educational coaches, mentors, and universally designed instruction. Some PSE options are linked to teacher or rehabilitation professional preparation programs at the host institution, and participants from these degree programs provide various supports to students with ID. Others develop student-mentoring programs that pair students without disabilities with a student who has an ID, to assist him or her in taking advantage of the wide range of academic and nonacademic offerings (e.g., recreation facilities, clubs, sports, evening events) that the college provides. These pairings can also help students with ID to be seen as a valued member of the college community and build an enhanced social network. Then there are PSE options that use education or life coaches to support students in academic and nonacademic pursuits. Table 3.5 (see p. 81) highlights many of these promising practices, which include but are not limited to the following list.

- *Interagency collaboration* is the cornerstone of good transition practice. It denotes a group of individuals from the local education agency, adult agencies, an IHE, family members, and students who come together to address common needs and pursue common goals for individual students. A team agrees to common values, sets clear goals and objectives, defines communication and operating procedures, and shares responsibilities through defined roles and activities (Johnson, Sharp, & Stodden, 2001; NCSPES–Hawai'i, 2003; Wehman, 1996; Whelley, Hart, & Zafft, 2002).
- *Resource mapping* is a process that assists a team of people in identifying and documenting resources within and across agencies or systems. It helps them to recognize duplication or gaps in services, then to reallocate duplicative resources to address identified gaps. This process creates a framework for cost sharing (e.g., blending of resources) and lays a foundation for strategic action planning (Chadsey, Leach, & Shelden, 2001; Crane & Skinner, 2003; NCSPES, 1999).
- *Person-centered planning* (e.g., Making Action Plans [MAPS], Planning Alternative Tomorrows with Hope [PATH], Whole Life Planning) assists students in planning for their future by defining desired outcomes in PSE education, work, social relationships, living, and leisure and by developing a plan to reach the individual's vision through informal and formal networks (Butterworth et al., 1993; Everson & Zhang, 2000).
- *Work-based learning* is one of the best ways to improve outcomes for youth with disabilities (Hughes, Moore, & Bailey, 1999). Work-based learning consists of real-world work experiences that help the student to apply what he or she is learning in the classroom and includes a broad range of opportunities, such as workplace mentoring, apprenticeships, and paid employment (Gramlich, Crane, Peterson, & Stenhjem, 2003). Participating faculty need professional development on how to integrate work-based learning into coursework.
- *Educational coaching* is a method of providing individual supports. Historically, educational coaching has been used with students with psychiatric challenges,

and, more recently, it has been applied to students with significant learning disabilities (Briel & Getzel, 2001). Through educational coaching, individual supports and accommodations are provided as needed, then phased out as students become familiar with coursework and expectations or as natural supports in the environment are provided.

- *Self-determination training* teaches students how to make decisions, choose whom to invite into the decision-making process, self-advocate, and, ultimately, take control of their lives (Powers et al., 1996; Wehmeyer, 1996, 1998, 2002).

- *Universal course design* (UCD) shifts old assumptions about teaching and learning in four ways: 1) students with ID fall along a continuum of learner differences rather than constituting a separate category; 2) faculty adjustments for learner differences should occur for all students, not just those with disabilities or ID; 3) curriculum materials should be varied and diverse, including digital and online resources, rather than centering on a single textbook; and 4) instead of "fixing" students so that they can learn from a set curriculum, the curriculum should be made more flexible to accommodate learner differences (Behling & Hart, 2008; Rose & Meyer, 2002). Participating faculty can be provided with training in UCD.

The Availability of Residential or Dorm Experiences

Few PSE programs offer the choice of a residential option on a college campus. In some cases this is done on a student-by-student basis. In other instances, students are housed in separate dormitories or a separate wing or section of a dormitory (e.g., Taft Transition to Independent Living Program, Venture Program at Bellevue Community College) or community-based apartments or houses (e.g., LifeLink PSU at Penn State College, UCLA Extension/Pathways Program) that are supported by the college, family, or a provider. For example, Students in the Pathways program (www.uclaextension.edu/pathway) live in private one- and two-bedroom apartments in an apartment building adjacent to the UCLA campus. The program employs two resident assistants, who also live in this apartment building, to provide oversight, counseling, and support to student residents.

Culminating Documentation

Generally, students in dual/concurrent-enrollment programs are awarded their high school diploma or a certificate of attendance from their school district upon exiting services, depending on district/state policies regarding graduation requirements. Adults with ID who participate in a PSE option but are not pursuing a traditional degree track may receive a certificate from the IHE, but many programs do not offer any valid credential. The Venture program at Bellevue Community College offers two kinds of nontransferable associates degrees, an Associate in Arts in General Studies and an Associate in Occupational and Life Skills. The second of these was specially created for students who participate in the Venture program curriculum. The degree is nontransferable and is not intended for students pursuing a baccalaureate degree. The Venture program is the only PSE option thus far that has an accredited degree program. To address the need for some credentialing option, the new Higher Education Opportunities Act (PL 110-315) contains authorization for a training and technical assistance center that will be charged with development of an authentic credential option for PSE programs to grant to students with ID who complete their course of study.

COMMON CHALLENGES AND BARRIERS

There are many challenges that students with ID and professionals face when creating access to PSE, which have been detailed in the discussion on the mixed/hybrid option. According to a national survey of PSE for students with ID, the most significant challenges that students with ID face are the "attitude" and "low expectations" of secondary and postsecondary professionals, families, and students themselves (Hart, 2008; Neubert, Moon, & Grigal, 2004; Uditsky & Hughson, 2008). Additional key challenges include a lack of student preparation; creating alternative pathways that circumvent placement tests, entrance criteria, ability-to-benefit tests, "otherwise qualified" requirements, and prerequisite requirements; and a lack of funding for tuition and the development and enhancement of services and supports. These challenges are described next.

Low Expectations and Lack of Preparation

In addition to the barriers individuals with ID have faced in seeking access to public education, employment, and independent living, the public profile that IHEs wish to cultivate makes this new arena of PSE education somewhat more challenging.

Students with ID who receive academic instruction in segregated or pull-out resource room classes when they are in high school are often not as well prepared for college. The curriculum used in these separate classes varies widely and can range from a life skills curriculum to a modified general education curriculum, neither of which is standardized or leads to the necessary skills students will need in college. Secondary general and special educators can use strategies, such as universal design for learning, that promote greater access to the general education curriculum in regular education classes. IHEs need to conduct outreach to sending school districts to make them aware of the need for better preparation—not just for students with ID, but for all students.

Otherwise Qualified

Two federal laws address equal access to a PSE for students with disabilities: the Rehabilitation Act of 1973 (PL 93-112) and the Americans with Disabilities Act (ADA) of 1990 (PL 101-336). Both prohibit discrimination against individuals with disabilities participating fully within their communities, including higher education and the workplace. Section 504 of the Rehabilitation Act prohibits discrimination against an individual, due to their disability, by persons, businesses, organizations, or government agencies that receive federal funds. To have any rights against discrimination under Section 504, a student with a disability who is pursuing a degree or certificate program must be an "otherwise qualified individual with a disability."

The definition of an "otherwise qualified individual with a disability" seeking access to a PSE program as a matriculating student refers to a person who meets the program's essential eligibility requirements for services. If an individual needs a reasonable accommodation to meet those requirements, he or she is also considered "otherwise qualified."

The primary question then becomes, does an IHE have to provide accommodations for nonmatriculating students with disabilities, including students with ID? The answer is yes. Students with disabilities, including ID, who are auditing classes or who otherwise are not enrolled in a degree or certificate program, must be provided accommodations to the same extent as students who are matriculating. A 1990 court decision held that requirements relating to accommodations apply to nondegree as well as degree programs (*United States v. University of Alabama at Birmingham*; http://www.cqc.state.ny.us/DisabilityRightsADA/RehabAct Sect504Post-SecEd.htm)

The district court held that the University of Alabama at Birmingham's (UAB's) accommodation policy violated Section 504 because it excluded "special" students from eligibility for assistance in the form of accommodations. "Special" students are those who are enrolled in noncredit or nondegree programs—in this case, those who were enrolled through UAB's Division of Special Studies (http://bulk.resource.org/courts.gov/c/F2/908/908.F2d.740.897148.html). Furthermore, the U.S. Department of Education, Office of Civil Rights (1998), states "students with disabilities who are auditing classes or who otherwise are not working for a degree must be provided auxiliary aids and services to the same extent as students who are in a degree-granting program."

Clearly, providing access to PSE for students with ID has ramifications for each IHE, and although the current procedures and guidelines should be maintained, they must also be viewed in a new light. Students with ID who are going to be matriculating and pursuing a traditional degree or certificate program should be held to the same entrance criteria and standards as a student without a disability, including ability-to-benefit tests, the "otherwise qualified" standard, and prerequisites for taking a course or entering a course of study. There are also a growing number of students with ID who are pursuing access to a PSE who will not be pursuing a traditional pathway because they will not meet these entrance criteria and are not seeking a degree. For the most part, students with ID need an alternative pathway to PSE because they will not be matriculating and will be auditing courses, taking noncredit courses, and/or continuing education courses with supports and needed accommodations. Those seeking this alternative path may secure assistance from the Disability Service Office, if they are supportive, to negotiate with individuals in the governance structure of the IHE to identify where changes or waivers to the entrance criteria can be established. The individual student's vision and career goals will guide course selection and drive needed services and supports. However, students with ID need to be held to the same code of conduct as every other student on campus. Figure 3.2 illustrates the alternative pathway in contrast to the traditional pathway.

Pathways to Access Postsecondary Education for Individuals with Intellectual Disabilities

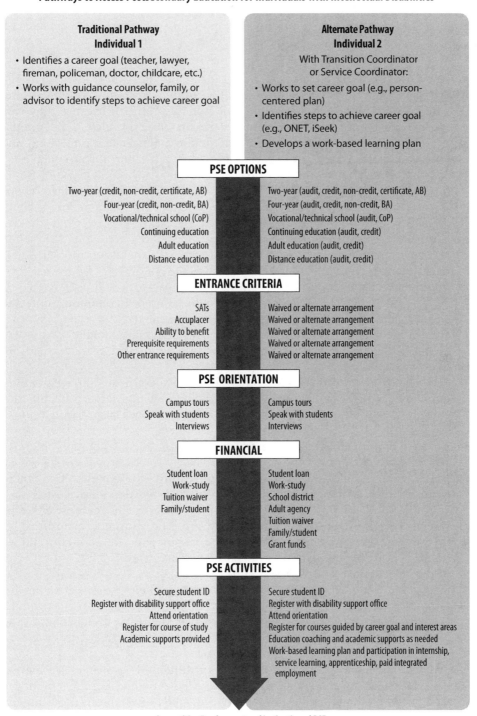

Figure 3.2. Alternative pathways to inclusive postsecondary education. (Created by Debra Hart and the Institute for Community Inclusion.)

Funding Services, Supports, and Tuition

There is a range of funding options for PSE for students with ID that include, but are not limited to the following list:

- Family funds: PSE options can be paid for by families and students. The recent passage of the Higher Education Opportunities Act will have a major impact on the funding of PSE options for students with ID, because they will soon be eligible for work-study and federal financial aid, such as Pell grants.
- IDEA funds: A school district might fund tuition and needed services and supports under IDEA/Free and Appropriate Public Education for programs that are dual/concurrent enrollment. IDEA 2004 does not prohibit use of funds for this purpose, and a dual/concurrent-enrollment option provides school districts with an age-appropriate, least restrictive environment for students with ID who are transitioning to adult life.
- Cost-sharing funds: The cost of funding can be shared across the IHE, adult service agencies, families, and school districts. This depends on the individual circumstances (e.g., the student is still in high school).
- Vocational rehabilitation (VR): If a student's course work is directly related to accessing employment, state VR funds might be used. In addition, some VR agencies may offer a tuition waiver for eligible students.
- Other rehabilitation organizations: State developmental disability or departments of mental retardation may provide funding to assist a student with ID in accessing PSE.
- Scholarships: Foundations or organizations provide scholarships to students enrolling in PSE, regardless of their financial or disability status, providing the student meets other requirements. Individual colleges also award annual scholarships based on demonstrated financial need.
- Corporation for National and Community Service: The Corporation administers AmeriCorps (http://www.americorps.gov/). AmeriCorps is composed of VISTA and the National Civilian Community Corps. It provides several financial benefits for PSE to individuals who have participated in service. After successfully completing a term of service, AmeriCorps members are eligible to receive a Segal AmeriCorps Education Award. The education award can be used to pay costs at qualified institutions of higher education, for educational training, or to repay qualified student loans. The award is $4,725 for a year of full-time service and is prorated for part-time service. The award can be accessed in full or in part, and an individual can take up to 7 years after the term of service has ended to claim the award. In addition, there are currently 76 colleges and universities that match the Segal AmeriCorps Education Award for their students (for more information, see http://www.americorps.org/for_individuals/benefits/benefits_ed_award.asp).
- Grant funds: State, federal, and foundation funding is available. The newly passed Higher Education Opportunities Act will be funding a number of model demonstrations nationwide and offers seed funds to establish a PSE option for students with ID.
- Plans for Achieving Self-Support (PASS Plans): PASS Plans were developed by the Social Security Administration as an incentive to encourage individuals who may be receiving Supplemental Security Income (SSI) or Supplemental

Security Disability Income (SSDI) to enter the workforce. This plan allows an individual to work and save money and not be penalized by a deduction from his or her SSI or SSDI check. There are restrictions on what the saved money may be used for, but college tuition and fees would be permissible if they are shown to relate to a career goal and outcome.

NATIONAL POSTSECONDARY EDUCATION SURVEY RESULTS

Next we examine the results of a national survey of PSE programs for students with ID. The overall purpose of the survey was to contribute to a further understanding of the range of programs that are available nationwide, given the paucity of information on these programs. It was conducted by the Institute for Community Inclusion at the University of Massachusetts in the fall of 2007. The survey identified 150 PSE programs that support students with ID who use a wide variety of supports and services across 31 states. It is likely that there are two to three times that number, if not more. They operate in wide-ranging environments and have been developed by schools, IHEs, VR programs, and community providers. Overall, the majority of these PSE options have developed in isolation from one another. The programs were identified with the use of a convenience sample (e.g., inquiries on national listservs, conferences, word of mouth, and telephone inquiry) with each of the 150 programs listed in the ThinkCollege web site (www.ThinkCollege.net) database of PSE programs for students with ID. The data presented are based on 75 survey respondents from the 150 programs. For the most part, this information does not reflect the countless number of individual students and their families who have managed to create access to a PSE option.

Types of Options

The majority of the programs offered a mixed/hybrid option (51%) wherein students with ID were supported, sometimes on a limited basis, in taking regular college courses. The second most frequent model offered segregated services (33%) with no real opportunity or supports to enable students to take regular courses. Only a very few of the models offered an inclusive individual support model (16%) of PSE options with adequate supports provided so that students with ID could participate (auditing or for credit) in regular college courses of their own choosing. Overall, the mixed and substantially separate program curricula tended to focus on functional life skills and employment experiences. The individual support model focused on establishing student career goals that directed the course of study and linked the student to integrated competitive employment.

Students Served

A slight majority of programs supported both students who were dually enrolled in high school and college, and students who were also served as adults. Another category of programs supported only students who were dually enrolled (i.e., still

Table 3.2.   Program type

Type	%
Dual enrollment students	35%
Adults no longer receiving IDEA/public school funding	28%
Both	37%

served by their public school system/local education agency (LEA) under IDEA, typically ages 18–21), and the last category supported only adults. Table 3.2 provides a breakout of the different types of programs.

The majority of programs were located in 2-year IHEs, followed by 4-year IHEs. The least frequent IHEs were tech/trade schools. Table 3.3 details the breakout for each category.

The number of years that programs indicated that they were in existence ranged from 3 months to 35 years. The majority of programs (56.7%) reported being established within the last 5 to 10 years. The substantially separate programs were some of the oldest. Most programs reported having begun as a result of parent advocacy and lobbying.

A majority of programs reported serving 10 to 20 students with ID at a time. There were 10 programs that reported serving 100 or more students with ID. These programs tended to be older and more segregated. A majority of programs (81.1%) reported that some students continued to take classes after exiting the program, compared with 18.8% that indicated that none of their students took courses upon exiting the program.

Funding

In terms of funding for these postsecondary education programs and services, the most frequently cited funding source for these was private pay, followed by school district/IDEA funds for transportation and instructional assistants or education coaches. Overall, programs indicated that they were not often involved in cost or resource sharing with their vocational rehabilitation agency, their college's Disability Services Office, or their Department of Mental Retardation/Developmental Disabilities. Table 3.4 provides a breakdown of funding sources.

Table 3.3.   Type of institute of higher education

Type of IHE	Percentage
2-year	51.3%
4-year	40.8%
Tech/trade school	6.6%
Total	100.0%

Table 3.4.   Funding source

Institute of higher education	17.1%
Adult service agency	11.8%
Private pay	51.3%
Scholarship	11.8%
Financial aid	18.4%
School district	39.5%

PROMISING PRACTICES FOR POSTSECONDARY EDUCATION EXPERIENCES

The growth and national interest in PSE for students with ID has fostered the need to draft a list of promising practices that can assist individuals interested in developing or enhancing PSE initiatives for students with ID. A listing of Promising Practices serves to avoid reinventing the wheel and to disseminate quality practices that are known to work. Based on this need, Grigal and Hart (2008) developed a set of suggested promising practices (see Table 3.5). These promising practices are aligned with and reflective of both applied and research-based practices on transition that have been identified in the literature and recognized by the National Alliance for Secondary Education and Transition (NASET) to positively affect the transition of students from secondary school to adult life (NASET,

Table 3.5.   Promising Practices

Student activities

All instruction, services, and supports are individualized and are provided in integrated college and/or community settings.

Students have opportunity to participate in regular college courses (credit and noncredit or continuing education) with necessary supports and accommodations (e.g., education coach, assistive technology).

All unpaid employment experiences (e.g., community service, internships, volunteer, job sampling/shadow) have specific short-term objectives based upon meeting students' specified career goals, are time-limited, and are similar/equal to internships and service learning experiences of students without disabilities.

Students are provided the opportunity to make meaningful social connections with peers and with mentors or a caring adult at college or in the community.

Students are supported to seek and sustain paid integrated competitive employment related to their career goal as soon as possible (e.g., within the first year).

Students' schedules include participation in inclusive campus activities such as clubs, use of athletic facilities, student center, community service, fraternities, sororities, and other generic college social activities.

Students are supported in developing and monitoring crucial self-determination skills, including self-advocacy, problem solving, goal setting, self-initiating, and self-knowledge.

(continued)

Table 3.5.   Promising Practices *(continued)*

Student outcomes

Students exit with paid work related to their career goal and are connected with the adult systems and long-term services that sustain their current level of integrated employment.

Students exit with self-determination skills that enable them to articulate their support needs in all major life domains (e.g., work, college, community).

Upon exit, students know how to access adult learning opportunities both at college and in the community (e.g., course selection, registration, payment, securing accommodations, scheduling, transportation).

Policies and practices

Person-centered planning is used to identify and address student goals (e.g., career, courses, social or personal development) and support needs, including natural supports, prior to entering PSE and annually thereafter.

All student goals are measurable and outcome based.

Students adhere to the academic schedule and the code of conduct set forth by the college for all students.

Families are provided with the information, training, and support needed to help their child navigate the postsecondary, employment, and adult community environments to which they are transitioning (e.g., transportation, benefits planning, housing, college requirements, and state agency supports).

Policies support student course access and address requirements such as placement tests (ability-to-benefit testing) and prerequisites to ensure that they are not barriers to participation.

Evaluation data (e.g., employment, college course participation, self-determination skill acquisition, exit and follow-up data) are compiled and reviewed annually to identify needed changes.

Staffing and oversight

An interagency team is established that includes representatives from disability-specific agencies and workforce development providers, college personnel, families, and students.

An interagency team continually evaluates (at a minimum biannually) the provision of services and student outcomes, as well as the partnerships that support those experiences.

A formal or informal memorandum of understanding is created between the collaborating entities that identifies a liaison who will facilitate communication between all organizations (e.g., institute of higher education, community rehabilitation providers, local school systems).

College faculty and disability support personnel are provided professional development on universal design principles and strategies that they integrate into their courses (e.g., accessible syllabi, varied instructional and assessment strategies).

Dedicated staff in clearly delineated position(s) are authorized to coordinate student services, monitor logistics and planning, and implement other administrative duties (e.g., interagency team meetings, person-centered planning, data collection, problem solving, outreach to families, evaluation).

2005). NASET was a national coalition of more than 40 organizations and advocacy groups representing special education, general education, career and technical education, youth development, multicultural perspectives, and parents, which established national standards for secondary education and transition for all youth in five key areas: schooling, career preparatory experiences, youth development and youth leadership, family involvement, and connecting activities and service coordination (NASET, 2005).

In addition to being aligned with multiple NASET standards, these objective and measurable promising practices are also informed by the culmination of work conducted by six model demonstration, outreach, and research and innovation projects funded over the past 10 years by the U.S. Department of Education, Office of Special Education Programs. These projects conducted outreach, research, training, and technical assistance to develop and improve PSE options for students with ID across several states, including California, Connecticut, Delaware, Florida, Hawaii, Illinois, Maryland, Massachusetts, Michigan, Minnesota, Mississippi, Montana, New Jersey, South Carolina, Tennessee, and Virginia.

The Promising Practices list has a number of purposes. Their overall purpose is to identify evidence-based, objective measures that can be used to define, create, or expand high-quality services to support positive postschool outcomes for students with ID. Grigal and Hart (2008) suggest the following potential uses for the Promising Practices by various stakeholders:

- A basis upon which to conduct and compare research of effective practices and to measure student outcomes.
- Guidance for local school systems creating new transition services, supports, or programs to serve students with ID in postsecondary settings.
- Guidance for IHEs that are creating new or expanding existing services for students with ID.
- A framework for reviewing, evaluating, and improving existing programs and services.
- A framework for guiding the creation of policy and legislation that affect PSE options for students with ID.
- Guidance in determining the quality of available services for students with ID and their families.

SUMMARY

The purpose of ensuring that students with ID have choices in and access to a PSE is to provide them with opportunities to establish a career path and to learn how to navigate their communities in the 21st century. As students with ID participate in PSE they begin to influence the low expectations of professionals, families, employers, and community members. History has demonstrated that individuals with ID have been drastically underestimated; they are far more capable than once thought. As PSE options for students with ID grow nationwide, so too will individuals' perceptions and expectations of them. We know that students with disabilities who have had access to the general curriculum, paid work, and high expectations are more likely to participate in PSE and to be employed as adults. Keeping college in the mix of possibilities as students with ID explore which steps to take after high school enhances their potential for success.

Given all the federal and state activity related to improving PSE access and services for students with ID, it is clear that these options are not going away. Professionals in secondary education, adult services, and IHEs have a choice. They can work together to determine how PSE options for students with ID can benefit both the students they serve and the systems they work in, or they can choose not to. This latter choice is one that will become difficult to maintain, as the call for change, access, partnership, and better outcomes is growing stronger with each passing year. The collective voice of students with ID will continue to rise, demanding not only attention, but action from those who hold control over their most sacred possession—their futures.

REFERENCES

Americans with Disabilities Act of 1990, PL 101-336, 42 U.S.C. §§ 12101 *et seq.*

Behling, K., & Hart, D. (2008). Universal course design: A model of professional development. Strategies for bringing UCD to a college campus and ensuring its sustainability. In S. Burgstahler (Ed.), *Universal design in post-secondary education: From principles to practice* (pp. 109–125). Cambridge: Harvard Education Press.

Briel, L.W., & Getzel, E.E. (2001). Internships in higher education: Promoting success for students with disabilities. *Disability Studies Quarterly, 21*(1), 38–48.

Butterworth, J., Hagner, D., Heikkinen, B., Faris, S., DeMello, S., & McDonough, K. (1993). *Whole life planning: A guide for organizers and facilitators.* Boston: Children's Hospital, Institute for Community Inclusion.

Casale-Giannola, D., & Wilson Kamens, M. (2006). Inclusion at a university: Experiences of a young woman with Down syndrome. *Mental Retardation, 44*(5), 344–352.

Chadsey, J., Leach, L., & Shelden, D. (2001). *Including youth with disabilities in education reform: Lessons learned from school-to-work states.* Champaign: University of Illinois at Urbana-Champaign, Transition Research Institute.

Crane, K., & Skinner, B. (2003). *Community resource mapping: A strategy for promoting successful transition for youth with disabilities* (Information Brief, Vol. 2, Issue 1). Minneapolis: University of Minnesota, Institute for Community Integration.

Everson, J., & Zhang, D. (2000). Person-centered planning: Characteristics, inhibitors, and supports. *Education and Training in Mental Retardation and Developmental Disabilities, 35,* 36–43.

Ginsberg, M., Johnson, J., & Moffett, C. (1997). *Educators supporting educators: A guide to organizing school support teams.* Alexandria, VA: Association for Supervision and Curriculum Development.

Gramlich, M., Crane, K., Peterson, K., & Stenhjem, P. (2003). *Work-based learning and future employment for youth: A guide for parents and guardians* (Information Brief, 2[2]). Minneapolis: National Center on Secondary Education and Transition.

Grigal, M., Dwyre, A., & Davis, H. (2006, December). Transition services for students aged 18–21 with intellectual disabilities in college and community settings: Models and implications of success, National Center on Secondary Education and Transition. *Information Brief: Addressing Trends and Developments in Secondary Education and Transition, 5*(5).

Grigal, M., & Hart, D. (2008). *Promising practices to support students with intellectual disabilities in inclusive postsecondary education options: A self-assessment.* Rockville: TransCen, Inc.

Grigal, M., Neubert, D.A., & Moon, M.S. (2001). Public school programs for students with significant disabilities in postsecondary settings. *Education and Training in Mental Retardation and Developmental Disabilities, 36,* 244–254.

Hall, M., Kleinert, H.L., & Kearns, J.F. (2000). Going to college! Postsecondary programs for students with moderate to severe disabilities. *Teaching Exceptional Children 32*, 58–65.

Hamill, L.B. (2003). Going to college: The experiences of a young woman with Down syndrome. *Mental Retardation, 41*(5), 340–353.

Hart, D. (2008). [National survey of postsecondary education programs that support students with intellectual disabilities]. Unpublished raw data.

Hart, D., Mele-McCarthy, J., Parker, D., Pasternack, R., & Zimbrich, K. (2004). Community college: A pathway to success for youth with learning, cognitive, and intellectual disabilities in secondary education. *Education and Training in Developmental Disabilities, 39*(1), 54–66.

Hart, D., Zafft, C., & Zimbrich, K. (2001). Creating access to college for all students. *Journal for Vocational Special Needs Education, 23*(2), 19–31.

Hart, D., Zimbrich, K., & Parker, D.R. (2006). Dual enrollment as a postsecondary education option for students with intellectual disabilities. In E.E. Getzel & P. Wehman (Eds.), *Going to college: Expanding opportunities for people with disabilities* (p. 260). Baltimore: Paul H. Brookes Publishing Co.

Higher Education Opportunity Act, Public Law 110-315, 122 Stat. 3078.

Hughes, K.L., Moore, D.T., & Bailey, T.R. (1999). *Work-based learning and academic skills.* Retrieved October 12, 2004, from http://www.teacherscollege.edu/iee/BRIEFS/Brief27.htm

Individuals with Disabilities Education Improvement Act (IDEA) of 2004, PL 108-446, 20 U.S.C. §§ 1400 *et seq.*

Johnson, D.R., Sharp, M., & Stodden, R. (2001). *The transition to postsecondary education for students with disabilities.* Minneapolis: University of Minnesota, Institute on Community Integration.

Karp, M., Calcagno, J., Hughes, K., Jeong, D.W., & Bailey, T. (2007). *The postsecondary achievement of participants in dual enrollment: An analysis of student outcomes in two states.* Community College Research Center. Retrieved November 27, 2007, from http://www.ecs.org/html/IssueSection.asp?issueid=214&s=Selected+Research+%26+Readings

National Alliance for Secondary Education and Transition. (2005). Part II. Supporting evidence and research. In *National standards and quality indicators: Transition toolkit for systems improvements.* Minneapolis: University of Minnesota, National Center for Secondary Education and Transition.

National Center for the Study of Postsecondary Educational Supports. (1999). *Students with disabilities in postsecondary education: A profile of preparation, participation and outcomes.* Retrieved February 7, 2007, from the U.S. Department of Education, National Center for Educational Statistics web site: http://nces.ed.gov/pubs99/1999187.pdf

National Center for the Study of Postsecondary Educational Supports. (2003). *Capacity building institute proceedings: Students with intellectual disabilities and postsecondary education: Discussions of developments in practice and policy.* Honolulu, HI: Center for Disability Studies.

National Center for Youth Transition. (n.d.). *Best practices.* Retrieved October 19, 2006, from http://ntacyt.fmhi.usf.edu/promisepractice/index.cfm

National Collaborative for Workforce Development—Youth. (2005). *Transition guideposts developed by the National Collaborative for Workforce Development—Youth.* Retrieved December 8, 2008, from http://www.ncwd-youth.info/index.html

Neubert, D.A., Moon, M.S., & Grigal, M. (2004). Activities of students with significant disabilities receiving services in postsecondary settings. *Education and Training in Developmental Disabilities, 39*(1), 16–25.

Powers, L., Wilson, R., Matuszewski, J., Phillips, A., Rein, C., Schumacher, D., et al. (1996). Facilitating adolescent self-determination: What does it take? In D.J. Sands & M.L. Wehmeyer (Eds.), *Self-determination across the life span: Independence and choice for people with disabilities* (pp. 257–284). Baltimore: Paul H. Brookes Publishing Co.

Rammler, L., & Wood, R. (1999). *College lifestyle for all!* Middlefield, CT: Rammler and Wood Consultants.

Rehabilitation Act of 1973, PL 93-112, 29 U.S.C. §§ 701 *et seq.*

Rose, D.H., & Meyer, A. (2002). *Teaching every student in the digital age: Universal design for learning.* Alexandria, VA: Association for Supervision and Curriculum Development.

Segal AmeriCorps Education Award. (n.d.). Retrieved December 8, 2008, from http://www.americorps.gov/for_individuals/benefits/benefits_ed_award.asp

Stodden, R.A., Brown, S.E., Galloway, L.M., Mrazek, S., & Noy, L. (2005). *Essential tools: Interagency transition team development and facilitation.* Minneapolis: National Center on Secondary Education and Transition.

Uditsky, B., & Hughson, A. (2008). *Inclusive postsecondary education for adults with developmental disabilities: A promising path to an inclusive life.* Calgary, Alberta: Alberta Association for Community Living.

U.S. Department of Education. Office of Civil Rights. (1998). *Auxiliary aids and services for postsecondary students with disabilities. Higher education's obligations under Section 504 and Title II of the ADA.* Retrieved December 10, 2008, from http://www.ed.gov/about/offices/list/ocr/docs/auxaids.html

United States v. Board of Trustees of the University of Alabama, 908 F.2d 740 (11th Cir. 1990).

Wehman, P. (1996). *Life beyond the classroom: Transition strategies for young people with disabilities.* Baltimore: Paul H. Brookes Publishing Co.

Wehmeyer, M.L. (1996). Self-determination as an educational outcome: Why is it important to children, youth, and adults with disabilities? In D.J. Sands & M.L. Wehmeyer (Eds.), *Self-determination across the lifespan: Independence and choices for people with disabilities* (pp. 17–35). Baltimore: Paul H. Brooks Publishing Co.

Wehmeyer, M.L. (1998). Self-determination and individuals with significant disabilities: Examining meanings and misinterpretations. *Journal of the Association for Persons with Severe Handicaps, 23,* 5–16.

Wehmeyer, M.L. (2002). *Self-determination and the education of students with disabilities* (Digest No. E632). Reston, VA: ERIC Clearinghouse on Disabilities and Gifted Education. (ERIC Document Reproduction Service No. ED470036)

Whelley, T., Hart, D., & Zafft, C. (2002). *Coordination and management of services and supports for individuals with disabilities from secondary to postsecondary education and employment.* Unpublished manuscript, Honolulu, HI.

Zafft, C., Hart, D., & Zimbrich, K. (2004). College career connection: A study of youth with intellectual disabilities and the impact of postsecondary education. *Education and Training in Developmental Disabilities, 1*(1), 45–54.

Local School System Perspectives

CHAPTER

4

Maria Paiewonsky and Jerri Roach Ostergard

This chapter describes the perspective of school systems as they approach the prospect of creating postsecondary education (PSE) experiences for students with intellectual disabilities (ID). We first identify the various benefits of providing students with ID the opportunity to receive transition services in the PSE environment. Issues related to planning, implementing, and evaluating services in PSE settings are addressed, and strategies for overcoming challenges are offered. Next, issues related to accessing coursework, employment, and social and recreational experiences on the college campus are explored; strategies for success are provided. Throughout this chapter, profiles and case studies are used to illustrate how these benefits and challenges have affected school systems. Recommendations and checklists are included for those interested in implementing a transition model to improve PSE outcomes for students with ID.

CURRENT STATUS FOR STUDENTS AGES 18–21 WITH INTELLECTUAL DISABILITIES IN SCHOOL SYSTEMS WITH NO POSTSECONDARY OPTIONS

Increasing numbers of students with ID are benefiting from improved access to elementary, secondary, and special education services as a result of federal legislation such as the No Child Left Behind Act of 2001 (PL 107-110) and the Individuals with Disabilities Education Improvement Act of 2004 (PL 108-446). There is an expectation that students with ID will experience improvements in transition planning, including participation in college, work, and community activities. For school systems this has meant reconsidering what transition education is and how and where it is taught (Gaumer, Morningstar, & Clark, 2004). The traditional transition curriculum has focused on teaching life skills, as needed for daily living, social situations, and career awareness, as well as possibly repeating high school curricula. Gaumer et al. (2004) recognized that this approach offers students valuable information and time to practice and reinforce skills but does not go far enough in preparing students for the type of postschool outcomes they and their parents expect, such as going to college and obtaining paid employment in the community (Cameto, Levine, & Wagner, 2004; Gaumer et al., 2004; Grigal & Neubert, 2004; Zhang, Ivester, & Katsiyannis, 2005). In addition, the majority of traditional transition instruction is provided in high school settings instead of being taught in real-life situations where students must apply these life skills. Because of this, students do not have opportunities to learn with their same-age peers without disabilities, who are preparing for the same transition to young adulthood in multiple settings, such as college classrooms, the workplace, and the greater community (Gaumer et al., 2004; Hart, Zafft, & Zimbrich, 2001). As a result, students with disabilities are underprepared to pursue their postsecondary goals (Johnson, Stodden, Emanuel, Luecking, & Mack, 2002). Some students do not stay in school to receive any transition support. Wagner, Newman, Camino, and Levine (2005) report that 30% of students with disabilities drop out of school, and in a national study of school leavers, including those with disabilities, former students indicated that the number one reason they left school is that their classes were not interesting or relevant to their lives (Bridgeton, DiJulio, & Morison, 2006).

In a report from the National Longitudinal Transition Study-2 (NLTS-2), in which the transition status of 3,000 youth is being tracked through interviews with parents, schools, and students, school staff indicate that for up to 20% of students with disabilities, the staff question the suitability of the student's school program to prepare them to achieve their transition goals (Cameto et al., 2004). Similarly, when asked how helpful transition planning was for their sons and daughters, parents of 18% of students with disabilities indicate that the planning experience was either "not very" or "not at all" useful in preparing students for postschool life. As for students' involvement in their own transition planning to discuss their postsecondary goals, only 15% of students with disabilities who are 18 or older take a lead in their own planning meetings, and for students with ID, the percentage of those taking the lead is just 3% (Cameto et al., 2004; Katsiyannis, Zhang, Woodruff, & Dixon, 2005).

Benefits of Providing Postsecondary Education Services for School Systems

Transition services that include PSE provide many benefits for school systems. These services give districts a way to address transition in a comprehensive manner with evidence-based practices; these include teaching youth to take the lead in their own postsecondary planning, involving families in transition planning, providing parents with the support they need to understand and promote their sons' and daughters' transition activities, and partnering with agencies and local colleges to provide transition experiences that prepare students for the types of postsecondary futures they and their families want (Grigal, Dwyre, & Davis, 2006; Neubert & Moon, 2006; Zafft, Hart, & Zimbrich, 2004).

The innovation of comprehensive student-centered transition services and their commitment to students with ID lead to improved postschool outcomes. These models promote partnerships between schools and local colleges that can build bridges and strengthen services for all students; this approach is now seen as the next step in preparing students for the 21st-century workplace (Cassner-Lotto & Barrington, 2006). Providing individualized transition services to students means working with teachers to develop skills and practices that prepare students for postsecondary planning (Wehmeyer & Palmer, 2003). Professional development for staff focuses on youth development and self-determination, job development and support, academic accommodations, person-centered planning (PCP), differences between high school and college, and interagency collaboration (Hart & Grigal, 2004; National Center on Secondary Education and Transition, 2005;

Timmons, 2007; Weir, 2004). Through their experiences with students' transition activities, staff determine the areas that younger students should address, such as understanding their disability and being able to discuss accommodation needs, developing reading skills, and taking advantage of opportunities to practice self-determination and self-advocacy. Interagency collaboration and participation can result in cost sharing between the schools and employment providers to develop jobs for students (Luecking & Certo, 2002; Timmons, 2007). Developing PSE transition models helps districts to expand postschool choices that align with available options to students with disabilities and meet federal indicators of postschool planning and outcomes. Furthermore, collaborating with institutes of higher education (IHEs) promotes a seamless system of preparing students for postsecondary success through strong partnerships and ongoing collaboration (Harris, Cobb, Pooler, & Perry, 2008). This system allows students to move to age-appropriate education options, rather than linger in high school (Luecking & Certo, 2002). Finally, developing a PSE transition model demonstrates to students and families a commitment to see students through to the next phase of their lives.

PLANNING POSTSECONDARY EDUCATION SERVICES FOR STUDENTS WITH INTELLECTUAL DISABILITIES

Preparing for PSE requires comprehensive planning and facing some challenges. First among these is the recruitment of members for the planning committee itself. School and agency personnel involved in special education and disability issues often complain that they are inundated with meetings. And college administrators who are already faced with many challenges in supporting a diverse student population may initially feel reluctant to discuss a new initiative. Working out the many logistics involved takes time and persistence. Issues such as prioritizing students for planning, transportation, hiring and training staff, and administrative concerns have to be addressed. In this section, we outline the steps in planning for PSE services, discuss the challenges involved in each step, and offer strategies to address those potential barriers.

Steps in Planning Postsecondary Education Services

As highlighted by Grigal, Neubert, and Moon (2005), preliminary planning includes 1) establishing a planning committee, 2) determining the student population that will be served, 3) identifying the setting or settings in which transition services will be offered, 4) agreeing on goals that will shape the direction of the new services, 5) choosing a model that includes PSE and best fits the goals of the district, and 6) broadening the planning committee to form interagency student support teams that address administrative issues, formal agreements for services, and support to students.

Establishing Planning Partners

For school personnel, the idea of dedicating time to yet one more initiative or committing to one more meeting can seem difficult or even impossible, considering the number of priorities they have to address in any given week. Yet, PSE experiences are most effectively established through interagency collaboration (Hart, Zimbrich, & Ghiloni, 2001, 2002; Grigal et al., 2005; Luecking & Certo; Morningstar, 2006; National Center for Secondary Education and Transition, 2005; Timmons, 2007). In fact, it is this collaboration that has proved to be the strongest predictor of transition policy compliance and best practice (McMahan & Baer, 2001). In anticipation of possible barriers, the planning facilitator who is recruiting members should be prepared to make clear the goals of the planning committee and the typical length of the meeting. The facilitator should ask members who work for agencies or organizations to host some of the meetings so that the location can be rotated. This not only eases the burden of schools that host transition-related meetings, but also helps members to become more familiar with other organizations.

Recruitment for a planning committee should focus on those individuals who have a demonstrated commitment to transition outcomes for youth with disabilities and come with diverse perspectives on the issues (Grigal et al., 2005). Membership may include parents, school administrators and teachers, employment providers, state agency personnel, and staff from local independent living and workforce development centers (see Table 4.1). Membership may change over time as more community members are invited to contribute to the plan. In these initial planning meetings, members consider what is and is not negotiable in identifying the key elements of their vision of PSE supports and services, the resources available, and the partnerships that need to be secured or developed to achieve the vision (Grigal et al., 2005).

Table 4.1. Potential candidates for membership on a planning committee

1. Local school system (LSS) director of special education and other special education administrators/coordinators
2. LSS teachers and department chairs of high schools sending students
3. LSS principal(s)
4. Personnel from other school systems who may want to collaborate in creating new services
5. Community-based instructors/work coordinators/transition specialists
6. Related services personnel, such as therapists, counselors, and paraprofessionals
7. Parents
8. Local agencies serving adults (e.g., not-for-profit community organizations, vocational or residential support providers, independent living centers)
9. Personnel from local community colleges or universities
10. Teachers or staff members of existing programs in postsecondary settings
11. Vocational rehabilitation or developmental disabilities case management representatives
12. Employment support organizations (e.g., local One-Stop Career Center)
13. Advocacy organization representatives
14. Recent graduate or student with severe disability
15. Other (list):

From Grigal, M., Neubert, D.A., & Moon, M.S. (2005). *Transition services for students with significant disabilities in college and community settings: Strategies for planning, implementation, and evaluation.* Austin, TX: PRO-ED; adapted by permission.

Determining the Students Who Will Receive Services

To successfully implement transition services in PSE environments, planning teams must clearly define the group of students who will be served. This process can be difficult for school personnel for several reasons; most of them agree that all students, whether or not they have a disability, would benefit from transition planning and access to PSE before leaving school. In addition, some committee members may feel that directing the available resources to the large number of students with disabilities who need less intense support is the most logical way to organize priorities. Other planning committee members may feel that with limited resources and personnel, it is important to select those students who are going to need the most support to achieve successful postschool outcomes. To address these concerns and varying opinions, the committee may find it helpful to conduct a needs assessment that takes into consideration the preparation and experiences potential students had during their high school years in preparation for their transition, the anticipated type of services and level of support from adult agencies their education team expects to recommend, and the options that are likely to be made available to those students without comprehensive transition services (see Appendix 4.1). From this list, the committee can determine which students to support and how many (Grigal et al., 2005). During the first year of implementation, a maximum of three to five students is recommended in order to pilot, adjust, and revise polices and strategies. This pilot year should include, at a minimum, the support of a transition coordinator who can serve as a case manager for the participating students.

Identifying the Location of Services

There are many internal issues that drive the choice for the location of services. Planning committee members who are focused on expanding transition services to include access to PSE must take into consideration the existing college connections within the school district, the support that can be expected from the college administration, the transportation available to students, the accessibility of the campus, and the available courses.

Existing College Connections

One issue to consider is the connections the school system already has with local colleges. These may be formal relationships, such as written agreements between the school and local colleges that provide concurrent enrollment opportunities to other identified students at the school. The district may also have informal relationships with specific colleges. For example, college faculty or staff may sit on vocational advisory boards or collaborate with the schools through teacher training programs. In these cases, a new program of services may be aligned with the existing initiatives or expand them. It may be that one or more of the colleges seek to establish more connections to the area high schools. The challenge for school personnel will be to encourage partners to be open to broadening these connections for students with disabilities, because historically concurrently enrolled high school students have come from honors programs (Karp, Bailey, Hughes, & Fermin, 2004).

Support from the College Administration

Determining the location of services may include reaching out to college administrators to learn more about the mission of the college and discuss the design and benefits of dual enrollment. When meeting with administrators, planning committee members should articulate how dual-enrollment initiatives for students with ID can address some of the college's mission or administrative needs. Initially, there may be some resistance from local colleges to such an initiative. Community colleges in particular are often described as being stressed by a number of factors, including increasing enrollments, a student population with diverse academic preparation for college, increased numbers of students who need remediation, and administrative pressure to increase degree completion rates (National Center for Public Policy and Higher Education, 2006). It is critical, in conversations with college personnel, that the mission of this initiative be shown to match the mission of the college to serve the community and to promote individuals for the workforce; examples that highlight how students with disabilities can benefit from a college experience would be helpful.

Transportation

An important part of accessibility is the ability to get to and from the campus. Determining the location of services should include a review of all transportation to the college, including public transportation, carpooling, subsidized transportation for targeted commuters such as college students and individuals with disabilities, and transportation offered through the school. Planning committee members should carefully consider avoiding school transportation, because it is the most costly option and does not help the student to develop more independent travel skills.

Accessibility of the Campus

Planning committee members should also consider the college's proximity to the school or community from which the students will be traveling. Especially for students who initially travel from a high school, it is important that there are public transportation routes to the college and that travel time does not take up the majority of the day.

Availability of Courses

In choosing the location of services, it is important to review the college's selection of courses that are available to students with ID who are not necessarily enrolling in a full course of study. The planning committee should determine which courses do not require prerequisites, which can be audited, and what noncredit classes are available. Because placement test scores are likely to prevent traditional access to some courses, it is important to investigate the procedures for waiving prerequisites.

Determining How Services Will Be Structured

The schedule and structure of services in the PSE setting should be based on students' individual transition goals. For many students with ID, transition goals include college courses, work, and participation in community activities. Therefore, activities and support services may be spread across several locations. This can be challenging for school districts that provide the majority of transition education activities in a high school setting. Thoughtful planning and scheduling are required, so that students can pursue individual transition goals with the support of staff across settings. This planning is usually directed by a transition or program coordinator who takes responsibility for developing student and staff schedules.

One way to begin is to start with just one student schedule. In the example presented in Figure 4.1, Julie indicated an interest in learning more about sales work. She had a community-based job, unpacking new deliveries of clothes in the back room of a large department store. After observing other workers at the store, Julie expressed an interest in working at the customer service counter. Her team suggested that while waiting for a job to open up, she should consider developing additional customer representative skills. At the local community college, a one-credit business course, Customer Service Skills, was offered in the spring. The transition coordinator helped Julie register for this class. In addition to her job and the college class, Julie was also going to learn to use Americans with Disability Act (ADA) of 1990 (PL 101-336) public transportation to get to her job, the college campus, and home. Figure 4.1 is Julie's weekly community-based transition schedule. A coach at college supported Julie while school staff

Figure 4.1. Julie: Spring 2009 schedule

Transition goals: Apply for job in customer service; develop related job skills; learn to use transportation to travel to and from job, college campus, and home

Time	Monday	Tuesday	Wednesday	Thursday	Friday
8:00–9:00	Travel to job	Travel to campus	Travel to job	Travel to campus	Travel to job
9:00–10:00	Work at department store	Customer service class	Work at department store	Customer service class	Work at department store
10:00–11:00		Homework center		Homework center	
11:00–12:00		11:15–12:00 Yoga class		11:15–12:00 Yoga class	
12:00–1:00	Lunch	12:15–1:00 Lunch in cafeteria	Lunch	12:15–1:00 Lunch in cafeteria	Lunch
1:00–2:00	Work	Travel training	Work	Travel training	Work
2:00–3:00		Home		Home	
3:00–4:00	Travel home		Travel home		Travel home

helped her to use public transportation. At work, a job coach checked in with her at least once during every shift.

Clearly, one student's schedule is fairly easy to manage. It is when schools try to plan for a larger number of students that it can seem impossible to provide all students with community-based transition services. However, if transition staff or coaches are trained to fade their support to some students while reserving time for those students who will always need more, it is possible to plan for transition staff to support more students in a PSE setting in the community. An example of how staff can support a number of transition-age students is illustrated in Figure 4.2. In this case, a transition coordinator splits her time between coordinating student and staff schedules, attending students' transition planning meetings, supervising transition staff, attending interagency transition planning meetings, and introducing students to college and job opportunities. A number of transition staff split their time between helping students at college and work and training students to use public transportation. In addition, transition staff may assist students meeting with adult agency staff to further prepare for their transition from school.

Many school districts choose to have a base on the college campus where staff can be available to help students prepare for or alter schedules or resolve problems. The base location may be at the community college, a workforce development center, or a community center. It is recommended that the base location not be at the local high school, primarily because the purpose of college- and community-based transition programming is to help students establish new connections and routines in the community.

Policy Issues Related to Flexible Student Schedules

School administrators involved in the development of flexible student schedules will need to discuss policies that differ from those of a typical high school, such as monitoring attendance of students who do not come to the high school, grading of students who are automatically enrolled in the school's computer system, and contingency plans for transition staff absence. These are all topics that may have to be addressed by the special education director or administrator, school principal, and, in some cases, school committee members. Any new policies that are proposed should also be presented to family members for review and feedback.

Integrating Related Services

An important issue school administrators are concerned about is how to address related transition services and individual education goals. Initially administrators may feel that students should take classes at college but must then return to the high school for related services and to participate in life skills practice or basic academic classes. This solution can lead to problems, such as the expense of trips to and from the home, college, and high school; tight schedules that have students rushing from one place to another; and stress created by an overloaded schedule. Another solution, which may take a semester or two to establish, is to work with the student and his or her team to shift the location of services entirely to the college setting. This strategy allows students to have quality time in age-appropriate settings and to receive any specialized instruction and related services in those settings where these functional skills need to be used.

Figure 4.2. Transition staff schedule for week of October 6–10

Staff	Monday	Tuesday	Wednesday	Thursday	Friday
Peg Trans. coord.	Justin's ITP meeting (Voc. Rehab. Office)	On campus all day: Meet with transition staff	8:50 To campus: Meet Ben 11:00 Check in with Jake at new job	AM: Interagency Transition Planning meeting PM: Train staff on travel training & fading	Tim's ITP meeting (DMR offices) Develop & e-mail staff schedules for next week
Carol Trans. coach	Drive to Lucy's job site for 8:00 Check in with Julie/Marge at jobs Leave at 12:00 to provide job support for Dan	7:50–11:15 Ed coaching with Lucy/Amy/Julie in a.m. courses 1:00 Travel training with Julie: college to home	7:50 Drive to job sites. Check in with Julie/Marge at jobs Meet Marge at 12:40: job prep at One Stop Career Center	7:50–11:15 Ed coaching with Lucy/Amy/Julie in a.m. courses 1:00 Travel training with Julie: college to home	Drive to college: Ed coach support to Rachel Check in with Julie/Marge at jobs Leave at 12:00 to provide job support for Dan
Missy Trans. coach	8:50 To college with Jen 11:00 Travel/job support to Rich	7:30 To college with Jake 11:30 Travel training (Jake)	8:50 To college with Jen 11:00 Travel/job support to Rich	7:30 To college with Jake 11:30 Travel training (Jake)	7:50 Job check-in with Don/Jake/Artie 11:00 to campus. Check in with students
Anne Trans. coach	7:30 Meet Richie at campus 11:00 Shadow Richie taking cab to work 11:45 Job coaching	7:30 Job check-in with Millie/Rose 12:30 Travel training with Rose	7:30 Meet Richie at campus 11:00 Shadow Richie taking cab to work 11:45 Job coaching	7:30 Job check-in with Millie/Rose 12:30 Travel training with Rose	7:30 Meet Richie at campus 11:00 Shadow Richie taking cab to work 11:45 Job coaching

Creating Measurable Goals

Establishing goals for transition services in PSE settings can be challenging. Transition goals such as enhancing self-determination, accessing community services, and developing a career plan are all plausible goals, but may be difficult for a planning committee to see as possible to promote for all students with ID. At the same time, goals can set the direction for new services and improved outcomes. The most important aspect of setting goals is to make them measurable and appropriate to each student. Goals should be determined by a review of what students need to improve their postschool outcomes. Information may be drawn from a transition needs assessment conducted by the planning committee, from focus groups with key stakeholders, and from resource mapping with an expanded planning group. In this way it is possible to determine what resources are available to transition-age students, locate gaps in or duplication of services, and create an action plan to develop a new model of services (Grigal et al., 2005; Hart, Zimbrich, et al., 2001). A sample resource map in Appendix 4.2 highlights how one district identified goals with this process.

An important consideration for planning committees is to limit the number of major goals to three to five. These may include a combination of systematic goals and individual student goals. An example of a systematic goal may be to develop a college-school partnership in a collaborative effort to provide college and work opportunities for students with disabilities. An example of an individual student goal is to secure paid employment based on students' preferences. These goals and the committee's efforts to adopt new transition policies and practices reflect a commitment from the district to make changes and therefore should be presented to school administrators and other key stakeholders, including the superintendent, school committee members, special education administration staff and teachers, the local parent advisory group, and others the planning committee deems appropriate. Advocacy and leadership are critical throughout the process as the model grows to support more students with ID. Feedback from participants will help ensure that the committee has considered concerns that potential partners may have about the new services. With goals set, the planning committee should develop an action plan, delineating roles and responsibilities, to bring the vision of services to life (Grigal et al., 2005).

Person-Centered Planning

PCP promotes the active engagement of the student in the identification of his or her strengths, preferences, and aspirations for the future. It has been useful in the transition planning process because it encourages students to articulate their dreams. What makes it different from an individual education or transition planning meeting is that the student is asked to identify people who they trust to become a part of the collaboration. Therefore, invited guests more likely include extended family, friends, and neighbors. Some but not all team members may be invited. In addition, the individual is asked to identify a comfortable place to have the PCP meeting, so often it is not held at school. An important distinction to make between PCP and other school-based transition planning is that PCP is focused on supporting individuals instead of on system-centered options, such as a segregated program (Amado & McBride, 2001). It may seem to school personnel that PCP is difficult to implement, because it requires that meetings be held away from school if the student prefers that option and that the meetings be held when it is convenient for the majority of guests the student has invited. This may involve meeting in the evening or on a weekend. In addition, school personnel are accustomed to preparing for meetings by reviewing objectives and data reports, which is not required and in fact is discouraged at PCP meetings. Despite these challenges, many teachers who have adopted PCP have found ways to incorporate it into their scope of work for transition planning and find the process empowering for students.

PCP is particularly helpful for students who 1) are unclear about what they want to do after high school, 2) have had unsatisfactory transition experiences in the past, 3) have had few or no transition experiences, 4) have a large support team whose members have different and/or conflicting priorities, and 5) need time to consider postsecondary aspirations with others. When student goals include work and/or college, the PCP facilitator asks students to describe how they learn best, what accommodations they use, and whether they have developed a resume. Initially staff may facilitate PCP with students, but as the program grows, other district personnel, including teachers and instructional assistants, may also be trained to facilitate planning. There are many types of PCP that are useful for students with ID, including Whole Life Planning, 5 Bold Steps, MAPS, and Essential Lifestyles Planning, to name a few.

As a result of PCP, a plan is developed that includes action steps for each student aspiration and a responsible person and a deadline for each step. Details of a sample action plan are listed in Figure 4.3: it identifies a student's

Figure 4.3.   Carmen: Person-centered planning action plan

Education vision: Study fashion design May 9, 2008			
Student vision	*Action step*	*Who is taking responsibility*	*Will report back to group by*
Study fashion design	• Research local schools that offer course of study • Work with family to arrange college visits • Research costs	• Mrs. Damaa (teacher) will help Carmen research schools during career skills class. • Mrs. Taule (guidance) and Mr. Cisco (Voc. Rehab.) will meet Carmen and parents to review financial aid options. • Carmen and parents will visit colleges in summer/fall.	June 16

aspiration to explore fashion design and lists the resulting action steps and a deadline for reporting back to the group, which agreed to reconvene on June 16.

Individualizing Student Schedules

A key element in developing and sustaining a PSE transition model is understanding the need for individualized, flexible student schedules. Activities take place in postsecondary environments like college campuses and workplaces. Other related education goals, such as learning to use public transportation to and from school or work, using communication technology, and accessing fitness and recreation facilities, are also addressed in natural settings. In some districts, during the first year of transition away from the high school, when a student's schedule is reflecting more transition-related activities in the community, transition staff encourage students to phase out their participation in high school–based activities in favor of community-based activities. Although this adjustment can be hard for some students and often requires some negotiation with parents and students, the benefits of establishing new networks of support and new age-appropriate postsecondary activities begin to outweigh the student's nostalgia for high school activities.

Figures 4.4 and 4.5 are two examples of how students' schedules look as they prepare for their transition out of school. In the first example, Angela's goals include getting a job working with children, taking some college classes, getting some regular exercise, and volunteering. Angela's schedule reflects her vision—she takes classes at the local community college, she has an internship connected to her desire to work with children, she takes swimming lessons at the local YWCA, she volunteers at the nursing home where her grandmother lives, and she is looking for paid work through the local workforce development center. Angela no longer goes to the high school, because her transition activities are based in the community.

In the second example, Victor is an 18-year-old student with ID who wants to pursue work as an auto mechanic. He has helped his father maintain the family car and recently had the opportunity to get some more hands-on experience by working once a week with a neighbor who works as a mechanic. Victor can read and write at the third-grade level and learned that he would have to increase his reading and writing skills if he wanted to be accepted into an auto mechanics training program. With the assistance of a transition coach and the disability support counselor at a local community college, Victor took the placement tests, and, based on his scores, he registered for the developmental reading class. In addition to auditing that class, the transition coordinator arranged for Victor to enroll in a one-credit auto mechanics orientation class through continuing education at the college. Victor also has an opportunity to do an internship at a local auto body shop 2 days a week. Although he is eager to apply to the auto mechanics program, he worked on building the skills he needed, through college classes and the internship, to further develop his reading skills and relevant work experience to pursue his aspirations.

Figure 4.4. Angela's schedule

Monday	Tuesday	Wednesday	Thursday	Friday
7:00–8:00 City ADA transportation to community college	8:00–9:00 City ADA transportation from home to internship	7:00–8:00 City ADA transportation to community college	8:00–9:00 City ADA transportation from home to internship	7:00–8:00 City ADA transportation to community college
8:00–9:00 Reading class	9:00–5:00 Childcare internship: Kennedy Elementary	8:00–9:00 Reading class	9:00–5:00 Childcare internship: Kennedy Elementary	8:00–9:00 Reading class
10:00–12:00 College child care class		10:00–12:00 College child care class		10:00–12:00 College child care class
12:00–12:30 Lunch on campus	12:30–1:00 Lunch at internship	12:00–12:30 Lunch on campus	12:30–1:00 Lunch at internship	12:00–12:30 Lunch on campus
12:30–1:00 City ADA transportation to internship		12:30–1:00 City ADA transportation to nursing home		12:30–1:00 City ADA transportation to One-stop career center
1:00–5:00 Child care internship: Kennedy Elementary	5:00 City ADA transportation home	1:00–5:00 Volunteer: nursing home	5:00 City ADA transportation home	1:00–3:30 One-stop career center
	6:00 YWCA water aerobics class	5:30 YWCA swimming lesson		3:30 City ADA transportation home

Determining How Supports Will Be Provided

Students receiving services in PSE settings may receive support from various people, including the transition coordinator, support staff (such as instructional assistants, job coaches, education coaches, peer mentors, and college disability services staff), and in some cases community services providers if the school has contracted with an agency for transition support. Student support needs will vary depending upon their level of integration at the college and skills. Students in programs that create separate curricula and coursework for students with ID at the college will likely not require as much or the same type of support in their classes as students who are taking a typical college course. Three recommended strategies for planning student support include an interagency student support team, formal interagency agreements, and ongoing interagency support for students.

Figure 4.5.   Victor's schedule

Monday	Tuesday	Wednesday	Thursday	Friday
7:00–8:00 City ADA transportation to community college	8:00–9:00 City ADA transportation from home to internship	7:00–8:00 City ADA transportation to community college	8:00–9:00 City ADA transportation from home to internship	7:00–8:00 City ADA transportation to community college
8:00–9:00 College: basic reading	9:00–1:00 Internship at auto detailing shop	8:00–9:00 College: basic reading	9:00–1:00 Internship at auto detailing shop	8:00–9:00 College: basic reading
9:15–11:15 Basic auto mechanics		9:15–11:15 Basic auto mechanics		9:00–10:00 Homework support at college tutoring center
11:15–12:30 Homework support at college tutoring center	1:00–1:30 Lunch at internship site	11:15–12:30 Homework support at college tutoring center	1:00–1:30 Lunch at internship site	10:00–11:30 Meet with transition counselor: job-seeking support
12:30–1:00 Lunch on campus		12:30–1:00 Lunch on campus		11:30–12:15 Lunch on campus
1:00–2:30 College fitness center	1:30–3:00 City ADA transportation home	1:00–2:30 College fitness center	1:30–3:00 City ADA transportation home	12:15–2:00 College fitness center
2:30–3:00 City ADA transportation home	3:00–3:30 Finish homework for next class	2:30–3:00 City ADA transportation home	3:00–3:30 Finish homework for next class	2:00–2:30 City ADA transportation home
				3:00–5:00 Volunteer at neighbor's garage sale

The Interagency Student Support Team

An interagency student support team is highly recommended (Hart et al., 2001; Luecking & Certo, 2002; Morningstar, 2006; Timmons, 2007). This group can collaborate to assist with the daily operations of the work. Once the interagency team is established, members can work as a group to 1) determine policies and procedures that must be in place before implementing new services; 2) pursue formal interagency agreements among partners that offer specific transition support to students, such as job development or job support; and 3) offer consistent interagency transition support to students. These activities operationalize the model by addressing the systemic and individual transition issues discussed next.

Administrative Policies and Procedures

There are a number of procedures that must be followed before transition services can be implemented. The interagency team should discuss and draw up guidelines that address the student population targeted by these services. Policy descriptions should then be distributed to all appropriate staff and administrators. Referral and application forms and the following information packets should be made available ahead of time:

- Emergency procedures
- How school and college schedules will be followed
- Staff and student schedules
- IEP and graduation policies and procedures
- Budget and funding source allocation
- Record keeping

Formal Interagency Agreements

At the system level, interagency team members may want to pursue formal agreements between organizations to address transition service goals. Examples of formal agreements made through such efforts include school/vendor agency partnerships that focus on employment outcomes for students; school district/IHE partnerships that work collaboratively to promote college access to students with ID; and partnerships between state agencies and city transportation companies that provide travel training for students (see Appendix 4.3). Generally, formal agreements include an outline of the responsibilities of each partner and a time line for activities.

Securing agreements or memoranda of understanding (MOUs) takes patience and diplomacy. Even when there are established contacts from each organization, determining who is authorized to sign an MOU or agreement often takes some persistence. If the authorized person is not someone who has been directly involved in the planning, additional conversations may be necessary to explain the collaboration and the importance of having a formal agreement for such a partnership.

Ongoing Interagency Transition Support for Students

The work of the interagency student support team is critical in supporting individual student aspirations. Members assist in coordinating many activities related to transition planning, including helping to facilitate PCP, working with students to determine how to proceed with college aspirations, coordinating work opportunities related to students' college and career interests, coordinating service delivery and supports, and evaluating the model for its effectiveness and its capacity to support more students. Students should be encouraged to present their transition goals to the interagency transition team and return to the team whenever they feel their transition has stalled or if they need more help from the team.

Identifying Resources

From an administrator's perspective, one concern that stalls implementation of PSE transition services is the perception that there are not enough resources or personnel to support this model as well as other initiatives in the district. Initially, school districts may identify one teacher or one instructional assistant to pilot the model with two or three students but have difficulty seeing how to expand the model without draining other resources. By examining existing resources within the district and with community partners and then working to combine resources, school districts can restructure responsibilities as well as resources. For example, the position of a teacher who is already working with transition-age students may be converted into a transition coordinator position. Support staff for this work often serve as educational and job coaches to the participating students.

Staff hired to work on community-based transition activities will need new training to prepare for their community-based work, and this should be made clear at their interviews. Transition staff will need support to understand that the traditional roles and responsibilities of special education teachers and instructional assistants (IAs) differ from these new positions, even though their former training and experience will be valuable. Administrators need to understand how these new positions differ from the traditional teacher and IA roles. Some issues that can be challenging to think about are how to prepare new staff to work more independently across community settings, how to explain these positions to current staff and possibly to the teachers' union, and the contingency plans and resources staff will need to do their work away from the school. Training topics for new staff often include student-centered planning, differences between high school versus college for students with disabilities, self-determination and self-advocacy support during the transition process, and universal design, which includes an explanation of accommodations. New staff should also be given information about any school policies that address community work. Examples might include district policies about transporting students, responding to emergencies, reporting student absences, and interacting with community partners as a representative of the school.

Transition Staff Roles and Responsibilities

Ideally, a program or services coordinator will have a background in special education and adult disability services. In this position, the coordinator will spearhead the interagency team, introduce PSE transition services to students and their families, coordinate PCP sessions, help establish individual schedules for students, and coordinate the supports students need to participate in activities, including staffing, transportation, and accommodations. The transition coaches may be expected to work a flexible schedule, undergo additional training in identifying natural supports, and phase out their own support to students in academic, work, and community activities as appropriate to help students assume responsibility for their postsecondary schedules (see Appendix 4.4).

Flexible Staff Schedules

Before staff are hired, it is important to plan how students will be supported when their classes or work schedules occur outside of typical school hours. For students with ID who might need short or continued support to take classes or might have work shifts that occur beyond school hours, no support usually means not participating in those activities. Some school districts create job descriptions for educational and job coaches that include a requirement to work more flexible hours. Transition support staff work the same number of hours as other instructional assistants in the district but have agreed to work hours that better support students whose schedules may no longer follow a typical school day. Some districts establish formal agreements with agency providers to provide extended support after typical school hours. Administrative staff coordinating this work should prepare to explain flexible staff schedules to other school personnel, such as the school principal and union representatives.

IMPLEMENTING TRANSITION SERVICES IN POSTSECONDARY EDUCATION SETTINGS

A primary task of implementing transition services in PSE settings is informing key stakeholders about the new services and providing each group—students, families, and school personnel—with the information and training they need to participate. Staff need to be made aware that new postsecondary options are available to students with ID and how these students can benefit from these options. To prepare students, their teachers need to understand how college differs from high school, including how students become eligible for accommodations and the role students need to take to advocate their needs. Both parents and teachers need to understand that students' schedules will require customization to reflect their transition goals and that this may have an impact on staffing. Students need support to understand how PSE can be accessed and the responsibilities they must assume to pursue this option. Finally, to evaluate the impact PSE has on student outcomes, school personnel and other partners need to be aware of ongoing and postimplementation data collection strategies that can shed light on this work.

Customizing Transition Services

Implementing PSE services for students with ID requires a commitment from the team and the district to support students as they customize their postsecondary planning. It also means that, from the start, school staff and families are partnering with students to develop skills they will need to pursue postsecondary plans. This can be a challenge for school systems for a number of reasons. First, securing a commitment from all stakeholders on the team will take time. Initially, there may be some apprehension about what access to college for students with ID really means and how viable it is. Some school personnel may question how feasible it is to customize transition services. In many cases, transition-age students with ID receive services in self-contained classrooms, which may or may not include community-based experiences. In these settings, students are often taught skills as a group. Some administrators argue that this model is the most cost-efficient way to provide services. They may argue that supporting students individually is not realistic. In these cases, it is important to let administrators know that some students need less support than others over time and that staff support to students can be distributed in a way that appropriately meets the needs of students while building their independence.

Recruitment Challenges

Teachers and parents may not be able to picture what accessing college means for students with ID. Staff should expect that some teachers and parents might have concerns about developing new services for PSE. Well-intentioned individuals who support students with disabilities may say that traditional options for individuals with severe disabilities such as segregated adult services models are the most realistic. In addressing those opinions, it is important to provide examples that illustrate what access to inclusive postsecondary education means for students with ID and to explain how PSE may influence transition success. Some marketing strategies that schools have used include 1) hosting an orientation to explain the new services to students for whom these services are being developed, as well as to their parents and teachers; 2) presenting information at parent advisory committee meetings; and 3) developing a brochure that highlights the new services (see Table 4.2). This type of marketing helps to allay fears and answer questions individuals may have about these services. Marketing can also serve as an effective way to introduce, advertise, and involve adult agencies.

Some school systems create profiles of students to help families and staff understand the background of students who might be most successfully served in PSE settings. In Table 4.3, a short story describing how a person with a developmental disability can participate in college has helped other families in his community to visualize how this might work.

Developing Application and Referral Processes

School systems need to create organizational structures and processes to ensure that students who wish to receive transition services in PSE settings know what is required of them and that staff and families know the process through which these services can be accessed. An application form may be required for students and their teachers to request transition services from the district. In this form, teachers may identify their reasons for wanting transition services, the education and work experiences students have had to date, and the accommodations they might need in college and at work (see Appendix 4.5).

An application process may seem to indicate that only selected students will participate in transition activities; this is not the case. Instituting an application process can mark the beginning of more intensive transition support for older students and signal to transition staff that a student will need assessments in the areas of vocational, travel, and safety skills. An application can also instruct students and their team to begin pulling together documents, such as the latest IEP, transition plans, and psychological evaluations that will be useful or necessary for transition activities. An important outcome of an application process is that it can be a first step the student takes in transition planning, much as any student prepares for his or her exit from high school.

Table 4.2. Worcester Public Schools transition services program description

The Transition Services Program originally established in 2000 by the Worcester Public Schools (WPS) is designed to prepare high school students with disabilities Grades 10–12 to pursue postsecondary activities based on their visions for their future careers and life. The students have the opportunity to explore careers through internships, employment (college or adult education when a grant is available), transportation training, and community activities. Internships and employment in local business and nonprofit agencies provide students with valued experiences in developing and reaching their career goals. These combined experiences help students to formulate a career plan and individual goals for their future. The WPS Transition Coordinator, in collaboration with educational and job coaches, assists students to develop career plans. A career plan would list students' employment/career goal, as well as any additional educational/training goals. It also lists students' strengths and learning style, their preferences for jobs and hours, etc. By the time a student is leaving high school, the goals are to have a clearer idea of a career path, to have completed a resume/portfolio detailing his or her experiences, and if possible to have secured and be working at a job.

Some students who need additional guidance in developing future goals may participate in Person-centered planning (PCP), which is an individual planning process driven by a student and the significant people in their lives. The PCP acknowledges a student's vision in the areas of education, career, home, and leisure and is then used to develop an action plan and guide for their future.

A citywide Student Support Team (SST) meets monthly comprised of staff from DMR, MRC, Work Force Central, and Disabilities Coordinator from QCC, ICI, and the WPS Transition Coordinator and individual students. The SST was established to develop and monitor procedures, referrals, identify services and resources, problem solves and brainstorms with and for students around their action plans. One of the major goals of the SST is to coordinate supports and resources across agencies on a systems level, as well as on an individual level for students.

Source: Worcester Public Schools Department of Special Education, Worcester, MA.

Coordinating the Referral Process

A referral process may include conversations with teachers, reviewing student applications, attending meetings with students that include IEP meetings, following up with students and parents, facilitating PCP, coordinating a site visit, and attending orientation meetings. In Table 4.4 we present a referral protocol for a large school district that serves over 30 transition-age students with severe disabilities each year.

The issue of referrals is important. Staff need to understand the expectations for transition so that they can 1) prepare students to succeed in the postsecondary experience and 2) make appropriate referrals for jobs and/or PSE classes. Teachers who make a referral for transition services that include PSE should be made aware of the criteria that students must meet. A sample list of criteria for students with ID may include 1) being between 18 and 22 years old, 2) having an ID, 3) having a short- or long-term goal of competitive employment, 4) expressing an interest in PSE, 5) demonstrating the ability to follow directions, and 6) being able to attend to activities that are, at a minimum, 30 minutes long. The

Table 4.3.   David's college experience

David was a 20-year-old man with developmental disabilities. He attended a segregated life skills program for students with significant ID in an urban high school. David had a number of academic challenges. Although he was able to perform basic math and had some basic knowledge of money and its value, he was also considered a non-reader and -writer.

David was referred to the district's transition coordinator for transition supports and services. After participating in person-centered planning meetings, he participated in internships, job shadowing, and informational interviews to further explore career interests. David was also invited to visit the local community college to look into a course that might interest him as well as build his employment skills. With some apprehension, David agreed to take a tour of the campus with the transition coordinator. While on campus, the coordinator arranged for David to sit in on a college class, hang around the student center, and talk to college students with and without disabilities about their college experience. Although David enjoyed the visit, he declined to take this any further—he said he was not a good student and really wasn't "college material." He chose to take a job at a local warehouse where he could pursue his dream of working alongside people unloading trucks. His big dream was to work with a shipping clerk.

About 6 months later, after watching some of his friends from school talk about going to college, David approached one of the transition coaches and said, "I think I'd like to try that college thing." With assistance from the transition staff, he attended an orientation on the campus and its services, completed an intake interview with a disability services counselor, and registered for a course called Customer Supports. He also received safety training for travel to and from college, work, and home, and staff integrated time management skills training throughout his day. As for his course accommodations, David had extended time for tests, a reader, and a scribe. His self-confidence grew, as he spoke in class and joined discussions about good and bad customer service experiences he has observed. He actively utilized the campus resources to play basketball and computer games and eat lunch with friends. After a few months, staff noted that David had picked up some reading skills, presumably from completing course assignments with a tutor and doing his homework with a friend. Although David received a C in the class, he and his team were satisfied that he had learned some new skills and was a far more confident and mature young man because of his college experience.

A year later, David reported that he now works full time in a retail store. He receives medical benefits and vacation time and has stock options from the company. He is proud of his achievements and credits his college and internship experiences with his success.

application forms may also include information about the steps the teacher and student should follow, and the documentation necessary to apply for jobs, seek disability support services, and register for classes (Grigal et al., 2005).

Preparing Students for Postsecondary Education Experiences

Students with ID who pursue inclusive PSE are often at a disadvantage because of academic and career development histories that may or may not have prepared them for college and work expectations (Cameto, et al., 2004; Zhang,

Table 4.4. PSE transition services referral protocol

1. Chairperson invites transition coordinator to IEP for 10th-grade students with significant disabilities. At this meeting the transition coordinator gives an overview of transition services.
2. Team chairperson submits the referral form with a copy of the student's current IEP, transition plan, and recent psychological evaluation to the transition coordinator.
3. Transition coordinator reviews student information.
4. Transition coordinator contacts classroom teacher to schedule an observation of student and discussion with student and teacher.
5. Classroom teacher completes the vocational screening and submits to transition coordinator.
6. Transition coordinator reviews all information and gathers any additional information necessary.
7. Transition coordinator reviews referrals with special education administration and a final decision is made.
8. Transition coordinator completes acceptance form and mails to student and parents. When the student is accepted, the transition services emergency forms will be sent home to be completed and returned. Copies of acceptance forms are given to classroom teacher, team chairperson, and assistant director for special projects.
9. When the student is accepted into the program, a start date will be determined, once the completed transition services emergency forms are completed and returned to the transition coordinator.

Ivester, & Katsiyannis, 2005). Whether they received their education in inclusive or segregated classes, they may have had much of their academic work modified, used different textbooks, or been expected to achieve modified goals to obtain grades (Wagner, Newman, & Cameto, 2004). Students may not have been offered the kinds of accommodations used in colleges or access to the same material as their peers in high school (Shaw & Madaus, 2008). In college, there are no modifications. Students who are deemed eligible for reasonable and appropriate accommodations must expect to encounter the same course content and are graded with the same expectations as their classmates. Students may not be aware of the option to audit a class or take noncredit classes. In addition to having academic disadvantages, students with ID are often excluded from career activities at their school (Guy, Sitlington, Larsen, & Frank, 2008). If schools create job development programs for students with disabilities, the work is often limited to unpaid, repetitive work that requires little skill, such as cleaning, sorting, and stocking. As a result, students with ID have limited exposure to competitive work environments and expectations. Transition team members who intend to support students in college and competitive community employment must continuously address the expected roles and responsibilities of college students and employees, not only with students, but also with parents, teachers, and educational and job coaches (see Appendix 4.6). Training topics for students, teachers, and families may include the differences between high school and college, including IDEA and ADA/Section 504, new postsecondary options for students with ID, student expectations for supports and services, the language of higher education and transition, and self-determination in PSE and the workplace. School administrators must be prepared to customize training for teachers and introduce new postsecondary options for students with ID that differ from traditional choices. These will be critical, because teachers often have a primary role in transition planning meetings and must be aware of these new options. For students in particular, training in these topics will help them to understand the role they must take to fully engage in their own postsecondary planning (Finn, Getzel, & McManus, 2008; Getzel & Thoma, 2008; Thoma & Getzel, 2005).

Communicating with Families

A key activity in postsecondary planning is maintaining consistent communication with the family (Morningstar, 2006; National Center for Secondary Education and Transition, 2005). From the first IEP or interagency transition planning meeting the transition coordinator attends with the student and family, communication about transition planning should be a priority. This can be a challenge for school teams when parents miss meetings or say little when they do attend. Remember that transition planning can be stressful for everyone, but most importantly for families, who are often anxious about the shift to adult service agencies, new eligibility requirements, different hours that might affect their work, and new personnel working with their son or daughter (Benz, Johnson, Mikkelsen, & Lindstrom, 1995; Cooney, 2002; Thompson, Fulk, & Piercy, 2000).

The transition coordinator should inform families about the differences between high school and college, transition schedules versus typical school schedules, and transportation options and review any district-required forms, including emergency contact forms (see Appendix 4.7). The coordinator should also describe youth-directed transition planning as the cornerstone of transition and, for those students who are unclear about what they want to do after high school, offer PCP (see description of person-centered planning).

Family Educational Rights and Privacy Act

The Family Educational Rights and Privacy Act (FERPA) of 1974 (PL 93-380) is a federal law that protects the privacy of student education records. It applies to all schools that receive funds under an applicable program of the U.S. Department of Education (2008). School personnel implementing new PSE services to students should include information about FERPA in their training and inform families of the impact of this law. FERPA gives parents certain rights with respect to their children's education records. These rights transfer to the student when he or she reaches the age of 18 or attends a school beyond the high school level. Students to whom these rights have been transferred are *eligible students*. For college students with ID, this means that the college may release student information only with the consent of the student, unless the student is not his or her own legal guardian. It is also important to highlight for students that this means their instructors do not have access to their files, including any information about their disability. The only information instructors can ask for is about specific accommodations students need, and they can ask for that information only with a student's permission (Barr, Hartman, & Spillane, 1995).

Addressing the Student's Desire to Participate in Graduation Activities

A challenge faced by many students with disabilities who are eligible for special education services beyond 4 years of high school is that many students who want to participate in graduation ceremonies with their peers may be told by school administrators that once they accept the diploma or certificate of high school completion, their special education services are over. In many cases, adult services organizations are not always prepared for referrals before students turn 22, because their funds are determined on a year-to-year basis and are appropriated by the state legislature. To address this issue, many states are advising school districts to allow students to participate in graduation activities such as the prom and other traditional senior activities before they begin postsecondary planning activities, because this mirrors the typical transition their peers from high school have undergone. They will still receive services until they turn 22, but in a different setting, depending on the model.

Dealing with Scheduling Issues

There are two scheduling issues that should be acknowledged in preparation for implementation of PSE services with transition-age students. First, an individualized PSE transition schedule will differ from the typical high school schedule, and this could affect staffing. One way to deal with this is to tap into the resources that members of the interagency team might be able to offer, especially if student support is needed in the late afternoon or evening. This might include contracting with community rehabilitation providers to provide support during nonschool hours. Another solution is to hire transition coaches with the understanding that their hours will differ from those of traditional instructional assistant staff. Depending on the needs of the student, a second issue relates to the different academic schedules that colleges and high schools follow; this is most evident during vacations. It is important to adapt to these differences with the creation of seminars or independent study projects.

Site Visits

A number of experiences can be offered to students to assist them with making a decision about college. The coordinator can arrange for students to visit the college and during this visit arrange for students to take a general college tour or a customized tour, depending on the needs of the student. In addition to the typical college tour stops, the customized tour might include a visit to the disability services office for an explanation of the supports and services offered and a stop at the campus police office, where students are directed to go if they are lost or need help. The coordinator can arrange for the student to sit in a class to experience firsthand what it means to take a college course. Coordinators may include a stop at the college bookstore so students can see the textbooks used for college classes and get a sense of the reading done for college classes. The students may be invited to eat lunch in the student cafeteria and talk to other students about their college experiences.

Evaluating Services and Outcomes

As recommended by Grigal et al. (2005), from its onset the development of new transition services should be documented so that the process can be monitored and evaluated. Documentation should focus on data collection on numerous factors, such as whether goals were met, how many students participated in each activity, the staff support that was needed to assist students, the outcomes of support services, and the perceptions of students, staff, parents, and members of the interagency team. This information will help the team to demonstrate to stakeholders what new transition services can provide to students with ID. It can help the team and school administrators determine how successfully proposed transition activities were implemented and what adjustments need to be made to improve services (Grigal et al., 2005).

Two strategies that should be considered for the evaluation of transition services are ongoing and postimplementation data collection. Both strategies should be developed in the planning stages so that data are collected before the school year ends. Ongoing data collection includes information on student and staff activities, such as students' postsecondary goals, the transition activities they participated in, and exactly how they participated in college.

There are a number of postimplementation data collection activities that are recommended not only for evaluation of the impact of the transition services for students, but also for documentation of the process and for the satisfaction of stakeholders, including members of the interagency team, staff, and parents. To collect data on the postschool outcomes of students, staff should refer to the process that their district uses to comply with required data on "the percent of youth who had IEPs, who are no longer in secondary school (graduated or aged out), and who have been competitively employed, enrolled in some type of postsecondary school, or both, within one year of leaving high school" (IDEA 2004) (20 U.S.C. 1416(a)(3)(B)). To document the process and satisfaction of stakeholders, interviews or surveys should be designed to gather information on how the services were implemented, the challenges that were encountered, which strategies were found to be the most effective and which ones were not, and concerns of students and staff. Parents should also be asked about their perceptions of the outreach activities to gauge how effective they were in preparing parents for their son's or daughter's transition activities and eventual move from school (Grigal et al., 2005).

PLANNING FOR SERVICES AND SUPPORTS

To plan for services and supports at the college, school personnel must understand the many differences between high school and college. These differences affect how supports and services are offered at the college. It is especially important to understand differences when students are dually supported by college and school transition staff. School staff needs to understand how different laws guide the supports and services to students with disabilities at college as well as student rights and responsibilities. Without an understanding of these differences, incorrect assumptions are made by school personnel about how students with ID can access college (see Appendix 4.8).

The laws that govern supports and services to students with disabilities also directly influence the language that is used in college to describe these supports. Given these differences, it should come as no surprise that school personnel working at a college campus are often surprised and challenged to accept the differences. In this section we review typical college activities where these challenges may occur and offer suggestions to address them.

Accessing Typical College Coursework

If transition staff are able to arrange a college class visit with a student, they are likely to observe some traditional teaching methods. Although there are faculty who incorporate innovative teaching practices into their courses, most of the college curriculum, especially core or required courses, is taught with traditional methods, including lectures, readings, term papers, and exams. For students with ID, these methods can be difficult to access, even with accommodations. Initially, transition staff may think that the course material can be modified to be more accessible to the students, but that is not the case. Whereas IDEA is about success in the general curriculum, Section 504 of the Rehabilitation Act of 1973 (PL 93-112), which guides the law for disability-related supports and services, is about access to the curriculum. This is a major shift in thinking for school personnel, who are rarely responsible for implementing Section 504 and have little training on the related policies and procedures (Shaw & Madaus, 2008). To the extent possible, students and transition staff need training in Section 504 compliance, and background on the classes they are interested in, to determine the instructor's methods, the course content, and their use of universal access principles in the course design.

The Role of Disability Support Services

When the student has decided to pursue college and plans to take general college classes, the coordinator needs to determine the extent to which the student can receive supports from the office of disability support services. School personnel may not be aware that often the first step for students who want to take a college class is to make an appointment to talk to a counselor in the disability services office, to learn what needs to be done to register for classes and apply for support services. It may also be the first time transition staff and students learn that it is the student's responsibility to answer all of the questions at the appointment. If disability support services provide support to dually enrolled students, transition staff may need to work with the student to practice answering questions the disability counselor will ask, such as How are your reading skills? How are your writing skills? What is your disability? What do you have a hard time doing in your classes? and What kinds of accommodations do you use? In addition, students must be prepared to fill out a questionnaire and provide their social security number, health insurance information, and emergency contact information. Students must work with the transition coordinator and their parents to provide the latest copy of their IEP and their most recent neurological/psychological evaluation, which must be less than 3 years old. Once the questionnaire is complete, the disability services counselor determines whether the student should take placement tests to determine his or her reading, writing, and math levels.

If the student decides to take a class for college credit, he or she may be required to take the placement tests. If so, disability services will help the student set up a time to take the test. Accommodations are provided to students as needed/requested. If a student is planning to audit a class or take a noncredit class or a credit class that does not have prerequisites, he or she should not have to take the placement tests. Within a few days, after the application is reviewed, the disability counselor will have a completed accommodations form to give to the student. This packet includes information about accommodations that the student must give to the instructor by the first day of class. If possible, it is most helpful if students make an appointment with the instructor before the first class to discuss their learning style, their accommodations, and the purpose of their educational coach, if they have that support.

> *One of the first things people can go to if they need help is the disability office on their campus. If you have a certain disability and want to go to college you need to sign up in the disability office if they have one. The student needs to have paperwork that documents their disability. After that, you can get help.*
>
> —Beth, age 21, dual enrollment student

The Role of Placement Tests

Many colleges require students who have not received a high school diploma or general equivalency diploma to take placement tests to determine their eligibility for financial aid and their ability to benefit from college. This can be a challenge for PSE transition staff who want to help students register for a class that matches their interests. If their placement test scores are low, students may be told that they cannot access other courses until they take remedial courses at the college.

Although students can receive accommodations to take tests, the result is often that students receive low scores and are then told that they are only eligible for developmental reading, writing, and math courses and courses with no prerequisites. Although these courses may be beneficial for many students, including those with ID, this also means that students have limited course options and are prevented from auditing courses that would help them to learn more about the specific careers they want to pursue. This issue of placement tests and determining ability to benefit remains one of the biggest barriers in the pursuit of PSE for students who do not have a diploma. College personnel should be encouraged to discuss their concerns, but they should make consistent efforts to show how this innovative model of transition planning requires nontraditional access to college if students with ID are going to benefit.

Additional Issues Related to Course Access

In addition to the specific challenges students with ID face in accessing college courses, they and the staff must also be aware of other access issues, especially at community colleges. Community colleges are growing much faster than 4-year colleges and universities, enrolling nearly half of all undergraduates (Merrow,

2007). With these increased enrollments, all students find that unless they register for courses early, usually the semester before the course is offered, they are likely to find that the course has filled and closed. If students need a teacher's signature of approval to take a course, it can be extremely difficult to track this person down, especially a member of the adjunct faculty. When students do register for a course, they may find that the course and/or instructor is not the right match. Because of the difficulty of getting into courses, often students will remain in such a class, just to have the experience of being in college. Students with ID should be helped to identify why they want to take a course, whether it is for developing skills or to explore an interest, and how they feel they will benefit from the course. Students also need to understand the expectations of the course, which can be found in most syllabi and reviewed in advance, as many professors post their syllabus online or maintain it on record with their department.

Registering for College Courses

When students have chosen their courses, they must register for classes. This seemingly simple task can be challenging for any student, but it is especially so for students with disabilities who may need to complete additional tasks to be eligible to take the class. For example, Kayla was a dually enrolled student who selected a course called Water Exercise (Table 4.5). Before registering for the class, she discovered that there was a reading and writing requirement for the class, which meant that Kayla had to take a placement test. Kayla arranged to do this herself, and while she was on campus to take the tests, she paid her application fee. Unfortunately, Kayla was doing all this during the winter break. Tracking down her results, which were considered too low to take the class, and finding the instructor to ask about waiving the academic requirement were difficult during a slow period on campus. When she finally resolved those problems, she then had to address an unexpected issue when the college temporarily had no record that Kayla had paid the application fee.

In many cases, students with disabilities need support to register for classes because of the additional requirements they must fulfill to access courses. It is important that the PSE coordinator or other support personnel help students prepare for both anticipated and unanticipated problems during the registration process. Regardless of the challenges, students should be involved in all aspects of registration. As Kayla's example highlights, it is important to understand the registration process and to learn how problems arising during this process can be resolved.

Audit or Credit Status

Students and staff should determine whether they want to take the course for credit or audit the class. In most cases, staff should encourage students to try taking a course for credit first, and if they do not feel prepared to fulfill the course requirements after the first 2 weeks, they can change their course status to audit. Staff should encourage students to complete course assignments whether or not they are taking it for credit.

Table 4.5. Steps taken/problems encountered by student taking credit class at a community college

---

Kayla Registering for Class

---

1. Kayla determined that she wanted to take an exercise class. She selected Water Exercise from the credit course listing.
2. Kayla learned more about Water Exercise from the college catalog, including the fact that the course had a reading and writing assessment requirement. She obtained testing information from the assessment center.
3. Kayla selected a time for walk-in testing before the winter break. With support she presented herself for testing and was checked in. She then went to the testing room on her own and completed the assessment testing. With support, she also applied for admission in person at Student Services, paying the fee of $25.
4. Kayla was unable to receive her test results immediately because the computers were down. She returned the following Monday, but at the assessment center she was told to go to Continuing Ed to obtain her results. At Continuing Ed she was told that she needed to make an appointment to speak with someone, and the next available appointment was several days later. She made the appointment, but in an effort to move things along a little faster, Kayla contacted a counselor who has helped her out in the past. The counselor was able to show Kayla her assessment results immediately. Because Kayla tested below the required assessment level, the counselor recommended that she speak with the professor and request an exception. With support, Kayla e-mailed the professor. When the professor did not reply within 24 hours, the counselor recommended that Kayla speak directly with the department chair. With support, Kayla visited the Department Chair, who had heard from the professor about Kayla. The Department Chair and professor were willing to waive the assessment requirement, and the Deparment Chair told Kayla that she had taken care of things via the computer.
5. Kayla intended to register for the course online during winter break but was unable to access the community college online registration system. She went on her own to register for the class at Student Services. At that time, the clerk told her that she hadn't met the required assessment level and needed to be enrolled in Pathways, a program for students who need to improve their test scores. Furthermore, the clerk found no evidence that the Department Chair had approved Kayla's taking the course. Kayla returned to the registration area with support, and it was determined from a different clerk that the Department Chair actually needed to sign a form giving Kayla permission to take the class.
6. Kayla went on her own to obtain the necessary signature. This required several trips because the college was still on winter break and the Department Chair wasn't in often.
7. Once Kayla had the signature, with support she returned to Student Services to attempt to register. This time, a third clerk stated that Kayla had never applied for admission to the college. With support, Kayla successfully persuaded the clerk to check further, and it was finally determined that she had applied and had received the appropriate permission to take the course. Kayla received the necessary paperwork and went to the cashier to pay for the class.
8. Kayla started class on January 22, six weeks after beginning the registration process.

Participating in College Courses

On the first day of class, students must give their accommodation form to the instructor if they have not met with him or her before the first day of class. This can be a challenge for staff because it is not always easy to track down faculty on campus. In addition, it may be an intimidating step for students to take. Taking some time to rehearse the conversation with the student will help to prepare him or her for the instructor's questions about the student's accommodations.

PSE transition staff will often serve as educational coaches in or out of the college classroom. Education coaches help students to adjust to the pace of a course, use appropriate classroom behavior, develop and use organizational skills to meet course expectations, and use appropriate time management skills to complete their coursework. If the student has difficulty meeting course expectations, the educational coach may advise the student to meet with his or her disability counselor and/or to seek out academic support offered through the college's academic support center. The educational coach also helps the student to work with the instructor to plan for any test-taking accommodations before the day of a test. After receiving test scores, the educational coach may work with the student to review how to prepare for the next test, depending on the grade. When students are discouraged or are not keeping up with homework, the educational coach may remind them about their commitment by reviewing their postsecondary goals (see Appendix 4.9).

One concern about education coaches is their presence in the college classroom. As in K–12 settings, many faculty members may question how appropriate it is to have another instructor in the room. In some cases, instructors are comfortable working with students with disabilities as long as they are aware of their accommodation needs. In other cases, the idea that there is another teaching professional in the room makes them uncomfortable. One way to deal with this is for the PSE transition coordinator to work with the instructor to find ways for the education coach to serve the whole class, not just the student who requires an education coach. This might include supporting small-group work, lab work, or field studies.

> *It's not scary. You can learn stuff there. It's good to try it. You're going to be a little scared but that's normal. Because you've never tried it before. There's a lot of people there and that looks scary at first. When you get to know the college, you're going to feel more confident and good about yourself. I was like that too. I was scared but I got more confident. It took a while. By the end, I was better and I'm not nervous about it anymore. I said I didn't like it and I wasn't coming back but then I changed my mind. I wanted to go back.*
>
> —Alex, 20, dual enrollment student

Accessing Noncredit or Community-Based Instruction

Some students may choose to take a noncredit class or a community education class outside of college. They may think this option is an easier first step, which may be more affordable and match the needs of the student more closely than the existing courses at the college. In any case, the principles outlined in this chapter should apply in these cases. Students benefit from some type of PCP process to determine the skills they need to pursue their aspirations. From there, they may find that a community-based course is a better match for their interests.

Planning for Paid Employment

Students enrolled in college classes are usually pursuing work goals. Therefore, related work experiences are often paired with college experiences. When school personnel include PCP in their transition services, it is usually easy to develop the link between students' career aspirations and related courses. In some cases, school districts use the campus only as a base location and focus the majority of their services on work-related transition goals.

Focusing on work can be very challenging for school personnel whose professional training has minimally covered career development or any other transition topics (Morningstar & Kleinhammer-Tramill, 2005; Roessler, Hennessey, & Rumrill, 2007). As a result, many special education teachers feel unprepared to include career development in their transition services, relying instead on a functional curriculum, social skills training, and school-based functional learning opportunities (Katsiyannis, Zhang, Woodruff, & Dixon, 2005; Zhang, Ivester, & Katsiyannis, 2005). In addition, supports students need in employment settings are different from what they need in academic settings. For instance, in work settings, students need more support to advocate for workplace accommodations, determine if and when to disclose a disability, apply social skills to develop relationships with co-workers, and use self-determination skills to discuss and evaluate their work. If students with disabilities are going to successfully prepare for work, they must have access to career development preparation that includes work experiences and a flexible schedule to support job training, travel and transportation training, and self-determination skill development (Getzel & Wehman, 2005; Roessler, Hennessey, & Rumrill, 2007; Wehman, 2006).

Determining Work Interests

The PSE transition coordinator and his or her staff often begin by confirming with students the type of work they are interested in exploring. Many students with ID have little or no work experience and are not sure what they want to do for work (Cameto, Levine, & Wagner, 2004). A number of career exploration activities, including internships, job shadows, informational interviews, paid work, and job preparation through the local workforce development office, can provide students with applicable skills (National Collaborative for Workforce Development and Youth, 2003). These efforts can be enhanced through formal agreements with employment providers, which is a collaborative effort a number of schools have pursued to strengthen their career development curriculum.

Internships

Internships are useful in helping students to narrow down or further explore work interests. Internship opportunities can be established formally through school connections or informally through processes such as PCP. These internships vary and support career interests in numerous fields such as child care, business and medical office management, animal care, clerical support, retail support, landscaping, elder care, and numerous jobs within a supermarket, including the bakery, florist, and produce departments. At the end of each internship, students should be asked to evaluate their experience. Feedback from these internships should inform planning for future experiences and job placements.

Job Shadows/Informational Interviews

For students who have some ideas about what they want to do for work, staff may arrange for them to explore that kind of work by shadowing someone for a few hours who is doing similar work, preparing for and conducting informational interviews with people in the field who can answer questions about the job, or researching career interests on Internet sites (such as Occupational Information Network, also known as O*NET Online) that describe occupations.

Job Readiness

PSE transition staff should make sure that students have an updated resume and/or portfolio and a minimum of two references, from other work experiences or from school. If a student does not have a resume, the coordinator or other staff members should work with him or her to prepare one. Students should be encouraged to participate in all aspects of the job search, including looking for work through generic employment resources such as the local workforce development office and personal connections. They can participate in workforce development workshops that highlight interviewing skills and resume critique. A word of warning about job training that does not necessarily lead to paid employment: these experiences are valuable for short-term skill development but should be time-limited to avoid the common outcome of leaving school without a competitive work experience. One way to avoid this problem is to coordinate a meeting between the student, employer, and job developer or job coach to develop three or four work goals that will help the student to develop competitive work skills. In Massachusetts, a work-based learning plan helps to organize these three-way meetings (Massachusetts Department of Elementary and Secondary Education, 2008).

Employment Agreements

School districts may pursue formal agreements with community providers to help students to find work related to their career interests. In these cases, the transition coordinator should communicate the mission of the PSE transition services to the potential partner to ensure that students will be helped to pursue work that is related to their vision. Through each stage of job development—gathering references, job shadowing, job searches—students should be required to keep track of their progress with worksheets and journals. Students should be prompted to reflect on their job search and to keep a record of the steps they are taking for future searches.

National and Community Service

There are opportunities for students with disabilities, including those with ID, to make a 1- or 2-year commitment to a service organization. From a transition perspective, volunteers can make a connection with their community, enhance their resume, and develop skills that benefit the community as well as the individual. Individuals who serve in Americorps, for example, upon completion of service, can earn an Americorps Education Award, which can be used to pay for college. Many school systems have incorporated service or community learning into their curriculum, and it may be that established agreements between the school and service groups already exist.

Planning for Transportation

The PSE transition coordinator should review the transportation options that will be explored with the student and the parents. Depending on the location, the options may include public transportation, carpooling, or, in the case of some students, walking to the campus or to a job. Regardless of the options available, the goal for transportation should be a shift from a reliance on school transportation to other options that peers typically rely on to get to a job, college campus, or community destination. All PSE programs and services must include transportation as a key element so that students can learn to transition from district-sponsored transportation to typical transportation in a community. Some students may live in districts where they can learn to use city buses, and the education or job coaches should work with these students to review schedules; determine arrival times at the bus, train, or subway station; and travel safely. In some cases, the coaches phase out support when the student is able to travel independently. For other students who need accessible transportation, transition staff may apply for the city's paratransit services. Once they are determined to be eligible, students can immediately learn to take responsibility for their transportation arrangements. One school district developed a simplified version of the ADA Paratransit Manual (see Appendix 4.10) to promote students' independent travel skills. Beginning with their first trip, students learn how to take ADA paratransit transportation and to be on time when the van arrives. Initially, the school district may purchase tickets to distribute to students who are involved in transition-related activities, including internships, college, and accessing community resources. Eventually, students can purchase their own tickets, learn the exact address of their destination to schedule rides (which they have been instructed to record in their personal ADA Paratransit Manual), and be on time for pickups.

Students are encouraged to carry cell phones and include the ADA paratransit number in their speed dial so they can call the company if they need to cancel a ride or to check up on a late pickup. In many districts there are guidelines for students who use paratransit services. For example, students must understand that their ride may come within 20 minutes before or after the scheduled time. Therefore, students need to be ready when their ride comes. For students who have difficulty telling time, accommodations can be provided. Some students may be instructed to set an alarm on their cell phones to remind them to get ready for a pickup. When students are first learning to arrange their own transportation, they may be instructed to report the transportation arrangements to one of the transition staff, but this step should be phased out as students demonstrate the ability to do this on their own.

For districts that elect to use school transportation, there are considerations to take into account, such as whether new routes will need to be developed to accommodate the students and what costs will be incurred to do so. In addition, the district may develop a transportation schedule to coordinate student and staff schedules and activities.

In a few cases, students with ID have successfully received their driver's license. These students drive to college and to their jobs. Transition staff can help students to study for the driver's permit test and to request any accommodations they need. Some rehabilitation agencies may pay for an evaluation to assess a student's readiness for driving. This comprehensive assessment includes vision, peripheral and cognitive ability, reaction times, knowledge and understanding of road signs, and physical and cognitive capability to handle a vehicle. Independent living centers may provide tutoring to students who are studying for a learner's permit. Vocational rehabilitation agencies may pay for driving lessons if the license is related to an employment outcome. From experience, some transition coordinators have reported that even when students have a driver's license, they often need some support to follow driving and parking regulations in the community.

Whether individuals live in urban, suburban, or rural communities, the issue of transportation comes with challenges. Students and parents in urban communities are often concerned about the safety of using public transportation. In suburban communities, students and parents have complained that public transportation is limited and inconsistent. In rural communities, where public transportation may be extremely limited, students and parents are hesitant to consider other options such as carpooling, and school personnel may worry about liability issues. Some city transportation authorities may provide travel training as well as vocational rehabilitation offices. For districts preparing to implement services in a PSE setting, it is important to be aware of the existing transportation options available in the community and to draft a training curriculum and action steps to help students develop safe travel skills.

Managing Risk on the College Campus

In many school districts, students are encouraged to use public transportation, walk to their classes, and get to work as independently as possible. Staff supporting students on college campuses take precautions to prepare students and parents for this emerging independence. One helpful precaution is to have students and their parents complete emergency contact forms that are available to staff (see Appendix 4.7). In some school districts, city lawyers review the forms to ensure that they comply with school policies (see Figure 4.6). In addition, students should be encouraged to carry a cell phone that includes emergency contacts and all PSE staff in their speed dial function. A final precaution is that students should be instructed on how to keep themselves safe in the community and how to seek help on campus. For additional discussion of risk management, see Chapter 6.

Participating in College Activities and Experiences

Taking courses on a college campus affords students with ID the opportunity to access college resources and activities. These include student clubs and organizations, health and fitness facilities, and numerous social events. Typically special

Figure 4.6. Sample letter addressing travel training

LMN Public Schools
Special Education Department
Transition Services Program
Community Travel Permission Form

The Transition Services Program (TSP) works with older students with disabilities. TSP offers educational services and may include work-related activities, postsecondary education, community training, and travel training, based on students' areas of need. Transportation may be provided to the student in a variety of ways, which may include school-contracted transportation, local/regional transportation, and walking.

As the parent/guardian of _____ ,
                                                        (Student Name)

_____ I agree to allow my son or daughter to participate in the Transition Services Program.

_____ I do not agree to allow my son or daughter to participate in the Transition Services Program.

Date: _____ **Parent/Guardian Signature:** _____

or

As a student who has reached the age of majority and has assumed decision-making

rights, I _____
                                                        (Student Name)

_____ agree to participate in the Transition Services Program.

_____ do not agree to participate in the Transition Services Program.

Date: _____ **Student Signature:** _____

Date: _____ **Director of Special Education Signature:** _____

---

events such as sports, theater, and social events are held in the evening and on weekends, when students are less likely to attend classes. For students with disabilities, there are some challenges that make participation in these campus activities difficult: staying informed about nonacademic activities that are available to students, building time into their schedules to attend them, and having the transportation and money needed to access the activities. Some students will need support at the events as well.

To build student awareness of nonacademic activities on campus, school and college partnerships have developed a number of strategies, including orientation sessions, typically held at the start of the academic year, where student clubs and college events are promoted. Another strategy is to send students a monthly calendar of events via e-mail or regular mail. In some PSE transition models, students are asked to choose one to three college activities or events per semester to attend as part of their college participation.

For students who need support while attending activities, some school/ college partnerships rely on peer mentors. This has proved to be successful in helping students understand the nuances of social situations (Adreon & Durocher, 2007; Moreno, 2005). Another solution is to share information with families about available campus activities and work with them to help their son or daughter to take advantage of these opportunities.

For all students, the transition away from friends at school and from high school extracurricular activities can be very difficult. This is not different for students with disabilities, particularly when they have been together for many years and have participated in the same recreational activities. Transition services that include PSE must also include strategies to help students develop skills to make new social connections on campus and at work (Adreon & Durocher, 2007; Casale-Giannola & Kamens, 2006; Thoma & Getzel, 2005). With time, students will establish new social connections and engage in recreational and community activities just like their peers without disabilities.

RECOMMENDATIONS FOR LOCAL SCHOOL SYSTEMS SEEKING TO EXPAND TRANSITION SERVICES TO POSTSECONDARY SETTINGS

The following recommendations are offered for individuals, teams, and districts that are interested in establishing transition services in PSE settings. These recommendations are based on the experiences and lessons of many school districts that have implemented such services and are continually refining and improving their work to promote school outcomes for students with disabilities that match their transition goals.

1. *Prepare students for transition and promote the development of self-determination skills.* Both professionals and students indicate that self-determination skills are critical for a successful PSE experience. Skills such as finding the right postsecondary supports, assuming responsibility for the workload, and working with professors must be learned early in transition planning (Adreon & Durocher, 2007; Sitlington, 2003; Thoma & Getzel, 2005; Thoma & Wehmeyer, 2005). Preparation at the middle and high school levels should include student participation and ideally their eventual leadership in their own IEP meetings. This provides them with opportunities to discuss their learning style and disability with college disability staff and future employers, gain access to more inclusive classes, use accommodations similar to those offered in college, manage their schedules, be responsible for completing class assignments, and evaluate their own progress (see Table 4.6).

Table 4.6.   Strategies for student success at college

1.   Learn your name, address, phone number, and SSI number to the best of your ability.
2.   Carry a picture I.D. card at all times with emergency information, including your college I.D. number.
3.   Be responsible for your own belongings—coat, books, pens, lunch, money, etc.
4.   Learn whom to ask for help in an emergency.
5.   If you don't understand something, ask for help.
6.   If you can, get a cell phone and learn to use it, carry it at all times, and remember to charge it.
7.   Follow your schedule to go to classes, work, and lunch and for transportation. If you can't tell time, learn other ways, such as cell phone, talking watches, or asking others.
8.   Know what your disability is—what are you good at, what might you need help with, and the best way to teach you something new.
9.   Decide what you want to do for your future, your vision, and let people know what it is.
10. Learn phone skills if you need to call for help or a ride, or how to ask someone to do that for you.
11. Learn how to use your transportation system to get to work, school, college, and so forth.
12. Talk to your parents/family members at home to update them on college homework and what you might need help with.
13. Pick up your accommodations packet at the disabilities office at the start of the semester and give a copy to your professor.
14. Keep your college information together—accommodation information, course syllabus, course selection form, and so forth.
15. Buy your textbooks at the bookstore before the first day of class. You will need your course selection form.
16. Learn how to get around campus—cafeteria, classroom, bookstore, campus police, student activity center, gym and track, disabilities office, registrar's office, library, homework/tutoring center, and computer lab.
17. Learn how to use the library, computer lab, and the homework tutoring center.
18. Know the name of your college disabilities coordinator—see him or her if you need help.
19. Learn how to sign up for test taking at the disabilities office ahead of time.
20. Read or have someone read the college paper and bulletin board to learn what student activities you might want to do.

2. Develop a PSE transition coordinator position. The PSE transition coordinator must have the wide array of skills needed to support students at numerous levels with an individualized approach, coordinate multiple staff schedules, establish and maintain partnerships, provide orientation and ongoing training and support to families, and facilitate regular meetings among partners. Ideally, a PSE transition coordinator has a background in adult services and special education, but at a minimum has a strong working knowledge of how both systems work and how they can combine to provide outcome-oriented transition services. This person is often seen as the face of the school system on the college campus and must be able to continually network with college faculty and staff to facilitate increased access and support for students with ID.

3. *Change instructional assistant positions into transition coach positions.* When assistant instructional positions become available, those positions should be restructured into transition coach positions. It may be useful to collaborate with the local teacher union, but it is important to be clear that the position does not require more hours, just a redistribution of hours over a week. As these positions are developed, it is necessary to understand that they will require independence in the community, relationship building with college and employer personnel, supporting students to promote independence, and flexibility in work hours that will differ from typical school hours. Transition coaches need specific training that will enable them to understand the differences between high school and college, encourage students' self-determination and self-advocacy in postsecondary settings, teach students to seek out and use academic support resources, and implement risk management policies and procedures in community-based settings.

4. *Establish an IHE liaison.* It is important to have a point person from the college who can help high school personnel understand and navigate college services. This person is usually a college employee or is closely linked to the disability services office. The IHE liaison should work with the PSE transition coordinator to ensure that the student is taking appropriate steps to complete the accommodations packet, has the appropriate accommodations, and is aware of the academic support resources available. The IHE liaison should be in a position to support students with ID in accessing the college resources available to help all students in their career development. An important responsibility of the IHE liaison is to ensure that the faculty has opportunities to participate in professional development related to universal course design and to collaborate with the liaison to resolve issues that may arise. The IHE liaison can also establish a network on campus to assist with logistics, such as early registration for returning students, resolving accessibility issues, and directing students to campus resources. The liaison may also market the model of services to key college personnel at campus meetings and events.

5. *Implement person-centered planning.* PCP encourages students from the start to share their short-term and long-term goals for the future. There are a number of ways that school districts can offer PCP for students. The most thorough way is to facilitate Whole Life Planning sessions with students and their invited network of support; another way is for students to fill out surveys or charts about their aspirations as well as their strengths and preferences. Some students may be able to identify their interests through a series of conversations with staff, and still others may need to experience some transition activities before they can pinpoint career preferences. PCP should guide the creation of all students' transition goals in their IEP and should guide the implementation of all services in the PSE setting.

6. *Understand the differences between high school and college.* Before and during the transition process, it is important for individuals to understand the differences between high school and college. Key differences that are highlighted throughout this chapter include 1) curriculum accommodations in college versus curriculum modifications in high school, 2) student responsibility to articulate needs versus the school personnel's responsibility to provide special education, 3) special education entitlements versus eligibility and budgetary limitations for adult services, 4) school schedules and vacations versus the academic calendar and semester breaks, and 5) higher expectations for student responsibility.

These differences come up many times during a student's PSE experience, and it is critical that staff highlight these differences to students, families, teachers, and interagency team members (see Appendix 4.8).

7. *Establish communication channels.* For everyone involved, communication is critically important. PSE transition staff must maintain consistent communication with students and families. Even as students take more responsibility for their post-secondary planning, they still need to touch base with staff. In some districts, staff meet with students individually every 1 to 2 weeks and as needed regarding their current transition activities and to help them plan the next steps. For example, in Table 4.7, the transition coordinator working with Lauren reviewed her long-term goal to have a paid job as clerical staff and her short-term goal of gaining related experience to achieve that goal. Together they developed a list of tasks that they could work on for 2 weeks until they met again. These included researching other places where Lauren might find clerical work, finding someone who could help them with these tasks, and identifying some goals to be met, such as increasing the number of times Lauren arranged for her own transportation to an internship.

Table 4.7.   Sample student career planning meeting

Lauren's* Career Plan/Meeting Notes

October 20, 2008

Long-term goal: To work in a paid position in the community where she can offer office skills, such as copying, scanning, mailings, collating, and so forth; social skills; and memory/directional skills. Lauren would like to work in a supportive environment where she can gain greater independence, reducing her need for a 1:1 job coach.

Short-term goal: Lauren is interested in exploring career options through internships that would utilize her office skills, such as copying, scanning, mailings, and collating; social skills; and memory/directional skills, in a supportive environment with greater independence.

Tasks for the next 2 weeks:

1.   Lauren will update her resume.
2.   Job coach will explore with family health coordinator the possibility of Lauren working at FH 2 days, doing consistent tasks.
3.   Transition coordinator to check with director of health center to see if they scan medical records and to find out who does their shredding.
4.   Coordinator and staff to check the different colleges in the area to find out what the staff at the information booths do, their job descriptions, when these positions are staffed—areas to look include the student union, library, bookstore (where students leave their backpacks), athletic facilities, and so forth. Group will focus on helping Lauren to try each one for a month to see if she likes it. Mom to check at private college where her husband works to see what may be available. Once we have found areas we think might be appropriate for internships, father will assist with connecting to the colleges to get a contact.
5.   The two areas to focus on initially are family health centers and college settings.
6.   Lauren will utilize the paratransit system more independently by calling in for her own transportation from one time to three times a week.

*This is not the student's real name.

In addition, PSE transition staff should establish regular communication with families to review transition updates and be available to answer questions about the process. In many cases, transition staff initially act as liaisons between school and adult agency staff until parents are comfortable sorting out the different roles and responsibilities of those who are connected to their son's or daughter's transition. As for the interagency team, in addition to posting the monthly meetings on a Listserv, contact information must be provided for each member, because a key purpose of this team is open communication between members during student transitions.

SUMMARY

With federal accountability measures in place to track transition planning and postschool outcomes of students with disabilities, increasing numbers of school district administrators are more closely examining the connection between students' academic, vocational, and community learning educational objectives and their postschool goals. This scrutiny is leading administrators to look beyond traditional transition models to more innovative supports and services that offer students and their families a model of support that includes PSE and employment experiences.

Planning, implementing, and evaluating a transition model that includes PSE and employment experiences for students with ID is not without its challenges. Restructuring services will initially take a lot of work, and it will look very different from the traditional models of transition. Establishing an interagency team, conducting a needs assessment or community or agency resource mapping, restructuring roles and responsibilities, and maintaining consistent communication and collaboration with students, families, teachers, and higher education personnel will promote successful outcomes. A PSE transition coordinator may be hired to take the lead in coordinating transition services for students, serving as the liaison between the school and the IHE and, along with the interagency team, establishing formal agreements for transition services and collaboration.

Increasingly, students with disabilities have aspirations that students without disabilities prepare for, including PSE, meaningful work, and, eventually, financial independence from their family. Transition services that include PSE, paid employment, and independent or supported living training must be developed and offered to ensure that students with ID have the skills and experiences to pursue their goals and to be adequately prepared for adult life.

REFERENCES

Adreon, D., & Durocher, J.S. (2007). Evaluating the college transition needs of individuals with high-functioning autism spectrum disorders. *Intervention in School and Clinic, 42*(5), 271–279.

Americans with Disabilities Act of 1990, PL 101-336, 42 U.S.C. §§ 12101 *et seq.*

Barr, V.M., Hartman, R.C., & Spillane, S.A. (1995). *Getting ready for college: Advising high school students with learning disabilities.* HEATH Resource Center. Washington, DC: American Council on Education.

Benz, M.R., Johnson, D.K., Mikkelsen, K.S., & Lindstrom, L.E. (1995). Improving collaboration between schools and vocational rehabilitation: Stakeholder identified barriers and strategies. *Career Development for Exceptional Children, 16,* 197–211.

Bridgeton, J.M., DiJulio, J.J., & Morison, K.B. (2006). *The silent epidemic: Perspectives of high school dropouts.* Washington, DC: Civic Enterprises & Peter D. Hart Research Associates for the Bill and Melinda Gates Foundation.

Cameto, R., Levine, P., & Wagner, M. (2004). *Transition planning for students with disabilities. A special topic report of findings from the National Longitudinal Transition Study-2 (NLTS2).* Menlo Park, CA: SRI International. Retrieved October 15, 2008, from www.nlts2.org/reports/2004_11/nlts2_report_2004_11_complete.pdf.

Casale-Giannola, D., & Kamens, M.W. (2006). Inclusion at a university: Experiences of a young woman with Down syndrome. *Mental Retardation, 44*(5), 344–352.

Cassner-Lotto, J., & Barrington, L. (2006). *Are they really ready to work? Employers' perspectives on the basic knowledge and applied skills of new entrants to the 21st century U.S. workforce.* New York: Conference Board, Society for Human Resource Management (U.S.), Corporate Voices for Working Families, Partnership for 21st Century Skills.

Cooney, B.F. (2002). Exploring perspectives on transition of youth with disabilities: Voices of young adults, parents, and professionals. *Mental Retardation, 40*(6), 425–435.

Family Educational Rights and Privacy Act of 1974, PL 93-380, 20 U.S.C. § 1232g, 34CFR Part 99.

Finn, D.E., Getzel, E.E., & McManus, S. (2008). Adapting the self-determined learning model of instruction for college students with disabilities. *Career Development for Exceptional Individuals, 31*(2).

Gaumer, A., Morningstar, M., & Clark, G.M. (2004). Status of community-based transition programs: A national database. *Career Development for Exceptional Individuals, 27*(2).

Getzel, E.E., & Thoma, C.A. (2008). Experiences of college students with disabilities and the importance of self-determination in higher education settings. *Career Development for Exceptional Individuals, 31*(2), 77–84.

Getzel, E.E., & Wehman, P. (2005). *Going to college: Expanding opportunities for people with disabilities.* Baltimore: Paul H. Brookes Publishing Co.

Grigal, M., Dwyer, A., & Davis, H. (2006). *Transition services for students aged 18–21 with intellectual disabilities in college and community settings: Models and implications of success* (Institute Brief: *Addressing Trends and Developments in Secondary Education and Transition, 6*[5]). Minneapolis: University of Minnesota, Institute on Community Integration.

Grigal, M., & Neubert, D.A. (2004). Parents' in-school values and post-school expectations for transition-aged youth with disabilities. *Career Development for Exceptional Individuals, 27,* 65–85.

Grigal, M., Neubert, D.A., & Moon, M.S. (2005). *Transition services for students with significant disabilities in college and community settings: Strategies for planning, implementation and evaluation.* Austin, TX: PRO-ED.

Guy, B., Sitlington, P.L., Larsen, M.D., & Frank, A.R. (2008). What are high schools offering as preparation for employment? *Career Development for Exceptional Individuals.* Retrieved February 28, 2009, from Sage Journal Online web site: http://cde.sagepub.com/cgi/content/abstract/0885728808318625v1

Harris, W.J., Cobb, R.A., Pooler, A.E., & Perry, C.M. (2008). Implications of P-16 for teacher education: Teacher education will be at the heart of a P-16 system. *Phi Delta Kappan, 89*(7), 493–497.

Hart, D., & Grigal, M. (2004). *Individual support to increase access to an inclusive college experience for students with intellectual disabilities* [online module]. College Park: University of Maryland, Department of Special Education. Retrieved on October 8, 2008, from On-Campus Outreach web site: http://www.education.umd.edu/oco/

Hart, D., Zafft, C., & Zimbrich, K. (2001). Creating access to college for all students. *Journal for Vocational Special Needs Education, 23*(2), 19–31.

Hart, D., Zimbrich, K., & Ghiloni, C. (2001). Interagency partnerships and funding: Individual supports for youth with significant disabilities as they move into postsecondary education and employment options. *Journal of Vocational Rehabilitation, 16*(3–4), 145–154.

Individuals with Disabilities Education Improvement Act of 2004, PL 108-446, 20 U.S.C. §§ 1400 *et seq.*

Johnson, D.R., Stodden, R.A., Emanuel, E.J., Luecking, R., & Mack, M. (2002). Current challenges facing secondary education and transition services: What research tells us. *Council for Exceptional Children, 68*(4), 519–531.

Karp, M.M., Bailey, T.R., Hughes, K.L., & Fermin, B.J. (2004). *State dual enrollment policies: Addressing access and quality.* New York: Community College Research Center, Teachers College, Columbia University.

Katsiyannis, A., Zhang, D., Woodruff, N., & Dixon, A. (2005). Transition supports to students with mental retardation: An examination of data from the National Longitudinal Transition Study 2. *Education and Training in Developmental Disabilities, 40*(2), 109–116.

Luecking, R.G., & Certo, N. (2002). *Integrating service systems at the point of transition for youth with significant disabilities: A model that works* (Information Brief: Addressing Trends and Developments in Secondary Education and Transition, 1[4]). Minneapolis: University of Minnesota, Institute on Community Integration, National Center for Secondary Education and Transition.

Massachusetts Department of Elementary and Secondary Education. (2008). *Massachusetts work-based learning plan.* Retrieved October 26, 2008, from http://www.skillslibrary.com/wbl.htm

McMahan, R., & Baer, R. (2001). IDEA transition policy compliance and best practice: Perceptions of transition stakeholders. *Career Development for Exceptional Individuals, 24,* 169–184.

Merrow, J. (2007, April 22). Dream catchers. *New York Times, Education Supplement.* Retrieved October 18, 2008, from http://www.nytimes.com/2007/04/22/education/edlife/merrow.html

Moreno, S. (2005, Winter). On the road to successful college experience: Preparations make the difference. *Autism Spectrum Quarterly,* 16–19.

Morringstar, M.E. & Kleinhammer-Tramill, P.J. (2005). *Professional development for transition personnel: current issues and strategies for success.* (National Center on Secondary Education and Transition Informatin Brief). Minneapolis: University of Minnesota.

Morningstar, M. (2006). *Quality indicators of exemplary transition programs.* Lawrence: University of Kansas, Beech Center on Families and Disability.

National Center for Public Policy and Higher Education. (2006). *Measuring up: A national report card on higher education.* Retrieved October 17, 2008, from http://measuringup.highereducation.org/default.cfm

National Center for Secondary Education and Transition. (2005). *National Alliance for Secondary Education and Transition: National standards and quality indicators.* Minneapolis, MN: Author.

National Collaborative for Workforce Development and Youth. (2003). *High schools/high tech program manual.* Washington, DC: Institute on Educational Leadership.

Neubert, D.A., & Moon, M.S. (2006). Postsecondary settings and transition services for students with intellectual disabilities: Models and research. *Focus on Exceptional Children, 39*(4), 1–9.

No Child Left Behind Act of 2001, PL 107-110, 115 Stat. 1425, 20 U.S.C. §§ 6301 *et seq.*

Rehabilitation Act of 1973, PL 93-112, 29 U.S.C. §§ 701 *et seq.*

Roessler, R.T., Hennessey, M.L., & Rumrill, P.D. (2007). Strategies for improving career services for postsecondary education students with disabilities: Results of a focus group study of key stakeholders. *Career Development for Exceptional Individuals, 30*(3), 158–170.

Shaw, S.F., & Madaus, J.W. (2008). Preparing school personnel to implement Section 504. *Intervention in School and Clinic, 43*(4), 226–230.

Sitlington, P. (2003). Postsecondary education: The other transition. *Exceptionality*, *11*(2), 103–113.

Thoma, C.A., & Getzel, E.E. (2005). "Self-determination is what it's all about": What postsecondary students with disabilities tell us are important considerations for success. *Education and Training in Developmental Disabilities, 4*(3), 234–242.

Thoma, C.A. & Wehmeyer, M.L. (2005). Self-determination and the transition to postsecondary education. In E.E. Getzel & P. Wehman. *Going to College* (pp. 49–68). Baltimore: Paul H. Brookes Publishing Co.

Thompson, J.R., Fulk, B., & Piercy, S. (2000). Do individualized transition plans match the postschool projections of students with learning disabilities and their parents? *Career Development for Exceptional Individuals, 23*(1), 2–25.

Timmons, J. (2007). *Models of collaboration and cost sharing in transition programming.* (Information Brief: Addressing Trends and Developments in Secondary Education and Transition, 6[1]). Minneapolis: University of Minnesota, Institute on Community Integration, National Center for Secondary Education and Transition.

U.S. Department of Education: *State Performance Plans* (20 U.S.C. 1416(a) (3) (B)) Indicator 14. 20 U.S.C §§ 1416. Monitoring, technical assistance, and enforcement.

Wagner, M., Newman, L., & Cameto, R. (2005). *Changes over time in the secondary school experiences of students with disabilities. A report of findings from the National Longitudinal Transition Study (NLTS) and the National Longitudinal Transition Study-2 (NLTS2).* Menlo Park, CA: SRI International. Available online at http://www.nlts2.org/reports/2004_04/nlts2_report_2004_04_complete.pdf

Wagner, M., Newman, L., Cameto, R., Garza, N., & Levine, P. (2005). *After high school: A first look at the postschool experiences of youth with disabilities. A report from the National Longitudinal Transition Study-2 (NLTS2).* Menlo Park, CA: SRI International. Available online at http://www.nlts2.org/reports/2005_04/nlts2_report_2005_04_complete.pdf

Wehman, P. (2006). *Life beyond the classroom: Transition strategies for young people with disabilities.* Baltimore: Paul H. Brookes Publishing Co.

Wehmeyer, M.L., & Palmer, S. (2003). Adult outcomes for students with cognitive disabilities three years after high school: The impact of self-determination. *Education and Training in Developmental Disabilities, 38*(2), 131–144.

Weir, C. (2004). Person-centered planning and collaborative supports for college success. *Education and Training in Developmental Disabilities, 1*(1), 67–73.

Zafft, C., Hart, D., & Zimbrich, K. (2004). College Career Connection: A study of youth with intellectual disabilities and the impact of postsecondary education. *Education and Training in Developmental Disabilities, 39*(1), 45–53.

Zhang, D., Ivester, J., & Katsiyannis, A. (2005). Teachers' views of transition services: Results from a statewide survey in South Carolina. *Education and Training in Developmental Disabilities, 40*(4), 360–367.

Student Services Needs Assessment

NAME OF SCHOOL: _____

SCHOOL YEAR: _____

Number of students who will receive special education services until they are 21 who are/have:

Age	1 Receive SSI/ SSDI	2 SSI/ SSDI Eligible	3 VR Eligible	4 DD/MR Eligible	5 Included in general education classes	Not included in general education classes	6 Received behavior support	7 Paid work	Unpaid work training	8 Extra curricular activities in school	Extra curricular activities outside of school	9 Received travel training	10 Required 1:1
21 =													
20 =													
19 =													
18 =													
17 =													

Are changes needed? _____

How many students or families have expressed an interest in receiving services in a college or community setting? _____

From Grigal, M., Neubert, D.A., & Moon, M.S. (2005). *Transition services for students with significant disabilities in college and community settings: Strategies for planning, implementation and evaluation* (p.27). PRO-ED Series on Transition. Austin, TX: PRO-ED Copyright 2005 by PRO-ED, Inc.; reprinted by permission.

Sample Resource Map for Transition Planning

SUMMARY

With the assistance of an outside facilitator, the South Shore Interagency Team (SSIT) participated in resource mapping to take stock of the career development services they collectively offered transition age students with intellectual disabilities as indicated in Question 1. They were also interested in more closely examining how frequently staff provide information to these students on postsecondary education options—if they pair those options with person-centered planning and whether or not formal agreements with postsecondary education institutes are established (see Question 2). Finally, SSIT members wanted to ask knowledgeable staff at each organization about the differences between laws that affect transition and postsecondary education activities (see Question 3).

Based on these questions, the SSIT analyzed the results to identify service duplication and gaps. The team then developed four goals based on their analysis to increase postsecondary options for students with disabilities. These include:

1. Increase opportunities for students with intellectual disabilities to receive career counseling (including information about postsecondary education options).
2. Provide training and technical assistance to all transition staff on person-centered planning and postsecondary education planning.
3. Establish a minimum of two formal agreements with institutes of higher education to coordinate transition activities.
4. Provide training to all staff on the differences between IDEA, ADA, and 504 and how they affect services students receive.

Question 1: Which of the following career development services does your organization offer? (a) career exploration, (b) situational assessment, (c) interview techniques, (d) job shadows, (e) resume development, (f) informational interviews, (g) work tours, (h) career counseling, (i) networking skills, (j) portfolio development, (k) traditional vocational assessments, (l) other service, or (m) no career development services.

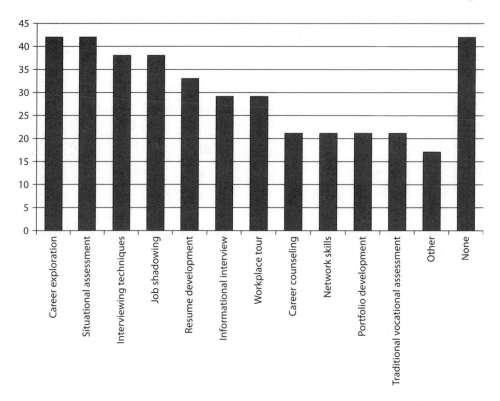

Question 2: My organization (a) provides information on postsecondary options; (b) pairs person-centered planning with postsecondary education planning and (c) has a formal agreement with a postsecondary institute to coordinate transition activities.

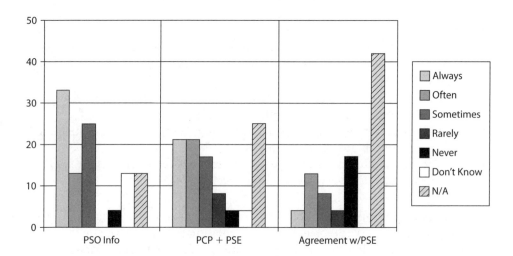

Question 3: Staff at my organization are knowledgeable about (a) the documentation students need to pursue postsecondary education and accommodations, (b) how IDEA, ADA, and 504 differ, and (c) educating students and families about how laws affect services students receive in high school versus college.

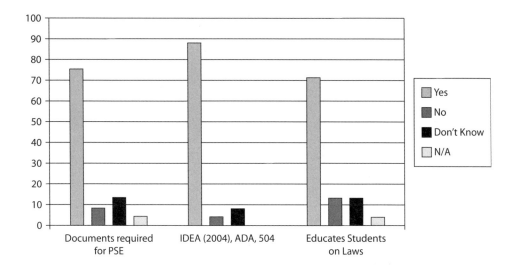

Sample Memorandum of Understanding (MOU) between a Community College and School System for a College-based Transition Program

April 29, 2005

About the Program

County ABC is a diverse, multicultural community that places a high value on the quality of life for all its citizens. Community College Y and School System X are ranked at the top of the list in excellence by local, state, and national standards. These two educational institutions work in partnership on a myriad of programs and initiatives to develop a strong future workforce for County ABC and the region. Specifically, School System X and Community College Y offer a continuum of services and programs to meet the needs of students with disabilities.

School System X acknowledges and supports the rights of all students to receive a free appropriate public education that will enable them to develop their unique talents and abilities, thus preparing them to participate in and serve their community with dignity and pride. For students ages 19–21, the college-based transition program (located at Community College Y) offers a range of instructional services which include academic, community, and vocational skills development. This partnership and objectives outline the agreement developed by Community College Y and School System X.

Curriculum Outline

This community-based post high school program is located on the campus of Community College Y and is designed for students with mild to moderate disabilities who are in their last years of public education. The curriculum includes:

- Personal management skills
- Consumer economics (money, banking, budgeting, and shopping)
- Self-Determination and social awareness
- Recreation and Leisure
- Including students in the least restrictive environment—the community

Characteristics of Students

Students who are 19 years of age

- Will receive a state high school certificate and *not* a Diploma
- Will have a minimum of four years in a high school setting
- Will have completed two semesters of the work study program and have demonstrated the ability to function independently with minimal supervision
- Will have IEP goals and transition plans that are appropriate
- Will have demonstrated satisfactory attendance and behavior

PARTNERSHIP DECLARATION

This agreement made on April 29, 2005 by and between School System X and Community College Y, the parties hereby agree as follows:

I.   SCOPE OF SERVICES

The School System X will provide transition services to individuals with developmental disabilities at Community College Y. Up to 20 persons ages 19–21 years who continue to need special education and who have continuing needs for transition as evidenced by individualized education programs (IEPs) will be considered for this placement. The School System X has sole responsibility for developing placement criteria to determine which School System X students will participate in the program.

II.   DUTIES OF THE SCHOOL SYSTEM X

A. The School System X shall provide special education instructors to implement the program at Community College Y.

B. The School System X shall provide staff support as determined by the students' Individual Education Program (IEPs).

C. The School System X shall be responsible for any costs associated with services including but not limited to, materials and equipment, transportation, and incidental costs.

D. The School System X agrees to provide school bus transportation to and from the Community College Y and each student's home.

E. If the students seek enrollment in the Community College Y credit, noncredit, audit or custom classes, these students will meet all admissions requirements, academic requirements, and all other policies related to enrolling and participating in classes including responsibility for costs of enrollment.

F. The School System X's instructor will familiarize himself or herself with the Institution's code of conduct and relate these standards to other School System X staff and students, and assume responsibility for enforcing and abiding by these standards.

G. Follow all School System X rules and regulations.

III. DUTIES OF THE COMMUNITY COLLEGE Y

A. Community College Y shall permit the School System X to use its facilities for educational purposes.

B. Community College Y shall provide one classroom for use by the School System X students that will be available from 7:30 a.m. to 10:00 a.m. (Monday through Friday) during the academic school year.

C. Community College Y shall provide one office area for use by the School System X during the academic year.

D. Community College Y shall provide the School System X with a telephone line and Internet access for School System X's use.

E. Community College Y shall permit the School System X to have access to Community College Y faculty or staff who agreed to assist the School System X in developing educational services for School System X students as well as Community College Y student interns who may wish to collaborate or support students.

F. Community College Y shall provide the School System X with information and access to job training opportunities at the Community College Y for School System X students.

G. Follow all Community College Y rules and regulations.

IV. INSURANCE AND INDEMNIFICATION

A. The School System X and Community College Y shall maintain property and liability coverage.

B. The School System X agrees to indemnify and hold harmless the Community College Y, its employees, agents, and officers against any and all claims which may be made against the Community College Y or its agents, for property damage or personal injuries sustained by any persons which may result from the use of said facilities, grounds or equipment by School System X, except in the case of gross negligence by Community College Y, its employees, agents, and officers. The indemnification agreed to by the School System X shall include (1) payment or reimbursement for attorneys' fees, court costs, and other defense costs; (2) full payment of any decree, award, decisions, compromise, or settlement rendered against the indemnities.

C. The School System X remains a separate public organization, independent from Community College Y and responsible for all other costs of its operation. The School System X and/or any employee of the School System X shall not be considered an employee, agent, or sub-agent of Community College Y. No acts performed or representation whether oral or written made by or with respect to third parties by the School System X shall be binding on Community College Y.

V. TERM AND TERMINATION

The effective date of the agreement shall be April 29, 2005 and this agreement shall terminate on June 23, 2009. At the conclusion of this agreement, Community College Y and the School System X shall collaborate to determine whether to continue this agreement annually.

We the undersigned do fully agree to the above stated Declaration of Partnership between Community College Y and the School System X.

Signatures and Titles:

_____

Superintendent
School System X

_____

Date

_____

President
Community College Y

_____

Date

Sample Job Description for Transition Coordinator, Education Coach

1. Oversee all functions and operations of the transition program.
2. Member of the special education management team (responsible for attending all department head meetings and trainings).
3. Collaborate with high school teachers, special education department heads, team chairpersons, and administrators in identifying students in need of transition services.
4. Oversee referral process to the transition program and determine student eligibility.
5. Responsible for developing and implementing individualized transition supports and services, including employment, postsecondary education, community training, and travel training for individuals ages 18–22 with disabilities.
6. Responsible for working with students utilizing a variety of methods (Person-Centered Planning, Career Planning, Interest Inventories, etc.) to assist them in developing a vision for their future and an action plan that may include career, postsecondary education, home, and leisure.
7. Oversee implementation of student action plans and review/revise as needed.
8. Active participant in student IEP and ITP meetings, providing information and goals as appropriate. Responsible for developing and coordinating the master schedule for all participating students and staff.
9. Responsible for the coordination of all transportation services, supports, and training using a variety of options based on student need.
10. Provide orientation and training to parents and students on transition topics, including self-determination, SSI benefits, ADA transportation, and adult service agencies, highlighting the difference between school and adult supports.
11. Hire, supervise, and train staff to work as educational and job coaches—paying particular attention to best practices in the field, with strong emphasis on individualized support model.
12. Responsible for organizing the monthly Student Support Team Meetings, including representatives from school, college, Massachusetts Rehabilitation Commission Area Office, the Department of Mental Retardation Area Office, Independent Living Center for Living and Working, One-Stop Career Center, students, family members, adult service agency staff, and other interested parties. This is a multi-agency resource team that collaborates on both systemic and individual transition issues.

13. Ensure that students are referred to adult funding sources and connections are made prior to them aging out.

14. Oversee all postsecondary education services for students at the local college—assisting students in intakes, registration, educational coaching, etc. Collaborate closely with the college disabilities office to ensure students' needs are being met.

15. Oversee all internship and job development activities and competitive employment placements.

Sample Career Development Screening

Vocational Screening

Student Name:	
Teacher Completing Form:	
Date Given:	Date Completed Form Received:

1. Transportation (check all that apply)

	Yes/No	COMMENTS
• Provides own transportation (car, bike, walking)		
• Lives near public bus route		
• Has access to specialized transportation (note what)		
• Family can assist with transportation		
• Has acquired RTA/PARATRANSIT pass		
• No available transportation		

2. Travel Skills (check all that apply)   Yes/No   COMMENTS

	Yes/No	COMMENTS
• Able to make own transportation arrangements		
• Uses public transportation independently (including transfers)		
• Uses public transportation independently (with no transfers)		
• Uses RTA paratransit system		
• Travels independently in familiar settings		
• Travels independently in unfamiliar settings		
• Crosses streets safely		
• Requires travel training (specify type)		

3. Safety Skills   Yes/No   COMMENTS

	Yes/No	COMMENTS
• List student's level of safety skills		
• Can remain home alone. List number of hours.		
• Carries an ID		
• Uses phone to dial emergency numbers		
• Asks for assistance if in need of help or lost		
• Seeks out help by showing ID or instruction card		
• Exhibits fears or behaviors that may affect interactions in the community		

4. Physical Mobility/Movement   Yes/No   COMMENTS

	Yes/No	COMMENTS
• No physical limitations		
• Functional ambulation/stairs/minor obstacles		
• Poor ambulation		
• Can sit or stand in one area		
• Other considerations		

5. Orientating/Movement   Yes/No   COMMENTS

	Yes/No	COMMENTS
• Independent travel in the community		
• Independent throughout buildings and grounds		
• Independent throughout building only		
• Independent movement through several rooms		
• Independent movement in classroom only		

6. Personal Care   Yes/No   COMMENTS

	Yes/No	COMMENTS
• Takes responsibility for own personal care		
• Needs cues or reminders to care for needs		
• Requires PCA (specify type)		

7. Communications   Yes/No   COMMENTS

	Yes/No	COMMENTS
• Communication is clearly understood		
• Uses key words/phrases		
• Uses sounds or gestures		
• Uses sign language		
• Uses picture communication		
• Uses augmentative speech device		
• Can demonstrate the need for help		

8. Functional Reading   Yes/No   COMMENTS

	Yes/No	COMMENTS
• Reads at _____ grade level		
• Uses sight words/symbols		
• None		

9. Functional Math   Yes/No   COMMENTS

	Yes/No	COMMENTS
• Completed math at _____ grade level		
• Uses basic addition/subtraction		
• Rote counts to _____		
• Can count _____ number of objects		
• Identifies numbers to _____		
• Identifies coins and bills		
• Makes change for up to a dollar		
• None		

**10. Time awareness (specify use of   Yes/No   COMMENTS
         digital or analog, or cell phone):**

	Yes/No	COMMENTS
• Tells time to the hour		
• Tells time to the half hour		
• Tells time to the quarter hour		
• Tells time to the minute		
• Follows school and work schedules		
• Unaware of time and clock functions		

11. Flexibility   Yes/No   COMMENTS

	Yes/No	COMMENTS
• Adapts to changes easily		
• Adapts with some difficulty		
• Adapts with great difficulty		

12. Handling Feedback/Stress   Yes/No   COMMENTS

	Yes/No	COMMENTS
• Accepts feedback/changes behavior		
• Accepts feedback/does not change behavior		
• Withdraws/no reaction		
• Reacts negatively to feedback		

Additional Comments:

Does the family want community-based education—employment, travel training, postsecondary education, etc.?
Will there be family support for appropriate attendance, dress, hygiene, etc.?

List student's learning style, effective teaching strategies, and behavioral interventions as related to community experiences and education:

List the individuals in the student's life who could help with career and
personal life planning:

List student's career aspirations:

List family's career aspirations for student:

Sample Student and Parent Postsecondary Checklists

STUDENT POSTSECONDARY CHECKLIST

YES/NO	SKILL
	1. Students participate in activities focusing on enhancing self - determination, social skills, and independence and interdependence skills.
	2. Students learn personal safety, emergency procedures, use of cell phone, name, address, phone number, SSN, birthdate and age. Students acquire a State Identification through the Registry of Motor Vehicles.
	3. While still in high school, students will begin to use the mode of transportation they will use once out of school. Many students will apply for the paratransit ADA transportation service if appropriate. Students gradually begin to use ADA transportation for transition activities.
	4. Students participate as members of their high school and college communities in activities and events.
	5. Students learn to develop friendships and plan events and activities with others, utilizing phone, e-mail and conversation. Students learn to work with others.
	6. Students learn about their disabilities and abilities— strengths, weaknesses, and learning style and how they may affect their learning.
	7. Students learn about the IEP and ITP process—to help them prepare for their meetings.
	8. Students develop a vision for their futures (consider person-centered planning as a tool).
	9. Students develop career, postsecondary education, and life goals as appropriate.

YES/NO	SKILL
	10. Students learn about change, transition—high school and life after high school, the adult service system, and the differences between the two. Talk about this often.
	11. Students are referred to adult funding sources prior to aging out of high school and begin to build a relationship.
	12. Students learn to advocate for themselves in high school, which will prepare them for postsecondary education and life.
	13. Student tours colleges prior to a decision.
	14. In making decision, student reviews all college information gathered and their vision for future—what makes the most sense?
	15. Student will receive assistance from the high school transition coordinator to obtain documentation of their disabilities, including IEP and psychological assessment completed within the last 3 years.
	16. Once decision is made, student meets with the college disabilities coordinator to complete an intake, discuss college life and how it differs from high school, and complete an accommodations packet. Also discuss level of supports that the college can provide (tutoring, homework center, note taker, etc.) based on student need.
	17. Plan and practice transportation to college prior to the start of the semester.
	18. Student attends college orientation.
	19. Student receives assistance from Transition Coordinator on understanding the difference in college schedule and commits to attending college during high school vacations.
	20. Student learns to take more responsibility in following his or her schedule, completing assignments, transportation, organizing his or her time, and communicating to family, college, and high school personnel when in need of assistance.

PARENT POSTSECONDARY CHECKLIST

YES/NO	SKILL
	1. Attend and encourage your child to attend all transition trainings and orientations that are offered by the school system in conjunction with adult service agencies.
	2. Encourage your child and teach self-determination, social skills, and independence and interdependence skills throughout his or her life.
	3. Educate your child on personal safety, emergency procedures, use of cell phone, name, address, phone number, SSN, birthdate, and age. Ensure your student receives a state identification through the registry of motor vehicles.
	4. Assist your child in applying for the Paratransit ADA transportation service if appropriate. Educate yourself and your child on the use of this transportation system.
	5. Encourage your child to be a part of his or her community at school and out of school. Teach and model relationship building—encourage friendships and relationships with a variety of people.
	6. Prior to and during high school, be a strong advocate for your child in ensuring she or he is enrolled in academic courses, which will prepare him or her for postsecondary education.
	7. Work closely with assistive technology staff, high school teacher, and learning specialists to ensure your child is receiving the learning strategies and tools needed to be successful and that they occur at the college level (audiobooks, screen reader, tape recorder, PDA, etc.).
	8. Educate your child on his or her disability and abilities—strengths, weaknesses, and learning style and how this disability may affect his or her learning.
	9. Educate your child on the IEP and ITP process.
	10. Encourage your child to attend and participate in his or her IEP and ITP.
	11. Work with your child on developing a vision for his or her future (consider person-centered planning as a tool).
	12. Assist your child in developing career, postsecondary education, and life goals as appropriate.

YES/NO	SKILL
	13. Educate your child on change, transition—high school and life after high school, the adult service system, and the differences between the two. Talk about this often. The differences between laws that govern secondary education (IDEA—entitlement) and laws that govern at the college level (ADA) should be discussed.
	14. Put your child in contact with adult funding sources and agencies prior to him or her leaving high school.
	15. Help your child to advocate for himself or herself in high school, which will prepare him or her for postsecondary education and life.
	16. Assist your child in obtaining course catalogs and review them with your child and high school personnel.
	17. Tour colleges prior to your child's making a decision.
	18. In making a decision with your child, review with your child all college information gathered and his or her vision for the future—what makes the most sense?
	19. Ensure that documentation of your child's disability is up to date, including IEP and psychological assessment completed within the last 3 years.
	20. Once decision is made, ensure that your child meets with the college disabilities coordinator to complete an intake interview, discuss college life and how it differs from high school, and complete an accommodations packet. Also discuss level of supports that the college can provide (tutoring, homework center, note taker, etc.) based on student need.
	21. Plan and practice transportation to college prior to the start of the semester.
	22. Ensure your child attends college orientation.
	23. Work with your child to understand the difference in college schedule and develop alternative supports if needed in order for your child to attend college while high school staff is on vacation.

YES/NO	SKILL
	24. Be aware that your child is working on increased independence and acceptance of responsibility and commitment—college staff may address issues with your child directly and may not always inform parents. Have the student take responsibility for communicating his or her college experience and needs to parents directly. At times this may mean a student doesn't complete an assignment or garner necessary school supplies because he or she did not communicate that need to the parents. It's a learning process—a work in progress.
	25. Throughout this process work closely with the school transition coordinator to coordinate all postsecondary activities.
	26. As a family member, you will need written consent from your child to obtain access to his or her records at the college.
	27. Applaud all efforts, dream, encourage dreaming—believe.

Sample Emergency Contact Form

LMN Public Schools

Special Education Department

Transition Services Program

Emergency Fact Sheet

Student Name:	D.O.B.:
Address:	Phone #:
In the event of an emergency requiring medical attention, I understand that every effort will be made to contact me. However, if I cannot be reached, I hereby authorize the school staff to transport and/or have _____ transported to the nearest medical facility, and secure medical treatment.	

EMERGENCY MEDICAL INFORMATION

Student's Physician's Name:
Physician's Address:
Physician's Phone #:
Health Insurance Coverage: Policy #:
Student's Social Security Number:
List of student's active medical problems:
List student's allergies (food, medication, pollen, latex, etc.) and explain any reactions:
List Medications (Frequency and Dosage):
List any unusual fears: (e.g. water, height, noise, etc.):

EMERGENCY CONTACT INFORMATION

Name:	Address:
Relationship to Student:	Phone #:
Name:	Address:
Relationship to Student:	Phone #:
Do you give permission for student to be released to these persons? YES _____ NO _____	

Parent(s) Name: _____

Phone #: Home _____ Work: _____

High School versus College

High School	College
Law is the Individuals with Disabilities Education Improvement Act (IDEA).	Laws are Americans with Disabilities Act (ADA) and Sections 504 and 508 of the Rehabilitation Act.
IDEA is about success.	ADA is about access.
Core modifications of classes and materials are required.	NO modifications are required—only accommodations.
School district must identify disability.	Student must self-identify.
School district develops individualized education program (IEPs) to determine school's plan.	Student must identify needs and ask for services. NO IEP exists and IEP is not considered legal documentation.
School district provides free assessments.	Student must obtain assessments at their own expense.
Student is helped by parents and teachers.	Student must seek help (as needed) from disability services office.
School is responsible for arranging for accommodations.	Student must self-advocate and arrange for accommodations.
Personal care services are required.	No personal care services are required.
Parent has access to student records.	Parent has no access to student records without student's written consent.
Parent advocates for student.	Student advocates for self.
School year runs from September to June.	School year is divided into two semesters: September to December and January to May.
Classes meet daily.	Classes meet 1, 2, 3, or 4 times a week.
Classes generally meet in the same building.	Classes are held in many different places on campus.

High School	College
Average length of class is 35–45 minutes.	Classes vary in length from 50 minutes to 3 hours.
Daily contact with teachers.	Classes meet less frequently so you will see your instructors and teacher assistants less frequently.
Students need parent's permission to participate in most activities.	Student is an adult and gives own permission.
Guidance counselors and other staff schedule support services for students.	Student must schedule all support services.
Main office is center of activity for building.	The student is responsible for knowing where to go to get information and assistance.
Classes consist of about 30 students.	Classes may consist of about 100 students.
Teachers often remind you of assignments and due dates.	Professors expect you to read the course syllabus. They do not remind you of upcoming events.
High school is free.	Student must pay for college through financial aid and other arrangements.

Postsecondary Goals and the Role of the Educational Job Coach

Lauren's Career Plan/Meeting Notes
From October 20, 2006

Long-Term Goal:

To work in a paid position in the community using office skills such as copying, scanning, mailings, collating, etc, social skills, and memory/directional skills in a supportive environment with greater independence (not requiring a constant 1:1 job coach).

Short-Term Goal:

Lauren is interested in exploring career options through internships that would use her office skills such as copying, scanning, mailings, collating, social skills, and memory/directional skills in a supportive environment with greater independence.

Steps to Achieving Short-Term Goal

Lauren and her career planning team will work on the following steps:

1. Lauren will update her resume.
2. Job coach will explore, with Family Health Coordinator, the possibility of Lauren working at Family Health 2 days doing consistent tasks.
3. Lauren's Mom to check with Director to see if they do the scanning of medical records and also to check who does their shredding.
4. Educational coach and staff to check the different colleges in the area to find out what the staff at the information booths do, what are their job descriptions, when are these positions staffed. Areas to look for an appropriate position include the Student Union, Library, bookstore (where students leave their backpacks), athletic facilities, etc. The idea is that Lauren will try each position for a month to see if she likes it. Mom will follow up to get a job description, etc. Once we have found areas we think might be appropriate for internships, Dad will assist with connecting to the colleges to get a contact.
5. The 3 areas to focus on initially are family health, college environment, and scanning (put this on back burner)—maybe something she does as a piece of her day.
6. Lauren will use the paratransit system more independently by calling in for her own transportation from 1 to 3 times a week.

Educational Coach Job Description

Qualifications:

- 2 years of college
- Undergraduate degree—preferred but not necessary
- Excellent communication and organizational skills
- Strong interpersonal skills with the ability to build positive relationships
- Ability to work with college students in a fast-paced, multitasking environment
- Higher education experience preferred

Purpose of the Position:

The purpose of the position is to facilitate and support the inclusion of students in the college course work and campus life.

Job Performance Responsibilities:

- Help to maintain a positive academic environment
- Academic tutor when needed
- Monitor students for health problems if assigned
- Assist students with assignments in courses as assigned
- Maintain accurate records regarding students
- Work as a member of the team
- Maintain confidentiality regarding educational information and records
- Willing to obtain added training
- Perform other duties and responsibilities as assigned
- Take notes when needed
- Foster independence
- Assist with organization of logistics everyday
- Help with time management
- Help with money skills
- Help with recording homework
- Help with understanding the social environment
- Relay all communication about student progress to staff
- Cover duties of other educational coaches in the event of an absence
- Perform other duties as specified

Sample Table of Contents Page from *A Guide to Using ADA Paratransit*

Woodbury Public Schools Transition Services

Shortcuts for Using ADA Paratransit Services

Contents

College Perspectives and Issues

Laura Eisenman and Karen Mancini

The purpose of this chapter is to provide professionals, individuals with disabilities, and their families with information from a postsecondary perspective that will assist them in creating a good fit between the goals of young adults with intellectual disabilities (ID) and those of postsecondary institutions. Special attention is given to common practical challenges and supports that are part of postsecondary environments.

Traditionally, educating students with ID has not been part of higher education's role. This is hardly surprising when we consider that only within the last 30 years have students with ID been guaranteed access to education at any level. However, educating youth with ID can fit squarely within the teaching, research, and service missions of postsecondary institutions. Students with ID are part of a growing constituency of traditionally underrepresented groups that have benefited from increased access to secondary education experiences and are now seeking opportunities across the life span to expand their knowledge and skills in pursuit of career and personal goals.

As colleges explore ways to educate and support this new consumer group, there are potential benefits for other students on campus who—both professionally and personally—are increasingly likely to work and live with people with disabilities in their communities. With increased campus diversity come opportunities to institute educational services and accommodations that benefit a variety of learners, not just students with disabilities. Raising awareness in the campus community of disability as a natural part of the human condition will foster understanding and inclusion of all individuals with disabilities. Engaging the institution's research and professional programs in the generation of new approaches to service delivery and supports for people with disabilities not only benefits the field of disabilities; it can also serve institutional goals of research and knowledge dissemination across disciplines. Finally, expanded partnerships with local schools and community groups that work with people who have ID can enhance the institution's reputation for service and responsiveness to community needs.

COMMON GROUND FOR LEARNING: A CASE STUDY

For more than a decade, the University of Delaware had a quiet, mutually supportive relationship with a local school district. School district staff who had a commitment to educating young adult students with significant ID in age-appropriate community environments collaborated with like-minded university staff involved in disability-focused research, training, and service. The partnership they developed resulted in a model campus- and community-based education program that each year served up to 25 of the school district's students who were between the ages of 18 and 21. The young adults were dually enrolled—they maintained their status as public school students and were participants in a university-recognized, nontraditional campus program. School district teachers and paraprofessionals provided educational services and activities in accordance with students' individualized education programs (IEPs) while also making use of social, recreational, and vocational opportunities that they found on and around campus. Through a district-funded contract, a university faculty member served as a liaison to the university community, coordinated a project advisory committee, and conducted periodic evaluations. The project would have been considered a substantially separate model (Hart, Grigal, Sax, Martinez, & Will, 2006). The students enjoyed a presence on campus as they interacted with university peers and staff in work settings, made use of their university identification cards to access the gym or campus shuttle, and participated in university students' transition-focused course projects. However, the primary focus was use of the campus environment to facilitate acquisition of important life skills, less focus was put on engaging the students in a typical college experience, and no focus was given to the pursuit of college-matriculated student status.

Recently, that has changed. Two more districts approached the faculty liaison about gaining access to the campus for their students, aged 18 to 21, who had ID. As a result, the three school districts provided funding for an alliance with the university, enabling the university to hire a part-time project coordinator and expand the project focus to include greater integration of academic, employment, and social opportunities on campus. As in a mixed/hybrid model that incorporates non-traditional and traditional campus programs, services, and activities (Hart et al., 2006), the programmatic lens was expanded to include campus activities that reflected more typical college experiences while continuing to offer separate life skills education. For example, students informally audited college courses, and a more systematic effort was made to match individuals to college–student-oriented social activities.

Over the years, parents familiar with this project or other community activities of the university independently contacted university staff and faculty to explore the possibility of establishing a residential college program for young adults with ID and to inquire about specific postsecondary education (PSE) opportunities. Although no formal PSE programs were established by the university specifically for people with ID, a few individuals found their way into college courses as continuing education students, took up residence in nearby apartments geared to college students, and connected with social and recreational groups on campus.

The fact that both formal and informal avenues into PSE developed on the campus points to an important theme of this chapter. Access to PSE environments for people with ID is often driven by individuals who are clear about their specific reasons for pursuing PSE, understand the multiple missions of postsecondary institutions, and use their professional and social networks to build alliances and find resources. The impetus may come from school or university professionals who want to expand educational opportunities for people with disabilities, as well as from individuals with disabilities or their families who recognize that PSE is a socially valued experience that can confer long-term social and employment benefits on people with ID (Hughson, Moodie, & Uditsky, 2006; Zafft, Hart, & Zimbrich, 2004).

OPTIONS FOR POSTSECONDARY EDUCATION

When thinking about going to college, it is important to consider the variety of options available and the differing missions of PSE institutions. Typical options include 4-year and 2-year institutions, postsecondary career- (or vocational-) technical schools, and adult education.

Four-year colleges or universities usually focus their programs and services on students who plan to complete a bachelor's degree. Some of these institutions also may offer advanced degrees (master's or doctorate) or 2-year associate's degrees. Typically, these colleges have admission requirements related to completion of high school programs, grades, aptitude or achievement test scores, or other indicators that prospective students are likely to succeed in an academic degree program. Four-year colleges are sometimes judged by their retention and graduation rates, the time it takes students to complete a degree, and their competitiveness in attracting students.

Four-year institutions are often residential schools. Some students may be required to live on campus, and the college may invest in on-campus housing and related services for many students. The cost for tuition and housing at a 4-year college varies dramatically. Students attending publicly funded colleges may pay less for tuition if they are in-state residents, but the costs are still considerable. In 2006–2007, undergraduate education at public institutions cost an average of $12,796 for annual tuition, room, and board; at private colleges the average was $30,367 (College Board, 2006). Enrollment of students with disabilities in 4-year colleges has risen recently, but the numbers remain low compared with those for their peers without disabilities—6% versus 28%, respectively. According to the second National Longitudinal Transition Survey (Newman, 2005), which examines the experiences of a nationally representative sample of adolescents and young adults in each IDEA disability category during and after departing from high school, none of the sampled students with IDs had taken courses at a 4-year college or university following high school. *Community colleges*, which are most often 2-year public institutions, also may serve academic degree-seeking students, primarily those interested in an associate's degree. However, community colleges are much more likely than 4-year institutions to provide a variety of career-oriented certificate programs. These schools may be especially attuned to the local labor market and design their PSE certificate programs to meet local needs. In addition, community colleges may have articulation agreements with local high schools and universities that provide certificate or degree pathways from one institution to the other, creating a formal mechanism for students to pursue the next step in their academic careers. Community colleges also offer individual courses for nontraditional students of all ages who want to learn more about a particular topic or develop a specific skill without pursuing a degree.

Community colleges tend to be publicly funded and relatively inexpensive. Campus housing and related services are not typical options. As of January 2007, the average annual cost for tuition and fees was $2,272 (American Association of Community Colleges, 2007). About 20% of all youth with disabilities enroll in classes at a 2-year or community college within 2 years of leaving high school. Students with disabilities are more likely to enroll in 2-year institutions than in any other type of PSE, and their current rate of enrollment is not substantially different from that of their peers without disabilities. However, youth with ID report only a 5% participation rate (Newman, 2005).

Career- (vocational-) technical schools may be part of public high schools or public or private 2- or 4-year colleges that offer academic credentials. They also may be stand-alone private institutions that focus on training and certification in single career areas (e.g., cosmetology, automotive technology). The costs of attending a career-technical school vary widely, depending on the type of institution (public versus private), degree and certificate options, and reputation. Almost two-thirds of career-technical programs are offered through private schools; about 40% are for-profit institutions (U.S. Department of Education, 2004a). Across categories of disability, about 6% of students report having attended a technical school within 2 years of exiting high school; however, 11% of students with ID report having attended this type of postsecondary program (Newman, 2005).

Adult education, like career-technical programs, may be offered through a variety of organizations, including local school districts, private nonprofit groups, community colleges, and volunteer literacy organizations. Adult education programs are intended for people who are over the age of 16, who do not have a high school diploma, and who are not currently enrolled in school. There are three major programs that are usually available through publicly funded adult education: 1) adult basic education for people who want to improve their basic literacy skills, 2) adult secondary education for those with more advanced literacy skills who want to get a high school equivalency credential, and 3) English literacy education for those who are learning the English language. Depending on the sponsoring organization, a variety of vocational, recreational, or academically focused programs might also be available. It is not known just how many people with disabilities participate in adult education programs, although directors of adult basic education programs believe that a major subset of participants have learning disabilities or attention deficit disorder (National Institute for Literacy, 1998).

A CRITICAL LEGAL TRANSITION

Each of these PSE options may be of interest to young adults with ID, depending on their academic and vocational goals. Regardless of the PSE option chosen, young adults and their families must be knowledgeable about a critical legal transition that is made when they move from secondary to postsecondary education. The Individuals with Disabilities Education Improvement Act (IDEA) of 2004 (PL 108-446), which is one of the primary laws governing the education of students with special education needs before graduation from high school, does *not* apply to PSE. The application of Section 504 of the Rehabilitation Act of 1973 (PL 93-112), a law that also guarantees a free and appropriate public education to students with disabilities, is drastically different in higher education. Instead, the Americans with Disabilities Act (ADA) of 1990 (PL 101-136) has the greatest influence on the legal rights and responsibilities of people with disabilities in PSE.

Entitlement versus Eligibility

IDEA guarantees an education to all students with disabilities until a maximum age of 21 in most states. IDEA mandates that the school and its representatives identify students with special needs, determine their needs, and provide specialized instruction and other services and supports to ensure a free and appropriate public education for all students with disabilities. Students with disabilities in K-12, are also eligible for accommodations and other services related to access under Section 504 of the Rehabilitation Act. Parents have the opportunity to advocate for their children through the IEP planning process or 504 plans. It is through the IEP process that parents and students can establish long-term transition goals that include a PSE experience. However, neither of these laws nor the ADA offers a guarantee of higher education. Table 5.1 highlights some of the major differences among these laws.

Students with ID who are dually enrolled at a college and continue to receive supports through their local school system are in a unique situation. They still receive educational services from the local education agency under IDEA as provided in their IEPs, but the higher education setting in which these services are delivered does not operate under IDEA. Therefore, these students and those who support them need to have a clear understanding of the truly dual nature of the laws that govern their experience: entitlement to IDEA services through the local education agency accompanied by access (but not entitlement) to higher education programs and services. Advocates for dually-enrolled students must take into consideration the availability of both sets of legal protections when negotiating services for such students.

Once students with disabilities exit the school system with a diploma or a certificate or by aging out at 21, their primary disability-related legal protection is under the ADA. The ADA does not guarantee an *education*, but it does guarantee *access* to programs and services for otherwise *qualified* individuals. Under the ADA, people with disabilities must become their own advocates; it is their responsibility to identify themselves, provide supporting documentation about their disabilities, and request needed accommodations. They will never age out of the protections afforded by ADA, but they must actively pursue their rights and carry out their responsibilities to ensure that protection.

Preparing for the Legal Transition

This legal transition can be difficult for parents who are accustomed to being the point person when advocating for the educational needs of their child. Parents must now take on a supporting role when seeking accommodations in college settings. In addition, parents who desire information about their child's progress and status in college coursework will often be surprised to find out that college personnel are not allowed to share such information without written authorization from their child. These rights are provided under the Family Educational Rights and Privacy Act (FERPA) of 1974 (PL 93-380), which is a federal law that protects the privacy of student education records. The law applies to all schools that receive funds under an applicable program of the U.S. Department of Education. FERPA gives parents certain rights with respect to their child's education

Table 5.1. IDEA, ADA and Section 504

IDEA	Americans with Disabilities Act and Section 504
Guarantees a free and appropriate public education. IDEA ensures entitlement—charges schools to ensure that students make progress in the general curriculum.	Guarantees access to all programs, services, and activities including all activities open to the public. Does not guarantee an education, but provides equal opportunity to individuals who are 'otherwise qualified' for the programs that they enter.
School district is responsible for identifying students and initiating services to address learning issues with students.	Students must identify themselves as a student with a disability to the appropriate office at the IHE.
It is the school's responsibility to assess and document the disability and the functional limitations that will be addressed with an individualized education program (IEP) or accommodations. Public schools are responsible for providing any diagnostic testing that is warranted.	The student must provide documentation for the disability that meets the IHE's documentation guidelines. IHE's are not required to offer testing. Those that do may offer it through a fee-based learning clinic. IEPs are generally not sufficient by themselves to document a disability.
Eligibility is based on age and disability. Students age out at 21.	Individuals with disabilities are eligible for reasonable accommodations as long as they are "otherwise qualified." There are no age restrictions.
IEP plans may include course waivers or substitutions. Untimed tests and alternative test formats are permitted. Specially designed instruction is appropriate.	Specially designed instruction is not considered a reasonable accommodation. Colleges are not required to change an integral part of a course or program. Students are offered access and are expected to meet requirements of the programs and courses in which they are enrolled. Extended-time exams are provided as reasonable accommodations.
The IEP team will include the student, professionals, and parents.	Students must request accommodations directly, most often via the Disability Services Office.
IDEA requires schools to provide a transition plan for students.	Some IHEs offer transition services and programs but these are not required under any law.
Schools may provide or coordinate personal support services, homework support, and tutoring.	IHEs are not required to provide services of a personal nature.
Assistive technology is provided as identified by the IEP team.	Assistive technology is only provided to give access and often varies across IHEs.

records while he or she is still in high school. These rights transfer to the student when he or she reaches the age of 18 or attends a school beyond the high school level. FERPA applies to any student taking courses at a college regardless of his or her age and therefore applies to students who are taking part in dual enrollment at a college.

This shift in primary responsibility for advocacy from parent to student, coupled with the different legal rights that govern access to PSE, means that prior to exiting high school, students must be equipped with specific dispositions, skills, and documentation. First, the development of self-determination skills is critical to the process of advocating for protections and accommodations in postsecondary schools. Students who have a clear understanding of their goals and the desire and determination to act reasonably and responsibly to pursue those goals are more likely to be successful. Students are expected to advocate for themselves in a variety of contexts that may include classrooms, social milieus, and employment placements. Second, to receive any accommodations in college, students need to self-identify (i.e., disclose the disability) at the disability support services (DSS) office and provide documentation of their disability and needed education supports. The role of DSS on college campuses and the nature of required disability documentation are both discussed in detail later in the chapter, but these issues bear repeating and should be embedded in the transition planning process for any student with a disability who plans to pursue PSE.

To self-identify at the DSS students must have a clear understanding of their learning style, the accommodations that they have received, and how those accommodations benefited them in the school and social environment. High school guidance counselors, teachers, and case workers need to educate their students about their learning style and related supports that they have offered to them. Students need to know which supports they will be expected to provide for themselves in postsecondary institutions and which accommodations may be available through an institution (e.g., see Table 5.2). Furthermore, information about accommodations must be tied to documentation of the student's disability. Typically the requirements for this documentation include a psychological evaluation that is less than 3 years old. However, colleges differ in their documentation requirements, and it is advisable to contact the college ahead of time to plan appropriately.

Unfortunately, many students leave high school unaware of the specific supports they have received both directly and behind the scenes and are unable to explain the nature of their disability and its impact on their functioning in different environments. One of the new requirements under the Individuals with Disabilities Education Improvement Act of 2004 (PL 108-446), the Summary of Performance, can become a tool for helping students in this regard. The Summary is an exit document that must be provided by schools to students. The Summary must describe a student's academic achievement and functional performance and include recommendations on how to help the student to meet previously identified postsecondary goals. Students, their families, and professionals should ensure that the most recent information about the nature of a student's disability and accommodations is incorporated into the Summary.

In this chapter the examples we give regarding the role of ADA and other important aspects of the college experience focus primarily on 4- and 2-year institutions, which traditionally have not been considered viable options for students with ID. However, because people with disabilities are protected by ADA in all types of PSE settings, these examples may serve as the basis for exploring a variety of alternative PSE options. Remember that the ADA provides guidance regarding the minimum response required of an institution. PSE institutions may do more, to the degree that their mission, policies, programs, and funding sources support them to do so. Students and their families or support team should shop around to find the college that best meets their personal and educational needs.

CHALLENGES AND OPPORTUNITIES

The Admissions Process

John and his family wanted a residential, 4-year college experience for him. Everyone in his family had attended college, and they were determined to give him a shot at the same social and educational experiences. When they approached an admissions counselor at a local university about the possibility of his attending, they were told that John would have to complete the same application process as any other person. The fact that John had a certificate of attendance instead of a high school diploma concerned the counselor, who suggested that the family visit the nearby community college, which she said might admit him into some remedial courses. She expressed doubt about whether John could be considered "qualified" for any PSE program. John's family was discouraged but decided to make some calls to other schools to find out more about their admissions policies.

John's situation is not unique. Traditional students matriculating into the college campus will submit an application with their high school grades, SAT or ACT test scores, and an essay articulating an attribute or experience that has influenced their life. Whereas community colleges may maintain an open-door policy, 4-year schools use a combination of criteria to determine acceptance into the institution. Colleges and universities look at course selection in high school, rank in class, activities and involvement, grades, application essay, standardized test scores, and possibly an interview. Acceptance as a full-time matriculated student establishes a student's status as qualified. This process is daunting for the average student, and for the student with an ID, the process may seem impossible.

Although students with ID may not qualify through the traditional admission process, there are other avenues through which students can access 4-year campuses; they need not limit themselves to open-enrollment schools. For example, options for part-time study are available through most continuing education programs within 4-year institutions. These programs do not have the same entrance requirements, and they often offer credit courses as well as noncredit courses or certificate programs. Whether they are attending a 4-year or 2-year institution, students with an ID could benefit from a reduced load of one or two courses in a semester while becoming familiar with college academic expectations. If matriculation into an academic degree program as a full-time student is not the primary goal, then the traditional application process does not need to be a barrier. In fact, this was the solution to John's situation. He learned that he could enroll in courses as a continuing education student. He audited two courses during his first semester, and, with the help of a private tutor, he successfully completed the coursework. He also moved into an apartment complex near campus that catered to college students and found a part-time job on campus.

The next semester he chose to audit two more courses and took another on a pass/fail basis.

Other PSE opportunities for students with ID include participation in an inclusive individually supported option or a nontraditional campus program, such as the dual-enrollment plan at the University of Delaware. Students with ID who have not yet exited the K–12 school system with a diploma or certificate continue to be eligible for services as indicated in their IEPs, including participation in community- and college-based transition options. Admission to a dual-enrollment plan may be at the discretion of the public school program and the IEP team or the result of a collaborative decision between the school and the institution of higher education.

Colleges may offer a variety of nontraditional options, which provide alternative paths into the college environment. These officially recognized, nondegree programs can serve a wide variety of people in many different ways. For example, older adults may be welcomed into courses or institutes that capitalize on their life experiences while engaging their desire to be lifelong learners. Students from underrepresented cultural groups may be invited to participate in a short-term intensive summer college experience as a way to encourage their interest in and connections to higher education. Participants in a university-recognized, nontraditional campus program have rights under ADA and Section 504 to any services and programs that are open to the public or for which they are qualified.

Although traditional college admissions criteria do not apply to nonmatriculated students in dual-enrollment transition programs, it is important that those criteria be used to set expectations and guide transition planning for students. One of the core ingredients of a successful postsecondary experience is the student's fit with the intended program of study. The program must match the individual goals and career objectives of the student. Thus, transition planning is an important vehicle for establishing those goals and objectives for the postsecondary experience, and planning should begin upon entrance into the high school setting, even for students with ID.

Funding for Postsecondary Education

An important benefit of full-time matriculated status is access to federal financial aid, which is not available to part-time or continuing education students. Even matriculated students without disabilities who take a reduced course load as they acclimate to college life run into this financial barrier. This is no different for students with ID. Although a part-time course load may be appropriate for an individual with ID, tuition becomes an out-of-pocket expense for the student and family. Moreover, federal financial aid is not available to students who lack a high school diploma or equivalency unless they can pass a federally approved ability-to-benefit test (U.S. Department of Education, 2006). These tests are intended to demonstrate that an individual has the potential to perform well in college despite a lack of typical credentials. The recent reauthorization of the Higher Education Opportunities Act of 2008 (PL 110-315), the law that governs federal financial aid, has focused on changing some of the rules that limit access to aid by students with ID.

For example, under previous regulations only full-time matriculated students were eligible for work-study funding. New amendments in the Higher Education Opportunity Act of 2008 would permit participation in college work-study programs by students with ID even if they are not full-time matriculating students (Association of University Centers on Disabilities, 2006). In addition, the new HEOA supports the creation of a national technical assistance center and model demonstration projects on PSE for students with ID. Implementation of these new HEA provisions depends upon development of corresponding federal regulations and authorization of funding by Congress. Although these developments offer a possible avenue to increased student access to funding, advocacy will continue to be needed to increase federal financial aid options for students with ID.

Aside from parents' own funds, funding for students with ID in postsecondary settings has traditionally come through grant programs, vocational rehabilitation agencies, partnerships with school districts, education awards from AmeriCorps for community service, and scholarships that target students with ID. Dually enrolled students who are 18 to 21 years old can use IDEA funds for college. With the support of the school district and the IEP team, this may be accomplished on an individual basis for a student whose transition plan calls for such experiences or through a dual-enrollment program designed to serve a number of students on a college campus. Once students have completed their high school program, families must look to outside funding resources. If the student's coursework and experiences are focused on career development and job skills enhancement, vocational rehabilitation agencies may provide funding to assist the student. Public benefits counselors can be of assistance in identifying and coordinating other sources of limited funding, such as a Social Security PASS plan. Because postsecondary funding is limited and fragmented across several agencies, students and families should begin early in the transition planning process to establish eligibility for their state or county developmental disabilities services, vocational rehabilitation, and other adult services that could provide future funding.

Especially for nontraditional campus programs, students and families should inquire about the possibility of other fees. Many college campuses require matriculated students to pay a yearly fee that covers the general costs of recreational activities. This can be as little as $100 or as high as several hundred dollars. For a dually enrolled student, these fees may be covered by the student's school district or state agencies or waived by the university. However, many campus activities are not fee based, so students may be able to participate simply by showing a campus identification card. A university has the authority to decide whether nontraditional students can have a student identification card, and what privileges will be associated with that card. For example, students in some dual-enrollment programs may have an ID card that gives them access to student recreation centers, campus buses, and the library, but they might need special permission to check out books.

Finally, given that research and program development on PSE for individuals with ID are still in their infancy, it may be worthwhile to explore collaborations with college faculty who are involved in research, teaching, or service in this area. As interest builds and programs or inclusive options become more available, privately or publicly funded research and demonstration projects could open up additional funding avenues for students who are willing to participate in related studies.

Disability Support Services and Accommodations

On one particular day the DSS received a call from an adjunct faculty
member. A professional in the field, this faculty member worked part time
for the university. Her panic and frustration were obvious. She explained
that she had received a message from a "program coordinator" that a student in her course would be taking the exam with a scribe and would require a separate location. She admitted that at first, she thought it would
be no big deal, but then worried. When classes are in full swing, where do
you find space to monitor a separate exam? She acknowledged that she
truly wanted to help, but expressed her frustration that as an adjunct faculty member she did not have the means, time, or contacts to figure out
how to manage this. She was traveling between locations and did not
know whom to call until she remembered that the DSS office sometimes
handled accommodations.

The director asked the name of the student and immediately determined that the student was not registered with the DSS office. In hearing
more about the course, the director recognized the student and went on
to explain that this student was probably taking courses with the support
of one of the nontraditional campus programs. Because the director had a
solid working relationship with the unit that sponsored the program and
knew the program coordinator, she was able to defuse the situation
quickly. The director explained that although this student had not directly
registered with the DSS office, because she was a participant in a recognized campus program, the DSS staff could assist with the accommodation
process. The director assured the adjunct that space could be provided by
the DSS office; faculty did not have to figure out the accommodations.
The director thanked her for her true concern over resolving the issues
and assured her that she would contact the program coordinator to ensure
that the student registered with the DSS office and space would be
arranged for the test.

On that day, the director was able to provide reassurance to a panicked
faculty member, educate the program coordinator, and ultimately make
helpful resources available to the student. On a busy college campus, communication is key, and the working relationship between the DSS provider,
students, faculty, and nontraditional programs can make all the difference.

Disability services on college campuses are the central support offices for students with disabilities. DSS staff can become strong allies who help students ensure that their rights to accommodations under ADA are being met. However,
there are several potential barriers in the accommodation process for students
with ID on a college campus. First, DSS offices are often overloaded and under-
staffed. In addition, the majority of their students have entered through the traditional admission process, and their otherwise qualified status has been con-
firmed through admission. When considering accommodations, DSS staff work
with faculty to reduce the barriers related to the disability while maintaining the
integrity of the course and programs. DSS providers are trained not to make any
change to the criteria or expectations of the course that would fundamentally
alter the course. Thus DSS providers need to be informed of the goals of a course

for nonmatriculated students. If a course is audited or part of a noncredit certificate program, then the process of deciding on reasonable accommodations may be different. In addition, the litmus test for "otherwise qualified" is tied to the purpose and eligibility requirements of the program in which the student is participating. The focus is on the student's need for reasonable accommodation with respect to the essential components of the course or program. The DSS providers should be part of the process and have a full understanding of the individual's career goals in order to provide effective guidance.

The Role of DSS

The organization and structure of DSS can vary by campus, and even the name of the office can be different: Disability Support Services, Disability Services Office, Academic Services Office, and ADA Office are all possible names. Although colleges can decide how to name the office or choose the department in which it is to be housed, the ADA is clear that there must be a designated individual on campus to address ADA issues. However, the experience and background of DSS professionals can vary. Although they may receive direct training and support for accommodating matriculated students, many may not have experience or awareness of the different needs and possible supports for students in nontraditional programs. Thus, it would not be surprising if a DSS professional were to respond to some requests with "That's not my job," not realizing that ADA legal requirements encompass nontraditional students as well. Education and advocacy are key in these situations. Lack of experience or knowledge regarding students who have ID is not an acceptable reason for not providing accommodations. If initial efforts fail to improve relations with a DSS office, students and families can file grievances, a procedure that each office is required by the ADA to have available.

Not all program coordinators will realize the role that DSS providers can play for nontraditional students. As in the example above, the DSS provider was aware of the program's existence on campus, but the coordinator had not contacted DSS about the student's situation, because she was unaware that the DSS office could also support nontraditional students. That situation became an excellent opportunity for the two offices to build a working relationship that had not existed previously. In some cases, the services and relationships grow as a result of requests made by students. In this case, the professionals were open to building new processes and supports.

Equipped with this knowledge, DSS providers can be great advocates. Their role is to ensure that all of the services and programs on campus are accessible. This includes any public programs or inclusive individual supports students may receive. For example, theater productions, campus activities, and facilities for recreation must be accessible to all students. Students with ID need to clarify their status on campus. Students, with the support of staff such as the DSS provider, must ensure that they have access to all campus facilities and activities from the start. DSS providers are the main contact for ensuring that physical access is available, in addition to assistive technology.

Access to Accommodations

In an academic setting, DSS personnel would provide access to assistive technology, extended time on tests, and other common accommodations such as those listed in Table 5.2. DSS providers can help with faculty education and assist co-ordinators of nontraditional options with integration of accommodations into the classroom. The DSS provider is there to provide accommodations as long as they are not of a personal nature. Personal assistants and educational coaches are not usually considered reasonable accommodations for the college or university to provide. In some cases tutoring services are available, but this varies across institutions.

Although they may not be readily provided, supports such as personal assistants, tutors, or educational and job coaches may be necessary for student participation in any of the models that we discuss. In predominantly separate dual-enrollment programs, staff who facilitate the program may be the source of those supports. In most of these cases, it is the school district that funds such programs and provides teachers and education/job coaches for the students. Students who are dually enrolled may also receive additional support, often through a liaison to the university services, that is either funded through grants or provided by the university. The ideal situation would be for the liaison to have a solid working relationship with several departments on campus, including the DSS office. In a hybrid model, students may participate in a variety of nonacademic activities such as job training or recreational programs, as well as enroll in college classes. These activities may require services or supports in the form of education/job coaches, student mentors, or other personal supports. These services would not necessarily be considered accommodations that are the responsibility of the university, and alternative sources of funding such as grants or adult service agencies might have to be considered. In an inclusive program, where students may be enrolled in more courses, there may be a need for an education coach, and, if students are living independently near or on the campus, they may need a life coach to assist with daily living; in many cases, this can be the same person. Funding for these supports can also vary. The university would not typically provide accommodations of a personal nature, so the cost of an educational

Table 5.2. Common accommodations in postsecondary education institutions

Extended exam time
Distraction-limited testing environment
Notetakers
Scribes
Readers
Proctors
Interpreters for the Deaf, C Print, or CART services
Texts on tape or e-text
Use of word processor for written exams
Enlarged or braille texts and other course materials
JAWS for Windows, ZOOM Text, and scanners in selected computer labs on campus
Use of the academic resource center
Use of the writing center
Faculty notification of accommodations
Consultations with faculty
Reduced course load
Classroom relocation for accessibility
Accessible transportation
Snow removal priority

and life coach would have to be met through state agencies or private funding. Because no formal network of disability-related coaches exists, families and students who want to locate a coach will need to consult with the DSS, state disability agencies, local advocacy groups, and their own informal support network.

Disability Documentation

Students who want to access accommodations on a college campus will need to follow the guidelines of that campus. The ADA mandates that public entities such as colleges and universities make available procedures for access and accommodations. The process begins with the student. Students are required to identify themselves as an individual with a disability, provide documentation that is less than 3 years old of any disability, and request reasonable accommodations. Colleges and universities publish their documentation requirements in much the same way that they publish their general procedures. In many cases, schools will look to the Association on Higher Education and Disability (AHEAD) for guidance in designing their documentation requirements. Students who are uncertain as to which school they would like to apply to can use the AHEAD (2004) guidelines to prepare documentation for future accommodations. AHEAD posts an array of information about disabilities and higher education, along with their standards for documentation. Their web site (see http://www.ahead.org) can be a good resource for students and their families.

Another excellent resource is the HEATH Resource Center of George Washington University, Graduate School of Education and Human Development. HEATH is an online clearinghouse that gathers and disseminates information to help people with disabilities reach their full potential through PSE and training. The HEATH web site is http://www.heath.gwu.edu/.

Residential Options

Carole was excited to learn that she had been accepted into the new transitional independent living program that was located in a house just a block from the university campus. Through a combination of grants, state agency funding, and university and private support, the university was able to offer three post–high school young adults with developmental disabilities the opportunity to engage in an intensive person-centered planning process that would assist them over 6 months to 2 years to acquire the services and supports needed to clarify and take action on their postsecondary goals. Carole had always dreamed of getting a job in a business office and living in her own place. The idea that she would be living so close to campus while working on her goals made her wonder if she could also take some college courses or go to the football games with her friends.

The model program sponsored by the university was not created as a residential option for university students, however its proximity to campus and the active involvement of university staff make it likely that Carole will have the chance to explore campus life and, if she wishes, consider enrollment as a continuing education student. Like Carole, students with ID who want the college living experience—but are not matriculated, full-time students—will generally need to live in near-campus housing, because most PSE institutions have not yet considered how to provide adequate housing supports to nontraditional students. Although many colleges are now more equipped to house a student with a personal assistant, on-campus housing is generally reserved for full-time matriculated students. Some colleges may make exceptions and provide accessible housing to nonmatriculated students, but a request would need to be made through the school's DSS office.

Although providing housing for nontraditional students may not be standard practice, informed students and families can advocate to create these opportunities on college campuses. DSS providers and college administration may be resistant to this increased level of accommodation, and thus the goal of advocacy would be to educate university personnel about the "otherwise qualified" status of the individual with ID based on the student's commitment to academic study. Institutions may have already provided campus housing to other nonmatriculated students under special circumstances and may not have considered this possibility for students with ID. Moreover, to be considered "otherwise qualified" by the college to live in the residence halls, a student with accommodations must be able to take care of him- or herself and meet the requirements of community living, which includes following the student code of conduct. The logical accommodation in this case would be a personal assistant, funded by the individual or a service agency, who helps the student function in the college community. Again, the important step before approaching the university would be to establish postsecondary student goals and the appropriate individualized supports. The student, in conjunction with his or her IEP team and family, must assess whether residential living is a good fit. For some students, living at home or in an off-campus supported living situation may be a better option.

The advantage to living in campus housing is threefold. First, it is a monitored community environment. Living with a large number of students in a community offers increased social opportunities and planned activities. Participation in campus activities can increase quality of life and build a sense of confidence about social processes. Second, the structured environment of the residence halls offers a more gradual transition to independent living. When they live on campus, students eat in the dining halls and are not responsible for meal preparation. Third, the residence halls are generally more secure than off-campus locations. Residential life staff members are available to assist with problems and crisis situations.

On the other hand, on-campus living requires a higher standard of behavior. The student code of conduct is strictly enforced, and students are expected to function independently in the community living environment. Schools may or may not have the ability to offer a living arrangement that supports a personal assistant comfortably in the residence halls. At some colleges, newly built residence halls are equipped with a two-room suite that would allow for a personal assistant to live in an adjoining room with an individual with a disability. Current thinking tends to focus on this arrangement as a support for individuals with extensive or complex physical and/or health-related needs. However, families and nontraditional students should ask administrators about the possibility of using these living accommodations for students with ID.

Another consideration that cannot be overlooked is that students are initially assigned to residence halls based on survey information and sometimes academic major. The goal is a close-knit community that is active on campus and provides a healthy environment. However, in some cases the community may not be healthy. This could be due to conflict in the hall, an antiestablishment philosophy among some students, or a focus on a party atmosphere as opposed to a community atmosphere. There is no way to gauge in advance the possibility of negative influences or to ensure a nondiscriminatory, inclusive, and welcoming environment. Generally, residential staff can establish a sense of openness to differences among students. Asking the residence hall staff about their approach and philosophy will give families a better sense of the quality of the living environment for an individual with ID.

In some areas, adult services agencies may provide alternative residential options (e.g., supported living services). Such residential options can offer an active and open environment to facilitate independent living for young adults with more extensive support needs. When these residences are staffed appropriately, students can learn independent skills for cooking, cleaning, and self-management under supervision. Students are near campus, they can participate in campus programs, and they can benefit from activities scheduled in the house. The oversight agency—often a state agency, a nonprofit organization, or a grant-funded university program—will provide the staff training but also may strongly influence the goals and agenda for the individuals who are supported.

Off-campus housing is also always available through direct contract with local landlords. The student will still have the opportunity to participate in campus activities but will not have built-in community supports or programs. When there is no university affiliation, students and families must arrange for personal assistants and create a living environment specific to the needs and desires of the student. A personal assistant can serve as an educator in the independent living areas of meal preparation, cleaning, house maintenance, and self-management, as well as assist with access to campus-based activities. In this case, the student and the family designate the goals and parameters for the personal assistant.

Working with Faculty

Fifteen minutes before class, a few students have already settled into their seats in the large theater-style lecture hall where the course, Evolution of Popular Music, 1950–1980, is held. Bill and Peter (nontraditional, dually enrolled students who are informally auditing a class for the first time) arrive right on time, followed by a paraeducator who is acting as an education coach. Because this is the first college academic experience for Bill and Peter, their sponsoring program has asked her to provide eyes-on supervision while they learn the ropes. She finds a seat in the back row near the door while Bill and Peter locate seats several rows farther down. By 8:00 am, when the class is scheduled to begin, more than 50 students have arrived, and a couple more quietly slide into seats after the lecture is under way.

The professor opens the class by loudly broadcasting a popular guitar riff from his computer. His lecture today includes information about the Beach Boys and their predecessors and ends in the middle of an explanation about how the Beatles influenced popular culture. In between he discusses musical terms and instruments, playing and recording techniques, historical events, and cultural trends. His lecture is punctuated with brief audio clips and diagrams on the chalkboard. Throughout the class, he projects a list of the day's topics onto a large screen at the front of the room.

Like many other students, Bill has a notebook with him. Some students are writing in their books; some, including Bill, are not. Other students are typing or playing games on laptops. Some students sit attentively and others occasionally doze. The paraeducator listens to the lecture while reading a paperback book, unobtrusively monitoring Bill and Peter's participation. Bill and Peter are attentive for most of the lecture and at least once raise a hand to answer a question. Although this time another student was called upon, the professor later explains that Bill has answered a question in the past. When the professor concludes the lecture and dismisses the class, Bill and Peter leave with the other students, indistinguishable from them in their appearance and demeanor. They meet the paraeducator in a nearby courtyard where students gather.

The instructor of this popular music course has become a new ally in an informal network of people in the campus community who are open to the possibilities of PSE for students with ID. Because of this informal auditing experience, the instructor learned that including Bill and Peter in his lecture course was easy, and he and the colleagues with whom he interacts are more likely to welcome other students with ID into their classrooms. Taking into account the typical concerns of faculty members and becoming knowledgeable about helpful strategies and resources increase the likelihood of a successful experience for both faculty and students.

A primary concern of faculty is maintaining the integrity of the course being taught. Especially when a course is part of a degree program, instructors want to ensure that the content meshes with other required courses and meets the overall goals of the program. Instructors may be required to teach specific content and grade students according to set standards. A student may not be permitted into a course unless prerequisite coursework has been completed or knowledge of background material is otherwise demonstrated. To ensure that the course's integrity is maintained for all students, faculty or programs may require students with ID to take placement or ability-to-benefit tests to prove they are ready to meet academic expectations.

If a student is taking a course to earn credit toward a degree, and prerequisite testing is required, then it must be successfully completed (with appropriate accommodations, if needed), and learning the essential content to the required standard is the basis upon which the student is evaluated. Continuing education students who participate in these courses are expected to meet the same standards and conduct themselves in the same manner as degree-seeking students. However, students who are taking a course on a noncredit basis as part of a nontraditional program may be able to negotiate access by speaking with the instructor individually. Likewise, instructors of courses that are not part of a degree program often have more flexibility in designing the course content and standards and may be more open to tailoring some elements of the course for individual students.

Students who are interested in a course but do not wish to be evaluated or receive a grade can audit a course. Students must still register for the course, which will appear on their transcripts but will not count for credits. Students who audit a course must talk with the instructor to determine the instructor's expectations for attendance, participation, and assignment completion. Another alternative is to informally audit a course, as was the case with the popular music course. Such an arrangement depends entirely on the goodwill of the instructor, and no official record of the student having taken the course is kept. Before pursuing an informal audit, it is important to consider the long-term career goals of the student. The lack of documentation could be a disadvantage if the student needs to demonstrate mastery of course material.

When approached by the transition program liaison about whether he would be open to having students informally audit his course, the professor imposed the conditions that Bill and Peter could participate on a space-available basis and that they would not submit assignments or exams, which would have created additional work for the instructor. In addition, the instructor was assured by the transition program liaison that Bill and Peter would be attentive students and would in no way detract from the conduct of the lecture-style class sessions. The demands for student interaction were low, which suited Bill and Peter, who were able to sit quietly for the duration of the lectures. Had the class been one that involved frequent group work, the instructor probably would have wanted some assurance that Bill and Peter could manage the student interactions independently. Additional issues could have arisen had in-class group work counted toward individual student grades.

A minor problem arose when Bill and Peter arrived for class one day when a test was being given. The instructor had used the classwide e-mail system, which only recognized registered students, to switch an exam date. Because they had not known how the professor communicated with students outside of class, they missed some important information. The problem could have easily been avoided by asking the professor (or a fellow student) at the beginning of the semester for information about how the professor communicated with students outside of class, and then developing an alternative for Bill and Peter. A clear understanding of the course content and standards, the behavioral expectations for participating students, and the communication methods used by the class can help nontraditional students negotiate entrance into a course and maintain satisfactory participation.

Some faculty members may suggest that students with ID do not have the ability to benefit and therefore should not participate in a college course. Ultimately, such a decision is not one the faculty member can make for any student. If students—with or without disabilities—meet the institution's requirements for course participation in accord with their status (e.g., matriculated, continuing education, nontraditional), then they must be given access to the course. Another concern that faculty members may have is whether accommodating students with disabilities will increase their workload. Because students with disabilities have not participated in PSE in large numbers, some faculty members have limited experience with accommodations. They may wonder if they will have to spend extra time making changes to lectures, activities, or tests. They may worry that an accommodation will disrupt the classroom environment or force them to change their teaching style. They may not be informed regarding the availability or role of DSS personnel on campus. Students can help to demystify the situation for instructors by becoming knowledgeable about the purpose of their accommodations and being able to explain in plain language how they work. Approaching the instructor in advance to offer information, including documentation from and contact information for the DSS office, will give the instructor an opportunity to ask questions and seek additional support if needed.

Providing information about an accommodation does not mean disclosing to the faculty one's disability label or diagnosis; doing so is not necessary or recommended in most cases. Faculty may be unfamiliar with disability terminology, or they may have misconceptions about disabilities. Both factors are more likely to raise barriers to postsecondary classrooms than to lower them. Staff supporting students with ID who are participants in nontraditional campus programs/options may be tempted to educate faculty members about disabilities in the hope that increased knowledge will lead to greater acceptance. Instead, we suggest an alternative approach that is more closely aligned with faculty interests. Explain why the course is of interest to students, how it relates to their academic and personal goals, and the mechanisms available to help students attain their goals.

Finally, when selecting a course or selecting between instructors for a particular course, students should tap into their informal social network of other students and faculty allies to identify instructors who have a reputation for flexibility and openness. These instructors create classrooms that are accessible and engaging to many students—not just those with disabilities—by using a variety of teaching methods to help students understand ideas and offering different opportunities for students to demonstrate what they know and can do. This approach may have developed over time as an instructor experimented with more flexible modes of teaching and learning. Or some instructors may have received training on universal design principles and practices.

Teachers who use a universal design approach assume that they will have students with diverse abilities and interests in their classrooms, and, accordingly, they plan multiple ways to represent important concepts to students, engage students in the learning process, and allow students to practice and demonstrate what they have learned. For example, the popular music instructor often played audio clips to supplement his verbal explanation of a musical technique, created graphic organizers on the chalkboard to help students understand the connections among the topics being discussed, and then referred students to web sites where they could hear other examples and read more about scholarship on popular music. Another professor, who taught an introductory communications course, made it possible for students to videotape their draft oral presentations and receive supportive feedback from peers and the instructor. A universal design approach does not completely eliminate the need to accommodate individuals, but it does increase the likelihood that improving access to learning is in the foreground of the instructional planning process rather than an afterthought. The following are web-based resources related to universal design in higher education:

- *Equity and Excellence in Higher Education* is designed to increase access and participation in college courses for all students, including those with disabilities (see www.eeonline.org).
- *DO-IT* serves to increase the participation of individuals with disabilities in challenging academic programs and careers (see http://www.washington.edu/doit/).

- *FacultyWare* provides examples of how college faculty can enhance access to learning (see http://www.facultyware.uconn.edu/UDI_examples.htm).
- *CAST* (n.d.) has a variety of online professional development resources for teachers at all grade levels (see http://www.cast.org/pd/resources/index.html).

Engaging Peers without Disabilities

Nate and Delia present their identification cards to the desk attendant in the lobby of the university sports center, where students and employees can take advantage of a variety of fitness activities. Delia is an undergraduate majoring in health sciences with a minor in disability studies. She responded to an advertisement from Nate's parents, who were willing to pay someone to serve as Nate's personal coach during his fitness workout twice each week after school. Inside the fitness center, Delia signs them in and they proceed upstairs to the cardio machines. It is a little before 3:00, and there are only three other people using the machines; two are reading while pedaling or walking on the machines. A popular music radio station is playing in the background. Nate chooses to start on an elliptical, which Delia programs for him. She stands to the side while he works out, offering occasional prompts and encouragement, such as "Remember to breathe." As Nate finishes on this machine, Delia records on his workout log what he has done and resets the machine for the next person. Nate gets a drink of water from the fountain and then selects another machine, a bike. Again, Delia programs the machine and coaches him as needed— she tells him to "go slow" when he accelerates too much, or to "sit up straight" when he slouches. Another person chooses the bike next to Nate's, glances at him, puts on some small earphones, and begins his workout. Nate continues quietly until the time on the machine runs out.

After a little more than 30 minutes on the cardio machines, Delia models some leg stretches and Nate follows her lead. Then they go downstairs to use the weight machines. The weight room is also uncrowded. Two co-workers chat while using the machines, and an attendant works in the small office near the entrance. For the next 20 minutes Nate works on five different machines. He has favorites and knows the order in which to use them. Each time Delia sets the weights and provides coaching as needed to ensure he is using proper form. Nate appears to be listening to the music, nodding his head in time with a song playing in the background. When his workout is done, Nate exits the fitness center, gets a soda from a machine in the hallway, and meets his father in the parking lot for a ride home.

Delia and Nate's relationship is an unusual one on campus. Not many students have a personal trainer! Although the arrangement may not be typical, Nate now has access to the campus athletic facilities with a same-age peer—rather than a parent or teacher—and he has established a relationship with someone who shares his interest in exercise. He is also attaining his personal fitness and recreation goals. This story points to an interesting challenge encountered when young adults with ID become part of a campus community that has little experience incorporating them into student life, academically and socially.

Like other new students, students with ID may need assistance navigating the new world of the campus and making academic and social connections with like-minded students. Unlike other students, they may need additional or more intensive supports to establish and maintain those connections (Hart et al., 2006; Neubert, Moon, & Grigal, 2004). Depending on the nature of their secondary schooling, they and their peers without disabilities may have had limited opportunities for reciprocal social relationships, or they may have been participants in peer buddy programs where their roles were defined in ways that were relevant to high school academic settings. In a college environment, what are the goals and possibilities for academic and social relationships with peers? How should supports be configured to maximize engagement, inclusion, and reciprocity?

One obvious approach is to take advantage of the same peer supports and activities as other college students. For example, students who want more academic help join peer study groups, do homework with a study buddy from class, and find peer tutors through the college's academic enrichment or DSS offices. Students who want to expand their social life attend college-sponsored student-life events, go to campus activities fairs, join hobby or special-interest clubs, and contribute to service organizations. Natural supports can be used to facilitate instrumental activities as well. For example, Ramona had to rely on her school district for transportation to the child care course she was taking because there was no public transportation from her home to the college campus. She felt that using transportation from her school district made her stand out, but she felt she had no choice. At the close of the first week of class, she became friends with another student in her class who drove to the college campus daily and happened to live near Ramona. Ramona coordinated her schedule with this classmate so she could drive with her to campus, which she did for the remainder of the course.

Some programs designed to increase engagement of young adults with ID on college campuses have supported these interactions by providing facilitators, who may be paid professionals affiliated with the program or volunteer peers recruited from the campus community by the program staff or by parents of youth with disabilities (Grantley, 2000; Greenholtz, Mosoff, & Hurtado, 2005; Neubert et al., 2004; Saloviita, n.d.). Personal assistants paid for by the person with a disability or their family and peers without disabilities may also facilitate access to activities. In Nate's case, family members contacted faculty members whom they knew advised students with interests in disability studies and special education. The faculty then shared information about the opportunity with their students.

The insertion of a paid or volunteer support person into the social equation requires attention to the same issue that arises when paraeducators, job coaches, or personal assistants are present in school, employment, or community settings—how to provide an appropriate level of support in the least intrusive manner (see, e.g., Giangreco, Edelman, Luiselli, & MacFarland, 1997; Rogan, Hagner, & Murphy, 1993). For example, assistants must consider the effect that their proximity to the student has on the likelihood that peers will engage the assistant instead of the student in a social interaction. Initially, an assistant may need to set the stage for a social interaction by starting an activity or conversation in which peers and the student can participate. But as quickly as possible, the assistant must step back from being an active element in the interaction. Assistants who hover too much run the risk of becoming the focus of the interaction, instead of the facilitator of the students' own relationships. Likewise, assistants need to ensure that peers direct questions and conversation to the student and that the student has the opportunity to speak for him- or herself.

College students may have observed personal assistants on campus who help individuals with physical disabilities, or they may have noticed individuals taking notes for a person with a disability. They are less likely to have experience interacting with assistants in social situations, however, and they may be reluctant to ask questions. The young person with the disability or his/her facilitator should be prepared to offer information and do so in a way that establishes the young adult with the ID as a peer who has academic and social goals in common with other students (Grantley, 2000; Greenholtz et al., 2005). Thus before a facilitator is brought into the process, some thought must be given to the goals of facilitation for the individual student, the role of the facilitator in various campus settings and situations, and plans for actively developing natural supports wherever possible.

Another method for increasing interaction among students with and without disabilities on college campuses, especially in the context of dual enrollment, is to work collaboratively with faculty and students who have a professional interest in disabilities. At the University of Delaware, for example, undergraduates and graduate students have worked with students participating in the campus-based transition program, through independent studies or regular courses, in research, and as peer mentors. These activities have included teaching a student the skills necessary to reach a vocational goal, adapting a goal attainment strategy for use by students with significant support needs, developing a community resource map for a student about to exit school, and regularly accompanying a student to the gym. Although we have seen benefits for students with and without disabilities, the danger in this approach is that the student with the disability may be perceived as a project rather than as a peer. At least one inclusive PSE program has intentionally avoided these situations for that very reason (Greenholtz et al., 2005).

Administrative and Logistical Concerns

In many respects colleges and universities operate like businesses; however, the structure of the administration and faculty tends to be decentralized. Because of this it is important to understand that the communication patterns and information flow at individual institutions will vary. DSS offices can be closely integrated into campus functions, or they can be run under the radar and work on a case-by-case basis with each department. This decentralized approach can be a benefit or a hindrance. University offices can work from a personal and one-on-one approach to solicit the supports needed to establish a program for a student with ID. However, without a strong and universal commitment to students with disabilities established across the campus, communication can break down and negative and restrictive attitudes may be encountered. To understand how this may play out on a college campus, it is important to review some of the reactions, attitudes, or myths that may be common to the administration or the faculty.

Maintaining Image and Rigor

First, presenting an elite or inviting image to incoming students and families may be a factor for some colleges. There may be a perception that having students with ID on the campus will negatively affect the image of the institution. There will be those administrators and faculty who do not see the benefits of an inclusive environment and will want these programs to be more hidden, strictly out of fear over the institution's image and reputation.

The administration may also share the concerns of some faculty that the provision of services to students with ID on campus will bring scrutiny to the academic rigor of the campus programs. The ADA is specific in stating that modifications that alter a fundamental or integral piece of the curriculum are not reasonable. Therefore, the rigor of the curriculum should not be affected. Students who receive a grade and traditional credit for the course will be held to the academic standards set by the faculty. However, when a course is audited, the student and the educational coach or program coordinator have the option of determining the standards of achievement, as the instructor will not be issuing a grade on assignments or exams.

Faculty and administration can be assured that their participation in campus programs for students with ID in no way jeopardizes the integrity of the curriculum, but in fact allows the courses to reach more diverse populations. Although they are more available at 2- and 4-year state institutions, postsecondary options for students with disabilities are offered at many highly regarded colleges and universities. These programs offer opportunities to nontraditional populations and do not detract from opportunities provided for students without disabilities.

Students without disabilities come to institutions of higher education with varying levels of experience with individuals who have disabilities. Inclusive education in elementary and secondary schools is becoming more common. As such, the image of a university that offers an inclusive opportunity to individuals with ID will be familiar and, in many cases, positive. Institutions that offer undergraduate programs in education will undoubtedly have a core group of faculty who acknowledge and articulate the benefits of an inclusive classroom. Colleges may receive positive press and accolades for their contributions made to the local community by promoting access to postsecondary education for underserved and traditionally underrepresented student groups, including those with disabilities. As families explore the fit between a college and their student's goals, they may want to ask administrators about the level of knowledge regarding the benefits of an inclusive and diverse campus. A strong commitment on the part of program administrators, DSS office staff, and participants in other significant programs on campus and the knowledge they bring to bear can offer a buffer between the student and negative perceptions held by the campus community.

From an administrative standpoint, there may be a degree of fear about the institution becoming disability friendly. If the institution builds a reputation for being proactive, responsive, and inclusive, this may draw more students with disabilities than the college feels prepared to manage. In some cases, accommodations for students with disabilities can be costly, and the administration might fear that recruiting more students will mean more expense. Students with ID, however, do not generally require costly accommodations that the university would be responsible to pay for. In most cases, it is personal assistants or education coaches who incur the most costs, and they are not usually the responsibility of the university. In addition, with the ADA now in place for more than 15 years, colleges in general have more accessible buildings and require less retrofitting. For example, at the University of Delaware, as new construction and building renovations have been completed in the last 15 years, most of the buildings are accessible and would require only a few modifications should an individual with a significant disability need architectural changes to provide access. Buildings that are currently not accessible house mostly administrative functions that could be moved if needed. In addition, most students with multiple disabilities who need extensive supports tend not to go out of state to school, so in most cases those students would have been attending the school regardless of the disability friendly reputation. As families and program coordinators advocate for access to PSE for individuals with ID, it is important to continue to emphasize the level of accommodations needed and the distinction between university-provided accommodations and those provided by the families or state agencies. In many cases, the university-provided accommodations are easily achievable and low cost.

Space Concerns

Campuses have space constraints as well. With limited space on campus, there may be resistance to designating office space for noncollege staff involved with nontraditional dual enrollment. Although space will always be an issue on college campuses, knowing how nontraditional programs are articulated and structured can alleviate this concern. Helping administrators to understand the benefits of such options for both the university and the community can positively change this outlook. Specifically, land-grant institutions, which most state universities are, include service to the community as part of their mission and may be more open to sharing space with their program partners. Because space constraints may be an area of concern for nontraditional programs, families will want to see how these constraints have either limited programs or forced more creative approaches to service provision. Some campuses have offered comprehensive, integrated programs with very limited space. One local school district, as an example, at the University of Delaware, preferred to have a home base where students and their instructors could meet and where school administrators could contact students and staff for dissemination of information. When space was not available on campus, the school district rented two apartments one block from campus to creatively address this need. For those implementing an inclusive individual support model, space is less of an issue, because there is no need for a dedicated classroom space. The DSS office can serve as a point of contact, and cell phones can be used to communicate about students' daily schedules and supports.

SUMMARY

Not unlike students without disabilities, students with ID and their families must seek the right institutional fit for their postsecondary goals, inquire about traditional and nontraditional campus opportunities, find allies, and create social networks on campus. Importantly, they must know their rights and responsibilities under ADA and Section 504 and be willing to work with DSS providers and other professionals on campus to educate the campus community. Some pertinent topics and questions that families and individuals with disabilities may want to consider when pursuing PSE are suggested in Table 5.3.

Table 5.3. Checklist for students and families exploring postsecondary education options

---

What are my goals for participating in a postsecondary education program?
Completing a certificate or degree
Paid community-integrated employment
Community navigation
Taking college courses (credit and continuing education)
Auditing courses
Social opportunities with other college-age students
Participation in specific campus activities or facilities
Independent living through a residential experience
> On-campus housing
> Near-campus group living home
> Near-campus apartment living
> Living at home

What types of postsecondary education options are available at each institution that I am considering?
Public or private
2-year community college or technical college
4-year institution
Adult education programs

What accommodations should I request or find?
Academic accommodations
Reader, scribe, interpreter services, physical access, assistive technology (FM systems/ computer software for text-to-voice access to books and/or internet information), books on CD, other adaptations
Other nonacademic supports
Job coach, education coach, personal assistant, life coach

Who are potential allies on campus?
DSS provider
University Center on Excellence in Developmental Disabilities
Disability-friendly faculty, administrators, staff members, and departments
Professional and student groups with an interest in disability issues

How can I fund my postsecondary education?
School district programs
IEP identified services
State and local agencies
> Eligibility requirements for agencies
> Timelines for eligibility with the state agencies
Federal student loan and work-study programs
Nonprofit grant opportunities
Grant opportunities at local institutions
Private loans
Part-time work
Personal savings

(continued)

Table 5.3.   Checklist for students and families exploring postsecondary education
options *(continued)*

Other questions to ask about nontraditional program options
What services or programs are offered on campus specifically for students with intellectual
    disabilities or for other underrepresented groups?
What department oversees those programs?
How large is the program staff, and what are its functions?
Who determines eligibility for the program?
What is the status of students in nontraditional programs on campus?
Do students have full access to campus facilities and activities?
What types of activities does the campus offer that would be of interest to the students?
What is the physical layout of the program?
Where is it located on campus?
What types of transportation are available to and from the campus?
How integrated is the program into the university community?
Is the DSS provider familiar with the program and the needs of the students within the
    program?

Preconceived attitudes regarding PSE for young people with ID may still exist among the administrators, faculty, staff, and students at any university or college. As more students with ID pursue a postsecondary experience, institutions
of higher education will become more practiced with educating and accommodating students with disabilities, and more research findings on outcomes associated with students' postsecondary experiences will become available. As a result, one can expect to see a national shift to more positive attitudes about the
value of PSE for students who previously have had limited access to higher education. Education is the key to changing attitudes.

REFERENCES

AHEAD. (2004). *AHEAD best practices: Disability documentation in higher education*. Retrieved
    July 3, 2007, from http://www.ahead.org/resources/bestpracticesdoc.htm
American Association of Community Colleges. (2007). *Facts 2007*. Washington, DC: Au-
    thor. Retrieved June 5, 2007, from http://www2.aacc.nche.edu/pdf/factsheet2007_
    updated.pdf
Americans with Disabilities Act of 1990, PL 101-336, 42 U.S.C. §§ 12101 *et seq.*
Association of University Centers on Disabilities. (2006). *Expanding postsecondary and em-
    ployment opportunities for students with intellectual disabilities through the Higher Education Act.*
    Retrieved June 5, 2007, from http://www.aucd.org/docs/policy/post_sec_ed/Fact_
    Sheet_%20on_Higher_Ed_Amends_5_06_07.doc
CAST. (n.d.). *Professional development resources*. Retrieved October 8, 2007, from CAST: Uni-
    versal Design for Learning web site, http://www.cast.org/pd/resources/index.html
College Board. (2006). *Trends in college pricing*. New York: Author. Retrieved June 5, 2007,
    from http://www.collegeboard.com/prod_downloads/press/cost06/trends_college_pricing_
    06.pdf
Family Educational Rights and Privacy Act (FERPA)of 1974, PL 93-380, 20 U.S.C. §§ 1232
    et seq.
Giangreco, M., Edelman, S., Luiselli, T., & MacFarland, S. (1997). Helping or hovering?
    Effects of instructional assistant proximity on students with disabilities. *Exceptional Chil-
    dren, 64,* 7–18.

Grantley, J. (2000). *Towards inclusion in university of people with intellectual disabilities.* Paper presented at the International Special Education Congress, University of Manchester, United Kingdom. Retrieved June 5, 2007, from http://www.stepsforward.homestead. com/R12ISEC2000FlindersUniversity.html

Greenholtz, J., Mosoff, J., & Hurtado, T. (2005). *STEPS Forward: Inclusive post-secondary education for young adults with intellectual disabilities.* Paper presented at Society for Research into Higher Education, University of Edinburgh, United Kingdom. Retrieved July 18, 2008, from http://www.stepsforward.homestead.com/Research/SRHE_Greenholtz_ STEPS_2006.pdf

Hart, D., Grigal, M., Sax, C., Martinez, D., & Will, M. (2006). Postsecondary education options for students with intellectual disabilities. *Research to Practice,* no. 45. Boston: University of Massachusetts, Institute for Community Inclusion. Retrieved June 5, 2007, from http://www.communityinclusion.org/article.php?article_id=178

Higher Education Opportunity Act of 2008, PL 110-315, 122 Stat. 3078.

Hughson, E.A., Moodie, S., & Uditsky, B. (2006). *The story of inclusive post secondary education in Alberta: Final research report 2004–2005.* Edmonton: Alberta Association for Community Living.

Individuals with Disabilities Education Improvement Act of 2004, PL 108-446, 20 U.S.C. §§ 1400 *et seq.*

National Institute for Literacy. (1998). *Disability & literacy: How disability issues are addressed in adult basic education programs: Findings of a national focus group.* Washington, DC: Author. (ERIC Document 427187)

Neubert, D., Moon, S., & Grigal, M. (2004). Activities of students with significant disabilities receiving services in postsecondary settings. *Education and Training in Developmental Disabilities, 39*(1), 16–25.

Newman, L. (2005). Postsecondary education participation of youth with disabilities. In M. Wagner, L. Newman, R. Cameto, N. Garza, & P. Levine (Eds.), *After high school: A first look at the postschool experiences of youth with disabilities* (pp. 4-1–4-17). Retrieved June 5, 2007, from http://www.nlts2.org/reports/2005_04/nlts2_report_2005_04_complete.pdf

Rehabilitation Act of 1973, PL 93-112, 29 U.S.C. §§ 701 *et seq.*

Rogan, P., Hagner, D., & Murphy, S. (1993). Natural supports: Reconceptualizing job coach roles. *Journal of The Association for Persons with Severe Handicaps, 18*, 275–281.

Saloviita, T. (n.d.). *An inclusive adult education program for students with mild to severe developmental disabilities: A pilot project in Finland.* Jyväskylä, Finland: University of Jyväskylä. Retrieved June 5, 2007, from http://www.steps-forward.org/Research-Finland.html

U.S. Department of Education. (2004a). *Career/technical education statistics (CTES): Postsecondary /college level tables.* Washington, DC: National Center for Education Statistics, Integrated Postsecondary Education Data System. Retrieved June 5, 2007, from http://nces.ed.gov/surveys/ctes/tables/index.asp?LEVEL=COLLEGE

U.S. Department of Education. (2004b). *Undergraduate enrollments in academic, career, and vocational education* (Issue Brief, NCES 2004–018). Washington, DC: Institute of Education Sciences. Retrieved June 5, 2007, from http://nces.ed.gov/pubs2004/2004018.pdf

U.S. Department of Education. (2006). *The guide to federal student aid: 2007-08.* Retrieved June 5, 2007, from http://www.studentaid.ed.gov/students/attachments/siteresources/ FundingEduBeyondHighSchool_0708.pdf

Zafft, C., Hart, D., & Zimbrich, K. (2004). College career connection: A study of youth with intellectual disabilities and the impact of postsecondary education. *Education and Training in Developmental Disabilities, 39*, 45–53.

Student and Family Perspectives

Amy Dwyre, Meg Grigal, and Janice Fialka

For years families of students with intellectual disabilities (ID) have heard the refrain, from their doctors, their teachers, and sometimes their relatives and friends:

> Your son or daughter can't . . .
> *Expect to have a normal life.*
> *Learn.*
> *Go to his or her neighborhood school.*
> *Get a job.*
> *Learn to use a bus.*
> *Live independently.*

And for every *can't*, these family members have remained resilient and have persisted with determination and lots of hard work and have proved again and again that their child can achieve all of these things. It is just this kind of determination and vision that has recently provided so many students with ID with another unforeseen accomplishment: participation in a college experience. Students with ID and their families have often been the sole initiator of many of the innovative programs and services that have been developed to serve students with ID in postsecondary settings over the past 10 years across the country (Grigal, Neubert, & Moon, 2001).

These parents and students, along with supportive and equally committed and visionary professionals, have created opportunity where there once was none. And now these opportunities have been expanded in many areas to become part of the continuum of services in special education. Yet, this path is still one of uncertainty, one that is not available to all students and their families, and one that requires a good deal of planning to negotiate successfully.

This chapter provides a guide to these paths, through insights from students, families, and professionals who have traveled this nearly uncharted territory. It also provides an overview of what historically have been the outcomes for youth with ID, what motivates anyone to go to college, the potential outcomes and pitfalls of students with ID going to college, the changing roles of families, and ways to navigate the process. Throughout the chapter, there are snapshots of students we have worked with over the years, along with tools and tips from students and families who have gone through this process to help others who are ready to take the next step toward a postsecondary education (PSE) experience.

189

PLANNING FOR THE FUTURE: WHAT THE RESEARCH SHOWS

Students without Disabilities: Endless Options

Imagine the lives of typical 17-year-olds. They are preparing for their senior prom and graduation. They are reviewing their prospects for college with their families and getting help with filling out all the applications. Or maybe they are getting ready to enter the military, or start a full-time job. Their families are proudly telling people at church or synagogue, in the grocery store line, at work, about their children's leap toward independence and their impending life adventures. They and their families are looking forward to the new challenges and adventures ahead and are feeling excited, hopeful, proud, energized, and a little anxious as they prepare to launch into the next big phase of their lives.

What Are the Typical Outcomes for This Population of Students?

The average student without disabilities graduates from high school with a diploma and moves away from home (60%) and then either goes directly into a job or the military or enters college (68%)—a 2-year community college, a 4-year higher education institution, or a trade school. As young people pursue any of these options, their main goals are to determine the kind of job they want and then set out to obtain that job. The result is that 79% of adults without disabilities have part-time or full-time jobs (Blumberg & Ferguson, 1999).

Students with Disabilities: Limited Options

Now imagine the lives of typical 17-year-olds with ID. They are possibly preparing to return to their high school—potentially for the next 3 years—while they watch their peers graduate and move on. If they have been included in general education classes, they will now be the oldest in many of their classes and will likely not be provided with an array of new learning experiences. If they have been served in a self-contained setting, they will likely return to it and more often than not have the same teacher for another 1–3 years.

Many students with ID remain in school until they are 21 years old, but some do not. What are the expectations for those who do leave? Often they leave high school with the prospect of either having nothing to do at home or perhaps attending an adult day center with organized activities only for people with disabilities. If they are especially lucky, they will eventually receive help finding a job, or keep the one they had during school. In any case, for any supports that they do need, they will now suddenly have to be deemed eligible for them. They are no longer *entitled* to receive disability services, but now enter the insecure world of adult *eligibility*. They and their families are likely to be overwhelmed, confused, and probably a little helpless as they attempt to maneuver through rough roads ahead in an entirely new system: the world of adult services.

What are the typical outcomes for students with ID after secondary school?

Students with ID typically have not been included in regular education classes. In fact, nationally, in 2002–2003, as presented by the U.S. Department of Education, less than 11% of students with ID were fully included in regular education classrooms (Smith, 2007).

All too often, as students with ID age and move from elementary to middle to high school, their level of inclusion diminishes. Beyond high school only 11% of students with ID attend any postsecondary education, which is the lowest percentage of any of the disability categories (National Longitudinal Transition Study-2 , 2003a). Looking at the larger, more general population, the Bureau of Labor Statistics of the U.S. Department of Labor (2008) reported that in October of 2007, 67.2 percent of high school graduates from the class of 2007 were enrolled in colleges or universities. In terms of employment after high school, according to the National Longitudinal Transition Study-2 (2003b), 58.6% of youth with ID have had some form of a paid job in the two years after exit from high school; this is the 2nd lowest percentage of all disability categories researched, with only youth with autism having a slightly lower percentage for the same finding. These data demonstrate that the population of youth with ID have fewer experiences in both postsecondary education and employment, as compared to other disability categories and youth in general.

Along with working less, only 37% of youth with disabilities are in some independent living situation 5 years out of school, as compared with 60% of the general population. And finally, youth with disabilities report a much higher level of social isolation after high school than the typical adult without disabilities (National Organization on Disability, 1998; U.S. Department of Education, 1996, 1999).

What does this mean? That the different expectations for youth with and without disabilities lead to different outcomes. What are recognized as viable options for the average student are still not presented as expected options or outcomes in the planning process for those students with ID, and therefore the systems are often not in place to help this population of youth to achieve what the typical youth does. Instead, there is roadblock after detour after gridlock. This is particularly true for the option of college.

I have a younger brother, Patrick, with ID. My parents fought hard for him to be included in general education classes and social activities while in high school. They encouraged him to get job experiences. They began planning for ways for Patrick to live away from Mom and Dad. They were often considered the "Problem Parents." They began raising their own expectations slowly, and Patrick began rising to them. Unfortunately, the rest of society—and Patrick's service providers in particular—did not. He exited high school, walking the stage with all his general education peers, and then he came home. For months, he waited until his service providers finally placed him in a sheltered workshop, where he was bored and as a result started developing inappropriate work habits and imitating other participants' bizarre behaviors at the workshop. As my mother fought to get him in competitive employment again, she was told that he clearly was not ready and referred back to the inappropriate behaviors—which my mother then pointed out he had only developed recently as a result of this terrible placement. It had become a vicious circle. It took many, many appeals for new service providers and many months of an uphill battle to get Patrick out of the workshop and doing something far more productive and enjoyable for him. Was this the exception to the rule? Unfortunately, this scenario is closer to the typical family experience than not.

—Amy Dwyre

Students with Intellectual Disabilities: New Options

Transition services for students with ID in college settings—community colleges, private 4-year institutions, technical and trade schools, or state universities—provide an alternative to the scenarios described above. Students can use the experiences they gain in these settings in a variety of ways:

- To build their independence
- To achieve their transition goals in a setting that is socially valued
- To learn with their age-appropriate peers
- To achieve their goals and learn in a typical, integrated community environment

In many instances, however, there are few services that offer these opportunities to students with ID. Often the students and their families have to be the catalyst for creating programs and services in postsecondary settings. The challenge in planning for the future—for both families and systems—includes understanding the options available beyond the typical expectations (most often the road less or rarely traveled), how to match goals and desired outcomes with appropriate services, and then how to make it all flow smoothly.

THE INFLUENCE OF EXPECTATIONS

The issue of expectations is influential, because expectations guide the paths of professionals, families, and the students they support, particularly as they work together to plan a student's future. As families and students with ID expand their expectations to include college, it is important for them to be aware of some of the pitfalls and roadblocks that await them.

Low Expectations

Sadly, our history of supporting individuals with ID is riddled with many examples of low expectations. The family of coauthor Amy Dwyre came face to face with this when her brother Patrick was born in 1970. Her parents were told that they should consider institutional living arrangements for Patrick, because the doctors never expected him to walk or talk. As they gathered more information about Patrick and his needs, they realized they needed to adjust their ideas of what to expect for their son. But rather than expecting Patrick to not do things, they learned to expect him to do things *differently*. With that frame of mind, and with much perseverance and untiring persistence, they sought out the services that would help Patrick learn to do things in the best way he could do them. Throughout his life, rather than saying no to things Patrick wanted to do, they asked how? So luckily for Patrick—who lives away from his family, has hiked the Grand Canyon, gone scuba diving in Hawaii, skied in Utah, has had several jobs he's loved, in addition to being a nonstop talker—his family did not take that initial advice from the doctors to heart.

> *Our daughter Katie was only six days old, and with tears in our eyes we uttered to the pediatrician our wish, that we be able to help her lead a life with dignity, while giving her the most independence possible. This conversation with the pediatrician was filled with his professional advice, mainly stressing the limitations for our daughter and how we were to now lower our expectations. She would never be able to lead "our kind of life," he uttered. Before the time Katie was one year old, even our relatives felt we were illogical for not understanding our daughter's limitations.*
>
> —Paulette Apostolides, mother of Katie, who attends Aloysius College and happens to have Down syndrome

Even with the strides in the field of special education and inclusion, and with numerous families proving their pediatricians wrong year after year, the idea of a young person with ID going to college is still not commonly accepted; it is still not an expected route for most students and their families.

In addition, according to a report from the National Longitudinal Transition Study-2, youth with disabilities in general are much less likely to be expected by their families to continue their education after leaving high school—only 62% compared with 92% of their peers in the general population (as calculated from the 1999 National Household Education Survey for 13- to 17-year-olds). In fact, only 36% of these parents expected their sons or daughters to complete a 4-year college program, as compared with 88% of parents of general education students. And not surprisingly, the type and severity of disability determined parents' levels of expectations, with the highest level of expectation for PSE enrollment from parents of youth with speech/language, visual, or hearing impairments, and the lowest level of expectations from parents of youth with intellectual or multiple disabilities, autism, or deaf-blindness (Newman, 2005).

Changing Expectations

In order for the college experience to become a reality for young adults with ID, expectations need to be changed on a variety of levels. Training and technical assistance (TTA) on the various PSE options and the potential for positive student outcomes could be used to change these expectations. Ideally this kind of TTA would be available to:

- Pediatricians and other medical personnel who often dispense advice to families at the earliest stages
- Professionals in school systems who coordinate key special education and transition services

- Families and students, so they can understand the wide spectrum of PSE opportunities available
- Community Service Providers, who should be natural partners in the development of these options
- Personnel in PSE institutions, such as community centers, adult learning programs, community colleges, and 4-year colleges and universities, who will be receiving these students into their educational communities
- Legislators and policymakers, who are responsible for supporting the best interests of everyone—including people with ID and their families—in this venture

Raising Expectations

In recent years, parents of students with ID and other low-incidence disabilities have indicated a growing interest in their children's participation in a college experience. Grigal and Neubert (2004) found that when asked to choose their most desired outcome for their children, given the choices of community college, 4-year college, military, part-time work, supported employment, and segregated workshop, 36.2% of parents of secondary students with low-incidence disabilities, including those with ID, desired a 4-year college, and 21.7% desired a community college. These findings demonstrate that parents' desires for their children with ID are now reflecting some of the changes we see in practice. However, desire alone is not enough to make a college experience possible. There also need to be opportunities and clear expectations on the part of the student and family members.

> We had to first and foremost listen to Micah's dream to go to college. He has always lived IN the community and participated in the same classes and activities as his peers. Thus, he internalized the same expectations as his peers had: that is, after high school you go to college. It is just what you do in our community! It never dawned on him that he wouldn't go to college. We also had to listen to [Micah's] dream initially without worrying about how we would make this happen. If we started with the barriers and the unlikelihood of his going to college, we would have stopped dead in our tracks. We had to always be guided by Micah's dream. Our mantra became "It isn't if he would go to college, it is how he would go to college." This didn't mean that we knew what we were doing or how to make it happen. We really had no idea about the first steps to get Micah to college. But we had to create the vision and move toward it.
>
> —Janice Fialka-Feldman, talking about her son Micah,
> who attends Oakland University in Michigan

In our society, when someone says "college student," a certain profile or image comes to mind for most people: hard-working, goal-oriented, smart, organized, and independent, among other things. The profile seldom includes an ID. There are people of all ages, characteristics, intelligence levels, and motivations in college settings. For parents of children with ID who want their child to go to college, it is important that they recognize the skills, characteristics, and desires of their children and how these may or may not match with the college experience.

The Issue of Motivation

The first thing that parents of students with ID who express a desire for their kids to go to college hear is "You're crazy! They can't do that!" But looking beyond the possibility or impossibility of a youth going to college, families need to understand their own motivations—and their child's—for going to college. This issue is not limited to families of students with ID, as all of us know a friend whose parents pressured him or her to go to college. And we all know a friend who went for the wrong reasons and it didn't work out. In order to create the most successful experience possible, families and students with ID and the people who are supporting them throughout the transition process need to have honest conversations about motivation.

Parent Motivation

It is very important, in fact, almost necessary, for families to be supportive of their children going to college in order for them to be successful—*if* going to college is what the young person *wants* to do. Parents need to ask themselves *why* they want their child to go to college. There are many common reasons why parents want to see their sons and daughters go off to college that are not related to the degree achieved or job obtained. Some common motivations include:

- Personal dreams: They have always wanted their child to go to their alma mater.
- Personal history: Because they went to college.
- Family history: Because an older sibling went to college.
- Pride: They want to talk about their child's college choice, because going to college represents a certain social status in our society.

There is nothing wrong with parents wanting their child to go to college. However, in order for a child to succeed in college—regardless of the existence of a disability—that child must want to be there. Parent motivation without student motivation makes it a difficult journey for everyone involved.

Student Motivation

Students also have varied reasons for wanting to go to college. Many know that they are destined for college at a very young age and are encouraged to think so by their parents. Others may have less certainty because of the struggles they have faced in high school, financial concerns, and an overall feeling of not knowing what they want to do with their lives. College is often a time when students, allowed for the first time to define their own experiences, try out different potential futures. But to do so, they first must clear that initial hurdle of wanting to go to college. For students with ID, being motivated to participate in a college experience may be difficult, because often these students have limited experiences from which they can draw an understanding of what college is. For other students with ID, it is the goal they have always wanted to pursue.

Students with ID may require some time, support, and repeated visits to a college to help them conceptualize what going to college means. Students should be provided with opportunities to meet with other college students to ask questions about their experiences. Providing students with ID a chance to think about what they might want to get out of a college experience will affect their motivation and allow them to better participate in setting up goals for that experience.

Although a lack of motivation can be based upon a lack of experience, it can also be a true reflection of a student's feelings, and this needs to be recognized by both family members and the transition support personnel who are assisting in planning. If a student does not have any interest in participating in a college experience, it is likely that if forced to do so, he or she will not succeed. It is important that families and school personnel have frank discussions with students about their motivation to ensure that the transition goals for students are truly reflective of the students' desires.

> *It was during the [early] years of Katie's education that we all wanted to give up, start down the traditional path of special education, and make life "easier" for our beautiful daughter. Yet, by not giving up and by struggling through many tears (Katie's and mine) we learned immeasurable lessons that would take us through the next 15 years of education and into her adult life. Lesson number one: Have high expectations and provide proper supports to reach Katie's goals. In "Mommy terms" this means treat Katie as a normal child first and support her special needs accordingly. She needed to learn how to behave in a classroom, work hard, take personal responsibility, and hear her inner voice to reach her true goals. Seems to me, these are lessons one continues to pursue throughout life.*
>
> *School for Katie was something she enjoyed and excelled in. Katie's work ethic allowed her to gain respect from even the most skeptical teachers along the way. Regular education teachers learned to forget the disability and teach to the child. During the difficult middle-school years, Katie began showing her independence and speaking her mind. Within the first year of high school, Katie announced to her parents that she was going to a REGULAR college and we had better get ready. She began taking the college prep classes at her high school, where, much to everyone's amazement, she continued to excel. There were classes that required extra team effort and math adaptations to accomplish. Yet, she persevered and grew more driven each year. In her second year of high school we insisted on meeting with the REGULAR guidance counselor to address her college choices and were told that all special education students were handled through the special education department. Not one special education student, in the entire history of her school, had ever worked in the traditional sense with their guidance counselor. This was about to change.*
>
> —Paulette Apostolides

COLLEGE: A NATURAL ENVIRONMENT FOR TRANSITION

Going to college: What does it mean? The most common first reaction is: Going to college means getting a degree. Period. But looking beyond this basic answer, we realize that the college *experience* is where many young adults learn the skills they need to be successful adults: How to manage time, how to balance work and social activities, how to get around new places, how to meet and interact with new people from different backgrounds, how to set goals and pursue activities to help achieve those goals, how to make decisions, how to navigate various uncharted paths (registering for classes, joining clubs, choosing dorms, applying for work, getting a student identification card, understanding the cafeteria, library, student center, etc.), how to ask for help and tell people what is needed, and many more, less tangible outcomes. Ask anyone who went to college if he or she can remember test scores or paper topics. Although some individuals might be able to resurrect that information, most people would likely draw a blank. However, if you ask people to talk about what they learned in college, you would likely find that these same people can talk for hours about all their great experiences, the friends they made for life, the new things they tried, and even the mistakes they made. These memories often reflect the real learning that occurs in college: life lessons. In this respect, like so many others, the college *experience* is not different for people with ID.

The college experience can be meaningful to students with ID in a variety of ways. Particularly significant is the opportunity to connect newly learned skills and information to real-life adult outcomes. When a student with ID decides to go to college, it is important for all of the parties involved to think about the elements of the college experience that are most vital, interesting, suited, and available for that student and what the outcomes of those experiences will be. For parents of young adults, college is a nice stepping-stone to the adult world. All parents want their children to become independent, happy, contributing citizens in the real world, and to branch out on their own. Yet, at the same time, it is difficult to suddenly let go, particularly after 17 or more years of hands-on monitoring and support. A college environment provides an ideal setting for transitioning into the adult world, with built-in supports, mentors, checks and balances, authority figures, rules and regulations, a subset of the real world to help build a sense of self, hone skills, and create some focused goals for the future.

Transition Goals Met at College

College campuses offer the opportunity to positively affect three important variables for successful transitioning into the adult world: employment, social networking, and postsecondary learning. With a basic foundation in these three areas, a student with ID can start out on the road to becoming a successful and independent citizen in the world beyond high school and special education; these are the building blocks for cultivating independence.

The Impact of College on Employment

All young people need to be prepared for work in the 21st century. A study by Ochs & Roessler (2001) compared career development levels of 95 special education students and 99 general education students, both with optimistic career outlooks. Unfortunately the special education students scored significantly lower on career decision-making efficacy, career outcome expectations, and career exploration intentions, showing that the special education students were either less prepared or had lower career expectations—or both. In addition, according to Dawn Rosenberg McKay (2006), the U.S. Department of Labor says that workers between the ages of 18 and 38 change jobs an average of 10 times. Yet all too often it is assumed that a young person with an ID who gets an entry-level job will stay at that job for many years. In fact, this situation is often applauded as a success story. In reality, many young people with and without disabilities do not know what they want to do as a career when they go off to college. In fact, from 1997 to 2001, the percentage of college-bound high school seniors who took the ACT college placement test and were undecided about their career path jumped from 9.6% to 11.1% (*ACT News Release*, 2001). They spend the next 4 (or more) years learning about things that interest them, developing a network, changing their minds, and gaining knowledge to help them discover a career— a way to get paid well for doing what they enjoy. Young people with ID are no different. With the chance to learn about new things that interest them, their opportunities for meaningful work multiply.

One thing that families and students need to discuss together throughout the transition planning process and when approaching a postsecondary experience, is to what extent are their goals related to employment. What type of career does the student want to pursue? The answer to this question can be simple or complicated, depending upon a number of variables.

Career Exploration in High School

Has the student experienced any form of career exploration while in high school? If a student has not had the opportunity to discover a variety of career options— through job-site tours, informational interviews, job shadowing, and so forth— he or she may have no tangible experience upon which to base a career area of interest. In that case, an employment goal would start with career exploration. This would include several steps:

- Completing a career interest inventory to find out in general what the student likes to do
- Locating people and places throughout the college campus and community related to those things the student likes to do
- Exploring, observing, and trying out the jobs related to their interests

Work Experience

Has the student ever worked before? While in high school, some students have the opportunity to have work experiences. This may be in the form of in-school jobs, work trial experiences at preset work sites, or paid jobs in the community. Depending on the level of experience—or if a student has had no work experience—an employment goal might be to develop work skills, and this might occur through internships or volunteer positions with the support of staff.

Differences between High School and College

How is college different from high school when it comes to employment? What can a college- or community-based experience offer in the area of employment that high schools cannot? There are a number of ways that a college experience can positively support and enhance career opportunities for students with ID.

Expanding Networks

The expanded networks of new situations and people that are available to the students on college campuses can lead to a wider, more diverse variety of experiences, and therefore open the door to more career opportunities. Social networks in general can positively affect a person's employment situation, even for people with ID (Eisenman, 2007). An example of this is shared in Snapshot A: Rodney, which demonstrates how one student transformed his love of photography into a paying job at a 4-year university in Connecticut through his expanded social network.

Snapshot A: Rodney
Rodney** was a young man with ID who participated in a local education agency (LEA)-sponsored dual-enrollment program on a state university campus and who was interested in photography. Through people he met on campus, he became involved with the campus newspaper. Rodney was given several photography assignments, which were published in the newspaper, and he was eventually listed as a staff photographer. By his second year on campus, this same young man left the dual enrollment program and enrolled directly in classes at the university. As a part-time undergraduate student taking courses for credit, Rodney was then eligible to work for pay on the campus newspaper. Rodney was elected photographic editor for two cycles and continues to hold this university-paid position, with hopes of pursuing photographic journalism as a career in the future.

Expanding Learning Opportunities

Another way that a college- or community-based experience can support a student's employment goal is through the learning environment and course offerings. In high school, the focus on reaching graduation and standardized testing requirements can often limit the selection of classes. There is little opportunity to take classes for personal interest. Postsecondary education offers students with and without disabilities the chance to take courses that are related to their interests. These courses may give them insights into a career area, arm them with basic skills to enter a career area, or build upon existing skills to help them advance within a specific career area. Snapshot B: Manny and Snapshot C: Julia illustrate how two students changed their job opportunities by accessing a class.

**All student names mentioned in case study snapshots have been changed.

Snapshot B: Manny

Manny** was a young man with ID who was receiving services in a college-based program. Manny was working at a local grocery store in the deli department. He enjoyed working at the store, but was not especially fond of working with meat and using cutting machines; he wanted instead to work in the bakery department. However, there were no entry-level positions available. With support from his college program, he investigated the evening adult learning courses offered through a partnership between the community college and the local public school system. He found a two-part cake-decorating series that resulted in a certificate upon completion. After completing the course and receiving the certificate, he was able to approach his supervisor at the grocery store—demonstrating not only his interest and skill level, but also his commitment to his own career growth—and was hired onto the bakery staff at a level higher than entry level. He now had a job he enjoyed, and earned more money as well.

Snapshot C: Julia

Julia** was a 20-year-old woman with ID in a community college-based dual-enrollment program. Her career interest was child care, but her only real experience had been babysitting siblings and cousins. Because this was a very competitive field in her community, she was finding difficulty getting a job as a child care aide. The community college she attended offered a child development certificate program, and with support she began exploring some of the classes that were offered within this program. Julia audited a different class within that program each semester and enrolled in a first aid course offered by a local community center. Although she did not receive the child development certificate, as she was auditing the courses, she was now able to present herself to employers as someone who was learning related skills, had completed first aid, and was an eager and committed potential employee. Julia was able to get a job as a child care aide at a local child care center. Her goal is to continue to audit the child development courses until she feels ready to take them for credit, and she will eventually achieve the certificate and be able to advance within her company.

Both of these examples show that being part of a larger community beyond high school opened the door to new opportunities that led directly into interesting career areas. Research has shown other positive employment outcomes related to postsecondary experiences.

A study in Massachusetts (Zafft, Hart, & Zimbrich, 2004) compared the outcomes of 20 students with ID who had PSE experiences with 20 similar students who had no PSE experience. The results showed that 100% of the students with PSE experiences who were working were in competitive work environments in the community, whereas only 42.9% of their cohorts who were working were working competitively; the majority were in noncompetitive or sheltered settings. In addition, they found that 66.7% of the students with postsecondary experience used no work-related supports (such as a job coach) to do their jobs, whereas only 28.6% of those with no postsecondary experience needed no work-related supports. And in terms of rate of pay, no student with postsecondary experience worked below the rate of $6.75 per hour, whereas several students with no postsecondary experience were either performing piecework and earning $.50 per hour or earning $4.10 per hour. This study shows that PSE experience potentially positively affects work settings, level of support needs, and rate of pay.

In PSE settings, students with ID can develop and pursue career goals through the people they have met and the resources they have accessed. They can access courses to enhance their careers through promotions or job changes. Given access, opportunity, and support, students with ID can have increased confidence and control over their employment outcomes.

The Impact of College on Social Networks

Another significant opportunity afforded by a college experience is the ability to develop and expand a social network—not just in numbers, but also in terms of diversity. Recall that statistics show that high school graduates with disabilities report a high level of social isolation once they exit school and usually participate in activities meant only for other people with disabilities (National Organization on Disability, 1998; U.S. Department of Education, 1996, 1999). This is the reality for the typical youth with ID, but it seems just the opposite occurs for the average college student. Suddenly, in college, young people are exposed to all types of peers with varying personalities, cultures, backgrounds, experiences, and values. There are planned activities all over campus with the goal of bringing college students together socially, both formally and informally. There are places on campus that exist for the sole purpose of allowing students to get together and "hang out."

No More Labels

Once a young person's social network expands, his or her identity can also expand and change. For many students with ID, college may be the first chance they have had since entering public education to *not* be defined by their disability. The college community, full of nontraditional students, can be the great equalizer. It is host to people of all races, academic levels, and religions, who come from a variety of different communities, cultural backgrounds, and family statuses. Diversity is welcomed. Given this access to a new identity and social network, young people with ID who previously may have relied solely on paid support staff to assist them in accessing transportation, receiving help in a class, purchasing materials, and so forth, may have access to natural forms of adult interdependence—friends helping out friends, peers supporting each other. And simply being a part of that community represents a certain status and recognition and can lead to a boost in self-confidence, as it did for Rhonda in Snapshot D.

Snapshot D: Rhonda
Rhonda,** a student with ID at a college program based at Johns Hopkins University in Baltimore, was waiting for a bus as part of her mobility

training with a program staff member. They were with several other Hopkins students, one of whom the young girl had met in the office where she interned on campus and who had agreed to accompany her on the campus bus until she learned the route herself. As they were waiting, a young man from her former high school showed up at the bus stop and recognized her. He asked her what she had been doing, and Rhonda responded that she goes to Johns Hopkins University. He did not believe her, so Rhonda pulled out her Johns Hopkins student identification card, and introduced him to her friend, a philosophy major from the Philippines. The young man's disbelief turned to amazement, and Rhonda's pride and confidence swelled. This was a young girl who was known in high school for being so shy she was almost considered nonverbal. That was the last day staff rode the bus with Rhonda; she asked her staff person not to come anymore, as her friends would help her out from that point on.

The Natural Social Environment at College

There are many opportunities for natural social interactions to occur on college campuses. The earlier example of the young man in Connecticut who now works for the campus newspaper all started when he met another young man in a class he was auditing who happened to work at the paper. Because he knew this person, he felt comfortable enough to approach the newspaper staff and ask about positions. This is an example of classic peer-to-peer networking. But not all students—with or without ID—have the skills, experience, or confidence to be able to do this type of networking and must learn to initiate and maintain social relationships on their own.

> One time I was asking my social worker, Kim, about finding people to do activities with me on campus. I thought it would be nice to have a peer to do to things with instead of my parents. She said we should make a flyer to put all across campus. Kim and I worked together to make the flyer. I interviewed five people a week later. She and I talked about what the people might do with me and thought it would be best to choose one boy and one girl.
>
> It felt strange to have a helper at first, so I talked to my parents about it. After a couple weeks I felt comfortable and I was having fun. Nate and Amanda helped me with my homework and drove me home from school sometimes. They also took me to events on campus such as basketball games, club meetings, hip-hop aerobics, and community services events. I got to experience a wide variety of things on campus. This helped me meet more people on campus and make many friends. I became more excited about college and it made my college experience better. I felt more like a real college student.
>
> Nate and Amanda also hung out with me off campus. When we weren't working on homework or going to events, Amanda and I went shopping for clothes, saw movies, got dinner or coffee, and went to the bank. One

time Amanda and I went to International Night on campus. We had fun learning about all of the cultures and trying all of the different foods; we even ate sushi. Also that night we joined the Polish Club. Nate and I went to concerts and played basketball. I even got to spend the night at his apartment. It helped me learn what I had to do in life outside of school and how to be more independent.

I also learned how to be a boss. I had to sign Nate and Amanda's time sheets and if I made a mistake they would not get paid. I had to be able to tell them what I wanted to do and explain myself clearly.

A year and a half later, Amanda is still helping me. I got Amanda to go to the student leadership retreat, but Amanda got me involved with Up 'til Dawn, a campus-wide fundraiser for St. Jude's Children's Research Hospital. We sent letters to friends and family asking if they would donate to St. Jude's. I really liked it because I was helping people who are sick. At the letter-writing party in 2006, I, with Amanda's help, sent out 113 letters and was able to raise $500.

In the fall semester Amanda arranged for me to show my film and PowerPoint to all of the sororities on campus. Because of this I met Sarah and Jamie, and they are my new friends. Jamie and I have lunch together sometimes and just talk and hang out. I have a class with Sarah and she is my peer tutor. I am happy that I was able to become friends with Sarah and Jamie, and they have told me they are happy to become my friends too. Also, Sarah, Amanda, and I are all joining Alpha Phi Omega coed community service fraternity. Some of the goals Amanda and I are working on right now are managing money, shopping for and preparing food, and increasing my reading skills.

—Micah Fialka-Feldman, Student at Oakland University in Michigan

Teaching Social Skills on a College Campus

Research has shown that the ability to interact socially with peers is an important skill associated with success in the real world—including maintaining employment (Andrews, 2005; Butterworth & Strauch, 1994). Therefore, developing social skills in PSE settings is an important goal for students with ID and can and should be supported by staff and families. Students with ID may need the chance to role-play or practice handling unfamiliar situations as illustrated in Snapshot E: Barbara. Because of the adult nature of the college environment, families should have frank conversations about how to cope with the potential presence of drugs and alcohol on campus. Students may need a specific time set aside to discuss how they are feeling about their social interactions. Some PSE programs employ social workers or counselors to hold group sessions to discuss issues related to social issues and relationships. Other programs ask peer mentors to work individually with students to help them better navigate the social realms of college. There are a number of techniques that have been studied to help teach students social skills and competence, such as developing task lists that break down the steps to introducing oneself, role playing, repetition, and simply creating opportunities for social interactions to develop where they may not have naturally (Sukhodolsky & Butter, 2007; Chadsey-Rusch, 1990; Foxx & Faw, 1992). It is important to remember that each student has different support needs.

Snapshot E: Barbara

Barbara** was the program coordinator at a school system-sponsored, dual-enrollment program based at a community college in Baltimore. She realized that during the week, when she was around to help facilitate social interactions, her students were doing quite well at developing new networks. But when they were away from her program—during the weekends or time off—the students were not initiating their own social lives. As a result, she developed planning cards related to various social events. For example, she helped some students develop movie cards that they kept in their wallets or purses. These cards included step-by-step instructions—sometimes written, sometimes using pictures or symbols—on how to pick a movie, find theater locations and times, call a friend, locate bus lines and times, discuss where to meet the friend, figure out the cost of a movie and food, and how to get home safely. During the week Barbara and her staff would practice with the students, reading movie and bus schedules, paying for purchases, learning what words to use to ask for a soda, and so forth. Role playing and practice with the cards were enough to help many of her students initiate their own evening out with a friend.

How Families Can Help

How can families support their children in expanding their social networks? In the scenario above, family members could work with their children to make sure they are reading the schedules correctly, or that they have enough money to participate in a planned activity. Families could also help with transportation, which can be a big barrier for students with ID participating in social events (Grigal et al., 2001). At colleges, many of the social events with other students—concerts, sporting events, plays, and so forth—take place in the evening. If students have difficulty getting back to campus in the evening because of limited transportation, they cannot take advantage of these social opportunities. Families that are able to provide or help to arrange transportation to and from social events on campus will help their child access additional opportunities for social networking. Encouragement and praise from home as well as from school can also help students feel more confident and willing to try out new social activities.

THE IMPACT OF COLLEGE ON LEARNING: A NEW VIEWPOINT

As was mentioned earlier, a significant difference between high school and college is the motivation for learning, as well as the types of learning available. Whereas high school learning is often driven by tests, standards, and credit requirements for graduation, postsecondary learning can be more reflective of personal interests. This is the first time, for many students with ID, to discover that learning can really be fun and that it can have meaning in their lives. For students with ID in college, simply the act of taking a college course may not have significant meaning. But understanding the *process and reason for* taking a course—understanding one's own interests, finding a class that matches that interest, learning how to enroll and pay for a class, figuring out how to get to the classroom, learning to schedule activities around a class, learning how to ask for help throughout, and simply knowing that this whole process is possible and desirable—is a huge life lesson and the first step to realizing that learning does not end with high school. Now these students have the tools to practice lifelong learning that can lead to personal enhancement, career enhancement, new skills and hobbies, and a new network of friends.

Students with ID, like everyone else, may wish to take a class for many reasons: They are interested in trying something new, they want to improve a skill they already have, they want to learn something that is related to a career goal and may help them get a job (or get a better job), or they want to experience something just for fun. Here are a couple of examples of students we have worked with and their very different reasons for wanting to take a class:

- Shannon** wanted to become healthier and lose some weight, so she enrolled in a nutrition class and took aerobics.
- Keisha** enjoyed babysitting and wanted to branch out to babysitting kids who were not just her relatives. She took a CPR/first aid class in order to have something extra to offer potential clients, and maybe charge a little more per hour.
- Nathan** wanted to work in an office setting because he enjoyed the environment and dressing nicely. He took several keyboarding and computer skills classes to improve his chances of getting a job in that field.
- Kerry,** who loved theater but never had the chance to perform in high school because of her use of a wheelchair, was able to take a theater course. In that class, she not only got to watch videos of performances and other students' performances, but she was given the chance to perform herself. She also made a number of friends who were all interested in theater, and she went to several performances on campus with that new group of friends.

Each of these students received some kind of support to be successful in his or her class, including

- being paired with a student mentor during class time
- receiving an assignment in a different format
- reviewing text with a tutor between classes
- using a map of the campus to locate a classroom

In all of these cases, the students ended up surprising others and themselves with how well they performed and how much they actually enjoyed what they were learning. Tip Sheet 6.1 offers some strategies for helping students to prepare for a successful experience.

TIP SHEET 6.1

HELPING YOUR CHILD PREPARE TO SUCCEED IN COLLEGE: THINGS STUDENTS AND FAMILIES CAN DO TO GET READY FOR THE COLLEGE EXPERIENCE

1. Become knowledgeable! By having a clear idea of what to expect, families can better prepare their children.

   We had to research what was happening. We wrote e-mails and letters to leaders in the field asking them what they knew about college for students with cognitive disabilities. We attended workshops at national conferences. We met with friends who taught at the local university and discussed Micah's dream.

   —Janice Fialka-Feldman

2. Be a part of the person-centered planning team. Families know their children better than most and therefore can give invaluable input into goal-setting for their child, offering their own support and ideas for other effective supports that will lead to success. In addition, it is important for families to learn about additional skills, talents, and characteristics of their children that may not be exhibited at home but are expressed with teachers and friends.

3. Begin planning for college early. Many families of students with ID do not expect PSE for their child. When it is an expectation as a potential option, there are a number of action steps that can be taken while students are still in middle school or earlier that will help the process along:
   - Encourage academic courses—The more experience a student has in academic class settings, the more prepared he or she will be for college settings.
   - Start financial planning—There may be several options for funding the college experience, from being supported by the local education agency (LEA), to accessing local, state, and federal financial aid and disability-specific (vocational rehabilitation, etc.) programs. Families need to research all possibilities early on.
   - Get in on the IEP transition plan early—Both the student and school personnel need to see college as an option in order for proper preparations to be made.

4. Visit colleges and look through course catalogues together—If a student has done this comfortably with family members, it won't seem so strange to be on a college campus later. Anything a family can do ahead of time to take the strangeness or newness out of the experience will make the transition easier for the student later.

5. Understand your child's disability, how it affects them, and the accommodations or supports that best help your child to succeed—and then make sure your child knows all this as well. Practice with your child in describing the disability and asking for supports. The more practice they have early on, the easier it will be for them to be a self-advocate in the college environment, where it is expected of them.

PAVING THE WAY TO INDEPENDENCE

For most young people going off to college, this is the first real step toward independence. Even if a student is not living on campus and may still be living at home with family, college students have much more individual responsibility, control over their schedules, freedom to explore, and a whole new level of opportunities afforded to them. In order to do all this successfully, young people—with and without disabilities—need to develop self-determination skills.

Self-determination and Postsecondary Education

Self-determination skills have been well documented as being an important attribute of transition planning (Agran, Snow, & Swaner, 1999; Eisenman & Chamberlin, 2001; Wehmeyer, Agran, & Hughes, 2000) and more recently have been correlated with successful postsecondary experiences for students with disabilities (Getzel & Thoma, 2008; Jameson, 2007; Thoma & Wehmeyer, 2005). Two of the most frequently used definitions of *self-determination* in the field of special education are:

> Acting as the primary causal agent in one's life and making choices and decisions regarding one's quality of life free from undue external influences or interference. (Wehmeyer, 1992, p. 305)
>
> The attitudes, abilities, and skills that allow a person to define personal goals and to take initiative in reaching those goals. (Ward, 1988, p. 2)

College environments are much like small communities. They provide many opportunities to spread one's wings, yet because of their organization and structure, they provide some safety nets for students. This combination makes them an ideal environment to help students with ID hone or even master their self-determination skills. The experiences of many students with ID in the world of public school special education are often very insular and protected. Public school special education may address the behaviors and interactions expected in adult settings, but there are few opportunities to actually practice these skills in the environments in which they will be occurring. Being a part of a college community, and all that it involves, can provide students with ID the chance to practice a variety of skills in real-life circumstances.

Students with ID, like all other college students, learn how to

- Determine their own schedules
- Choose their own courses appropriately—matching interests, skills, and time availability
- Manage free time—where to go, how to meet new people, how to safely get around a college campus alone
- Ask for help when it is needed from instructors, disability support services personnel, tutors, employers, and friends
- Solve problems
- Describe needed accommodations

Just as the experiences and responsibilities of these young people change, so do those of their families. As all children in families leave one phase and enter another, it is important to remember that the family members have to adjust to the changes as well—including adjusting their perspectives, their attitudes, their level and types of interventions, and even their emotions.

The Changing Role of Families

For families, going to college is often the event that triggers a change in how they view a child. Suddenly, that child is seen as an adult, with new roles and new responsibilities. What is interesting is that this also must change the role of the parent from primary advocate to one of support and guidance. This is often hard for parents of the typical young adult, but it can be extremely challenging for parents of young adults with ID to make that distinction. Where once family members played the role of guardian, overseer, protector, and decision maker, they must learn to step back and support their child in taking more control. This may mean watching their child make new and different and potentially less optimal choices, and watching him or her stumble and learn to recover. The family continues to protect, but from a distance, and by guiding the student away from dangerous decisions rather than by making decisions for him or her. The earlier that family members move to a support role rather than a primary role as decision maker the better. This may sound like a subtle difference, but for parents who have spent their child's lifetime playing a very hands-on role, letting go can be extremely difficult.

Ask any parent who is about to send a child into a college experience how they are feeling, and surely they will have mixed feelings: pride, excitement, joy, and even relief, alongside fear, anxiety, nervousness, and uncertainty. Ask a parent of a child with ID starting a college experience, and these same feelings are merely amplified. Children who have been in special education programs for their entire educational career have often experienced much nurturing, hand-holding, security, and protection—and often segregation. Although these students learn about appropriate behavior and life skills, they do much of this in a somewhat sheltered environment. For many of these students and families, entering an experience in a college setting—even with the help of a school system—is the first step into the real world. And that is scary and risky.

The Dignity of Risk

The dignity of risk was a concept first introduced in the 1970s by Robert Perske (1972) and Wolf Wolfensberg. The term refers to how appropriate and reasonable risk taking can and should be worked into the daily living experiences of people with ID. "Many of our best achievements came the hard way: We took risks, fell flat, suffered, picked ourselves up, and tried again. Sometimes we made it and sometimes we did not. Even so, we were given the chance to try. Persons with special needs need these chances, too" (Perske, 1972, p. 26).

Risk can be defined as "potential peril," "danger," and "jeopardy"; but risk can also be defined as the basis of opportunity, such as "taking a gamble with the hopes of a favorable outcome" (www.wordnet.princeton.edu, *Webster's New*

World Thesaurus). Taking calculated and prudent risks is the way most people learn. The sense of uncertainty about the exact outcome of a venture is what gives us pride and a feeling of accomplishment when the result is favorable. And when a failure does occur—one that does not involve physical harm or danger—we learn life lessons and how to adapt. Everyone who goes to college is exposed to uncertainty and the unknown. With more responsibility, freedom, opportunities for making choices, and control over daily schedules—all that was discussed earlier as the potential benefits of college—comes risk. For those students with ID, who have had fewer experiences and perhaps fewer skills in decision making and adaptability, the level of risk is higher. That is why the necessary supports and guidance must be built into the service provision of PSE experiences for students with ID. The harmful aspects of risk can be reduced by anticipating and preparing for potential pitfalls.

> When we tell the story of Micah's journey to college and in general his story to live inclusively in a world that has great expectations and opportunities for him, we are acutely aware that it is a story of risk taking—over and over again. It is a story of pushing the limits and stepping out of our comfort zone on a regular basis. If he, we, or the community around Micah did not take risks, did not allow him to try walking to school with a friend in fourth grade, did not allow him to have a speaking part in the school play (would he remember his lines?), or did not permit him to stay out until 1:30 am with a friend when he was 21 years old, then this would be a much different story—one I fear that would be less joyful, less exciting, and less meaningful. Every risk taken was well thought out, involved deliberation, discussion of the pros and cons, with a conscious plan to reduce danger. Every risk was founded on the principle that we must build community and connections every chance we have.
>
> There are no guarantees in life. Risk taking abounds. We don't know how things will turn out. Each family must determine their limits for risk taking. But we have learned certain fundamentals to this risk-taking business.
>
> What our family is learning over and over is that the more connections you make in the community, the more we reach out, the more living in the community we do, the greater the likelihood that responsible, kind people will come forth. Equally important is that by trying new things (with careful planning and deliberation) Micah has learned how to negotiate some complicated moments; he is often comfortable asking for help. He is better able to access his need for help. Micah walks more confidently and competently because he has tried new things, made some mistakes, reevaluated them with the support of others, and has succeeded in meeting many new challenges.
>
> —Janice Fialka

Managing the Risk

The key factor in controlling the level of risk for students with ID going off to college is uncertainty, and the uncertainty in a situation can be countered by the anticipation of potentially risky situations and a plan to address them. In order to fully prepare for a student to enter this new situation, all stakeholders in the student's life should be part of the planning process, including

- Family members
- The student
- School system personnel
- College personnel
- Other relevant community organizations

Each party must bring to the table all the knowledge they have about the particular student who will be participating in this new venture—including skills, interests, support needs, fears, and personality traits—and knowledge about the new environments the student will be entering into—including campus culture, code of conduct, activities, safe and unsafe areas, schedules, resources (or lack of resources), and locations. Because every student is different, individualized supports must be set up to minimize potential risks, such as

- Getting around campus safely and effectively
- Getting around the community safely and effectively
- Asking for help appropriately when needed (how and who)
- Learning to take cues in social situations

Some supports that have worked and are based on individual needs and abilities include such things as simple as a

- color-coded map
- cheat sheet of phrased questions
- checklist
- cell phone with programmed phone numbers and/or color coding

and as intensive as a

- one-on-one education coach, companion, or mentor
- structured and repetitive mobility training with a palm pilot, ipod, or picture charts

As illustrated in Snapshot F: Kai, with careful planning, potential risks can be managed and/or avoided, providing students with ID the opportunity to access new, challenging experiences, accomplish new tasks, and enjoy new freedoms while being safe.

Snapshot F: Kai

Kai** was a young man in an LEA-sponsored city college program who was learning to take public transportation for the first time. He could not read or write, and his speech was often difficult to understand. His family was very concerned that he would get easily confused or lost and would not be able to figure out a solution on his own. As a result of these concerns, many plans and backup plans were developed to make him and his family feel comfortable. Along with a regular map and photos of the route, he carried a prepared script of how to ask for help from a bus driver and tell that person exactly where he needed go. All of these supports were put to use on the day the bus was rerouted because of a water main break; Kai was aware he was going a different route because the scenery did not match his photos, and he was able to pull out his list of questions and ask the bus driver what he needed to do. Kai told us later he got very flustered, but he pointed to his question and the bus driver read it and made sure he got to where he was going.

With so many opportunities and potential outcomes offered by a college experience, planning and preparation for managing it all safely with the individual student's needs and desires in mind are essential for a successful journey. Support teams can help students and families safely plan for and achieve social, academic, self-advocacy, employment, and many other goals by focusing on student-centered planning with continual open communication and readjustment of goals and plans.

When my brother Patrick finally got out of the sheltered workshop, my parents fought hard for him to participate in a new, innovative program supported by the Los Angeles County School System. It was the radical idea of supporting a classroom of students with ID on a local community college campus. When Patrick finished his tenure at the Mt. San Antonio Community College in Walnut, CA—known locally as Mt. SAC—he had audited a variety of classes (including American Languages, Spanish, and several travel courses), worked at the Campus Inn bussing tables alongside other college students, and was trained on public buses and campus transportation to get to and from home and between classes and work on campus. They had a college graduation ceremony on campus with caps and gown in the college colors, and the keynote speaker for the day was Chris Burke, the actor who played Corky from the hit T.V. series Life Goes On *(it pays to be close to Hollywood!). According to my mom, this is where Patrick learned his work ethic, developed his self-confidence, and for one of the first times in his life felt proud to be just like everyone else. He now lives away from my parents in a group home, has been competitively employed for 10 years (including promotions and several pay raises), is an avid gambler and show-goer in Las Vegas, travels annually to the Grand Canyon or Hawaii (or both!), and has been dating the same woman for over 10 years. And if you ask Patrick today about all the things he has done in his life that are important to him or have real meaning, he will always tell you that he went to college.*

—Amy Dwyre

PLANNING A COLLEGE EXPERIENCE: GETTING READY FOR THE TRIP AHEAD

Determining what the college experience can offer your child is important, and it can vary, depending on the student's needs, desires, and skills as well as his or her choice of postsecondary environment. First and foremost, there must be supports in place to ensure the safety of students while allowing for independence and growth. Students must also have goals in place, and a plan to achieve those goals.

Person-Centered Planning

As the whole family heads down this new road of the college experience, everyone needs to be able to express their fears and concerns right alongside their expectations and desires. Lack of clear communication can lead to misunderstandings and can ultimately interfere with a student's success. For example, if a family has concerns about their child getting a job and they do not express those concerns during the planning process, a likely outcome is that a student will not be successful in getting or keeping a job.

Person-centered planning is an excellent way to gather input from all parties involved with a student's planning, as well as to discover a student's interests, skills, needs, values, and much more—all necessary elements in developing goals with a student. Person-centered planning (Garner & Dietz, 1996) can come in many forms. According to Cornell University's Person-Centered Planning Education web site (http://www.ilr.cornell.edu/edi/pcp/), person-centered planning is a process that helps to empower people with disabilities by focusing on their needs. It puts the person with a disability in the driver's seat, as opposed to letting available services and resources control the outcomes. This works most effectively when team and family members support the student in making personal goals happen. There are many approaches to person-centered planning, including making action plans, known as MAPS (Forest & Lusthaus, 1990); group action planning, known as GAP (Turnbull & Turnbull, 1992); planning alternative tomorrows with hope, known as PATH (Pearpoint, O'Brien, & Forest, 1993); Whole Life Planning (Butterworth et al., 1993); and the positive personal profile or PPP (Tilson, Cuozzo, & Coppola, 2001). No matter what process is used, the key elements include

- Gathering a group of key stakeholders to the person for whom the plan is being developed. This can include the individual, family members, friends and peers, school personnel, community members, neighbors, other service providers, and so forth. Just as we discussed the importance of all stakeholders assisting in risk management, it is just as important to include everyone in the overall planning process (Benz & Blalock, 1999).
- Regular meetings of the group or team to explore the individual's strengths, needs, interests, and skills
- Remembering that the individual is the focal person and is in control of the process
- The individual developing a plan of action, with the support of this group

A study by Miner and Bates (1997) found that increased parental participation and overall family satisfaction with the transition planning process occurred for those families who participated in person-centered planning. In addition, they found that families who did go through person-centered planning reported more preparation, and family and student participation in the overall process.

Snapshot G: Manny (continued)

Manny,** whose story about moving from the deli to the bakery is discussed earlier in this chapter, used the positive personal profile format (Tilson et al., 2001) to conduct his person-centered planning session. He and his family invited all of the key stakeholders, including school personnel, relatives, and friends, to come to a meeting at Manny's house. A facilitator guided these team members through a brainstorming session around a list of specific topics related to Manny, including his dreams and goals, his positive personality traits, his work environment preferences, and values (see Figure 6.1). They also addressed his challenges and possible solutions. From this brainstorming session, an action plan (see Figure 6.2) was developed to identify goals and ways to help Manny reach those goals.

Writing Student Goals

Because each student's interests, skills, and support needs are unique, each student accessing a college experience should have his or her own goals. Whereas for some the ultimate goal of college might be to develop career skills and get a job, others may be focused on other outcomes, such as expanding personal knowledge and skills, meeting others with similar interests, or determining future topics of interest. Manny and those supporting his planning initially chose three main goals that came out of his person-centered planning session; these were employment, PSE, and community participation. Each of his goals in these areas were relevant and specifically meaningful to his life. As students who are dually enrolled in high school and college leave the high school environment and begin a college experience, their IEP goals should be revised to ensure that they are appropriate to the new setting and potential outcomes. For example, an IEP goal of participating in the high school band or having a work experience in the high school front office are no longer relevant to the college campus setting and may no longer match a student's desired outcome for attendance in a college program.

NAVIGATING THE SYSTEM

Students with ID and their families seeking a PSE experience have different options based upon a number of factors: their age, where they live, the involvement (or not) of public school, and the kinds of services they are seeking. In some cases, going through the typical channels of application and admission may be possible, and in other cases, students and their families may need to seek an alternative path. As indicated in Chapter 3, there is a wide array of services and support for students with ID seeking PSE experiences throughout the country,

Figure 6.1.   An example of Manny's positive personal profile.

Positive Personal Profile
Name: Manny

Dreams and goals
- To move his mom to a better house
- To get a good job
- To get around the city himself
- To get married and have kids

Interests
- Cooking and baking; wants to work in a bakery
- Playing sports
- Watching TV or going to the movies with friends
- Listening to music on his headphones

Talents, skills, and knowledge
- Cooking and baking
- Detail-oriented
- Works hard and focuses on completing a task well
- Asks questions when he needs help
- Very friendly; good with customers
- Follows instructions well
- Playing basketball

Learning styles
- Interpersonal and linguistic
- Takes information in best if shown; once shown, a simple checklist is a good reminder
- Needs to go at own pace
- Enjoys working with others
- Slow and methodical, but final product is always good

Values
- Doing what you say you are going to do
- Doing things well, even if it takes time
- Being respectful
- Learning new things
- Hard work

Positive Personality Traits
- Has a great smile and connects with people; very gentle
- Focused on things he likes
- Autonomous; independent
- Problem-solver
- Is willing to take criticism and learn
- Perseveres

Environmental preferences
- Active environment
- Working with other people
- Prefers indoors mostly

Dislikes
- Being rushed
- When things are unfair
- Difficulty with reading; gets frustrated easily with that
- Being bored
- Where he and his mom live

Work experiences
- Volunteer position at a Children's Museum
- Volunteer at a local food shelter
- Deli counter at XYZ Grocery Store

Support system
- Mother
- Aunts and cousins
- Friends
- Teachers

Career ideas and possibilities to explore: local bakeries, family restaurants, grocery stores, movie theaters

---

and each of these may or may not be available in every locality. One of the first steps students and their families can take when seeking access to PSE is to determine *what* kind of services or program they are looking for and then determine whether it is available in their community. One of the first determining factors in this process will be whether the student with ID is still receiving services under the IDEA.

Figure 6.2. An example of Manny's action plan, developed as a result of his person-centered planning session.

Goal	Action steps/tasks	People responsible	Date
To get a job in a bakery	1. Investigate bakery positions at the grocery store 2. Find local bakeries that are hiring 3. Take a cake decorating course; locate affordable courses on a bus line	Manny, with help of mom and teacher	
Be more mobile in the community	1. Learn the city bus routes 2. Practice reading city map 3. Learn to take public transportation independently	Manny, instructional assistant, mom	
Meet new people	1. Investigate local clubs on campus and eligibility requirements 2. Role play introducing self to a new person 3. Practice calling a friend on the phone and asking him or her to go to a movie	Manny, college mentor, instructor	

Options for Students Aged 18–21 Still Receiving Services under IDEA

Local Education Agency-Supported Programs and Services

There are many different models and variations of PSE programs—each focusing on different goals and service delivery approaches—and not every program will be appropriate or match the goals and desired outcomes of every student and family. The first step for students and families is to understand their own needs, preferences, goals, and desired outcomes of a postsecondary experience; in other words, they should know what they want to get out of a PSE experience. Is the student looking for a full-time residential college experience or does he or she just want to audit a few courses? Once everyone is on the same page about the type of postsecondary experience they are looking for, families should research their options. Usually information about LEA-sponsored dual-enrollment options is provided to students and their families during the IEP meeting. In other cases, parents may hear about a PSE option through other parents or at a transition conference. Some school systems may have a variety of college-based options for their transitioning youth, whereas others may have only one option. Sometimes it will be a perfect fit—the goals match the student and family goals. Other times, parts of the PSE option match the student and family's needs and other aspects do not. In this case, the student and family need to work with the transition specialist or special education team and related LEA personnel to determine what adjustments can be made to better match the student's needs. For example, in Snapshot H: *Jose*, a compromise was reached between the family and school system that best matched the student's current needs and goals.

Snapshot H: Jose

Jose's** family was concerned that their son was not provided all the services he was entitled to under his current IEP, most importantly related to his transition from secondary school to adult life, including orientation and mobility training to travel from his home to the community college and then navigating the corridors of the college to his classes and then work. Jose began auditing courses at a local community college that would support his career goals of being a radio dispatcher for a taxi company or a disc jockey at a radio station when he was 19 years old and still in high school. He took a number of computer related and public speaking courses and simultaneously was supported in several job audit options and then two internships related to these employment goals.

He is a young man who is blind and who has an intellectual disability and as a result, needed a range of services and supports to be successful. These services included orientation and mobility training in new adult environments that Jose would participant in, and educational coaching and/or tutoring to be successful with his course work. Because he was still being served by his high school for services, he was eligible for a Free and Appropriate Public Education (FAPE) from his school district and had these services included in his Individualized Education Plan. To this end, his school district provided some of the related services, including orientation and mobility training, and educational coaching to support him in his academic courses and internships.

Providing a modified schedule, adjusting the level or frequency of supports available, or offering services in environments in which they will actually be used are some ways in which school systems can allow students to access currently available PSE services. In other cases, some school systems that do not have the capacity to support students in a college setting may partner with other local school systems to meet students' needs. For example, the Western Connection Program at Western Connecticut State University is operated by the Danbury Public Schools, but students from six other school systems access the program as an out of district placement. Another example is Massachusetts Bay Community College, which supports students with ID in accessing inclusive college courses and all aspects of college life. This PSE option is open to any student with an ID from any school district. That programs and services are not currently available does not mean that a student cannot access PSE; it means that other paths need to be pursued.

Local Education Agency-Supported Individual Support Model

Of the available PSE options, the inclusive individual support model is the least frequently offered. The ISM model often uses some type of a person-centered planning process (e.g., Whole Life Planning, 5 Bold Steps, PATH, MAPS) to assist the student in articulating a career goal and other goals for adult life. The goals are then used to inform the student transition plan if students are still in high school or their adult service plan if they are receiving adult services. The student's career goal helps guide his or her course selection and to identify needed supports for each student who is interested in going to college or pursuing some type of PSE education option. Then a variety of support services and funding sources (e.g., the local school system, vocational rehabilitation, intellectual disability/developmental disability agencies, one-stop career centers, and social security) are combined to provide the student's needed supports in college, employment, and the community at large. The curriculum consists of the experiences that students have in the college and the community: learning how to maneuver throughout the campus, taking public transportation, registering for and participating in courses, and solving problems as they arise. The student, their family, the school district, IHEs, and/or adult service agencies may elect to implement this inclusive approach to supporting students with ID in PSE, especially if the district has been inclusive in their K–12 service delivery and/or if the IHE has a philosophical underpinning of inclusion. This might also be an option for families to pursue if there is no existing school-supported program offered. Up front, this model might be more challenging to implement because it requires keeping track of individual student schedules, creating alternative paths to higher education such as negotiating access to courses requiring prerequisites, waiving the need for placement tests, mechanisms for bypassing developmental/remedial courses, and "otherwise qualified" requirements. Snapshot I describes one student's experience of receiving individual supports.

Snapshot I: Jamalin

Jamalin,** who has a label of intellectual disability and is now 26 years old, is employed full time as a dog groomer for a large national pet company and has been employed there since she turned 22. She earns well over $10 an hour and receives full benefits. Jamalin's path to this employment began when her school district, Worcester, Massachusetts, started supporting students who were 18 years of age and older and who were going to continue to be served by the district until they turned 22, in more age-appropriate options, including PSE. First, Jamalin, with support from staff, convened a Whole Life Planning meeting with her friends, family, and some adult service agency personnel that she thought might help her pursue her goals for adult life. Jamalin was extremely shy, so having her friends and family at the meeting really helped her. She was able to identify what she was interested in and develop an action plan of what needed to happen so she could achieve her goals. For example, one friend indicated that Jamalin had an incredible way with animals, especially dogs. Jamalin confirmed that she would really like to work with dogs but was not sure what the next steps were. A representative from the Office of Disability Support services at a local community college indicated that she had just seen a brochure from Becker College that listed a certificate in kennel management and would share the brochure with Jamalin. Jamalin's mother indicated that she would be happy to take Jamalin to visit Becker College to get more information and so both of them could get a real sense of what the college and students were like.

What happened next?

- Jamalin, her mother, and the district transition coordinator visited the college and actually met with the dog grooming course instructor. Jamalin stated that she was really excited and wanted to take Dog Grooming I as her first course. She registered for the course and chose to audit it. At the end of the course the instructor encouraged Jamalin to take the course again, but for credit.
- Jamalin ended up taking Dog Grooming I and II and a kennel management course. She also had two internships with her dog grooming course instructor, who happened to own a kennel.
- After four semesters of courses and several internships, the instructor hired Jamalin to work full time at her kennel. Jamalin was very happy but soon realized that because there was no public transportation to the kennel she had to rely on family to transport her to work, because there were no co-workers who lived close to her. During her internships, the school district covered the cost of transportation. She continued to work at the kennel for the summer while she worked with her transition coordinator from her school district and her vocational rehabilitation (VR) case manager to find work that was located near public transportation so that she could travel to work independently.
- Six months before her 22nd birthday her VR counselor found a job opening at a national pet company, which was near public transportation. Jamalin was extremely excited, but scared. Her transition coordinator and job coach (paid by VR) assisted her in applying for the job and then, when she got it, helped her in her transition. She has been there for the last 6 years and is doing well.

WORKING WITH A SCHOOL SYSTEM

All options that have been discussed so far have been for students with ID between the ages of 18 and 21 whose school system is currently providing services or a program in a postsecondary setting. What if your local school system is unaware of these PSE options? How do you work with a school system that is interested in expanding transition opportunities to the world of PSE but has nothing in place? And what is even harder, how do you work with a system whose initial response is no?

The first step to making a change is gaining knowledge. Often a school system may not offer PSE options for students with ID simply because its staff is not aware of the possibilities. Families can increase awareness by sharing information they have found on existing programs and services, funding sources, and community partnerships that have worked in other locations. It is also vital for both parents and students to clearly communicate that access to PSE is not only a real possibility, but a real *need* and *expectation*. Parents and students should make sure that goals related to accessing PSE or adult learning are included in students' IEPs as early as possible. This will provide a consistent message that the student and his family expect that this student will access education outside of the high school as part of their transition services. Tip Sheet 6.2 offers some strategies for accessing PSE.

It is possible that school system staff and administrators who are uninformed of the potential benefits of PSEs for students with ID may initially respond negatively. Many parents reading this who have been down this road are probably nodding, smiling to themselves, or saying, "That's an understatement!" Parents

— **TIP SHEET 6.2**

THE CONTINUUM OF NO, AND HOW TO RESPOND

Given the structure of most school systems, when approached with a novel idea, the response often falls on a continuum of "no." It is often up to the families to raise the expectations of professionals within a system. In every system we come across, there are obstacles, a tough one being the attitudinal barrier. There are several reasons that a person within a system would say, "You can't!"

- It is too difficult.
- It has never been done before.
- I don't understand how that would work/ I can't picture how that would work.
- I truly believe that cannot work.

It Is Too Difficult and It Has Never Been Done Before

People working within systems might tell you that the current system or status quo is not set up to accommodate your request. Things that can help influence a system to change include

- Support from many families making their desires heard
- Statistics and examples of the idea working somewhere else
- A list of benefits to the system overall if the change were made
- Willingness to contribute much of the work: A system is more likely to support families if they can show they are truly invested and making contributions.

I Don't Understand How That Would Work

Often people or systems do not afford opportunities merely because it did not occur to them, or it is simply not in their background of experiences. Lack of awareness does not necessarily mean lack of ability. Submit a proposal that clearly explains or describes

- How this has worked in other systems
- How it can work in this system
- How successful it has been in other places
- How good a system's outcomes will look if they give it a try

I Truly Believe This Cannot Work

If a professional is aware of an idea, how it works, and how it can benefit all parties, and he or she still simply does not *believe* in the idea, then this is a tough barrier. In all likelihood, the goal will have to be achieved without this person, or simply by another route that avoids this big bump in the road.

of students with ID who propose partnerships with colleges will often hear phrases like "unrealistic expectations," "crazy," as well as "we don't do that for kids without disabilities," or "college isn't for kids with ID." Whether families are dealing with school systems that are eager or not so eager to support students with ID in postsecondary settings, it is helpful to heed the wisdom and encouragement of those who have been down this path. Janice Fialka's son Micah attends Oakland University in Michigan. Her journey in support of Micah's dream of going to college has been a long one. She wrote the following list of tips for other parents based on her years of experience trying to get the system to recognize and support Micah's college potential.

Things All Families CAN Do When Seeking Access to PSE Experiences

- Have high expectations.
- Create the vision.
- Reach out to others locally and nationally.
- Do the research.
- Out of the blue, phone strangers who have expertise and experience.
- Ask for help.
- Try not to let the naysayers overwhelm you.
- Get support from friends and family.
- Take breaks.
- Remember that you are in it for the long run.
- Remember that it is very hard work and that it will not come easy.
- Do not be deterred by a lost battle or two.
- View the obstacles as bumps in the road, not the end of the road.
- Thank those who have helped (and recognize that most people value being able to help).
- Find the key decision makers who can support you and open doors (or at least crack a door open), and make sure the key decision makers come from different places in the system.
- Recruit a variety of key stakeholders (see Tip Sheet 6.3).
- Bring a positive attitude (even when it is excruciatingly hard to do).
- Ask people to share their worries and questions so that the issues can be addressed head-on, and then do not cut them off when they share a different perspective or identify barriers.
- Try to see perceived obstacles as clues to the issues that might have to be tackled next.
- Ask for the involvement of your child's peers. They have terrific ideas and often say the right thing just when you need it, such as, "Why wouldn't Micah go to college?!"

Options for Students No Longer in School: Over Age 21

Once a student exits the public school system, his or her involvement in IDEA-funded dual enrollment or individual support services coordinated by a LEA in PSE will end. Some students who have had such experiences may wish to con-

TIP SHEET 6.3

THE STEPS TO GAINING SCHOOL SYSTEM SUPPORT

Many school systems are eager to expand their PSE services for students with ID, with guidance. Following are steps to engage the school system in the idea of supporting students with ID in PSE experiences:

1. Become knowledgeable. Do research to learn about other programs nationally and locally. Contact people who are accessing PSE elsewhere to get their input and testimonials.
2. Identify school personnel who play a significant role in the transitioning of students with ID. These are the people who need to be targeted, fully informed, and brought on board.
3. Form a group or task force made up of several families, students, and professionals—all with the same vision. This group will need to be the driving force, the momentum maintainer, and the guide.
4. Develop a program plan—almost like a business plan—that outlines the *why*, *who*, *when*, *where*, and, specifically, the *how*, with documentation of existing success stories, research, testimonials, and backup plans. Explain how risk will be minimized, how costs will be covered, and especially how higher outcomes will be achieved. An excellent resource to help anyone get started in this process is the following book:

Transition Services for Students with Severe Disabilities in College and Community Settings, by Meg Grigal, Debra A. Neubert, and M. Sherrill Moon. Available from PRO-ED Publishers at www.proedinc.com.

1. Present this plan to the appropriate decision makers at the school and college or community-based organization.
2. Once accepted, it is now important to
   a. Conduct a needs assessment. Find out exactly where there are gaps in transition services for students with ID within the school system and where (and *if*) in the community would be the best option for meeting those needs.
   b. Prioritize the goals.
   c. Monitor the progress of the plan and program. In order to maintain success, a program needs to adapt, and only through monitoring successes and failures can the right changes be made.
   d. Expand partnerships. As needs arise, so should opportunities—more partnerships can translate into more and different opportunities.

tinue their access to PSE. Other students with ID may exit their secondary special education program without having had *any* PSE experience, but are interested in trying to find opportunities for such experiences now that they are done with high school. What options are available for adults with ID seeking PSE?

Formal Options

There are a variety of options for students with ID seeking access to PSE, some with a focus on independent living, others on employment, and still others on a more traditional college academic experience. Each college that provides access to students with ID determines the extent to which they will provide these services within the context of the typical course offerings. Some colleges have created special programs for students with ID that provide access to a set of coursework specifically designed for students with disabilities. Many of these programs have developed in the past few years and are supporting students with ID in developing independent living and employment skills. For example, the Pathways program at UCLA is a 2-year PSE program for young adults with ID. Students live near the UCLA campus and receive independent living skill training and undergo vocational exploration, in addition to taking classes through UCLA Extension, which offers continuing education courses. The fees for this program are similar to those of a typical private state college and run approximately $35,000 per year for tuition, room and board, meals, books, and supplies.

Similar programs have been developed around the country, such as the Career & Community Studies Program at the College of New Jersey, the Transition to Independent Living Program at Taft College, and the REACH Program at the University of Iowa. Each of these programs has a slightly different focus, but they are similar in that they have been initiated by a college, with a goal of helping students with ID between the ages of 18 and 25 gain skills to help them successfully transition into adulthood. In response to the growing need for services, there has been a great deal of program development in recent years. With the passage of the Higher Education Opportunity Act of 2008 (PL 110-315) (for more information, please see Chapter 2), more are sure to follow.

Other college-sponsored programs choose not to create separate classes, but integrate students with ID into their typical college course offerings. Students access the same courses as other college students. One such program was created in New Jersey in 2006 at Mercer Community College. The Dream Program is a demonstration project funded by a grant from Laura and Steve Riggio, through the National Down Syndrome Society. Each student in the Dream Program, along with access to typical courses, participates in an Introduction to Student Success Seminar, which gives new students a chance to meet with each other to discuss experiences under the guidance of a counselor. The Dream Program, like many others, relies on peer mentors, who are current community college students, to assist students with ID with their coursework. In addition, Dream students are supported by the college's academic support services staff, who provide all students with disabilities on campus with advocacy, accommodations, and referral to tutoring and other services to help students get the most out of their college experience.

Informal Options

Students and their families are not limited to attending a 2- or 4-year, specially designed program at a college. There are other, more informal options as well. Students with ID and their families may access a college experience by using the individual support model. Using this approach, students seek to enroll in a local college of their choice, and they and their family determine a method to coordinate the necessary supports (such as educational coaches) through collaboration with vocational rehabilitation, the college, and adult service agencies. (For more information about the individual support model, see Chapter 3.) Students with ID need not limit themselves only to courses designed for students with disabilities, but may register for any college course that meets their interests and learning needs and is available to them.

The decision about what courses to take should not hinge on the fact that the course is or is not designed for people with disabilities, but instead on what the student's goals are and whether they can be met by the course. It also may hinge on gaining access to the course, as prerequisites and placement tests often pose challenges for students with ID. Students with ID and their families need to recognize that some courses may not be suited to their needs and/or abilities. In some cases students with ID may need to audit a course instead of taking it for credit, or may need to repeat a course to have sufficient time to master the content. As illustrated in Snapshot J: Howard Community College, some colleges have made access to their credit courses easier by creating a new custom type of registration.

Snapshot J: Howard Community College

Howard Community College in Maryland offers all students, including those with ID, a registration option called CustomClass. This option provides a noncredit way to take most of the credit courses listed in the schedule of classes. CustomClass students sit in the same classes as credit students; however, they are enrolled as noncredit or continuing education students. Students receive the same instruction but do not get a grade/transcript. This option is different from auditing a class in that a student who audits must still meet prerequisites, take placement tests, fill out the credit application, and pay the consolidated fee. CustomClass students do not take placement tests or fulfill prerequisites. The student also determines whether to take tests or complete assignments. If you choose to take the tests or do the assignments, the instructor will grade your projects/tests but will not assign an overall grade for the course. This kind of flexibility provides students with ID a chance to take a variety of classes that might not have been available to them because of prerequisites.

Other informal options exist outside of the college setting and should not be overlooked by adults with ID seeking to access learning experiences. There are a variety of non–college-based adult education options in every community that offer opportunities for learning about a wide array of topics. Local parks and recreation departments offer courses on such topics such as musical theater, history, photography, cooking, crafts, dance, languages, business etiquette, martial arts, and outdoor recreation. This list is by no means exhaustive. All learning endeavors should be viewed as PSE opportunities, and each has is own value and related outcomes. Another driving force for many students with ID and their families is the cost of seeking a PSE experience.

College is expensive. This is not a surprise to most people, and this reality will not be different for students with ID. In some cases, the costs of accessing a program for students with ID may be greater than the cost of a typical college program, as tuition for some specialized programs, like the Chapel Haven program for students with autism, can be as high as $80,000 a year (www.chapelhaven.org). An additional barrier is that parents of students with ID are not able to save for college with the state-sponsored 529 investment plans, nor are they eligible to apply for or receive traditional federal financial aid, though this latter limitation may soon change because of the recent passage of Higher Education Opportunity Act of 2008. However, the fact remains that students whose families have limited resources may also have more limited postsecondary options.

SUMMARY

This chapter shows that the road to college for individuals with ID and their families is not always a smooth one. Families have worked hard to break down long-held myths and misconceptions about their children with ID and have begun to build their hopes, dreams, and expectations. In order for the college experience to become a reality for more young adults with ID, there are a number of variables that need to be addressed. First, all stakeholders should be trained beforehand to understand that PSE options exist and that they lead to positive outcomes. Such training should be provided to

- Pediatricians and other medical personnel, who are often the ones dispensing advice to families at the earliest stages
- Families, through parent training and information centers, so they can understand there is a wide spectrum of PSE opportunities available for their children
- Professionals in the LEAs who coordinate secondary and transition services
- Community service providers, who partner in the development of these options
- Personnel in PSE institutions, such as community centers, adult learning programs, community colleges, and 4-year colleges and universities, who will be receiving these students into their communities
- Legislators, who need to understand the possibilities for this population and are responsible for supporting the best interests of everyone—including people with ID and their families—in this venture.

In addition to changing expectations in people, we must begin to integrate change into systems. PSE must be presented early on as an *option* in transition services within local school systems so that students with ID can be *prepared* to experience college successfully.

The families who have chosen to take this bumpy, rarely traveled road toward a college experience for their child with ID are paving the way for many other young people with ID in the future. Over time, our society will start to see where this road leads: to productive, better educated, and well-adjusted lives for its citizens with ID. The college experience is different for each person, whether a person has a disability or not. Why someone seeks a college experience, how they get there, and what they learn depend a lot upon the planning and supports that are put into place. A young adult with an ID may need different and perhaps more supports in place to minimize risks and access opportunities than a student without an ID. But with motivation, person-centered planning, self-advocacy training, a cohesive and supportive team, and the belief that it is possible, young adults with ID can participate in exciting new PSE learning opportunities that lead to improved employment outcomes and expanded social networks.

REFERENCES

Agran, M., Snow, K., & Swaner, J. (1999). Teacher Perceptions of Self-Determination: Benefits, Characteristics, Strategies. *Education and Training in Mental Retardation and Developmental Disabilities*, 34(3), 293-301.

Andrews, L.W. (2005). Hiring people with intellectual disabilities: employers are discovering that with a little help, workers with such disabilities can take on a wide array of jobs. *H R Magazine*, 50 (7). July 2005.

Benz, M., & Blalock, G. (1999). Community transition teams: Enhancing student involvement in transition through community transition teams. *The Journal for Vocational Special Needs Education, 21*(3), 4–12.

Blumberg, R., & Ferguson, P. (1999). *On transition Services for Youth with Disabilities*. Retrieved from http://www.spannj.org/transition/transition_onpoint.htm.

Bureau of Labor Statistics. United States Department of Labor (2008). *College Enrollment and Work Activity of 2007 High School Graduates*. (Economic News Release No. USDL 08-0559). Washington, DC: Author.

Butterworth, J., Hagner, D., Heikkinen, B., Faris, S., DeMello, S., & McDonough, K. (1993). *Whole Life Planning: A Guide for Organizers and Facilitators*. Children's Hospital, Boston, MA. Institute for Community Inclusion, Massachusetts University, Boston. Sponsored by the Office of the Assistant Secretary for Planning and Evaluation (DHHS), Washington, DC.

Butterworth, Jr., J., & Strauch, J.D. (1994). The relationship between social competence and success in the competitive workplace for persons with mental retardation. *Education and Training in Mental Retardation and Developmental Disabilities, 29*, 118–133.

Chadsey-Rusch, J. (1990). Social interactions of secondary-aged students with severe handicaps: Implications for facilitating the transition from school to work. *Journal of the Association of Persons with Severe Handicaps, 15*, 69–78.

Eisenman, L.T. (2007). Social networks and careers of young adults with intellectual disabilities. *Intellectual and Developmental Disabilities, 45*(3), 199–208.

Eisenman, T., & Chamberlin, M. (2001). Implementing Self-Determination Activities: Lessons from Schools. *Remedial and Special Education, 22*(3), 138-147.

Forest, M., & Lusthaus, E. (1990). Everyone belongs with MAPS action planning system. *Teaching Exceptional Children, 22*, 32–35.

Foxx, R.M., & Faw, G.D. (1992). An eight-year follow-up of three social skills training studies. *Mental Retardation, 30*, 63–66.

Garner, H., & Dietz, L. (1996). Person-centered planning: Maps and paths to the future. *Four Runner, 11*(2), 1–2.

Getzel, E., & Thoma, C. (2008). Experiences of college students with disabilities and the importance of self-determination. In *Career Development for Exceptional Individuals* 31, 77–84.

Grigal, M., & Neubert, D. (2004). Parents' in-school values and post-school expectations for transition-aged youth with disabilities. *Career Development for Exceptional Individuals, 27*(1), 65–86.

Grigal, M., Neubert, D., & Moon, M.S. (2001). Public school programs for students with severe disabilities in post-secondary settings. *Education and Training in Mental Retardation and Developmental Disabilities, 36*(3), 244–254.

Grigal, M., Neubert, D., & Moon, M.S. (2005). *Transition services for students with severe disabilities in college and community settings: Strategies for planning, implementation and evaluation*. Austin, TX: PRO-ED.

Higher Education Opportunity Act of 2008, Pub. L. No. 110-315 § 122 STAT. 3078 (2008). ACT News Release. (2001). *Hot Jobs Get Cool Response from High School Grads*. August 15. ACT, Inc.

Individuals with Disabilities Education Improvement Act of 2004, PL 108-446, 20 U.S.C. §§ 1400 *et seq.*

Jameson, D. (2007). Self-determination and success outcomes of two-year college students with disabilities. *Journal of College Reading and Learning, 37* (2), 26-46.

McKay, D.R. (2006). *About.com Career Planning Newsletter*. Retrieved on July 18, 2008, from http://careerplanning.about.com/b/a/257170.htm

Miner, C., & Bates, P. (1997). The effect of person-centered planning activities on the IEP/transition planning process. *Education and Training in Mental Retardation and Developmental Disabilities, 32*, 105–112.

National Longitudinal Transition Study-2 (NLTS2) (2003a). *Parent/Youth Report of Postsecondary Education* (Table 257) [Data File]. Available from National Longitudinal Transition Study-2 (NLTS2) Web Site, http://www.nlts2.org

National Longitudinal Transition Study-2 (NLTS2) (2003b). *Parent/Youth Report of Youth Employment After Secondary School* (Table 274) [Data File]. Available from National Longitudinal Transition Study-2 (NLTS2) Web Site, http://www.nlts2.org

National Organization on Disability. (1998). *Harris survey of Americans with disabilities*. New York: Author.

Newman, L. (2005). *Family expectations and involvement for youth with disabilities* (NLTS2 Data Brief). *Reports from the National Longitudinal Transition Study, 4*(2).

Ochs, L., & Roessler, R. (2001). Students with disabilities: How ready are they for the 21st century? *Rehabilitation Counseling Bulletin, 44*(3), 170–176.

Pearpoint, J., O'Brien, J., & Forest, M. (1993). *Path: A workbook for planning possible positive futures: Planning alternative tomorrows with hope for schools, organizations, businesses, families*. Toronto: Inclusion Press.

Perske, R. (1972). The dignity of risk and the mentally retarded. *Mental Retardation, 10*(1), 24–27.

Rosemergy, J. (2007). Higher education options for intellectually disabled explored. *The Reporter, Vanderbilt University Medical Center*. (Week of May 18-25).

Salembier, G., & Furney, K. (2000). Rhetoric and reality: A review of the literature on parent and student participation in the IEP and transition planning process. Issues influencing the future of transition programs and services for students with disabilities (Ch. 7, pp. 111-126). In *Issues Influencing the Future of Transition Programs and Services in the United States*. Edited by Johnson, D., R., & Emanuel, E., J.Minneapolis, MN: University of Minnesota, Institute on Community Integration.

Sanders, M.G., & Epstein, J.L. (2000). Building school-family-community partnerships in middle and high school. In M.G. Sanders (Ed.), *School students placed at risk: Research, policy, and practice in the education of poor and minority adolescents* (pp. 339–361). Mahwah, NJ: Lawrence Erlbaum.

Smith, P. (2007). Have we made any progress? Including students with intellectual disabilities in regular education classrooms. *Intellectual and Developmental Disabilities, 45*(5), 297–309.

Sukhodolsky, D.G., & Butter, E.M. (2007). Social skills training for children with intellectual disabilities. In J. Jacobsen, J. Mulick, & J. Rojahn (Eds.), *Handbook of intellectual disabilities* (pp. 601–618). New York: Springer.

Thoma, C.A. & Wehmeyer, M.L. (2005). Self-determination and the transition to postsecondary education. In E.E. Getzel & P. Wehman. *Going to college* (pp. 49-68). Baltimore: Paul H. Brookes.

Tilson, G., Cuozzo, L., Coppola, J. (2001). *Positive Personal Profile: Helping all students become active participants in the post-high school transition planning process.* TransCen, Inc., 451 Hungerford Drive, Ste. 700, Rockville, MD 20850.

Turnbull, A., & Turnbull, R. (1992). Group action planning (GAP). *Families and Disability Newsletter*, 1–13.

U.S. Department of Education, Office of Special Education Programs. (1996, 1999). *Annual report to Congress.* Washington, DC: Author.

Ward, M.J. (1988). The many facets of self-determination. *NICHCY Transition Summary*, 5, 2-3. National Center for Children and Youth with Disabilities, Washington, D.C.

Wehmeyer, M.L., (1992). Self-determination and the education of students with mental retardation. Education and Training in Mental Retardation, 27, 302-314.

Wehmeyer, M., Agran, M., Hughes, C. (2000). A National Survey of Teachers' Promotion of Self-Determination and Student-Directed Learning. *The Journal of Special Education,* 34, (2), 58-68.

Wehmeyer, M.L., Kelchner, K., & Richards, S. (1996). Essential characteristics of self-determined behavior of individuals with mental retardation. *American Journal on Mental Retardation, 100*(6), 632–642.

Winsor, J.E., & Butterworth, J. (2007). *National day and employment service trends in MR/DD agencies* (Data Note #11b). Boston: University of Massachusetts, Institute on Community Inclusion.

Zafft, C., Hart, D., Zimbrich, K. (2004). College career connection: A study of youth with intellectual disabilities and the impact of PSE. *Education & Training in Developmental Disabilities, 39*(1), 45–53.

Critical Components for Planning and Implementing Dual Enrollment and Other Postsecondary Education Experiences

Meg Grigal and Debra Hart

Over the past 10 years we have delved into frontline activities supporting access to postsecondary education (PSE) for students with intellectual disabilities (ID) across the nation. Federally funded outreach, model demonstration, and research projects have allowed us to work directly with students with ID and their families who are preparing to access PSE, and to work with local school systems, adult service agencies, and two- and four-year colleges and universities to plan for, implement, and evaluate PSE services. Much of this work has centered around creating and supporting dual enrollment programs that serve transitioning students with ID ages 18–21 in college settings. This chapter highlights key lessons learned from our collective experiences concerning a) the need to prepare students with ID academically and emotionally for PSE, b) strategies for planning and implementing PSE services, c) practices that show promise to create the best chance of sustainable success for students with ID, and d) ongoing evaluation and data collection that inform each phase from preparing students to sustaining the PSE initiative.

LESSONS LEARNED ABOUT PREPARING STUDENTS WITH INTELLECTUAL DISABILITIES FOR POSTSECONDARY EDUCATION

Critical factors that must be considered when preparing students with ID for PSE include student motivation, student preparation, Universal Design for Learning, self-determination, and setting family and student expectations. In this section, we'll discuss the impact of each.

Student Motivation

Successful student experiences in PSE require a good deal of planning (Grigal, Neubert, & Moon, 2005), yet even the best planning cannot make an experience successful for a student who is not interested. One of the most crucial components of student success in PSE is the student's motivation to be there and his or her desire to learn. A lack of interest could be related to many factors; for example, if students have not been able to connect their previous learning experiences to any meaningful outcome, it may be difficult for them to see the benefit of continuing their learning experiences at college. It is vital that students be shown that what they learn in college can make a difference in their lives.

Students need to have the opportunity to hear from other students, like Elaine Cox (see Vignette 7.1), who used her experiences in a college-based program to achieve the independence she desired.

> *For our students, we've kind of developed a "predictors of success" list . . . . one predictor is that the students want to be in class, they want to try to do the work. Now they might not be competitive in the class, they might struggle with the work, but they have to be motivated enough to want to be there. And I would say that the two students who, in our five years, have not been successful here—it's been due to lack of motivation in class.*

> —Rich Emmett, Program Coordinator, Western Connecticut State
> University (WCSU)

There are many factors that play into whether a student lacks motivation, including parent input and support, previous experience, and fear of the unknown. Addressing the issue of motivation requires a little bit of digging and sometimes a bit of learning.

Vignette 7.1: Elaine's Story

Elaine Cox is almost 26 years old. She has worked at a local grocery store in Baltimore, Maryland, since September 2001 and is on her fourth raise—she started at $6.15 an hour and is now making $8.95, working 40 hours most weeks. Over the years, Elaine has saved more than $8,000 and just moved this past spring into her own apartment overlooking a large city park with a lake, where she finally dipped into savings to spend $3,000 on a living room set, kitchen table, bedroom furniture, and two televisions. She also paid her rent in full through the end of the year. She is not the typical 26-year-old in today's world: She has no debt and has enough of a nest egg to live comfortably for a very long time should she lose her job or not be able to work, showing more forethought and planning than many people in today's society!

What is also interesting about Elaine's story is that she has faced more barriers than the typical person. She was raised with several siblings by a single mother in the inner city of Baltimore, living in a neighborhood not known for its safe streets but more for its violence and drug dealing. Elaine also has an intellectual disability; a degenerative visual impairment; and a shunt in her brain that needs regular medical attention, can give her nearly unbearable headaches, and can put her in the hospital for weeks every several years. In many ways, she was at a disadvantage for succeeding in the real world.

But one advantage she did have was that she graduated from a transition program at a college setting. Through the Baltimore City Public Schools, through a program called the Baltimore Transition Connection, Elaine spent 3 years at Coppin State University and graduated in 2003. She became involved with campus life, had a student ID so she could access the library and computer labs and events, ate in the student cafeteria, shopped at the campus bookstore, and attended a class at Coppin State as well as classes at Baltimore City Community College and the YMCA. The program also spent a lot of time teaching Elaine how to get around the city on public transportation and through the door-to-door mobility program, how to budget and save money, how to shop and pay bills, how to find fun things to do in the community—and then get there and pay for them. The program also helped her open her first savings account—the same account she now has over $5,000 saved in, and helped her find her first job—the same job she still holds today, a promotion and four raises later. They also taught her how to keep a calendar with work schedules and important appointments, and how to make lists of things she needs. Elaine still uses those techniques and insists she has never gotten her work schedule confused in 7 years, and her pantry is almost always stocked with what she needs!

Elaine was connected to an adult service provider upon exit from the Baltimore Transition Connection at Coppin State. She continues to meet regularly with her job coach from that same agency, away from work, to discuss issues and even ideas for finding a new job. When she comes home from work late or doesn't feel safe, she knows how to schedule mobility services that will take her to her front door rather than take the normal bus route. With the help of her mom, she completed all the forms necessary to apply for subsidized housing through the city housing department. When they showed her three options from the waiting list, she was able to pick the one in a part of the city near Coppin State University because she was familiar with the neighborhood and the bus routes and knew she would be comfortable acclimating to these surroundings by herself. She goes to festivals at the park near her house and to the movies with friends.

Elaine is very open about saying that she and her mom would never have thought all this was possible before she went to Coppin State. She says she needed to learn first that it was even a possibility and then, of course, how to do it! With a lot of hard work, much love and support from her teachers and family, and the belief in opportunity, Elaine is a very happy, independent, and successful young woman in her community.

Parent Input and Support

Parents of students with ID may have less than positive experiences with the public school system (Mueller, Singer, & Draper, 2008; Esquivel, Ryan, & Bonner, 2008). All too often parents are given little support concerning their dreams for their child, if, in fact, anyone ever asked them what their dreams were. Given the prevalence of low expectations for students in special education (McGrew & Evans, 2003; Olson, 2004), parents may not believe it possible for their child to pursue additional education beyond high school. When parents of students with ID have negative feelings about past education experience or future outcomes, it is unlikely that their child will be encouraged to be motivated toward such experiences.

Previous Experiences

When asking a student whether he or she wants to go to college, it is important to acknowledge the previous experience of the person being asked and whether he or she has had any exposure to higher education. Students with ID who have had only high school learning experiences may not know what college is all about. They might have had friends or a sibling who has graduated from high school and gone to college. Depending upon what they have heard, college could represent anything from endless studying and an overwhelming workload to constant partying with little or no adult supervision. Just as college visits are recommended for students without disabilities, visiting a college or two can help students with ID understand what it means to go to college. Students with ID should be encouraged to speak with college students who attend a college of interest to gain some first-hand knowledge about what they can expect at that IHE. It may also be helpful to sit in on a few different types of classes.

Another influential aspect of a student's previous experience is whether he or she connects learning environments to being labeled as having a disability. Students involved in transition may see the end of their high school career as a welcome end of having to be labeled as mentally retarded or cognitively impaired or one of the many other terms that stigmatize students receiving special education services. In a recent interview one student who had been in a dual-enrollment program called the Western Connection at Western Connecticut State University related her reticence about letting her friends know that she was participating in a "program":

> *Interviewer:* What did you think going to Western Connection would be like?
>
> *Student:* I've been really enjoying it. It's been a good thing for me. Not a lot of kids I know in my high school know I'm here. 'Cause I didn't want to tell them about the program. I don't like to tell people about being learning disabled. I didn't want them to know I was coming to a special program.
>
> *Interviewer:* So where do your friends think you're going?
>
> *Student:* They know I'm going to West Conn. And I'm taking credits. They don't really know what the program's about.

If students see college as just one more place that they will be pigeonholed with a label, this may affect their motivation to go there. This phenomenon is not limited to students with ID, as only 40% of postsecondary students with disabilities identify themselves as having a disability and have informed their postsecondary schools of that disability (Wagner, Newman, Cameto, Garza, & Levine, 2005).

Fear of the Unknown

Another factor that can contribute to a student's motivation regarding postsecondary education is fear. College campuses, whether large or small, are typically vastly different from a high school building. Navigating between classes is also very different. There are no bells; no one is assigned to help students get around the campus, and there is no resource room or homeroom to provide support or direction in dealing with problems. It is important to define what a college experience might look like prior to a student with ID embarking on that path. Without this knowledge, a student could not be expected to make informed choices about their desire to go or not go to college. Students with ID, not unlike many other students with and without disabilities, may have no idea of the broad range of classes available at a college. Reviewing course options may be an eye-opening experience for both the student and the parents. When students are provided with information about the types of academic and nonacademic courses available, they will have some basis to be motivated to pursue or not to pursue such options. Table 7.1 provides some tips that parents can use to help students with ID become more familiar with college.

Student Preparation

Students with ID considering a PSE experience generally have had one of three previous histories. Some students will have participated in life skill classes or in

Table 7.1. Transition to college: tips for parents to help students with intellectual disabilities think about college

- Talk about what college is and how it is different from high school. There are no bells, study hall, or principals. Students are expected to do what they need to do with little supervision or assistance.
- College is also a place where the student decides what they want to learn, not the teachers or their parents. Students have the opportunity to choose to learn about a topic or subject that interests them.
- Visit a local college—or two. Eat lunch there, go to the library, and talk with some students. If you can, sit in on a class or two to see what it is like. Try to get a feel for the culture and where the students hang out and spend time together.
- Look at the different types of continuing education courses that are available for all students.
- Encourage your child to take a class while still in high school to see how the adult learning experience is different from high school.
- Discuss the things that your child would like to learn about. Although these things may not be academic, they may certainly be meaningful to him or her. See if a local course is available on this topic.
- Discuss all types of adult learning opportunities, including community college, continuing education, park and recreation classes, and training/classes offered through local stores (Michaels, Home Depot, Jo-Ann Fabrics). Many stores offer classes on crafts and home improvement projects that might be of interest to students.
- Help your child make the connection between his or her learning goals and his or her life: A cooking class could help a student become more independent in the kitchen; a cake decorating class could help a student get a job in the bakery at the local grocery store; a computer class could help to get a job in an office; classes taken just for fun allow you to meet people who have similar interests.
- Find out what accommodations are being provided in high school to help your child succeed.
- Work with your child to help practice asking for support from people your child doesn't know in different environments. If your child has difficulty communicating, help create other appropriate ways to indicate a need.

From the Postsecondary Education Research Center (PERC) Project; reprinted by permission.

self-contained special education classes in high school, using a functional curriculum that focuses on daily living skills, community-based instruction, and employment. Others may have participated in some general nonacademic classes and been "pulled out" for academic courses typically taught in resource rooms or substantially separate classes. Finally, but less frequently, other students with ID will have been fully included in their high school experience, taking the same classes as their peers without disabilities. Each of these scenarios provides valuable skill sets for success in PSE, but none provides all the crucial elements necessary to ensure a positive outcome.

Students from the first two experiences, who have been supported in self-contained classrooms or resource room classes are not generally prepared for the expectations associated with college learning experiences. These students have not been asked to work independently, take tests, write papers, or collaborate with peers on projects. Many have not possessed a textbook or been given the chance to work with computers or other forms of technology (Getzel, McManus & Briel, 2004).

Wehman and Yasuda (2005) suggest that the reasons that students with disabilities are unable to achieve sufficient academic success are substandard content; lack of expectation; lack of qualified teachers; standards-based curricula and standardized testing; and lack of self-advocacy skills. These drawbacks may be magnified for students with ID, who early in their education careers may have been "tracked" away from any academic pursuits. Students with ID may garner undeniable practical benefits from some life skill classes and exposure to functional curricula. However, exposure to *only* these types of learning experiences fails to prepare them for most of the kinds of learning that will occur in college classes.

On the other hand, while access to the general education curriculum in an inclusive setting allows students with ID to be better prepared when accessing coursework and navigating social interactions in PSE, one drawback of such experiences is that often these students have had minimal exposure to the world of work. Students with ID who are fully included may have had some work experience; these are typically comprised of after-school or summer jobs that are not supported during the school day (Moon, Neubert, & Grigal, 2002). More often, however, many fully included students will find themselves in their fourth year of high school at age 18, never having participated in work-based instruction, employment internships, or any job sampling or career awareness activities. These students will have a steeper learning curve when faced with the prospect of obtaining and keeping paid competitive employment in conjunction with, or following, a PSE experience.

Both of these scenarios have implications for staff who support students in PSE settings. Students whose background is described by the first two scenarios may require additional support, both academically and socially, when first accessing and participating in college classes. Providing students with ID with a clear idea of what they will be expected to do in a college class is vital to their success. Students should review their course syllabus with support staff and/or their education coach to identify the assignments; review, when applicable, the required readings; and develop a schedule for how each will be addressed throughout the semester. Setting up a matrix to clearly organize expectations, roles, and responsibilities and weekly monitoring of progress and challenges will ensure that any issue that comes up is addressed quickly and appropriately.

Inset 7.1 provides an overview of a process used by one program coordinator to ensure that students are engaged and supported in their college courses.

Students with ID who were fully included in high school may also require additional attention on the part of the staff. Students who have had little or no experience in work-based learning or exposure to employment will likely need some initial assessment related to career awareness and interests. Students may have difficulty transferring their academic skills to employment settings (Briel & Getzel, 2005) and may need support to connect what they learn in college to a career path. Building this bridge is important for all students. Richard Luecking, in Chapter 9 of this book, explores the essential nature of this connection, stating, "Without a clear connection between PSE experiences

---

INSET 7.1. SUMMARY COURSE REVIEWS AT THE WESTERN CONNECTION PROGRAM

We would schedule a weekly meeting (or more frequent meetings with individuals who might require it), always at the same time and on the same day of the week, during which the student would meet with my teaching assistant or me. At this meeting the student was required to have his or her course syllabus; textbook(s) (if applicable); notes/handouts; and any papers, quizzes, and so on, that were handed back by instructors during the past week. The staff member would review all work/assignments and discuss progress and offer suggestions for improvement as needed. Then, over time, we encouraged the student to verbalize his or her own strategies for improvement and work/study goals for the next week.

During the student's mentoring sessions similar reviews took place, to familiarize all staff members with the student's progress. If mentors felt that there might be a problem, they were instructed to immediately involve a staff member. Because all staff were involved with reviewing the student's work and were in communication with one another, students quickly became aware that there was no way that they could neglect or put off their work.

Most students looked forward to these course reviews because it gave them an opportunity to show or verbalize their work ethic and achievements, as well as the chance to brag a little about themselves. Most students took even more pride in their improved confidence in being able to independently think through any problems they might have and to make their own decisions, right or wrong, about how they could rectify those problems. This was a huge step for those students, and the staff reinforced the notion that such thinking and decision making would only help them be better prepared for dealing with hurdles they could encounter in a postsecondary classroom or on the job after they left the Western Connection Program.

Rich Emmett, Coordinator
The Western Connection Program
Western Connecticut State University

and adult employment and life goals, these youth are still vulnerable to the pervasive unemployment or underemployment that is unfortunately common among adults with ID."

Universal Design for Learning

The advent of Universal Design for Learning (UDL) and related principles (Behling & Hart, 2008; Rose & Meyer, 2002) has made it possible for students with differing learning styles, abilities, and preparedness to have greater access to college course material. UDL is the design of culturally responsive learning opportunities, including *curriculum, instruction, assessment*, and *environment*, to make them usable by all students, to the greatest extent possible, without the need for accommodations. Faculty trained in the application of UDL

- Vary presentation of content to accommodate all learning styles
- Provide multiple means for students to engage with the content/activity
- Provide multiple options that allow students to demonstrate competency/ knowledge of material

Overall, a UDL approach levels the playing field for many students and benefits all students. Faculty become proactive about integrating the use of a wide range of technology (e.g., screen readers, voice recognition software) that allows students to access course content. They also employ nontechnological strategies, such as varying instruction so as not to be reliant on lectures and to include video clips, project-based instruction, and service learning opportunities, where students have the opportunity to apply what they are learning in the classroom and to demonstrate their mastery of skills.

Self-Determination

A major factor that influences successful access to postsecondary experience is the student's ability to advocate for needed services and supports. Due to a lack of opportunity to practice self-determination skills in high school, many students with disabilities are ill-equipped to request and negotiate accommodations at the postsecondary level (Izzo & Lamb, 2002). This means that students who wish to pursue a postsecondary experience will need training and support in the area of self-determination and self-advocacy (Thoma & Wehmeyer, 2005). Chapter 5 highlights the need for college students with disabilities to self-identify at the disability support services office upon entering college, as well as other expectations related to disability documentation and accommodation requests. However, none of these behaviors are expected of high school students, let alone high school students with ID. Making a successful transition into the world of PSE will require staff to rethink how students with disabilities gain access to their academic supports and are involved in the planning and monitoring of their goals (Getzel & Thoma, 2008). Students with ID need repeated opportunities to practice self-determination and self-advocacy skills with their high school teachers, guidance counselors, family, and friends. Students with ID can focus on three major areas to improve their ability to self-advocate in a college setting. At a minimum, students should

1. *Know their disability.* All too often students are not made aware of their disability and what it implies to others about them. Students should be supported to be able to identify their disability in functional terms, describing how it affects their interactions and support needs in the context of a college learning experience or, at a minimum, have a written explanation. For example, knowing that your disability is labeled "Down syndrome" does little to inform your instructor about what you would require to be successful in his or her class. But students with that label could inform their instructor of their support needs by saying, "I have an intellectual disability. That means I have trouble reading and it takes me some time to ask my questions. I use a screen reader so I need to have my course material in digital form, and that includes class notes. Also, I would need to take any exams orally."

2. *Know supports/accommodations needed in adult environments.* What a student needs in a college class to be successful may be different from what he or she needs to be successful in a work environment (Briel & Wehman, 2005). And it may be that neither of these resembles what is needed in a social or family environment. Providing students with the knowledge of their learning style and the supports that they have been given in high school is a good first step. However, the modifications provided in secondary environments will seldom match up to the accommodations allowable in a postsecondary environment. Those family members and professionals who make accommodations or provide supports for students with ID in any adult environment (educational, employment, or social) need to communicate on a regular basis with the student about this. Students should be informed of how and why the accommodation was made, and how it is intended to help them.

3. *Support students as they practice asking for accommodations.* Typically, students with ID are provided curriculum modifications in secondary school unless they are on a 504 plan; they rarely have the need for accommodations. Therefore, the prospect of asking a professor or employer to provide an accommodation can be daunting, especially if these authority figures are not familiar to the student. Because they are rarely given the opportunity or expectation, students with ID often require additional practice in articulating their needs. Once students are given information about the accommodations and/or supports they need and have been able to express them (either verbally or in writing) to a familiar person, they need to be provided with opportunities to practice these requests with individuals with whom they are less familiar. Figure 7.1 provides one example of a tool that can be used to help students to monitor different aspects of articulating their support needs with individuals of varying levels of familiarity.

> Once students have the skills to explain their disabilities, negotiate their accommodations assertively, and assist in the coordination of those accommodations, they can become change agents. They can participate in the quality of the education they receive. Students can meet with faculty members, explain their disabilities and accommodations, and negotiate how to best coordinate delivery of those accommodations. When students take active roles in coordinating their accommodations, not only are they assisting faculty members (in gaining the skills to deliver a high quality education to a more diverse group of students), but students are getting the skills they will need in future employment settings. (Izzo, Hertzfeld, Simmons-Reed, & Aaron, 2001, p. 7)

Postsecondary Education Research Center Self-Advocacy Checklist

Student's Name

Setting	Steps	Teacher/ mentor	Date	Acquaintance	Date	New person	Date	Real-life situation	Date
Classroom	Introduce self								
	Describe strengths								
	Describe disability								
	Describe support needs								
	Present documentation								
Employment	Introduce self								
	Describe strengths								
	Describe disability								
	Describe support needs								
	Present documentation								
Social/Community	Introduce self								
	Describe strengths								
	Describe disability								
	Describe support needs								
	Present documentation								

Figure 7.1. PERC self-advocacy checklist. (From the PERC Project; reprinted by permission.)

Figure 7.1. Postsecondary Education Research Center Self-Advocacy Checklist *(continued)*

Directions for Using the PERC Self-Advocacy Checklist

Work with your teacher or peer mentor to practice the listed self-advocacy skills in each setting with:

1. Your mentor, or your teacher, or someone you know well
2. An acquaintance (someone you may have met, but do not know well)
3. Someone you have never met before (arranged by your teacher or mentor)
4. The appropriate person in the real-life situation

Once you feel that you can do this very well without any help, put a check mark in the box and write down the date.

Helpful Hints

- You don't have to use your disability label if you don't feel comfortable with it. Just describe what you can do well and what you need help doing.
- When you find words that feel good to you, write them down to help you remember them and then practice using them again next time.
- Remember that it is okay to be nervous when talking about yourself; everyone feels that way. Practice will make it easier.

Some words or phrases that might help describe your disability:

In a class
I have difficulty hearing/seeing and need to sit in the front of the room.
I have a learning disability that makes it hard for me to process lectures.
My disability makes it difficult for me to read and write.

On the job
I have a learning disability that makes it hard for me to remember instructions when you tell them to me.
My disability makes it hard for me to quickly count money.
I have a seizure disorder that is controlled by medication.

In a social/community situation
I have a hearing impairment that makes it difficult for me to understand everything.
My disability makes it hard for me to read and understand the instructions on my medicine.
I have cerebral palsy and sometimes get tired after walking for a while.

Some words or phrases that might help describe your strengths:

In a class
I am very excited about being in your class.
I have always been interested in child development and I am a quick learner.
I have always had an interest in art and am good at sketching.
I have a really good memory.

On the job
I am very excited to be working here.
I am very organized and detail oriented.
I am very outgoing and work well with customers.

(continued)

Figure 7.1. Postsecondary Education Research Center Self-Advocacy Checklist
(continued)

In a social/community situation
I really enjoy meeting new people.
I'm really good at figuring out how to take the bus.

Some words or phrases that might help describe your support needs:

In a class
In order to be successful in your class, I need to get notes ahead of time.
I have learned that these accommodations have worked best for me.
To hear everything you are saying clearly, I need to sit in the front row.
In the past, I have been most successful when given extra time on a test.

On the job
In order to be successful on the job, I need to have my daily instructions written down.
In the past, I have done a great job at the cash register if I have a practice guide next to me.
In case I have a question, I need to know to whom I should go first.

In a social/community situation
Sometimes I have difficulty understanding people when they talk too fast; could you speak
     a little slower?
I have trouble reading that menu board. Could you help me pick out lunch?
I don't understand these forms very well. I have all the information with me—could
     someone help me fill this out?

Some words or phrases that might help in presenting documentation, if necessary:

In a class
Here are the forms that show my documented disability and the accommodations that
     work best for me in a class.

On the job
Here are the forms that show my documented disability and the accommodations that
     work best for me in the workplace.

In a social/community situation
Here are the forms that show my documented disability and the assistance I need.

Setting Expectations

There are many kinds of services and activities available in PSE settings and it
can sometimes be difficult for families to know exactly what a program is providing to their child. Some PSE options focus their services on accessing college
coursework while others provide students with access to specially designed classes
that mirror some college courses. In some cases, students will access both typical and specialized courses. Students and their families should be provided with
information about the expectations in each class and the anticipated outcome. If
students are expected to register for typical classes, points of discussion should
include whether a course will be taken for credit or noncredit or audited; whether
a course is related to a certificate (e.g., auto mechanics, office management/
clerical, child care), and how students will manage the anticipated workload and
balance it with other activities in their schedule.

Other PSE options, though based at a college, focus more on employment or independent living skills than on accessing college courses. Staff from independent living programs on college campuses should help students and families understand what to expect with regard to level of support, independence, behavior, and safety. One such program, the College Living Experience, offers a 3-week summer program at one campus that provides incoming students with a preview of what living independently in a college environment will be like. It addresses situations like sharing a dormitory suite with a roommate, planning and preparing many of their own meals, keeping their suite clean, and doing their own laundry with assistance. During this time students take "Introduction to College" for credit. They can also take remedial math and English classes in addition to a variety of noncredit courses as they explore academic and career possibilities (http://www.cleinc.net).

If the focus of services on the college campus is related to employment, families need to be prepared for the type of employment that will be pursued and how it may affect the family schedule and/or the student's disability benefits under Social Security. The issue of benefits is one that is frequently overlooked by school systems and PSE services. Many parents of students with disabilities may not want their child to work because they fear that a paying job may endanger the student's Supplemental Security Income (SSI) or Social Security Disability Insurance (SSDI). Parents and students need to have access to benefits specialists who are able to address these concerns and describe the everchanging and very confusing array of work incentives that are used by the Social Security Administration, such as the Student Earned Income Exclusion, the Plans for Achieving Self-Support (PASS), and the Impairment Related Work Expenses (IRWEs).

Ideally the student and his or her family have an opportunity, prior to enrolling, to visit the college and ask questions regarding the schedule, activities, and expectations. It is vital that students and their parents are provided with information on how the provision of services and supports in college is different from that in high school (see Chapter 5 for an extended discussion related to this). Parents expecting high levels of student supervision, personal contact with professors, and daily or weekly updates from staff may find that these are not realistic expectations in most college-based programs. In addition, associated costs and related responsibilities should be reviewed prior to enrollment. These may include the cost of tuition, student fees, and transportation to or from classes, work, and/or social activities. In some cases, programs have created a list of parent, student, and program responsibilities that are reviewed prior to a student's enrollment to clearly articulate what will be expected from each party during a student's attendance.

LESSONS LEARNED ABOUT PLANNING POSTSECONDARY EDUCATION SERVICES

Planning for new services or programs in a postsecondary education setting requires a great deal of planning (Grigal et al., 2005). Such planning must take into account the anticipated student needs, the goals and outcomes of these services, and also the philosophical beliefs and values that will guide the creation of services and activities. The following provides an overview of some common pitfalls that can be avoided while planning activities occur.

Pitfall 1: The Bandwagon Approach

The grass is always greener, even in education. Parents, educators and other professionals hear about a new college program for students with ID in a neighboring community or state and think it sounds like a good idea. So they return to their community and say, "Let's do that, too. We have a college right down the street from our high school." Then they uproot their existing self-contained classroom in which students with ID are learning functional academics, life skills, and vocational training, and they move it to a college campus. This example might be a bit extreme, but it is not that far removed from how some programs have started. Thoughtful and deliberate planning (as described in Chapter 4) is needed to ensure that PSE experiences not only will meet students' needs but will improve student outcomes.

Planning activities can take a year or more, and there are a variety of resources available to assist in the development of dual-enrollment programs (Grigal et al., 2005; Grigal, 2003; Hart & Grigal, 2004) and inclusive college initiated programs (www.innovationsnow.net). Site visits can often be useful for ascertaining the range of services that others are able to provide. In addition, many programs provide examples of their application for services, sample schedules, and mission statements on web sites. As recently as five years ago, many may have felt that they needed to reinvent the wheel when it came to establishing PSE services; now more resources and strategies are available to help stakeholders carefully assess students' needs, establish needed partnerships, and effectively plan new PSE options for students with ID (see a list of web site resources in the Chapter Appendix). One such strategy is Resource Mapping (Crane & Mooney, 2005).

Resource Mapping is a collaborative process designed to identify resources and assets in a community that are available for a specified area or goal (e.g., improved transition outcomes for youth with ID). Once resources are identified, a strategic action plan is created to catalog how resources may be streamlined for more effective service delivery or combined to eliminate duplication, and how gaps may be addressed. This approach is designed to be a catalyst for collaboration, and resource and cost sharing.

Resource Mapping typically includes four major components:

1. Customization of an online survey of PSE and transition-related services and practices based on the National Alliance of Secondary Education Standards and the Transition Guideposts for Success. This component involves survey development, administration, synthesis, and analysis.
2. On-site facilitation (meeting 1), including an overview of what Resource Mapping is all about and a review of survey results to determine area PSE resources and practices, service overlaps, and gaps in services, and to set priorities.
3. On-site facilitation (meeting 2) for development of a PSE strategic action plan, which includes identification of goals, tasks, measurable milestones, roles and responsibilities of team members, and articulation of timelines.
4. Compilation of a PSE strategic action plan that is monitored biannually at a minimum.

Pitfall 2: Poorly Defined Program Goals

Goals are something that we hear a lot about in special education. As Chapter 2 detailed, the Individuals with Disabilities Education Improvement Act (IDEIA) of 2004 (PL 108-446) provides significant changes regarding what is required to be documented about transition services in student IEPs. In addition, State Performance Plans (SPP) Indicators 13 and 14 add a new level of accountability for states when reporting how these goals are documented and implemented, and how they affect student outcomes. Yet many of the programs that have been created to support students with ID in PSE settings have not been successful in setting measurable goals to guide implementation of services.

PSE options range widely across the country, but there are some similarities in how they describe their services. In general, most would indicate that their purpose is to

- Increase student independence
- Access postsecondary learning
- Learn the use of life skills in the environment in which they will be needed
- Promote self-determination, advocacy, and communication skills
- Secure and maintain integrated competitive employment
- Participate in aspects of the college community

All these goals have merit. In fact, many high school transition programs may also list these types of goals for the students with ID whom they support. However, many of these goals will never be actualized. They will remain, like far too many IEP goals, on the student's official to-do list without ever being done. Why? Because they are written in such a way that it is difficult to determine what success would look like. How do you know when you have expanded functional life skills? How are enhanced self-determination and self-advocacy measured? Employment seems to be an easier goal to judge objectively, yet even in this area, many programs retain their high school roots and perpetuate the rotating structure of endless job training experiences for students, without a plan to get them to the next level of paid employment. If PSE initiatives for students with ID are to fulfill their potential, the critical elements of service have to be addressed in the establishment of *measurable* goals.

How Can You Create "Program Goals" and Still Make a Student's Plan Individualized?

The idea of creating program goals may seem counterintuitive to some. It might appear that we are suggesting that all students who receive services in PSE should have the same goals; and, in a way, we are. All students' goals should be similar in that they are measurable, related to their personal needs, and described such that others can easily understand what each student will be expected to do. There is no magic bullet for success. But a sure-fire path to failure is to not know what you are trying to achieve. Without clearly articulated goals, there is no way to ascertain whether students are making progress, whether they are achieving the expected outcomes, and whether the services are successful. The first step to establishing goals is knowing what you are trying to accomplish,

INSET 7.2. WESTERN CONNECTION AT WESTERN CONNECTICUT STATE UNIVERSITY: PROGRAM GOALS

1. Students will annually participate in person-centered planning to identify dreams and determine goals and support needs for the upcoming year.
2. Students will explore job opportunities in three areas of interest through informational interviews, job shadows, and/or business tours.
3. Students will obtain paid integrated community supported or competitive employment in a field of interest.
4. Students will attend 1–2 audited college courses per year and monitor progress using a curriculum matrix.
5. Students will demonstrate the ability to choose continuing education or a college course that fits their schedule and interests, register for that course, and determine transportation to and from the class independently.
6. Students will demonstrate the ability to articulate their support needs in employment settings, college classrooms, community settings, and at home.
7. Students will monitor personal progress toward goals on a quarterly basis.
8. Students will demonstrate the ability to access public transportation, when needed, to travel in the community.
9. Students will participate in their IEP meetings to the best of their ability and at a minimum share their names, accomplishments, support needs, and goals for the upcoming year.
10. Students will make the transition out of the program to adult service providers that will sustain their level of integrated employment.

exactly. What will students get out of this experience? Inset 7.2 provides an example of how one program created measurable goals that could be individualized for each student.

Being able to clearly articulate the expected outcomes will drive every aspect of the services provided. Program goals provide guidance for the information you need to collect on incoming students: their knowledge base; their previous experience related to self-advocacy and self-determination; their previous job status; and what supports or strategies have helped them to succeed in their high school classes. Program goals impact how the PSE program is marketed to students and their families. They will also affect students' schedules, determine how, when, and where students receive services and supports and the location of instruction, as each will be determined by what the program is trying to achieve. Finally, program goals ultimately guide the creation of outcome measures. Did you achieve what you and your student set out to achieve? Without these goals, it will not be possible to determine the successes and failures of the experience.

Pitfall 3: Limiting the Integration of Student Experiences

A final pitfall that can be avoided when planning PSE initiatives is limiting students to segregated learning opportunities. Those spearheading planning efforts should not assume that simply because a student has an ID, he or she will not be able to derive meaningful knowledge from or participate effectively in inclusive college classes and all other aspects of college life. Will their accomplishments sometimes be different? Yes, perhaps, but we need only look at the success of students with ID who have been included in pre-K–12 options, integrated employment, and other areas of adult living, and the failure of past segregated learning opportunities to compare the long-term outcomes of each approach. History repeatedly shows us that individuals with ID have been drastically underestimated. The knee-jerk approach to separate students with disabilities, especially individuals with ID, is a path that need not be revisited in PSE. It is all too easy to imagine postsecondary education options that mirror those created in the K–12 system, with separate courses, specially designed curricula, and an abundance of support personnel. We know how to do that, as its been done before. Creating inclusive learning opportunities in institutes of higher education is a more difficult task, as is demonstrated by an examination of the known 150 PSE options nationwide and the discovery that only 16% are inclusive (Hart & Grigal, 2008). Yes, there are abundant first-hand accounts and experiences of individuals with ID to guide the direction of PSE options toward more inclusive choices.

Inclusive experiences for students with ID who are dually enrolled in high school and PSE have demonstrated an increased chance of attaining paid integrated employment (Zafft, Hart, & Zimbrich, 2004). The recent amendments to the Higher Education Opportunity Act of 2008 (PL 110-315) emphasize the need for inclusive learning experiences to be part of programs serving students with ID to be eligible to receive financial aid. In a Joint Explanatory Statement of the Committee of Conference, the House and the Senate recommended that "The Conferees intend to encourage such programs to integrate students with intellectual disabilities into inclusive activities, coursework and campus settings with nondisabled postsecondary students, and that such programs include measurable outcomes, such as attainment of a degree or certificate."

LESSONS LEARNED ABOUT IMPLEMENTING SERVICES IN PSE FOR STUDENTS WITH INTELLECTUAL DISABILITIES

Those who support students with ID as they access PSE must approach the implementation of services with the high expectation that students are capable of being involved in the planning, monitoring, and achievement of the goals and activities. Outcomes of such high expectations will include enhancing students' ability to access paid work and transition to new and better jobs, and increasing their capacity to participate to the greatest extent possible in typical college courses. As services in PSE settings are provided, the sponsoring entities need to develop methods to monitor student activities and evaluate the satisfaction level of both the people and systems involved.

The Need for High Expectations for Students with Intellectual Disabilities

One consistent theme in Chapters 4 and 6 is the need to use a person-centered planning process to ascertain what a student wants to gain by participating in PSE. This allows students, in partnership with their family, friends, and support personnel, to articulate their needs, fears, and desires, which will drive the creation of services and assist in identifying the level of supports that will be needed. This process may at first be somewhat foreign to students who are accustomed to sitting at IEP meetings but contributing little or nothing to the conversation about future goals.

Students need to be exposed to a wide range of experiences, because without knowledge of the range of possible options it may be difficult for students to choose personal goals or evaluate their progress toward those goals (Wehmeyer, Agran, & Hughes, 1998). As school systems and colleges seek to create services, the first step in establishing high expectations is to involve students in the process of creating goals. Wehmeyer et al. asserted, "Individuals who have lived restricted or live with little opportunity to sample a range of employment, social, educational or community experience may have a limited repertoire from which to draw when choosing personal goals" (p. 189).

In working with students who have had little or no real experience with setting or monitoring goals, one strategy is to keep things simple. Have the student set one goal for a semester and help him or her set up a schedule to monitor that goal. Self-selected goals may be as effective, if not more effective, than teacher-selected goals at enhancing a student's academic performance (Wehmeyer et al., 1998). While the goal might be academic or job-related, it also might relate to a personal desire (e.g., "I want to get some new clothes," "I want to have some friends on campus"). Allowing students to connect goal setting to a real, achievable outcome that actually affects their lives makes the process more meaningful. It can also help students to perceive themselves as someone who can set and achieve goals. Agran (1997) also connected goal setting to motivation, asserting,

> Students need to be involved in selecting and setting their own academic and social goals and desired levels of performances. Direct involvement of the student is very important. Students who have identified their own goals or who agree with the goals selected for them are more likely to engage in the desired behavior. Setting goals may motivate students to search for strategies to accomplish them.

Student Participation in IEP Meetings

As each of the other chapter authors indicates, there are no IEPs in higher education since it is not governed by the IDEIA. However, students who are dually enrolled and receiving transition services in PSE settings will continue to have the need for an IEP. Developing IEP goals for students who will be or are in PSE can be a challenge in the beginning. Matching the IEP requirements to the context of higher education often challenges local education agency personnel. Under IDEIA 2004, school systems are required to assist the student in identifying measurable postschool goals in training, education, employment, and, where appropriate, independent living skills. As previously discussed, person-centered planning techniques can be used to assist students and their families in identifying goals in these areas. But goal creation should not be the end of a student's involvement in his or her IEP. A great deal of preparation, practice, and follow-up is necessary to engage students as active participants in their IEP meetings. Students should be able to choose how they would like to participate in their IEP meeting. For example, some may want to introduce themselves, discuss how they are doing in each of their classes, and discuss the goals and vision they have for the future. This level of participation might include assisting them to create a digital story of what they envision for their future, a PowerPoint handout, or a short summary from their person-centered planning. See Inset 7.3, which shows how one student shared her input during her IEP meeting.

Students should be supported to share their vision for the future, even if, to some, it may seem unattainable. The information gleaned provides vital insight into students' goals and motivations. They should not be told that they are being unrealistic or that they could never achieve a particular goal or career path. Instead, students can be helped to identify the necessary skills that are required for a chosen career by using online occupational databases such as O'Net (http://onlinecenter.org), job shadowing, and/or informational interviews. A guided inquiry process assists students in coming to the realization for themselves that a certain career may not be as interesting or attainable to them as they once thought. Additionally, a guided inquiry process may help to identify related careers. For example, a young woman wanted to be a veterinarian, but once she identified what she would have to do to accomplish that goal, especially all the years of education, she opted not to pursue that career path. Instead, she decided that working with animals in another capacity would be preferable, so she audited three college courses: Pet Grooming I and II and Kennel Management. She now works full time for a national pet supply company as a dog groomer and is fully benefited.

Student Involvement in Course Choice and Registration

Part of establishing and maintaining high expectations for students with ID is determining from the outset how students will be involved in each aspect of their PSE experience. All students, whether they have a disability or not, may have had limited experience in choosing high school courses. Typically, they have been limited to a set of predetermined courses during high school which may be driven by the functional life skills curriculum or by the general education curriculum. Given the limitations placed on students in high school regarding course selection, students with ID may have some difficulty determining the courses they would like to take in a college setting. Many students *without* disabilities attend college because they want to be able to get a good job in an area of interest. The goal is often the same for students with ID, and their career aspirations can help guide their course selection. In PSE, students are assigned to an academic advisor who assists them with registration and choosing courses that are related to a declared major, degree, or certificate program that they are enrolled in. Depending upon the structure of the PSE initiative, students with ID may or may not have access to a traditional college advisor. Those students with ID who do receive academic advising may wish to also seek input from the institution's disability support services

Inset 7.3
Keisha X
IEP Meeting
Thursday, March 29, 2009

Summary of my likes and preferences

I would like to stay one more year at the
    university site.
I like classroom work.
I like community outings (especially
    assignments at the mall).
I like my classmates, and I like the students on campus.
I like my job.
I like being able to choose where I eat on campus.

My strengths

I always participate in class.
I always pay close attention in class.
I follow directions well.
I am a nice and friendly person.
I work well independently or in a team
    with others.
I am good at reading people's moods.
I am good at vocabulary lessons.
I am a pretty good reader.
I ask questions when I need help.

_____

_____

Things I need to work on

Math
Money concepts
Understanding difficult words when I'm reading
Listening to instructions and writing them
    down if I need to
Riding the MTA
Using my left arm more often
Not breaking my braces

_____

_____

I want to …

Learn how to ride the MTA
Visit work sites and take tours of different
    jobs, in the following areas:
    Office jobs
    Computer jobs
    Construction work
    Airport jobs
Get a paid job in an office setting
Go out with friends more

My future

I want to learn how to ride the MTA to college by myself.
I want a full-time job.
I want to continue living with my aunt for a while.
Eventually, I would like to live on my own, near my aunt.
I would like to always visit my friends from
    college.
In the faraway future, I would like to get
    married and have two kids (but no pets!).
I want to get my driver's license and buy
    a car.

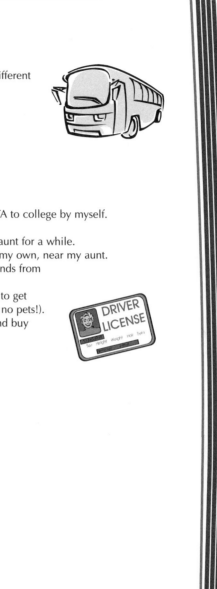

staff, who can identify professors and courses that match a student's learning style. It is helpful to find college instructors who employ different instructional strategies and who have previously had students with disabilities in their classes. Students should consider the benefits of auditing a course before taking it for credit if they are taking a rigorous academic course for the first time.

Considerations relevant to choosing courses include

- The student's career goals
- Teaching style and overall openness of the instructor to diverse learners
- The availability of internships, apprenticeships, and service learning opportunities offered by the college
- Transportation options
- Availability of educational coaches and tutors
- Availability of classroom accommodations
- The student's employment schedule

Course registration presents a variety of learning opportunities. Students will be expected to know how to determine the course offerings (by using the course catalog or a web site), determine whether they are taking a course for credit or auditing and what that means, fill out the required paperwork, and pay for the class. Tuition is one area in which PSE initiatives vary widely. Some programs charge tuition by the semester, and these bills are sent to the students' families. Other programs that work with dually enrolled students with ID, charge school systems a predetermined fee for each class taken. Some community colleges provide tuition waivers for students who are receiving Supplemental Security Income (SSI) from the Social Security Administration. Regardless of the system used, students need to know the process that is in place and their role in the course registration process. How do you determine the cost of a class? Who do you pay? The program needs to have a systematic way to support students and families through this process, and students should be made aware that a process exists. Ultimately one of the biggest potential outcomes of participating in a PSE experience is learning *how to access knowledge as an adult*. Helping students with ID learn the steps in this process and how to navigate through them to achieve a personal learning goal is a vital outcome of any PSE experience. If achieved, this skill will allow students with ID to access desired learning even after their tenure in a program is over.

The Importance of Employment

For youth with disabilities, paid work experiences have been consistently shown to be the strongest predictor of postsecondary employment (Brewer, 2005; Brown, Shiraga, & Kessler, 2006; Colley & Jamison, 1998; Fabian, Lent, & Willis, 1998; Luecking & Fabian, 2000). Wagner, Newman, Cameto, Levine, and Garza's (2006) report, *Changes Over Time in the Early Postschool Outcomes of Youth with Disabilities: A Report of Findings from the National Longitudinal Transition Study-2*, demonstrated that secondary school students with disabilities who worked for pay outside the home in the preceding year before exit and/or participated in a work-study program at school had an increased chance for employment in their postschool years. Yet our most recent national data demonstrate low levels of paid employment for students with ID before they leave high school (Wagner, Cadwallader, & Marder et al., 2003). Of paramount concern as we move the PSE agenda forward for students with ID is the possibility of doing so in a manner that divorces those college experiences from employment. We must strive to address both access to college *and* employment if we hope to make a lasting impact on the lives of students with ID. Chapters 8 and 9 provide an extended discussion of the importance of engaging students with ID in integrated paid supported or competitive employment experiences as part of their college experience.

Monitoring and Evaluation of Student Activities and Outcomes

Within the current climate of standards-based reform, state performance plans, and higher levels of accountability for educational outcomes, program evaluation activities need to be incorporated into new models of service delivery, including PSE for students with ID. Collecting student outcome data and using these results to determine strategies for systemic improvement and related professional development needs (Hasazi, Furney, & DeStefano, 1999; Test, Eddy, Neale, & Wood, 2004) can help to ensure that the needs of students with ID are met, that postschool outcomes are enhanced, and that collaborative relationships (e.g., the public school, postsecondary institution, and community agencies) support student success. However, school systems often have difficulty providing such evaluation services because of a lack of personnel, expertise, and funding (Johnson, 1998; Levesque, Bradby, & Rossi, 1996; McLaughlin, 1993; Test et al., 2004). Colleges have historically collected outcome data, but it usually relates to retention and degree achievement. College personnel supporting adult students with ID in PSE may also not have experience with program evaluation methods. In fact, in a national survey, Hart, Mele-McCarthy, Pasternack, Zimbrich, & Parker (2004) found that the majority of PSE programs do not collect evaluation data or outcome data on their students with ID.

Grigal et al. (2005) suggested three central areas in which data can be collected about students' activities in the course of operations: college course access, employment, and participation in social or recreational activities afforded to all students. They suggested that compiling and reviewing these data on a regular basis can

- Demonstrate student achievement of goals
- Document staff time used to support students in various learning environments
- Provide a record of successful partnerships in employment and PSE
- Document whether the goals of the program have been achieved
- Identify areas in which students are not actively participating

However, it is important to note that these suggestions may be easier to implement in certain types of PSE programs. Those programs that are supporting dually enrolled students and those that have been specifically designed to support adult students with ID are more likely to have the staff resources to address these monitoring activities.

Documenting College Course Participation

A major impetus for serving students with ID on a college campus is to access college courses. However, Neubert, Moon, & Grigal (2004) did not find that this practice was universal in the programs they surveyed. Only 36% of the 163 students served in programs were taking a college course. The majority of these students were enrolled in noncredit or audited courses, primarily in health and fitness or art-related areas. If a stated program goal is that students with ID will access college courses, the frequency and outcome of such participation must be monitored. Grigal et al. (2005) suggested that the following information be compiled about students' access to college courses: name of course taken, instructor, semester, whether the course was taken for credit or audited, student grade, and the type of educational supports provided to the student. Documenting student participation in college classes provides data that can be used to demonstrate to college personnel and administrators, families, and education professionals the ability of students with ID to participate in and benefit from accessing college classes. These data should be reviewed by staff to determine whether students' interests and goals are reflected in course participation, whether staff need to assist students in selecting a broader range of courses, and what types of educational supports are needed by students in this setting.

Documenting Employment

Not all PSE initiatives will include a focus on employment. Those that do are likely seeking outcomes related to paid employment and connecting students, as needed, to adult provider agencies that might continue to provide support after the student exits the program. Zafft, Hart, & Zimbrich (2004) documented that students with ID who participate in PSE experiences have better employment outcomes than those who do not participate in PSE. However, to draw such a conclusion it is necessary to capture and compile student employment data on a regular basis. Grigal et al. (2005) suggested that at a minimum the following relevant employment information be compiled: job title(s), whether the job is paid or unpaid, the rate of pay, the hours worked per week, who provided job support, the kinds of supports that were most effective, and the transportation used to get to and from the job. In addition, as students move between jobs, it is helpful to document the reason for these transitions. Did the student quit? And if so, why? Did they leave under other circumstances? This kind of work history provides staff with relevant information that can be useful in future job development activities and shared with future adult community rehabilitation providers.

Once these data are compiled, staff should review them to identify the types of jobs students are accessing and whether these jobs match students' expressed interests and goals for employment. Staff can consider how to expand job opportunities if necessary, how to develop job sites that have the potential to offer benefits if needed, and whether transportation needs that promote independence have been addressed. These data can be shared with supervisors, college administrators, and parents to justify the need for additional support staff to provide on-the-job training, travel training if necessary, or to document progress toward established program employment goals.

Documenting College and Community Activities

One advantage of serving students with ID in PSE is to increase opportunities to interact with same-age peers without disabilities (Dolyniuk et al., 2002; Hall, Kleinert, & Kearns, 2000). However, there has been little research that supports this assumption, with the exception of the work of Neubert et al. (2004), who found that 64% of 163 students attended college events after school hours. Grigal et al. (2005) suggested that staff compile information about students' participation in college or community activities, including type of activity, location, frequency, time of day, and transportation used. This information can provide staff and administrators with an accurate picture of the activities that students are accessing regularly, and perhaps even more importantly, highlight students who are *not* participating in *any* activities. Reviewing this information throughout the year can provide an indication of the emphasis placed on and outcomes related to social engagement on campus.

The Importance of Scheduling Data Collection and Review

To ensure that data are collected, regularly reviewed, and used to inform better practice, we suggest that PSE programs create a schedule for all program evaluation activities for relevant staff. This schedule should include the kinds of data that are to be collected (e.g., employment, college course access, participation in social or recreational activities), the person assigned to collect the data (e.g., coordinator, job coach, education coach), and when it will be collected (e.g., monthly, quarterly, as needed). These evaluation activities should be known by all and embedded in staff calendars. A final aspect of evaluation is how these data will be used. Evaluation data should be used to determine the strengths of the program and identify areas that need improvement. This will not occur unless two things happen: the data are reviewed and discussed, and this discussion leads to the development of an action plan to effect positive change.

Using Data to Drive Change

Often a great deal of time and energy has been put into creating and planning programs and services in PSE. However, once implementation begins, attention to program improvement and expansion wanes as staff members become involved with day-to-day operations. As shown in Chapter 3, there are many different models used to support student access to PSE. Currently, there are no standards in place for the creation of PSE programs or implementation of services, though initial work has been done to create and validate a set of quality indicators (Grigal & Hart, 2008). Furthermore, there are no commercially available evaluation tools designed to assess the services provided in, or outcomes of, PSE programs for students with ID.

To address this need, the PostSecondary Education Research Center (PERC) Project, coordinated through TransCen, Inc., created the PERC Postsecondary Program Evaluation Tool (see Chapter 1, Figure 1.1). This tool provides a snapshot of the quality of existing services and provides users with a concise evaluation report and the option to create an itemized action plan to address areas in need of improvement. The PERC Postsecondary Program Evaluation Tool consists of 10 sections, including program planning, staffing, administration, student planning, student activities, employment, self-determination, interagency collaboration, monitoring, and evaluation. In addition, the tool provides users with the opportunity to compile detailed information about the employment experiences in which their students participate. It is available free of charge on the PERC project web site (www.transitiontocollege.net).

Evaluation cannot be conducted in a vacuum. The goal of all evaluation activities should be to review, advance, or improve current services and outcomes. There are multiple forms of data that can be collected about PSE programs and services for students with ID. Below is a list of various areas in which data can also be compiled:

- Satisfaction of students, families, college personnel, and community personnel with PSE initiatives, collected through written or personal interviews
- Changes in students' quality of life (e.g., more independent, more self-determined, more connected to the community)
- Documentation of how logistics are handled (e.g., transportation to and from PSE, dispensing of medication, free and reduced lunches, location of IEP meetings, discipline, and adherence to the IHE code of conduct)
- Documentation of how PSE staff spend their time (e.g., type of activity, amount of time)
- Documentation of formal or informal partnerships with PSE and community personnel
- Documentation of student goal attainment, including IEP goals, goals for PSE participation, and goals identified through person-centered planning
- Record of exit data as each student prepares to exit the PSE initiative (e.g., SSI, employment placement, referral or acceptance to adult agency, goals for future)
- Record of follow-up activities (e.g., documentation of former student outcomes concerning employment, independent living, participation with adult agency, and social activities)
- Documentation of PSE program goals (e.g., if the purpose is to provide employment support and opportunities, is this happening for the majority of students?)

If the impetus for access to PSE for students with ID is to improve their lives, be it through expanded education opportunities, enhanced employment outcomes, or increased social networks and connections, then we owe it to this group of individuals to ensure these outcomes occur. We must encourage students and their families to anticipate that college is an option and support the development of academic and self-advocacy skills throughout elementary, middle, and high school. We must meet their fears and misconceptions with information and experiences and quell their misgivings with stories of success. We must guide students with ID to consider what knowledge they would seek in a college and reinforce this vision with action. We must provide them the opportunity to cultivate the skills needed to seek further learning as the need or desire arises in their adult lives. Finally, we must capture the outcomes of these experiences to demonstrate that PSE can make a difference in the lives of individuals—young and old—with ID. We hope that these lessons learned and shared in this chapter can serve to inform all who are planning to support or are supporting helping students with ID in PSE settings to create, implement, and evaluate these services in a more thoughtful and deliberate manner.

REFERENCES

Agran, M. (Ed.). (1997). *Student-directed learning: Teaching self-determination skills.* Thousand Oaks, CA: Brooks/Cole.

Behling, K., & Hart, D. (2008). Universal course design: A model of professional development. Strategies for bringing UCD to a college campus and ensuring its sustainability. In S. Burgstahler (Ed.), *Universal design in post-secondary education: From principles to practice.* Cambridge: Harvard Education Press, pp. 109-125.

Brewer, D. (2005). *Working my way through high school: The impact of paid employment on transitioning students with disabilities.* Ithaca, NY: Cornell University, School of Industrial and Labor Relations Extension, Employment and Disability Institute. Retrieved November 6, 2008, from http://digitalcommons.ilr.cornell.edu/edicollect/109

Briel, L.W., & Getzel, E.E. (2005). Internships and field experiences. In E.E. Getzel & P. Wehman (Eds.), *Going to college: Expanding opportunities for people with disabilities* (pp. 271–290). Baltimore: Paul H. Brookes Publishing Co.

Briel, L.W., & Wehman, P. (2005). Career planning and placement. In E.E. Getzel & P. Wehman (Eds.), *Going to college: Expanding opportunities for people with disabilities* (pp. 291–305). Baltimore: Paul H. Brookes Publishing Co.

Brown, L., Shiraga, B., & Kessler, K. (2006). The quest for ordinary lives: The integrated post-school vocational functioning of 50 workers with significant disabilities. *Journal of Research and Practice for Persons with Severe Disabilities, 31*(2), 93–126.

Colley, D.A., & Jamison, D. (1998). Postschool results for youth with disabilities: Key indicators and policy implications. *Career Development for Exceptional Individuals, 21*(2), 145–160.

Crane, K., & Mooney, M. (2005). *Essential tools: Community resource mapping.* Minneapolis: University of Minnesota, Institute on Community Integration, National Center on Secondary Education and Transition.

Dolyniuk, C.A., Kamens, M.W., Corman, H., DiNardo, P.O., Totaro, R.M., & Rockoff, J.C. (2002). Students with developmental disabilities go to college: Description of a collaborative transition project. *Focus on Autism and Other Developmental Disabilities,7*(4), 236–241.

Esquivel, S.L., Ryan, C.S., & Bonner, M. (2008) Involved parents' perceptions of their experiences in school-based team meetings. *Journal of Educational and Psychological Consultation, 18*(3), 236–258.

Fabian, E.S., Lent, R.L., & Willis, S.P. (1998). Predicting work transition outcomes for students with disabilities: Implications for counselors. *Journal of Counseling & Development, 76,* 311–315.

Getzel E.E., McManus, S., & Briel, L.W. (2004). An effective model for college students with learning disabilities and attention deficit hyperactivity disorders. *Research to Practice,* 3(1). Retrieved January 14, 2008 from http://www.ncset.org/publications/researchtopractice/NCSETResearch Brief_3.1.pdf.

Getzel, E.E., & Thoma, C.A. (2008). Experiences of college students with disabilities and the importance of self-determination in higher education settings. *Career Development for Exceptional Individuals, 31*(2), 77–84.

Grigal, M. (2003). Needs assessment for students with significant disabilities. In *Online training modules from the University of Maryland On-Campus Outreach*. Retrieved June 17, 2008, from http://www.education.umd.edu/oco/training/oco_training_modules/start. html

Grigal, M. & Hart, D. (2008). *Quality Indicators of Postsecondary Education Services for students with intellectual disabilities*. Presentation at the Division on Career Development and Transition International Conference. Milwaukee, WI.

Grigal, M., Neubert, D., & Moon, M.S. (2005). *Transition services for students with severe disabilities in college and community settings: Strategies for planning, implementation and evaluation*. Austin, TX: PRO-ED.

Hall, M., Kleinert, H.L., & Kearns, J.F. (2000). Going to college! Postsecondary programs for students with moderate and severe disabilities. *Teaching Exceptional Children, 32*(3), 58–65.

Hart, D. (2008). [National survey of postsecondary education programs that support students with intellectual disabilities]. Unpublished raw data.

Hart, D., & Grigal, M. (2004). Individual support to increase access to an inclusive college experience for students with intellectual disabilities. In *Online training modules from the University of Maryland On-Campus Outreach*. Retrieved June 17, 2008, from http://www. education.umd.edu/oco/training/oco_training_modules/IndividualSupports/start.html

Hart, D., & Grigal, M. (2008, March). New frontier: Postsecondary education for youth with intellectual disabilities. *Section 504 Compliance Handbook*, 10–11.

Hart, D., Mele-McCarthy, J., Pasternack, R.H., Zimbrich, K., & Parker, D.R. (2004). Community college: A pathway to success for youth with learning, cognitive, and intellectual disabilities in secondary settings. *Education and Training in Developmental Disabilities, 1*(1), 54–66.

Hasazi, S.B., Furney, K.S., & DeStefano, L. (1999). Implementing the IDEA transition mandates. *Exceptional Children, 65*(4), 555–566.

Higher Education Opportunity Act of 2008, Pub. L. No. 110-315 § 122 STAT. 3078 (2008).

Individuals with Disabilities Education Improvement Act of 2004, PL 108-446, 20 U.S.C. §§ 1400 *et seq.*

Izzo, M., Hertzfeld, J., Simmons-Reed, G., & Aaron, J. (2001). *Promising practices: Improving the quality of higher education for students with disabilities*. National Center for Postsecondary Educational Supports, Center on Disability Studies. Available from http://devtest.cds.hawaii.edu/rrtc/products/phaseII/pdf/022d(1)-H01.pdf

Izzo, M., & Lamb, M. (2002). Self-determination and career development: Skills fur successful transitions to postsecondary education and employment. Unpublished manuscript.

Johnson, L.R. (1998). *Program evaluation in special education: An examination of the practices utilized by local education agencies*. Jonesboro: Arkansas State University. (ERIC Document ED424291)

Joint Explanatory Statement of the Committee of Conference, the House and the Senate (2008). H.R. 110-803 at 592. Higher Education Opportunity Act Conference Report.

Levesque, K., Bradby, D., & Rossi, K. (1996). *Using data for program improvement: How do we encourage schools to do it?* (Centerfocus No. 12). Berkeley: University of California at Berkeley, National Center for Research in Vocational Education. Retrieved June 24, 2002, from http://vocserve.berkeley.edu/CenterFocus/CF12.html

Luecking, R., & Fabian, E. (2000). Paid internships and employment success for youth in transition. *Career Development for Exceptional Individuals, 23*, 205–222.

McGrew, K.S., & Evans, J. (2003). *Expectations for students with cognitive disabilities: Is the cup half empty or half full? Can the cup flow over?* (Synthesis Report 55). Minneapolis: University of Minnesota, National Center on Educational Outcomes. Retrieved January 18, 2009, from http://education.umn.edu/NCEO/OnlinePubs/Synthesis55.html

McLaughlin, M.J. (1993). Promising practices and future directions for special education. *NICHCY News Digest, 2.*

Moon, M.S., Neubert, D.A., & Grigal, M. (2002). Postsecondary education and transition services for students ages 18–21 with significant disabilities. *Focus on Exceptional Children, 34*, 1–11.

Mueller, T.G., Singer, G.H.S., & Draper, L.M. (2008). Reducing parental dissatisfaction with special education in two school districts: Implementing conflict prevention and alternative dispute resolution. *Journal of Educational and Psychological Consultation, 18*(3), 191–233.

Neubert, D.A., Moon, M.S., & Grigal, M. (2004). Activities of students with significant disabilities receiving services in postsecondary settings. *Education and Training in Developmental Disabilities, 39*(1), 16–25.

Olson, L. (2004). Enveloping expectations. *Education Week, 23*(17), 8–20.

Rose, D.H., & Meyer, A. (2002). *Teaching every student in the digital age: Universal design for learning.* Alexandria, VA: ASCD.

Test, D.W., Eddy, S., Neale, M., & Wood, W.M. (2004). A survey of data collected by transition teachers. *Career Development for Exceptional Individuals, 27*, 87–100.

Thoma, C.A., & Wehmeyer, M.L. (2005). Self-determination and the transition to postsecondary education. In E.E. Getzel & P. Wehman (Eds.), *Going to college: Expanding opportunities for people with disabilities* (pp. 49–68). Baltimore: Paul H. Brookes Publishing Co.

Wagner, M., Cadwallader, T., & Marder, C. (with Cameto, R., Cardoso, D., Garza, N., Levine, P., & Newman, L.). (2003). *Life outside the classroom for youth with disabilities. A report from the National Longitudinal Transition Study-2* (NLTS2). Menlo Park, CA: SRI International. Available at www.nlts2.org/reports/2003_04-2/nlts2_report_2003_04-2_complete.pdf.

Wagner, M., Newman, L., Cameto, R., Garza, N., & Levine, P. (2005). *After high school: A first look at the postschool experiences of youth with disabilities. A report from the National Longitudinal Transition Study-2 (NLTS2).* Menlo Park, CA: SRI International. Available at www.nlts2.org/reports/2005_04/nlts2_report_2005_04_complete.pdf.

Wagner, M., Newman, L., Cameto, R., & Levine, P. (2005, June). *Changes over time in the early post-school outcomes of youth with disabilities. A Report from the National Longitudinal Transition Study-2* (SRI Project P11182). U.S. Department of Education, Office of Special Education Programs. Menlo Park, CA: SRI International.

Wagner, M., Newman, L., Cameto, R., Levine, P., & Garza, N. (2006). *An Overview of Findings from Wave 2 of the National Longitudinal Transition Study-2 (NLTS2).* Menlo Park, CA: SRI International. Available at www.nlts2.org/reports/2006_08/nlts2_report_2006_08_complete.pdf.

Wehman, P., & Yasuda, S. (2005). The need and the challenges associated with going to college. In L. Getzel & P. Wehman (Eds.), *Going to college: Expanded opportunities for individuals with disabilities* (pp. 3–23). Baltimore: Paul H. Brookes Publishing Co.

Wehmeyer, M., Agran, M., & Hughes, C. (1998). *Teaching self-determination skills to students with disabilities: Basic skills for successful transition.* Baltimore: Paul H. Brookes Publishing Co.

Wehmeyer, M.L., & Palmer, S.B. (2003). Adult outcomes for students with cognitive disabilities three years after high school: The impact of self determination. *Education and Training in Developmental Disabilities, 38*(2), 131–144.

Zafft, C., Hart, D., Zimbrich, K., & Kiernan, W. (2004). College career connection: A study of youth with intellectual disabilities and the impact of postsecondary education. *Education and Training in Developmental Disabilities, 39*(1), 45–53.

Web Resources on PSE Options for Students with ID

www.ThinkCollege.net

www.transitiontocollege.net

www.education.umd.edu/oco

www.transitioncoalition.org

www.STEPS-Forward.org

www.heath.gwu.edu

www.innovationsnow.net

www.ahead.org

www.inclusioninstitutes.org

The Missing Link: The Importance of Employment

Meg Grigal and Debra Hart

CHAPTER

8

While there are countless advantages related to the pursuit of postsecondary education, one undeniable benefit of seeking higher learning is that it can lead to improved employment outcomes. Students with and without disabilities and their adult counterparts have consistently demonstrated that further education correlates with successful employment or career outcomes (Wehman & Yasuda, 2005). Individuals with disabilities who have had any PSE are employed at double the rate of those with just a high school diploma (Gilmore, Bose, & Hart, 2001). Youth with ID who participated in PSE were 26% more likely to exit their vocational rehabilitation program with employment and earned a 73% higher weekly income (Migliore & Butterworth, 2008). So we know postsecondary education leads to better jobs. Why then is there a disconnect between what we know and the outcomes students with ID experience? And how can we ensure that our efforts related to increasing the participation of students with ID in college actually lead to better employment outcomes? The answer to the first question is that employment opportunities and outcomes for individuals with disabilities, and in particular individuals with ID, are negatively influenced by a variety of factors that are widely acknowledged, but seldom targeted for change. These include the overuse of vocational training experiences, inadequate training of transition and rehabilitation staff, and little emphasis on helping students with ID learn to transition "between" jobs. This chapter provides an overview of these challenges and how they reflect the need for change in how employment experiences are approached in the context of PSE programs for students with ID. Some suggestions for answering the second question, how to ensure better employment outcomes, are presented at the conclusion of the chapter with an example of how one PSE program in Connecticut was able to address some of these issues and improve student employment.

STARTING WITH PAID EMPLOYMENT

In 2006, the State Employment Leadership Network (SELN) (www.selnmembers. org) was launched by the National Association of State Directors of Developmental Disabilities Services (NASDDDS) and the Institute for Community Inclusion at the University of Massachusetts Boston (ICI) to facilitate collaboration between and within state developmental disability agencies working to maximize resources and develop more effective employment systems. Many states in conjunction with the SELN have created coalitions within their respective states to cultivate

259

Employment First initiatives under which employment is considered the first service provided to individuals with developmental disabilities and high support needs.

These Employment First initiatives focus on adults receiving services via their State Mental Retardation and Developmental Disabilities agencies. However, no such similar initiative is happening for students with ID within secondary education (Wehman, 2006). Paid employment is too seldom experienced by students with ID while in high school, although it has consistently been demonstrated to predict postschool employment success (Brewer, 2005; Wagner, Newman, Cameto, & Levine, 2005). When paid employment is deemed an expectation for students with ID, it is frequently seen as the culminating outcome of the transition-planning process, and thus, only sought at the end of a student's high school experience.

Given the freedom from a high school setting and the associated limitations related to scheduling, transportation, and staffing, PSE programs provide students with ID an ideal opportunity to focus both on accessing further education and on engagement in employment, much like their counterparts without disabilities. The employment component of PSE experiences for students with ID should *start* from the premise that the student can and should obtain integrated paid employment in the community as soon as possible (Wehman, 2006).

However, too many PSE initiatives for students with ID, whether operated by school systems or initiated by colleges, fall prey to a failed traditional secondary school vocational training model (Neubert & Redd, 2008). This model provides vocational training to students by rotating them through pre-established work experiences or internships in an array of different employment areas (e.g., culinary, maintenance, landscaping, clerical, retail, child care). The assumption is that these vocational training experiences give students a broad exposure to potential types of employment, help them to focus their personal career goals, and, perhaps, provide an opportunity to gain some work-related skills along the way (Hutchins & Renzaglia, 2002).

This type of programming has been conducted for years by special educators and transition and work-study coordinators in high schools nationwide, and is currently being replicated in some newly developed dual enrollment and college-initiated PSE programs, though it is not an evidence-based practice and has not been documented to result in a paid employment outcome for students with ID. In a recent unpublished survey of personnel from 14 PSE programs serving students with ID in one East Coast state, when asked the greatest challenges faced, respondents listed "establishing more stipend work opportunities on campus," "getting a 'stipend' program/process started," and "finding job sites that are willing to take 3-4 students per site" (Grigal, 2008). These responses reflect a continued commitment to the development of creating new job *training* experiences in lieu of focusing on increasing paid employment opportunities for students. Not surprisingly, the outcomes of the programs across this same state are reflective of the practices used. Of the 129 students served in 2007–2008 by these 14 programs, only 15 students with ID were in paid employment positions (Grigal, 2008).

Hutchins and Renzaglia (2002, p. 91) assert:

> There is no indication that this laissez-faire strategy is successful, in which vocational instruction is provided in a splintered manner with minimal regard for assessing community employment opportunities, evaluating the individual's

strengths and preferences in work, assessing family concerns and systemati-
cally teaching all relevant work and work-related skills necessary for successful
employment.

That is not to say that well-designed work-based learning experiences are not vital to the career development process of assisting students in obtaining paid employment. Luecking and Gramlich (2003) state that some indicators of quality
work-based learning experiences are 1) clear expectations of student activity at
the workplace, 2) clearly defined roles of teachers and work-site supervisors, and
3) well-structured feedback on student performance. The use of such experiences
to support the development of employment and work-related behavioral skills
for high school students with ID has great value. Countless publications have
documented that high-quality, goal-oriented work-based learning experiences are
vital, in that they help students with disabilities gain necessary employment skills
and broaden the experiences from which they could determine future desired
employment goals (Guy, Sitlington, Larsen, & Frank, 2008; Luecking, 2009;
Wehman, 2006). But it would be a stretch to call many of the rotating vocational
training experiences that are being implemented in PSE programs for students
with ID "well designed" and seldom do they result in paid competitive employment.

In the next chapter, Richard Luecking discusses how one of the ultimate
goals of PSE is to create a foundation for students with ID that leads to paid employment. He outlines the necessary characteristics of quality work-based experiences, characteristics that are all too frequently absent from the classic vocational training programs implemented by high schools and now being replicated
in PSE initiatives for students with ID. Most of these vocational training experiences are not created in response to a student's expressed desire, need, or interest, but instead are based upon what is available, nearby, or already established.
Most of the tasks involved in these experiences fall into stereotypical job categories for students with disabilities, such as the aforementioned culinary, ground
maintenance, custodial, landscaping, clerical, stocking, or child care. This is not
to imply that these types of jobs are without merit. Many individuals may find
long-lasting and fulfilling careers in these industries. However, when students
with ID are *only* offered experiences in these types of jobs, without regard to their
individual preferences, their chance of success is diminished. Additionally, these
experiences are seldom used to glean meaningful assessment data or implemented
to support the development of specific skills that students need to acquire in order to obtain paid employment in a career of their choice.

Some students with ID may have never engaged in work-based learning activities during their years prior to entering a PSE program. In such cases, it may
be necessary to assess their skills and identify their interests by engaging in job
shadowing, informational interviews, and perhaps in a well-designed, structured,
time-limited job training or internship experience. But the key words here are
time-limited. These experiences should not be used as time fillers in a student's
schedule or placeholders until a good paid job opportunity comes along. These
experiences need to be used strategically to help students do one of two things:
1) confirm a commitment to an area of interest in which they have little experience or 2) work on specific job skills so that the student can improve his or her
chances of seeking paid employment in that field.

Once the student has had the opportunity to ascertain whether he or she would like to pursue a career path in a specific area, and staff have gathered the assessment data needed to determine the student's skills and support needs, the focus should turn from job training to establishing paid employment—the earlier, the better. Participating in repeated and revolving job-training experiences unrelated to specific goals or outcomes is a model that should *not* be used when supporting students with ID in PSE settings because vocational training will never truly replicate a real job or demonstrate the student's capacity for paid employment.

Accessing Vocational Training Experiences

Students who are participating in vocational training experiences are often placed into these experiences without their input. Staff may assign students to a particular training site for a variety of reasons: availability of transportation, proximity, or an available slot. Students are told where they will be going and are expected to show up and do what they are told. Eventually, in a period of weeks or months, staff inform students that the experience is now over and tell them where their next experience will be. Although this is an oversimplification of the process, the description highlights an important issue. In a paid job, you don't just show up. There are many steps to seeking and gaining employment, and the job seeker is the central figure in each of them. The steps of choosing a career of interest, finding a job opening, filling out an application, and scheduling an interview entail skills that are not required of students participating in rotating vocational training or internship experiences.

Expectations

Expectations of both students and employers will also be vastly different in vocational training or internship experiences. Students involved in job training do not have to worry about being fired and are not, by necessity as required under the Fair Labor Standards Act's definition of a trainee, being asked to do what a typical employee would do (Simon & Halloran, 1994). Students in vocational training are not always expected to be responsible for monitoring their time with time cards, filling out time sheets, or calling in for days off or sick time. Moreover, because of the temporary nature of the experience, the expectations of the employer will differ substantially in vocational training. It is unlikely that an employer will have a great deal of investment in how well the student does or create long-term expectations for the student's outcome. Employers are not typically expected to provide the same level of supervision, feedback, or training as they would for a paid employee. Finally, and not insignificantly, vocational training and paid employment differ in their ultimate reward system. Student motivation to excel at the job and an employer's motivation to set high expectations are undoubtedly connected to a tangible financial outcome—the paycheck. A paycheck is what motivates most of the employed population without disabilities; it is what most employers use to reward good work; and it has equal bearing and influence on the employment of students with ID. One should not underestimate the power a paycheck may play in a student's motivation to do well at work.

The transition between the vocational training and paid employment experience is also very different. When a vocational training experience ends, students are simply rerouted to the training location. When a real job ends, students either have submitted their resignation or have been laid off or fired. None of these difficult experiences is replicated through the vocational training or internship experience.

THE TRANSITION BETWEEN JOBS

The phrase "the transition from school to work" has become commonplace in the world of special education; however, it doesn't reflect one of the most important transition skills that students with ID need to learn: how to transition between jobs. With the best of intentions, many school systems engage students in a wide array of unpaid vocational training or internship experiences throughout their high school career and then, as their culminating activity, seek to place a student in a paid job prior to their exit. In some cases this may be done in conjunction with an adult service provider or with the state vocational rehabilitation provider (Redd, 2004; National Council on Disability, 2008). Exiting high school with a paid job is a positive outcome, but it is also an outcome that cannot be expected to last forever. As Dwyre et al. suggested in Chapter 6, too often school systems glorify stories about students staying at the same job for many years as success stories. In some cases, this may be true and a student's job retention may be a true reflection of a high level of job satisfaction. However, longevity does not always mean that the employee is happy with his or her job. It is likely that there are just as many cases where students with ID remain in a job that they are unsatisfied with because they don't know how to transition to a new job.

A Bureau of Labor Statistics news release published in June 2008 examined the number of jobs that people born in the years 1957 to 1964 held from age 18 to age 42. These younger baby boomers held an average of 10.8 jobs during this 24-year period of time. The majority of these jobs were at the beginning of their working lives—when they were teenagers and in their early twenties. If job changes for people without disabilities occur most frequently in their teens and twenties, it would seem reasonable to assume that students with ID should reflect a similar pattern. Paid employment experience early in a student's postsecondary education provides an opportunity for students to navigate the uncharted and often scary experience of transitioning between jobs while still receiving support and guidance from staff who are familiar with their goals. There are three major components of transitioning between jobs that require support; losing a job, leaving a job, and getting a new job.

How to Handle Getting Fired or Being Laid Off

Losing a job is difficult for everyone. No one feels good about being fired or told that his or her services are no longer needed. This can be especially difficult if the person is being fired from his or her *first* job. Unfortunately job terminations for students with ID are fairly common (Moran, McDermott, & Butkus, 2002; Wehman, Inge, Revell, & Brooke, 2007) and may lead to extended periods of unemployment or a return to a segregated setting (Wehman et al., 2007). Difficult questions emerge when you are fired. How do you handle yourself? What should you say to your employer or to your family? How do you use the experience when looking for your next job? And what do you say during an interview when asked about why you left your previous job? The answers to all of these questions will depend to a large extent upon the person and his or her particular experience. Ideally, if PSE programs encourage students to engage in paid work early in their experience, then students who lose their job will be able to process this difficult transition with someone who knows them, has witnessed their employment history, and can help them use what they have learned in future employment experiences. However, if the student acquired the job as he or she is leaving the PSE experience, it is more likely that the support provider will be someone who has little history with the student and a large case management load. It is unlikely that the student with ID will be provided with the same level of support or be able to navigate the job loss experience as effectively.

How to Identify the Desire to Change Jobs

Another positive outcome of engaging students with ID in paid employment sooner rather than later is the potential to help them determine when a job isn't working out and how to engage in the job change process. Students with ID, like any other employee, may start out liking a job and in time determine that it is no longer right for them. Sometimes they may be able to articulate this; other times it may be evident in their job performance. Support staff that have been able to observe a student's changing attitude and performance would be able to intervene and begin a conversation with the student about what isn't working and why. Staff could also help the student think through the potential consequences of leaving his or her current job immediately and perhaps avoid a rash decision. Should you quit right now or look for a job while you are still employed? How should you tell your boss you are leaving? What kind of notice do you need to give? Anyone who has decided to leave his or her job will tell you that submitting your resignation to an employer is not the easiest of tasks for even the most experienced of workers. This task can be all the more challenging for students with ID, who have little work experience and even less experience changing jobs. Engaging students in paid employment as soon as possible leaves open the potential for them to deal with the feelings and logistics of changing jobs with the support and guidance of trusted support personnel. Most importantly, students with ID can also learn how to ask for and get support when seeking a new job in the future.

Gaining New Employment

Ideally, all job development activities conducted by staff in PSE programs and initiatives actively involve students in the process of seeking and obtaining employment. Students with ID should be creating their resumes or portfolios, filling out applications, scheduling and participating in interviews, and determining when and how to disclose their disability to employers. It may take time for students to become adept at handling questions during an interview, articulating their skills and abilities to an employer, describing what makes them a good candidate for employment or, if they have difficulty communicating, using a portfolio to assist them in communicating with an employer. They also may need to make decisions about future jobs based upon what worked and didn't work in previous employment experiences. The transition that students undergo when they leave one job to go to another is where things often fall apart. All too often, when students with ID obtain paid employment, the expectation is that the job will last for a very long time. Employment services in PSE programs should start not only with the presumption that students will be able to seek and gain *paid* employment, but also with the expectation that students will likely have more than one job during their postsecondary experience. Job change should be seen as an expected and welcome part of transitioning into the world of work. Supporting students as they begin to identify, navigate, *and alter* their career path should be part and parcel of the services provided in postsecondary education.

LACK OF ADEQUATELY TRAINED JOB DEVELOPERS

Perhaps the reason that PSE programs for students with ID engage in a vocational training model is that they take their lead from the professionals who they believe are the experts when it comes to addressing employment for people with disabilities. Often these "experts" are the special education teachers, transition specialists, and vocational rehabilitation professionals with whom they collaborate. However, few of these kinds of service providers have had extensive training on how to effectively develop jobs for students with ID. In a summary of the state of transition services for youth with disabilities in New York City, Mueller (2002, p. 40) reported:

> There is no requirement that a transition linkage coordinator have any specialized training in transition issues. Neither is there a state certification nor endorsement for a transition specialist. Indeed, the state does not even require coursework in transition as a requirement for a special education teaching certificate. This allows any certified teacher who wishes to apply for a transition linkage coordinator position to be considered qualified for the job.

A recent multistate survey of special education teachers' perceptions of their transition competencies indicated that teachers felt that they were reasonably prepared to plan and develop transition IEPs but lacked knowledge and skills related to any other key transition areas, including employment (Benitez, Morningstar, & Frey, 2008). The issue of adequately trained transition personnel is exacerbated by the reality that many times in community-based vocational instruction, the staff person directly helping students to get and keep jobs is not the transition coordinator or special education teacher, but instead is a paraprofessional or instructional assistant who serves as a job coach in the community. These paraprofessionals or instructional assistants usually have even less training than the transition coordinator or special education teacher. In a survey of special education teachers or transition coordinators in South Carolina, Whitaker (2000) found that half of the school districts employed one or more paraprofessionals to assist students with disabilities in occupational education classes. Only one-third of districts reported that they provided training, though almost all respondents felt that training was especially needed in job coaching.

There are many books (Griffin, Hammis, & Geary, 2007; Luecking, 2009; Wehman, Inge, Revell, & Brooke, 2007) and organizations (e.g., The Training Resource Network Inc., Virginia Commonwealth Universities Rehabilitation Research Center, Technical Assistance and Continuing Education grantees, Institute for Community Inclusion, TransCen, Inc.) that provide comprehensive information and training regarding the skills necessary to conduct effective job development, training, and support for students with ID. But seldom is this knowledge accessed and implemented by those who are involved in employment-related aspects of transition or rehabilitation services. In secondary education, the task of accessing jobs for students with disabilities is not given the same credence or value as the task of teaching students academics (Guy et al., 2008). When describing the lack of credentials necessary for transition coordinators, Sitlington, Clark, and Kolstoe (2000, p. 197) state:

> It borders on the bizarre that the vast majority of states across the nation do not value the professional role enough to recognize it as a legitimate, highly desirable public school position with appropriate certification requirements. It borders on malpractice that state and local education agencies permit individuals to function in such critical outcome areas with no more than some type of academic teaching endorsement.

Therefore, one of the major causes of under- and unemployment of students with ID is likely directly related to the lack of adequate training and expertise of the staff charged with helping them seek employment (Benitez et al., 2008). Too often staff who support students operate under the premise that their responsibility is to get the students *ready* to work and that someone else will cover the other part of the equation. Hutchins and Renzaglia (2002, p. 68) conclude that

> School programs that terminate in individual education suggesting he or she is "employment ready" are not facing the potential gap in services and the likely scenario that there is no one to effectively provide the necessary services to ensure and support long term community employment.

This pattern of behavior is beginning to emerge in PSE programs around the country and will likely lead to the same unfortunate outcome for students with ID—unemployment.

However, lack of training and expertise in job development skills is not limited to the transition or secondary special education personnel employed by local school systems. The employment specialists, job developers, and vocation support personnel employed by community rehabilitation providers who support transitioning students with ID once they exit school are also undertrained and often ineffective in placing students with ID in paid integrated employment. This could be due to the fact that according to the Rehabilitation Services Administration web site, there are no educational requirements for the position of employment specialist (http://www.ed.gov/students/college/adi/rehabv/carsupem.html).

In addition to a lack of credentialing, the prevailing methods used by rehabilitation professionals to engage employment opportunities for individuals with ID often lead to failure (Metzel, Boeltzig, Butterworth, Sulewski, & Gilmore, 2007). However, there are numerous professional organizations (e.g., Association for Persons in Supported Employment) and professional development providers (e.g., TransCen, Inc., VCU–RRTC) that are aware of these issues and are trying to provide quality training and technical assistance to remediate this situation.

A recent report from the United States Department of Labor, Office of Disability Employment Policy (Domzal, Houtenville, & Sharma, 2008) reflected results from a survey on employer perspectives on the employment of people with disabilities. It revealed that when asked about the type of information that would persuade them to recruit people with a disability, companies cited information about performance, productivity, and how hiring people with disabilities can benefit a company's bottom line as the most persuasive information. Unfortunately, many rehabilitation professionals charged with assisting individuals with ID to get jobs fail to emphasize the potential contributions of those they represent and instead approach employers with cold calls, offers of tax credits, or use of negative descriptions or deficit *marketing* (Riehle & Daston, 2006) to "sell" potential employees.

In addition to a lack of training and bad marketing strategies, staff turnover and inaccurate historical information can also impede successful outcomes from rehabilitation service providers. In a recent National Council on Disability (2008) report, a parent was quoted about how her son's experience reflected these issues.

> I did not see [the Department of Rehabilitative Services counselor] again until the summer before graduation when my son was invited to participate in the center-based week-long rehabilitative assessment process. . . . The assessment findings concluded that my son was eligible for segregated facility-based or supported employment but that he would not be a candidate for competitive employment. By this time he had been employed competitively for 18 months [through the IEP process in which VR participated].

A lack of funding and personnel resources often prevents community rehabilitation providers from addressing the needs of consumers (Hutchins & Renzaglia, 2002). Targett (2007, p. 94) asserts:

> Without adequate training and development, employment specialists will not be able to adequately meet the needs of those individuals with the most severe disabilities. Ill-equipped staff will be less effective and efficient, affecting both the quality of service delivery and costs. The bottom line is staff must receive the skills training necessary to provide high-quality and effective supported employment services.

Certainly the poor employment outcomes that have been observed for adults with ID bear out this statement.

In a recent state survey of 26 program representatives at 10 agencies serving transition youth with disabilities between the ages of 16 and 26 in Maryland, the final report indicated that employment services that required any kind of customizations rarely happened. In addition, few agencies or programs provided job coaches, supported employment, or customized employment. The report demonstrated that equal numbers of agencies placed youth in unpaid and paid employment opportunities and that some of the unpaid work experiences were not in competitive environments and did not transfer to paid employment (TransCen, Inc., 2006). Focus group findings from the same report reiterated these survey findings. Several focus group participants indicated career preparation and job placements were not individualized or based on students' personal preferences, interests, or abilities. Instead placement was based upon the availability and space at a facility. When youth were employed, they often were not given the necessary on-the-job supports (e.g., workplace accommodations) to successfully maintain that employment (TransCen, Inc., 2006).

So, not only are school system transition personnel often poorly trained to guide students toward competitive paid employment, but the adult service personnel to whom the school system traditionally transition students with the assumption that they will continue to support or take care of assisting students in securing paid employment, are just as ill-prepared.

The National Council on Disability (2008) responded to this need for additional training for providers by recommending that

> The Rehabilitation Services Administration (RSA) and state VR agencies
> should allocate additional staff development resources for the preparation of
> current and future rehabilitation counselors to meet the needs of transition-
> age youth, and target recruitment and professional development activities to
> attract qualified people with disabilities to the field. Current personnel prepa-
> ration efforts are not able to fully equip all VR transition counselors and adult
> counselors with the knowledge and skills necessary to address the complex
> support needs of the young adults with disabilities exiting school. These staff-
> development efforts should be based on comprehensive needs assessment and
> competency-based training programs that empirically identify the professional
> characteristics and qualifications needed for success as a VR transition coun-
> selor or adult counselor working with transition-age youth.

SUGGESTIONS FOR IMPROVING EMPLOYMENT OUTCOMES FOR STUDENTS WITH ID

Without guidance and leadership regarding the importance of establishing paid integrated employment as the hallmark of success, personnel who help students to access PSE programs and services will continue to perpetuate student involvement in job training experiences that lead to little more than increased unemployment or underemployment. However, it *is* possible to change the direction of services and derive better employment experiences and outcomes for students with ID. The following example provides a description of how one PSE program, which had initially used a vocational training model, was able to change their practices and by doing so increase its students' rate of paid employment from 0% to 90% in 1 year.

The Western Connection Program at Western Connecticut State University was established in 2003 with a planning grant from the Connecticut State Department of Education. The program has supported between seven and thirteen students each year over the past six years. When the program started, it served students from seven different school systems who were able to take a class at college each semester and received access to vocational training sites on the college campus and at a nearby hospital. In 2005, as part of an Office of Special Education Programs–funded Research and Innovation project, the Western Connection program became involved with the Postsecondary Education Research Center (PERC) project. Through this collaboration, the Western Connection Program conducted an intensive program evaluation using the PERC Postsecondary Programs Evaluation Tool (see Figure 1.1). The results of this evaluation indicated that there were a variety of strengths in the Western Connection program, but also some areas of need. One of these areas of need was paid employment—none of the students supported in the program was involved in paid work.

This evaluation led to a discussion about the purpose of the program and the anticipated outcomes and finally to the creation of an action plan focused on implementing some desired changes in the program. In partnership with PERC, the Western Connection staff determined that there were three major impediments to students gaining paid employment. The first problem was that students in the program were from a variety of different school systems. Each sending district had retained ownership of the student's career development services; therefore, there was no centralized entity or person who was monitoring the employment situation of each student. The second problem was that paid employment had never been articulated as a program goal, activity, or outcome. This was an issue that was not addressed during the planning stages of the program, and therefore the default activity was to continue the job training practices that had previously been implemented in the school system. The third issue was a lack of adequately trained job development staff. The program coordinator felt that he was not in a position to be off campus and did not currently have a staff member who was capable of developing paid employment experiences in the community.

These issues were resolved via the creation and implementation of an action plan. First, the program coordinator worked with the sending districts to reallocate ownership and supervision of the employment services that students in the program would receive, from the sending district to the Western Connection staff. Second, the program expanded its focus and identified paid employment as one of the major activities. Another important change related to the priority given to paid employment. Initially, program staff presumed that students would enter the program and remain in job training placements until they were ready to exit. During the final semester the staff would begin the search for a paid job. Instead of this last-minute approach, the program staff determined that they would instead begin each student's first year by working with him or her to determine what kind of paid job might be possible. The default plan would be to seek paid employment as soon as possible. Some students who had little or no employment experiences would be placed in a vocational training position to gauge their interests and provide a baseline for assessing their employment skills. But these placements would be done in conjunction with a search for paid employment.

The final and perhaps most important action taken by the program staff to address the need for paid employment was the creation of a part-time job developer position for the program. This person would have the flexible schedule that was needed to create and support paid student employment throughout each semester. In addition, this person received extensive job development training and was provided with field-based modeling of how to conduct quality job development activities by PERC staff. This formula of centralizing the provision of employment services, setting paid employment "first" as goal, and hiring and training dedicated staff allowed this program to rapidly increase the paid employment rate of its students. During the 2006–2007 school year, 92% (or 12 of 13 students) had paid, competitive jobs. This trend continued even through some staffing changes, and in the 2007–2008 school year, nine of the ten students served had paid jobs, one student had two paid jobs, and five students had one paid job and a second stipend-paid job training experience. On average, the working students were paid $8.40 an hour (up an average of $1.00 from the previous year) and worked in retail clothing stores, restaurants, an ice rink, and grocery stores in their communities.

SUMMARY

Is competitive employment readily available to people with ID? All too often, the answer is no (Wehman, Revell, & Brooke, 2003) for many of the reasons discussed in this chapter. The real potential in any PSE experience lies not only in what it offers during a student's attendance, but also in what it can lead to. Part of the mission of a PSE program for students with ID has to be to connect its education experiences to paid employment outcomes. The time is long overdue for the cessation of rotating students with ID through unrelated experiences in vocational training sites and expecting them to suddenly—almost miraculously—become employed. Additionally, we need to stop expecting special education, transition, and rehabilitation professionals, who have little training or experience, to successfully help students with ID get paid jobs. Proper training, guided practice, and, most of all, experience are what are required for someone to become a skilled employment specialist or job developer. So how does this inform activities conducted as part of a PSE program experience?

- Using untrained personnel to assist in job development does a disservice to the student and can lead to a poor reputation among employers.
- Staff, regardless of their background, should undergo quality training related to establishing job development strategies and techniques.
- Graduate students, peer mentors, educational coaches, and instructional assistants may all be available, but not necessarily capable or qualified. Do not assume that anyone can be an effective job developer.

PSE programs and services must not only emphasize and honor the importance of paid work experiences for students with ID in practice; they must also recognize the best way to achieve this outcome is to hire and train skilled employment specialists and job coaches to work with students. To do otherwise will likely lead to the same poor outcomes that students with ID have experienced in the past. We need to stop talking about getting students "ready to work." Students with ID, given the opportunity and the proper support, are *ready* to work. It is up to us to make it happen.

REFERENCES

Benitez, D.T., Morningstar, M.E., & Frey, B.B. (2008). A multistate survey of special education teachers' perceptions of their transition competencies. *Career Development for Exceptional Individuals.* First published September 8, 2008, as doi:10.1177/0885728808323945

Brewer, D. (2005, February). *Working my way through high school: The impact of paid employment on transitioning students with disabilities.* Ithaca, NY: Cornell University, School of Industrial and Labor Relations Extension, Employment and Disability Institute. http://digitalcommons.ilr.cornell.edu/edicollect/109

Domzal, C., Houtenville, A., & Sharma, R. (2008). *Survey of Employer Perspectives on the Employment of People with Disabilities: Technical Report.* (Prepared under contract to the Office of Disability and Employment Policy, U.S. Department of Labor). McLean, VA: CESSI.

Gilmore, S., Bose, J., & Hart, D. (2001). Postsecondary education as a critical step toward meaningful employment: Vocational rehabilitation's role. *Research to Practice, 7*(4).

Grigal, M. (2008). [The Postsecondary Education Research Center Project]. Unpublished raw data. Rockville, MD: TransCen.

Guy, B.A., Sitlington, P.L., Larsen, M.D., & Frank, A.R. (2008). What are high schools offering as preparation for employment? *Career Development for Exceptional Individuals.* First published May 29, 2008, as doi:10.1177/0885728808318625

Hutchins, M.P., & Renzaglia, A. (2002). Career development: Developing basic work skills and employment preferences. In K. Story, P. Bates, & D. Hunter (Eds.), *The road ahead: Transition to adult life for persons with disabilities.* St. Augustine, FL: TRN, Inc.

Luecking, R. (2009). *The way to work: How to facilitate work experiences for youth in transition.* Baltimore: Paul H. Brookes Publishing Co.

Luecking, R., & Fabian, E. (2000). Paid internships and employment success for youth in transition. *Career Development for Exceptional Individuals, 23*(2), 205–221.

Luecking, R., & Gramlich, M. (2003). *Quality work-based learning and postschool employment success* (Issue Brief 2[2]). National Center on Secondary Education and Transition.

Metzel, D.S., Boeltzig, H., Butterworth, J., Sulewski, S., & Gilmore, D.S. (2007). Achieving community membership through community rehabilitation providers services: Are we there yet? *Intellectual and Developmental Disabilities, 45*(3), 149-160.

Migliore, A. & Butterworth, J. (2008). Postsecondary Education and Employment Outcomes for Youth with Intellectual Disabilities. Data Note Series, Data Note XXI. Boston: Institute for Community Inclusion.

Moran, R., McDermott, S., & Butkus, S. (2002). Getting, sustaining and losing a job for individuals with mental retardation. *Journal of Vocational Rehabilitation, 16*(3, 4), 237–244.

Mueller, R. (2002). *Missed opportunities: The state of transition services for youth with disabilities in New York City.* New York: New York Lawyers for the Public Interest. Retrieved October 5, 2008, from www.nylpi.org/pub/NYLPI_Transition_Report.pdf

National Council on Disability. (2008). *The Rehabilitation Act: Outcomes for transition-age youth.* Washington, DC: Author. Retrieved October 28, 2008, from http://www.ncd.gov/newsroom/publications/index.htm

Neubert, D.A., & Redd, V.A. (2008). Transition services for students with intellectual disabilities: A case study of a public school program on a community college campus. *Exceptionality, 16*, 220 – 234.

Redd, V. (2004). *A public school-sponsored program for students ages 18 to 21 with significant disabilities located on a community college campus: A case study.* Unpublished doctoral dissertation, University of Maryland, College Park.

Riehle, J.E., & Daston, M. (2006). Deficit marketing: Good intentions, bad results. *Journal of Vocational Rehabilitation, 25*, 69-70.

Simon, M., & Halloran, W.D. (1994). Community-based vocational education: Guidelines for complying with the Fair Labor Standards Act. *Journal of the Association for Persons with Severe Handicaps, 19*, 52-61.

Sitlington, P. L., Clark, G.M., & Kolstoe, O.P. (2000). *Transition education and services for adolescents with disabilities.* Boston: Allyn and Bacon.

Targett, P.S. (2007). Staff selection, training, and development for community rehabilitation programs. In P. Wehman, K.J. Inge, W.G. Revell, & V.A. Brookes. *Real work for real pay.* (pp 75-103). Baltimore: Paul H. Brookes Publishing Co.

TransCen, Inc. (2006). *Final report on Maryland Resource Mapping Initiative.* Retrieved February 27, 2007, from http://www.mdtransition.org

U.S. Department of Labor, Bureau of Labor Statistics. (2008). *Number of jobs held, labor market activity, and earnings growth among the youngest baby boomers: Results from a longitudinal survey.* Report. Washington, DC: Author. Retrieved October 18, 2008, from http://www.bls.gov/news.release/nlsoy.nr0.htm

Wagner, M., Newman, L., Cameto, R., & Levine, P. (2005, June). *Changes over time in the early post-school outcomes of youth with disabilities. A Report from the National Longitudinal Transition Study-2* (SRI Project P11182). U.S. Department of Education, Office of Special Education Programs. Menlo Park, CA: SRI International.

Wehman, P. (2006). Integrated Employment: If not now, when? If not us, who? *Research & Practice for Persons with Severe Disabilities, 31(2),* 122–126.

Wehman, P., Inge, K.J., Revell, W.G., & Brooke, V.A. (2007). *Real work for real pay: Inclusive employment for people with disabilities.* Baltimore: Paul H. Brookes Publishing Co.

Wehman, P., Revell, W.G., & Brooke, V. (2003). Competitive employment: Has it become the "first choice" yet? *Journal of Disability Policy Studies, 14(3),* 163–173.

Wehman, P., & Yasuda, S. (2005). The need and the challenges associated with going to college. In E.E. Getzel & P. Wehman (Eds.), *Going to college: Expanding opportunities for individuals with disabilities* (pp. 3–23). Baltimore: Paul H. Brookes Publishing Co.

Whitaker, S.D. (2000). Training needs of paraprofessionals in occupational education classes. *Career Development for Exceptional Individuals, 23,* 173–185.

Preparing for What? Postsecondary Education, Employment, and Community Participation

Richard Luecking

CHAPTER

9

Previous chapters address the important elements of designing and implementing the preparatory and support features that ensure successful postsecondary education (PSE) experiences for youth with intellectual disabilities (ID). Although PSE experiences offer significant opportunity and promise for these individuals, this promise will be unfulfilled unless there is a simultaneous focus on the outcomes of these experiences. Without a clear connection between PSE experiences and adult employment and life goals, these young adults are still vulnerable to the pervasive unemployment or underemployment that is unfortunately common among adults with ID. What comes next? should be a question on the mind of everyone the moment the young adult enters the PSE setting. The student's course selection should be guided by his or her career goal for the most part, and work-based learning opportunities should be planned.

This chapter outlines and discusses the rationale and the strategies for developing meaningful, targeted work and community participation experiences during PSE enrollment that will ultimately lead to long-term jobs and active community lives. It presents the case for including work-related experiences and, even more importantly, paid work as integral features of PSE. It also offers strategies for organizing work experiences, recruiting employers to offer these experiences, integrating these experiences into the curriculum, and supporting students in their workplaces. The chapter presents considerations and strategies for making connections with sources of ongoing support for these employment and life activities after exit from PSE.

Given the array of different PSE options available for students with ID, it is not surprising that there is a correspondingly wide array of potential services and supports that could be needed. The people who provide these services and supports have many different job titles, such as transition coordinator or education liaison, and could be funded through various entities, such as the local school system or the state vocational rehabilitation agency. For the purposes of this chapter, the term *transition coordinator* is used to describe an individual whose primary job function is to support students with ID in PSE experiences, as well as to find integrated employment opportunities and paid employment, and to link the students to the appropriate adult service agencies (e.g., vocational rehabilitation), community rehabilitation providers, and generic community supports (e.g., one-stop career centers, college career services).

WHY WORK IS IMPORTANT

The culmination of any student's educational experience can and should be the beginning of a productive adult life. For most people this means a job or, even better, a career. There is every reason to expect, therefore, that individuals with ID, participating in a PSE experience, and their families can look forward to the day when they enter the workforce for what ideally will be the start of a long career. The statistics, however, suggest that these expectations are still not the norm and that employment is still an elusive postschool outcome for young people with ID. Luecking (2009) noted the following circumstances that illustrate the challenges of elevating employment outcomes:

- The latest national survey of young people with ID transitioning from public education to adult life indicates that a low percentage of these individuals have jobs when they leave school (National Longitudinal Transition Study-2, 2003).
- Postschool employment support services are not sufficient to meet the demand from transitioning young people, and the quality of these services is widely variable (Braddock, Rizzolo, & Hemp, 2004; Mank, Cioffi, & Yovanoff 2003; Wehman, 2006).
- Community employment service agencies struggle to provide quality supported employment to young people and adults with ID (Boeltzig, Gilmore, & Butterworth, 2006; Braddock et al., 2004; Connelly, 2003).
- Seventy-five percent of adult community rehabilitation services participants, most of whom have an ID, receive services in some type of segregated, congregate setting (Braddock et al., 2004).
- Subminimum wage and sheltered employment are the fate of thousands of people with ID (U.S. General Accounting Office, 2001.)

It is not sufficient, then, for the focus of PSE experiences to be limited to college courses and community access, as valuable as they are. There must be a simultaneous focus on competitive employment as an outcome, or else the fate of students in PSE will mirror previously cited poor employment outcomes. The good news is that young adults and their families do not have to be satisfied with these historically disappointing results. It has been shown repeatedly that work-based experiences such as job shadowing, internships, cooperative work placements, service learning, and volunteer work are effective and important elements to successful postschool employment success (Colley & Jamison, 1998; Sitlington & Clark, 2005; Wehman, 2006). Moreover, when paid work is paired with education, either as an ancillary activity or as an integral aspect of curriculum, all young people with disabilities are considerably more likely to obtain and retain employment as adults (Hart, Zafft, & Zimbrich, 2001; Wagner, Newman, Cameto, Garza, & Levine, 2005).

There are several studies that illustrate the value of paid work experience as an educational adjunct. For example, Luecking and Fabian (2001) found that youth with ID in their last year of secondary school who had opportunities for a paid internship with a cooperating company fared as well as youth with other disabilities, not only in obtaining and succeeding in the internships, but also in receiving offers of postinternship employment. Moreover, those youth who completed the internship were highly likely to remain successfully employed up to 2 years after school completion. In another study, young people with ID who participated in a targeted community work experience in secondary school (and who were followed for up to 20 years after leaving school) were noted to be significantly more successful in adult employment compared with the typical employment rates of this population (Brown, Shiraga, & Kessler, 2006).

It is clear from these studies and others (see, e.g., Tymchuk, Lakin, & Luckasson, 2001; Walker & Rogan, 2007) that it is imperative that any school experience, including PSE, for youth and young adults with ID include a strong focus on the ultimate outcome of that experience. This is especially important for young people with ID whose life experience up to the point of postsecondary enrollment may not have provided opportunities for exposure to areas of potential interest so they could develop job and career goals. The remainder of this chapter explores ways to prepare students in PSE for work.

TYPES OF WORK-BASED EXPERIENCE

There are several types of work-based experiences that can be valuable in exposing students to workplace expectations, helping them develop specific and general work skills, and identifying work environments and workplace accommodations that are optimal for individual youth. These experiences offer opportunities for students to learn the soft skills needed to succeed in the workplace, such as being on time, following directions, accepting supervision, and getting along with co-workers. They also help students identify employment and career preferences. Of equal importance, work-based experiences help students identify supports and accommodations that might be essential to eventual long-term workplace success, including the management of social and health issues that may affect work attendance and performance. Any opportunity for students to come in contact with the workplace and employers can be considered a work-based experience. The various types of work-based experiences are summarized in Table 9.1.

For the reasons identified above that point to the value of work experience for young people who are preparing for a postschool life as an employed adult, exposure to work-based experiences has ideally occurred in high school before the student enrolls in PSE. When it has not, the postsecondary educators involved with the students will need to organize such exposure. However, those experiences that are unpaid or not related to a course of study in PSE should be extremely focused and short-lived, so that paid employment can begin as soon as possible. Indeed, the gold standard is paid employment. Of all the types of work experiences the literature explicitly identifies, paid work in authentic workplace settings during the years of formal education is the strongest predictor of postschool employment success. This is true for young people without disabilities (Haimson & Bellotti, 2001) and young people with disabilities (Luecking & Fabian, 2001), including those with ID (Brown et al., 2006). For this reason alone, every PSE program should find ways to organize and facilitate paid work experiences (i.e., real jobs in real workplaces) as integral components of the student's course of study. In addition to all of the general advantages identified above for all work-based experiences, paid work helps youth build resumes along with valuable skills that will be important foundations for successful long-term

Table 9.1.   Types of work-based experiences

Career exploration	Visits by youth to workplaces to learn about jobs and the skills required to perform them.
	Visits and meetings with employers and people in identified occupations outside of the workplace are also types of career exploration activities from which youth can learn about jobs and careers. Typically, such visits are accompanied by discussions with youth about what they saw, heard, and learned.
Job shadowing	Extended time, often a full workday or several workdays, spent by a youth in a workplace accompanying an employee in the performance of his or her daily duties.
	Many companies have "take your son or daughter to work days" and some companies organize annual official job shadow days when they invite youth to spend time at the company.
Volunteer work	Unpaid work by a youth that does not materially benefit the employer but allows the youth to spend meaningful time in a work environment to learn aspects of potential careers and to learn soft skills required in the workplace.
	It is important for transition coordinators to be familiar with the Fair Labor Standards Act of 1938 (PL 75-718) requirements for volunteer activity.
Service learning	Hands-on volunteer service to the community that integrates with course objectives.
	This is a structured process that provides time for reflection on the service experience and demonstration of the skills and knowledge acquired.
Internships	Formal arrangements whereby a youth is assigned specific tasks in a workplace over a predetermined period of time.
	Internships may be paid or unpaid, depending on the nature of the agreement with the company and the nature of the tasks. Many postsecondary institutions help organize these experiences with local companies as adjuncts to specific degree programs; they are alternatively called "cooperative education experience," "cooperative work," or simply "co-ops."
Apprenticeships	Formal, sanctioned work experiences of extended duration in which an apprentice learns specific occupational skills related to a standardized trade, such as carpentry, plumbing, drafting, etc.
	Many apprenticeships also include paid work components.
Paid employment	May include existing standard jobs in a company or customized work assignments that are negotiated with an employer, but always feature a wage paid directly to the youth.
	Such work may be scheduled during or after the school day. It may be integral to a course of study or may simply be a separate adjunctive experience.

postschool employment and careers. The next section explains the process for making this happen.

STRATEGIES FOR DEVELOPING MEANINGFUL WORK EXPERIENCES

Whether a transition coordinator is helping students find work-based experiences such as internships or jobs targeted for long-term adult employment, there are strategies that can be commonly applied. There is an extensive body of literature about work experience and job development strategies, and there are many approaches to helping people with ID identify and secure jobs (e.g., Griffin, Hammis, & Geary, 2007; Luecking, Fabian, & Tilson, 2004; National Center on Workforce and Disability/Adult, 2005; Wehman, 2001). This section outlines features common to this process that can be adapted by educational personnel, career development personnel, and others interested in and involved with youth in the PSE education setting.

Getting to Know Students

Whatever the type of work-based experience the student seeks, it is important to use knowledge of the student as the starting point for the process. This is critical for many reasons, not the least of which is to make sure the experience contributes to the student's self-knowledge, which is so critical to a successful career search. Thus, it is important to avoid the common practice of finding just any jobsite where there is an employer who is amenable to hosting a student with a disability. The most successful work experiences and jobs are those that take into account the particular circumstances of the student, that is, interests, skills, desired career goals, and need for support and accommodations in the job search and on the job. This often requires assisting the student in a process that identifies these traits.

A useful process for getting to know the student as a prelude to a work experience or a job search includes person-centered planning and the development of a positive personal profile. Person-centered planning, as the name implies, focuses on the student and his or her unique attributes. It is a way to have the student, along with people who best know him or her, identify traits, preferences, interests, and support needs. There are a number of tools that are available to accomplish this, such as Making Action Plans (Mount, 1992) and Planning Alternative Tomorrows with Hope (PATH) (Pearpoint, O'Brien, & Forest, 1993). These tools can be used to help the student identify a career goal and plan for work experiences and jobs.

A practical tool for organizing the information obtained in a person-centered plan and/or from other sources of information about the student is called a positive personal profile (Luecking et al., 2004; Luecking, 2009). It is especially useful for preparing for the student's job search. The focus of the profile is those traits and personal circumstances that are likely to make the student marketable to prospective employers. The purpose of the profile, then, is to help students identify as much positive information about themselves as possible, so that the presentation to prospective employers is based on student strengths rather than focused or driven by perceived deficits. Students and transition coordinators can use this information to develop an individual job search plan.

A job search plan includes

- A summary of the student's interests and preferences, gleaned from the positive personal profile
- Preferred geographical locations of work, for example, places near a bus stop or near the school
- A preferred schedule, for example, part time, mornings, or evenings
- Transportation resources, that is, what might be available means for getting to and from work
- A summary of situations to avoid, for example, loud environments for individuals who dislike noise
- Potential accommodations needed, such as job coaching or visual prompts
- Most important, a list of employers to begin contacting

Armed with this information, the student and transition coordinator are ready to begin looking for job prospects. The plan also serves as a way of identifying points that may be important for eventual negotiation with an employer. This would include such things as work hours, productivity requirements, and pay.

Self-determination in the Search for Work Experiences and Jobs

Job development for students with ID has often been characterized by stereotypical jobs, such as janitorial and food service positions, because of the mistaken belief that these jobs were the best they could do, not to mention plentiful and convenient to find (Griffin et al., 2007). We now know that for work experience and job success to occur, students must be actively involved in the process of identifying and choosing their experiences. There is considerable research to support the importance of job seeker choice and control over the search process (Wehmeyer, Gragoudas, & Shogren, 2006). This is commonly referred to as self-determination. In the context of employment development, self-determination means people with disabilities having access to knowledge upon which vocational choices are made and being empowered to act freely on those choices. This is why work-based experiences are so helpful, because various experiences will expose students to workplaces, working conditions, and working environments that become the basis for making later job and career choices as well as academic course selections. When these opportunities have not occurred prior to PSE enrollment, they are important to organize as preludes to self-determined paid employment.

Using knowledge about the student gleaned in developing a positive personal profile and taking the lead from self-determined students, the transition coordinator is ready to help the student find work experiences and jobs that will contribute to eventual long-term employment and a career (see Sidebar 9.1). In order for this to happen, however, there must be available employers willing to host the student in the workplace. The next section outlines how to go about identifying and negotiating with employers for this purpose.

> ### Sidebar 9.1
>
> #### Theresa
>
> Theresa loves theater and dreams of being an actress. As part of her postsecondary education experience, Theresa audited an introductory acting class with support from an education coach. The class fueled her desire to work in theater. In her high school she had work experiences as a cafeteria service worker, which she hated. She insisted in her IEP meeting that she wanted a job in her area of interest, not "wiping tables!"
>
> As a result of her strongly stated preferences, her job search plan included a list of local community theater companies and organizations that would be contacted. With Theresa's permission, her transition coordinator contacted three of the organizations and conducted an informational interview with management staff at each one. One theater company said it needed help in three different departments, depending on the season. The marketing department needed help with collating and distributing marketing materials for new productions. The costume department needed help when plays were in production. The personnel department needed help during busy hiring times. Theresa and her transition coordinator met with people in each department, and a job was created for her to rotate through each department to help out whichever department needed the most help. Previously the company hired temporary help for each of these needs. Hiring Theresa made this no longer necessary.
>
> It was Theresa's strongly stated preference for a job in theater that led to this particular job. She is not yet an actress, but she is working in a place where she is close to the kind of activity that greatly interests her and that may lead to her dream job. Her self-advocacy and pursuit of personal choice served her well, as she is now on track for a career that complements her experience at the community college.

Getting to Know Employers and What They Want

There are three reasons that employers cite for hosting youth with disabilities in the workplace (Luecking, 2004). In order of importance, they are 1) meeting a specific company need, such as filling a job opening or addressing a production or service need; 2) meeting an industrywide need, such as preparing potential new workers in a technology industry; and/or 3) meeting a community need, such as helping youth become productive citizens. The implication of these motivating factors is that it is best to avoid appeals to employer benevolence; that is, avoid trying to convince employers of the value of hiring people with disabilities. The most effective ways to find and recruit employers to provide work experiences and jobs for individual students is to find out what most matters to prospective employers in their operation and in the people they hire. A good way to accomplish this is to arrange and structure workplace visits to conduct informational interviews.

When structured properly, informational interviews are usually easy to arrange, because most employers are very willing to talk about their enterprise. The purpose of the informational interview is to get to know the employer's needs, not to sell the employer on hosting or hiring a student. That will come later. First, it's necessary to get one's foot in the door. Simple requests that are easy to fulfill are best, such as, "I would like to learn more about your industry so that I can assist students to prepare for employment. Can I schedule a time to come by and have a brief meeting with you?" or "A friend told me of your company and its need for workers. I'd like to meet with you so I can learn more about your hiring needs."

Once the meeting is arranged, the tone should be informal and conversational, so that a relationship is established and the employer is comfortable talking about the company. If a few rules are followed, the informational interview can be a very productive experience, and the table will have been set for later negotiations with the employer for bringing the student into the workplace for a work experience or job.

Making the Match

Once a potential jobsite is identified through the use of informational interviews, the next step is to begin negotiations with the employer. The student should be included in the negotiation, either conducting the negotiation, supported in doing so by the transition coordinator, or occasionally initially represented by the transition coordinator with the student's permission when self-representation is not possible because of communication or other accommodation requirements. Most often this is an informal exchange in which the employer is presented with information about what the student has to offer in the workplace, that is, the highlights of his or her skills; how those skills will translate into benefits to the employer's enterprise; and what accommodations might be necessary to support the student's success in the workplace. Mutual benefit is the hallmark of all good job matches.

Consider Jason, a student with an ID enrolled in a community college who wanted to work in a setting that would complement his interest in video arts. He and his transition coordinator used his experience in a video arts class and a volunteer experience in a video store as a basis for outlining a job search plan. After contacting several video editing companies, they discovered one that needed someone to help duplicate DVDs and to time recordings for archiving. The negotiations with the employer hinged on Jason demonstrating that he could do the tasks and on proposing to the employer that his work on these tasks would enable other employees to spend time on more complicated video editing. Thus, the employer could fulfill customer orders faster and increase business volume. The obvious benefit to Jason was a job in his area of interest. The benefit to the company was the potential for improving operations and making more money. This negotiation was based on Jason's contribution to the company, not on his disability or association with an institution of higher education. As of this writing, Jason has been working at this video editing company for 2 years.

Disclosure, Accommodation, and Postplacement Support

Disclosure of disability is a personal issue. It is critical that the student have the final say about whether or not, or the manner in which, his or her disability is disclosed to a prospective employer. If the talent, skills, and positive attributes—and how these contribute to the employer's operation—are the primary focus of the negotiation with the employer, the disability is ultimately a secondary consideration. However, in order to receive accommodations from the employer, such as extended time for task completion or allowing a coach on-site to help the student learn the job, disclosure in some fashion is important and necessary. A good resource for the transition coordinator and student to work through decisions on disclosure is called "The 411 on Disclosure," published by the National Collaborative on Workforce and Disability/Youth (2005).

As discussed in the previous section, the need for and type of accommodations are often part of the negotiation with employers. The employer, however, is only legally bound to provide them if they are necessary for the employee to perform the *essential* functions of the job, that is, those tasks that are required as identified in a formal job description. Some students will be able to perform jobs and the tasks associated with them as stated in the job's formal job descriptions, with or without accommodations. In these cases, if accommodations for a student's disability are needed, then the employer must offer them if they are not an undue hardship for the company. This is the case even when such accommodations might be extensive, such as wheelchair accessibility, modified keyboards, or other accommodations that insure workplace accessibility and satisfactory job performance. Many students with ID, however, may be able to perform only some of the tasks mentioned in a standard job description. In these cases, the employer is under no obligation to provide accommodations or to hire the youth. This is plainly different from education settings which, according to the Individuals with Disabilities Education Act (IDEA) of 1990 (PL 101-476), must provide physical and learning accommodations when students require it. However, it is most frequently the case that employers will regard whatever accommodations are necessary as minimally intrusive when they ultimately lead to desired performance on the job. Thus, when transition coordinators are prepared to negotiate with prospective employers based on student positive traits and the potential contribution to the company, the result is that employers are amenable to hosting students in their workplaces, regardless of accommodation requirements.

As a way of making the student's initial presence in a workplace comfortable and welcoming, and to ensure long-term job success, it is often helpful to provide specific information or training about disability to workplace personnel and co-workers. Ways of clearing the way for student workplace success include providing information about specific accommodations required by the student (with the student's permission, of course), asking employers what further information they want in order to be comfortable supporting and accommodating the student, and modeling interaction and support appropriate for the student (Luecking, 2005). Sometimes it is helpful to provide disability awareness training. For example, one employer was particularly concerned about having a young man with autism in the workplace, especially how the co-workers would react. She asked the transition coordinator to present information to the staff about autism and ways to communicate with this young man. The transition coordinator offered specific techniques to the co-workers on how to interact effectively with the youth. As a result the co-workers became more comfortable with the youth's presence at that company and the work experience was successful for both the youth and the employer. Again, any sharing of information about the student's disability is done only with express permission from the student. There are several useful resources for disability awareness information that can be provided to, or adapted for sharing with, employers (see, e.g., ADA & IT Information Center, 2004).

Job Change and Job Loss

Like just about everyone who has ever had a job, students with ID will occasionally be faced with how to manage problems that arise on the job that may necessitate a change from that workplace. They may grow tired of the assigned tasks, they may have difficulty with a co-worker, they may experience a change in supervisor, or they may even be fired. Or they simply may want to find a better job. Whatever the case, it will sometimes be necessary for the transition coordinator to help students effectively navigate these circumstances. What help will the student need in finding a new job? How will the employment experience influence the next job search? What can transition coordinators and their partners do to ensure the success of the next placement?

All of the strategies discussed above about how to find jobs and work experiences apply here. In other words, start with what is known about the youth's interests, particular skills and strengths, and need for accommodation and support. With each job change, there is new and important information available for a new job search, because with the most recent work experience, the student and the transition coordinator know more about what kind of work environment should be avoided, what kind of work environment would be ideal, how accommodations should be identified and implemented, and the kind of tasks at which the student excels. This is a real advantage in locating the next job.

In fact, the logical place to begin is with a new positive personal profile and a new job search plan. Other strategies about finding and negotiating with employers (remember the informational interview!), making the match, determining disclosure strategies, follow-up support, and so forth are as applicable to new job searches as they are to the initial job search. It is important to recognize that there is something new learned in every job experience, whether it is new job skills, enhanced work behaviors, or simply heightened awareness of workplace expectations. Even unsuccessful work experiences are useful in all of these regards. The important thing to keep in mind is that a transition coordinator should be ready to assist and guide students when they need or want to change work experience sites or jobs.

QUALITY WORK-BASED LEARNING

The strategies discussed in the chapter thus far can be applied to help youth identify and secure either nonpaid work experiences or direct-hire jobs. In the most ideal of circumstances, these work experiences and jobs have a close link to the course of study and/or are organized in conjunction with the PSE experience. In order to ensure that youth get the maximum benefit from these work experiences, there are several factors that require consideration. Among these are connections between the job and school-based learning, clear expectations of student activity at the workplace, clearly defined roles of transition coordinators and worksite supervisors, and well-structured feedback on student performance.

There has been considerable research over the last 2 decades that suggests what must be considered in developing and nurturing quality work-based experiences (Benz & Lindstrom, 1997; Haimson & Bellotti, 2001; Hamilton & Hamilton, 1997; Hoerner & Wehrley, 1995; Wehman, 2006). Prominent among these factors is the task of ensuring that performance and support expectations at the workplace are well defined and that the respective roles of everyone involved are clearly delineated. However, a key issue pertinent to youth with ID in PSE settings is whether the work-based experience relates to the instructional curriculum. Many students with ID in PSE will be co-enrolled in mandated public school education through age 21. For these students it is advisable to include goals on the individual education plan (IEP) that incorporate work-based learning experiences. That, however, is only part of the consideration. When students engage in work-based learning, including paid jobs, it is desirable that the student have the opportunity to relate what is learned in the workplace to what is learned in the classroom and other venues of PSE, regardless of whether they are co-enrolled in publicly supported secondary education.

For example, JaMarcus is a 20-year-old student who is co-enrolled in his school district's special education services and a PSE experience at the local community college. His IEP included a goal to have an employment experience to complement his interest in baking. His transition coordinator helped him find a part-time job at a bakery near his neighborhood. Each day when he returned from his job, his transition coordinator set aside time to review what he did on the job. He was performing well but did not like the work he was assigned to, mostly clean-up tasks. He really wanted to decorate cakes, but his supervisor would not allow him to do that unless he completed a certified class. His high school transition coordinator helped him enroll in a cake-decorating class offered through the community college's adult education department. When he completed the class, and demonstrated to his employer what he had learned, he was offered a job as a cake decorator. In this case, his experience in PSE not only directly related to his work experience, but JaMarcus's work experience even influenced what courses he took at the community college. His career as a baker and cake decorator was well under way by the time he completed his education.

Even for those students who are not co-enrolled in secondary special education services, it is still important to connect relevant learning in the workplace to other PSE instruction. If students are involved in a specific occupational training program, for example, then ideally work experience not only relates to that program but also provides opportunities to relate classroom instruction with what the student is experiencing in the workplace. Or, if the student is aiming for a career in a specific industry, such as health care, then there should be ample opportunity for the student and the transition coordinator to discuss how a work experience is helping to gain skills and knowledge that will transfer to jobs in that field. Regardless of the focus of the curriculum, many aspects of workplace learning, especially the acquisition of soft skills such as following directions and getting along with co-workers, can be reinforced in nonwork settings. Thus, opportunities for students to review, discuss, and even practice what is learned in the workplace are important to integrate into other instruction. Conversely, it is also important to identify ways in which lessons taught in the classroom are reinforced at the worksite. Then, the pairing of work-based and other PSE instruction builds a strong set of skills that will serve the student well on the job long

Table 9.2.   Quality Work-Based Learning Characteristics

- Clear program goals
- Clear roles and responsibilities for worksite supervisors, mentors, transition coordinators, support personnel, and other partners
- Training plans that specify learning goals tailored to individual students with specific outcomes connected to student learning
- Convenient links between students, schools, and employers
- On-the-job learning
- Range of work-based learning opportunities, especially those outside traditional youth employing industries (e.g., restaurants, retail)
- Mentor(s) at the worksite
- Clear expectations and feedback to assess progress toward goals
- Assessments to identify skills, interests, and support needs at the worksite
- Reinforcement of work-based learning outside of work
- Appropriate academic, social, and administrative support for students, employers, and all partners

From Luecking, R., & Gramlich, M. (2003). *Quality work-based learning and postschool employment success.* Minneapolis: University of Minnesota, Institute on Community Integration, National Center on Secondary Education and Transition; reprinted by permission.

after exit from PSE. Table 9.2 summarizes characteristics of well-designed work-based experiences that promote acquisition of work behavior and skills.

CONNECTING WITH POSTSCHOOL SUPPORT AND SERVICES

For most students, the end of PSE will not necessarily mean the end of the need for support in the workplace or support in participating in other activities in their community. At work, they may need periodic coaching to maintain performance and good work behavior or to learn new job tasks. They may require assistance obtaining new employment if they are interested in a job change or if they lose their job. They may need help managing transportation to work. They may need assistance that maintains their current level of community integration and participation. They may also have nonwork life challenges that periodically affect work attendance and performance if they are not attended to, such as housing needs, family crises, or managing personal finances. And they may need ongoing help for managing public benefits such as Supplemental Security Income and Medical Assistance.

For these reasons, it is important for the transition coordinator to be prepared to help students link to those services and programs that offer support and assistance in one or more of these areas. Listed below are various services and programs that youth, families, and transition coordinators should be aware of so that students are able to access them, preferably long before the students' formal exit from PSE. The list is by no means all-inclusive, but information is provided here on those services most typically accessed by youth with ID who are in transition from education to adult employment.

Employment Support

Two primary resources for postschool employment support are the state vocational rehabilitation (VR) agency and local community rehabilitation providers (CRPs). CRPs are often also called adult employment service agencies. VR can facilitate and pay for such services as job coaching, assistive devices, and other accommodations needed for finding and keeping employment. Often VR will refer students to CRPs that are available to provide help finding a job and/or long-term job coaching support paid for by VR and the state developmental disabilities (DD) agency. Referral to postschool support services available through the VR and CRPs must be done early so that there is plenty of time for the services to be arranged prior to school exit. Even better, early referral will often result in partnerships with these agencies in joint efforts to help students find and keep jobs, especially those jobs that are targeted for the youth after they leave school. This type of collaboration leads to the ideal of seamless transition; that is, the student exits high school with a job in place and with the supports available to remain successful in that job. Many high schools, including those where youth are dually enrolled in public schools and PSE, have worked to implement a model such that the first day after school exit is not different from the last day of school (Rogan, Luecking, & Grossi, 2007).

One example is the Baltimore Transition Connection, established by the Baltimore City Public School System, local 2- and 4-year colleges, VR, and CRPs (Grigal, Dwyre & Davis, 2006). Students enrolled in the Baltimore Transition Connection receive instruction in age-appropriate environments, including one of three college campuses and various worksites throughout the community. Before their last year of eligibility for services from their school district, students are referred to VR and the state DD agency so that eligibility can be established and support arranged for postschool supported employment services. Through a cooperative agreement between the school district and a local CRP, the CRP helps students find job opportunities to supplement classroom instruction during the last year of school. The CRP also is available to provide ongoing job coaching if it is needed immediately upon school exit, ensuring a successful and seamless transition from postsecondary education to a working adult life.

Benefits Counseling

Many youth with ID will be eligible for, or are already receiving, Supplemental Security Income (SSI). This is a government benefit available to people with disabilities who are considered financially needy. After the age of 18, more individuals with disabilities become eligible for this benefit because their family's income and assets are no longer included in the determination of financial need. Youth on SSI and their families are often concerned about the potential effect of work earnings on SSI and the associated medical insurance called Medicaid. Because of work incentives offered by the Social Security Administration (SSA), it is most often the case that students will have more money if they work than if they do not.

However, it is common for students and their families to be concerned about the effect of job earnings on their SSI check and on their eligibility for medical benefits. For this reason, and because there are often complicated procedures for determining how, and the conditions under which, SSI benefits are affected by work, it is useful for students and their families to contact local experts, called work incentives program assistants (WIPA) for advice and help. These individuals are affiliated with different agencies in different communities, but local SSA offices can help transition coordinators contact the WIPA assigned to their area. The transition coordinator should become familiar with this resource in their community in order to connect students and their families. Introductory resources on SSI and relevant work incentives can be obtained from several resources, including the local SSA office.

One-Stop Career Centers

Every community has a designated location, most often called a one-stop career center, where anyone in that community, including youth with disabilities, can access job search and career information and where multiple services are available in one place. They may also offer such job search enhancements as resume writing and interviewing skills classes, as well as job training and youth employment programs for eligible customers. Because state VR agencies often are also located there, it is useful for the transition coordinator to become familiar with one-stop services. They can often find service enhancements that contribute to the students' transition plans, such as additional sources of career development information and expanded opportunities to find employer contacts for work-based opportunities and jobs. Other employment service agencies may also be located in one-stop career centers. Through youth programs and other services of the One-Stop Career Centers, young people with disabilities have the option of participating in a host of activities that are designed to give them exposure to work experiences that can be key adjuncts to, or integral parts of, their academic curriculum (Luecking & Crane, 2002). Core services of the one-stop centers are available to any individual over 18 at any time in his or her career. This opportunity allows youth to return for career and job search assistance without waiting for eligibility determination or designated program referrals once they leave school.

Ancillary Social and Community Services Linkages

Throughout the PSE years and beyond, youth with ID will often require support in order to access and use resources essential to address life circumstances that may affect employment success. There are a host of such situations that occur in anyone's life, but young adults with ID often need support to properly address them. These situations may include access to or support in maintaining housing, dealing with financial challenges, coping with health issues, and managing relationship, family, or marital issues, to name only a few.

In addition, participation in community activities outside of work and access to inclusive social activities will often be important to rounding out the young adult's working life (Walker & Rogan, 2007).

For these reasons, the transition coordinator will need to be aware of and help link students to supportive services that will help students address these issues outside of school and work. In many cases these services will be important partners in helping students and their families plan for the transition from PSE to adult life, as these supports may be needed at the point of transition and intermittently throughout the students' adult lives. These services include but are not limited to agencies that support people with developmental disabilities in maintaining housing, social services agencies, counseling and mental health services, and community recreation and leisure programs. Just as each student's employment and career path is unique, so too will other life circumstances be unique. Thus, linking to any of these types of services will necessarily be individually determined.

Roles of Postsecondary Education Transition Partners

There are many potential partners who may work collaboratively with students, families, and transition coordinators as they plan for what's next. Below is a summary of each of these potential partners and the roles they each may play in ensuring that students exit PSE on a path to an adult life characterized by successful employment and careers.

STUDENTS
- Develop self-advocacy and self-determination skills
- Direct IEP (if co-enrolled)
- Direct employment choices
- Learn responsible work behaviors
- Perform work to the employer's satisfaction

FAMILIES
- Support student in self-advocacy and self-determination
- Encourage and support student in work experience and jobs
- Help student navigate ancillary supportive services

PUBLIC SCHOOL DISTRICT (TRANSITION COORDINATOR)
- Include work-based experiences and jobs in curriculum
- Link these experiences to IEP goals
- Make early referral to postschool support services
- Convene partners as necessary
- Link students to necessary ancillary services
- Help link former students to ongoing adult education offerings and lifelong learning opportunities

VOCATIONAL REHABILITATION
- Open cases on referred students well before school exit
- Facilitate and fund services that contribute to employment goals, such as career-related courses, assistive devices, job development, and job coaching

COMMUNITY REHABILITATION PROGRAMS
- Accept early referrals prior to end of PSE
- Cooperatively develop work experiences and jobs with transition coordinator
- Support students in jobs and community life upon school exit as needed

ANCILLARY SOCIAL SERVICE PROGRAMS
- Attend planning meetings when invited and as appropriate
- Cooperate with other partners in service delivery
- Deliver services as needed to eligible students

EMPLOYERS
- Collaborate with PSE program in providing work opportunities
- Set student performance expectations
- Provide accommodations as needed

These are only a handful of possible partners, but they are likely the most frequently involved. Certainly the student should be in control of the process of determining which partners are involved and the role they play in planning, developing, and finalizing work experiences and jobs. In this process, transition coordinators are in an important position to help students identify their choices and support them in managing the roles of and interactions between partners.

SUMMARY

For the PSE experience to provide the maximum benefit to students with ID, it is important to keep the end in mind. That is, what will be the ideal culmination of that experience? For most people that will be a job that is the start of a long career. For many that will also mean the support available to succeed in the workplace and to participate in a full community life. This chapter provides the rationale for including work experiences and jobs as adjunctive activities that are ideally connected to students' courses of study. It also addresses what might need to be in place to ensure ongoing employment and career success.

The guiding philosophy should be that there is a job that can be found for everyone, regardless of disability, their need for support, or the economic vitality of their community. What youth learn in the PSE setting will contribute a great deal to making this happen, especially if the curriculum in that setting is complemented by real job experience. When school and work experiences are effectively paired, there is every reason to expect that the culmination of PSE will be adult employment and careers.

REFERENCES

ADA & IT Information Center. (2004). *Workforce discovery: Diversity and disability in the workplace*. Rockville, MD: TransCen, Inc.

Benz, M., & Lindstrom, L. (1997). *Building school-to-work programs: Strategies for youth with special needs*. Austin, TX: PRO-ED.

Boeltzig, H., Gilmore, D., & Butterworth, J. (2006, July). *The national survey of community rehabilitation providers, FY 2004–2005: Employment outcomes of people with developmental disabilities in integrated employment*. Boston: Institute for Community Inclusion, University of Massachusetts.

Braddock, D., Rizzolo, M., & Hemp, R. (2004). Most employment services growth in developmental disabilities during 1988–2002 was in segregated settings. *Mental Retardation, 42,* 317–320.

Brown, L., Shiraga, B., & Kessler, K. (2006). The quest for ordinary lives: The integrated post-school vocational functioning of 50 workers with significant disabilities. *Journal of Research and Practice for Persons with Severe Disabilities, 31,* 93–126.

Colley, D.A., & Jamison, D. (1998). Postschool results for youth with disabilities: Key indicators and policy implications. *Career Development for Exceptional Individuals, 21*(2).

Connelly, R. (2003). Supported employment in Maryland: Successes and issues. *Mental Retardation, 41,* 237–249.

Fair Labor Standards Act of 1938, PL 75-718, 29 U.S.C. 203(g).

Griffin, C., Hammis, D., & Geary, T. (2007). *The job developer's handbook: Practical tactics for customized employment.* Baltimore: Paul H. Brookes Publishing Co.

Grigal, M., Dwyre, A., & Davis, H. (2006). *Transition service for students aged 19–21 with intellectual disabilities in college and community settings: Models and implications for success.* Minneapolis: National Center on Secondary Education and Transition, University of Minnesota.

Haimson, J., & Bellotti, J. (2001). *Schooling in the workplace: Increasing the scale and quality of work-based learning.* Final report. Princeton, NJ: Mathematica Policy Research, Inc.

Hamilton, M., & Hamilton, S. (1997). *Learning well at work: Choices for quality.* New York: Cornell University Press.

Hart, D., Zafft, C., & Zimbrich, K. (2001). Creating access to college for all students. *The Journal for Vocational Special Needs Education, 23*(2), 19–31.

Hoerner, J., & Wehrley, J. (1995). *Work-based learning: The key to school-to-work transition.* New York: Glencoe/McGraw-Hill.

Individuals with Disabilities Education Act (IDEA) of 1990, PL 101-476, 20 U.S.C. §§ *1400 et seq.*

Luecking, R. (2004). *In their own words: Employer perspectives on youth with disabilities in the workplace.* Minneapolis: University of Minnesota, Institute on Community Integration, National Center on Secondary Education and Transition.

Luecking, R. (2005). *Strategies for youth workforce programs to become employer-friendly intermediaries* (Info Brief 12[1]). Washington, DC: Institute for Educational Leadership, National Collaborative on Workforce and Disability/Youth.

Luecking, R. (2009). *The way to work: How to facilitate work experiences for youth in transition.* Baltimore: Paul H. Brookes Publishing Co.

Luecking, R., & Crane, K. (2002). *Addressing the transition needs of youth with disabilities through the WIA system.* Minneapolis: University of Minnesota, Institute on Community Integration, National Center on Secondary Education and Transition.

Luecking, R., & Fabian, E. (2001). Paid internships and employment success for youth in transition. *Career Development for Exceptional Individuals, 23,* 205–221.

Luecking, R., Fabian, E., & Tilson, G. (2004). *Working relationships: Creating career opportunities for job seekers with disabilities through employer partnerships.* Baltimore: Paul H. Brookes Publishing Co.

Luecking, R., & Gramlich, M. (2003). *Quality work-based learning and postschool employment success.* Minneapolis: University of Minnesota, Institute on Community Integration, National Center on Secondary Education and Transition.

Mank, D., Cioffi, A., & Yovanoff, P. (2003). Supported employment outcomes across a decade: Is there evidence of improvement in the quality of implementation? *Mental Retardation, 41,* 188–197.

Mount, B. (1992). *Person-centered planning: Finding directions for change using personal futures planning.* New York: Graphics Futures.

National Center on Workforce and Disability/Adult. (2005). *Customized employment: A new competitive edge.* Boston: Institute for Community Inclusion, University of Massachusetts.

National Collaborative on Workforce and Disability/Youth. (2005). *The 411 on disclosure.* Washington, DC: Institute on Educational Leadership.

National Longitudinal Transition Study-2. (2003, December). *NLTS2 data brief: Youth employment, a report from the national longitudinal transition study-2.* Retrieved August 2007, from www.ncset.org/publications/default.asp#nlts2

Pearpoint, J., O'Brien, J., & Forest, M. (1993). *PATH: A workbook for planning positive possible futures and planning alternative tomorrows with hope for schools, organizations, businesses, and families* (2nd ed.). Toronto: Inclusion Press.

Rogan, P., Luecking, R., & Grossi, T. (2007). Preparing for meaningful adult lives through school and transition experiences. In P. Walker & P. Rogan (Eds.), *Make the day matter! Promoting typical lifestyles for adults with significant disabilities.* Baltimore: Paul H. Brookes Publishing Co.

Sitlington, P., & Clark, G. (2005). *Transition education and services for students with disbilities* (4th ed.). Boston: Allyn & Bacon.

Tymchuk, A., Lakin, L.C., & Luckasson, R. (2001). *The forgotten generation: The status and challenges of adults with mild cognitive limitations in American society.* Baltimore: Paul H. Brookes Publishing Company.

U.S. General Accounting Office. (2001). *Special minimum wage program: Centers offer employment and support services to workers with disabilities, but labor should improve oversight.* Washington, DC: Author.

Wagner, M., Newman, L., Cameto, R., Garza, N., & Levine, P. (2005). *After high school: A first look at the postschool experiences of youth with disabilities. A report from the National Longitudinal Transition Study-2 (NLTS2).* Menlo Park, CA: SRI International.

Walker, P., & Rogan, P. (2007). *Make the day matter: Promoting typical lifestyles for adults with significant disabilities.* Baltimore: Paul H. Brookes Publishing Co.

Wehman, P. (2001). *Supported employment in business.* St. Augustine, FL: TRN, Inc.

Wehman, P. (2006). *Life beyond the classroom: Transition strategies for young people with disabilities* (4th ed.). Baltimore: Paul H. Brookes Publishing Co.

Wehmeyer, M., Gragoudas, S., & Shogren, K. (2006). Self-determination, student involvement, and leadership development. In P. Wehman (Ed.), *Life beyond the classroom: Transition strategies for young people with disabilities* (4th ed.). Baltimore: Paul H. Brookes Publishing Co.

What the Future Holds

Meg Grigal and Debra Hart

This final chapter looks to the future, describing some of the next generation of issues likely to result from the increased demand for and supply of postsecondary education (PSE) options for students with intellectual disabilities (ID). The chapter highlights possible impacts that serving this new student population will have at national and state levels, the need to align with higher education initiatives related to diversity, and the associated ramifications on transition legislation and models of practice. The editors conclude with implications for students, research, and practice.

THE IMPACT OF POSTSECONDARY OPTIONS AT THE NATIONAL AND STATE LEVELS

There have been a variety of federal initiatives in the past few years that demonstrate an expanding interest in supporting access to PSE for students with ID. As is often the case with new practices, the federal government has supported a variety of grant-funded research and model demonstration projects focused on establishing services or gathering baseline data about these practices. Both of the editors of this book are currently receiving federal funds under the Office of Special Education Programs, research and innovation priority, for research on PSE initiatives for students with ID. A number of earlier model demonstration and outreach projects were funded in the late 1990s. Additional recent federal and state funding initiatives further reflect growing awareness of this area. In 2007, U.S. Secretary of Education Margaret Spellings delivered the following remarks at the Special Olympics Global Policy Summit in Shanghai:

> Now that we're making strong progress in K–12 schools, the next frontier is college. Especially now that higher education is becoming more and more essential for everyone in our global knowledge economy. That's why I'm pleased to announce that my department will provide 1.5 million dollars to create a Technical Assistance Center to help colleges and universities develop and expand programs for students with intellectual disabilities. By collecting and sharing information about effective coursework, supports and services, and community outreach strategies, the center will help more students enjoy a meaningful and rewarding college education.

In October 2008, this promise came to fruition, as the National Institute on Disability Rehabilitation Research, under the Department of Education, awarded a Center on Postsecondary Education for Students with Intellectual Disabilities

291

to the Institute for Community Inclusion at the University of Massachusetts and TransCen, Inc. This center will receive 3 years of funding, execute a national survey to collect data on existing PSE services, conduct secondary data analysis on three existing national data sets that include students with ID (National Longitudinal Transition Survey-2, Rehabilitation Services Administration 911, American Community Survey), and compile, create, and disseminate training and technical assistance materials to support increased access to PSE for students with ID. Simultaneously, the Administration on Developmental Disabilities awarded a different 5-year national training initiative to develop a consortium of University Centers for Excellence in Developmental Disabilities (UCEDDs). The Institute for Community Inclusion at the University of Massachusetts heads the consortium in partnership with seven UCEDDs (Delaware, Minnesota, Hawaii, South Carolina, Tennessee [Vanderbilt], Ohio, California) and the Association of University Centers on Disabilities. The consortium will conduct qualitative research with a participatory action research framework with students, families, and personnel from the institute of higher learning (IHE). It will use multimedia tools to describe each consumer's experience with PSE for students with developmental disabilities (DD), identify gaps, provide training and technical assistance to address these gaps, launch a nationwide effort to disseminate materials via the project web site (www.thinkcollege.net) and use established networks of all consortium members and the project's executive and advisory committees.

Together, these two national initiatives are designed to create sustainable change at both the national and local levels. Ideally the outcomes of these initiatives may lead to modifications in current federal legislation such as Individuals with Disabilities Education Improvement Act of 2004 (PL 108-446), the Workforce Investment Act of 1998 (PL 105-220), and the subsumed Rehabilitation Act of 1973 (PL 93-112), aligning them with the new amendments contained within the Higher Education Opportunity Act of 2008 (HEOA) (PL 110-315), which have language that includes students with ID. Overall, the HEOA contains language that provides for the creation of model demonstration programs that promote the successful transition of students with ID into higher education. Additionally, the HEOA supports the establishment of a coordinating center for technical assistance to oversee the creation and evaluation of such demonstration projects and to develop accreditation standards. The bill also contains language that would provide students enrolled in PSE initiatives access to financial aid work-study funds that they were previously prohibited from using. As this book goes to print, the HEOA awaits completion of a negotiated rule-making process and appropriations (for a more detailed discussion of the HEOA amendments, see Chapter 2). Finally, these efforts will lay a solid foundation for the future research agenda in this arena.

The issue of PSE for students with ID has finally found a voice, albeit a quiet one, on the national stage. What does this mean? The implications of such initiatives will affect states and local communities, colleges, and local school systems. Each has a stake in what will be developed and supported by these initiatives, and each will have to determine the extent to which it is interested in or willing to change its current practice, policies, and attitudes regarding postsecondary access for students with ID. For some, this will entail a complete overhaul of their current service delivery systems. For others, this will simply be an expansion of their existing practices of inclusion (at the high school level) or disability support services (at the IHE level).

State Impacts

Currently, 250 known PSE initiatives across 37 states have either dual-enrollment programs or services for students with ID. Some states have monitored and supported the creation of these programs through their state departments of education. In other states, these programs run independently through the school system or college and do not receive support or supervision at the state level. As the number of these programs increases, states will likely have to increase their monitoring of the activities and outcomes of these programs. One example of a state that has been very directive about the development of postsecondary programs for students with ID is Connecticut. In 2002–2003 the Connecticut State Department of Education (DOE) funded five local school districts with $10,000 of planning funds. Districts had up to 18 months to plan for the implementation of comprehensive transition programs in integrated, age-appropriate environments for students (aged 18–21) with disabilities. These programs served students with ID and significant learning and/or social-emotional disabilities in a program based in a college/university environment.

In 2004 the Connecticut DOE awarded each district which completed the planning process a sliver grant of $40,000 for implementation. Some of the programs established during this initiative took root and are still operating today; others were unable to continue because they had not planned for sustainability. Currently, the Connecticut DOE, in collaboration with the State Education Resource Center (SERC), continues to provide support for the existing and emerging college programs for students with ID by offering trainings and networking opportunities several times a year. The Connecticut DOE and SERC have also partnered with the PERC project at TransCen, Inc. to provide technical assistance, training, and evaluation activities for teams across the state (see Chapter 1 for a description). Finally, the Connecticut DOE and SERC hosted a recognition breakfast for the existing programs to honor the employers and colleges that are collaborating to serve students in postsecondary and community settings.

The state of California has also done considerable work to establish its infrastructure around postsecondary access for students with ID and developmental disabilities (DD). The California Consortium for PostSecondary Options for People with Developmental Disabilities and the newer initiative, Opening the Door to Postsecondary Education, are examples of a statewide consortium designed to grow and sustain PSE options for students with ID/DD (see Sidebar 10.1).

States that do not currently provide PSE options to students with ID have used a variety of strategies to generate interest. For example, in 2007 Vanderbilt University, in conjunction with a key stakeholder task force, hosted a full-day meeting to discuss PSE for students with ID and how to begin planning for and supporting students with ID in PSE. The task force was composed of representatives from the State Developmental Disabilities (DD) Council, the Vocational Rehabilitation Division, and the State Division of Mental Retardation Services. Outcomes from this stakeholder meeting included:

- The Tennessee Council on Developmental Disabilities awarded Vanderbilt University a planning and implementation grant. The leadership demonstrated at the state level by the DD Council executive director has moved the council to support such an initiative.

Sidebar 10.1: California Consortium for Postsecondary Education Options for Individuals with Developmental Disabilities

The California Consortium for Postsecondary Education Options for Individuals with Developmental Disabilities is a statewide network of 40 professionals from the developmental disabilities service system, education, and rehabilitation; parents; and students. Members include representatives from higher education (including the University of California, State University, Community College, and Continuing Education Divisions), the Department of Developmental Services and their Regional Centers, the California Department of Education, the State Council on Developmental Disabilities, school district transition coordinators and specialists, the University Center for Excellence in Developmental Disabilities, and the California Department of Rehabilitation. The consortium established the vision that by 2012, students with intellectual/developmental disabilities (ID/DD) will have the opportunity and support to pursue postsecondary learning opportunities that bring personal, social, vocational, and economic fulfillment. Consortium members share core values related to choice, equality, economic independence, and full community participation of people with DD. The consortium provides an opportunity for peer support and learning, as well as in-depth discussions of challenges, opportunities, and emerging practices and program models. Subcommittees have been established that focus on transition services, data gathering, new program development, public policy, and a future statewide conference.

Consortium Activities

In June of 2007, under the administration of the Tarjan Center at UCLA, the Consortium received an initial 12 months of funding from the California State Council on Developmental Disabilities for the Open the Doors to College Project. This grant provided the initial funding to hire designated staff to carry out some of the work of the consortium. The Open the Doors to College Project was recently awarded a new contract from the California Community College Chancellor's Office to provide technical assistance to the 110 California Community Colleges Disabled Students Programs and Services offices. The work of Open the Doors to College includes promoting public policy and systems change, gathering information about existing postsecondary program models in California, providing technical assistance to transition programs and colleges to modify existing programs or support emerging programs; and the creation of a web site with information about available PSE programs in California and resources for students, parents, and professionals. Currently the staff provide technical assistance to colleges on site as well as by telephone. In the future we will be hosting topic specific webinars. In several local communities, staff facilitate meetings with key representatives from education (transition specialists or coordinators from special education, as well as representatives from the local college), Department of Rehabilitation offices, and regional centers; students; parents; and others to encourage resource sharing, identification of community assets, and strategic planning of local PSE efforts.

Impact

1. One of the most important functions of the consortium is the regular opportunity for stakeholders to come together and address strategies being used by state and local agencies, professionals, and parents to expand opportunities and increase participation of individuals with ID/DD in PSE. Members report feeling empowered to make changes within their own programs and use their participation in the consortium to leverage additional resources and support. Within several local communities parents play a pivotal role initiating relationships and facilitating program development efforts at colleges.

2. Consortium members speak in a unified voice for change within the DD and higher education systems. Consortium members have made numerous presentations at legislative forums, during training for consumers and family members (i.e., Partners in Policymaking), and at state and regional conferences. Over the last year, representatives from the consortium had the opportunity to provide guidance and testimony to policy makers regarding state legislation aimed at reforming California's Lanterman Developmental Disabilities Services Act.*

3. California's higher education system (and community colleges in particular) are going to continue to be affected by the sheer numbers and growing desire of students with DD who want to attend college. Already there is an increased demand by community colleges for technical assistance to provide adequate instruction, supports, and services for these students. The consortium intends to continue its focus on encouraging public and state agency support for PSE, identify statewide opportunities, and provide leadership to programs to create model transition and PSE education programs.

Olivia Raynor, PhD
Wilbert Francis, MBA
Tarjan Center
University of California, Los Angeles

*Lanterman Developmental Disabilities Services Act, California Welfare and Institutions Code §§ 4500 et seq. (1969).

- A graduate student at Vanderbilt is conducting a statewide survey on what individuals with disabilities and families want in the area of PSE.
- Vanderbilt University will be a partner in the Administration on Developmental Disabilities National Training Initiative on PSE for students with ID/DD.

State legislation has also affected the development of services for students with ID in higher education. Both Massachusetts and South Carolina have funds allocated in their state budgets to support the creation of PSE initiatives, demonstrating both states' commitment, which resulted from clear efforts of the grassroots parent and legal advocacy community (see Sidebar 10.2 for language and summary from Massachusetts).

Sidebar 10.2: Line-item 7061-9600: Inclusive Concurrent Enrollment Programs for Students with Disabilities

This line item reads as follows:

For a discretionary grant pilot program with the purpose of providing monies to school districts and state public institutions of higher education partnering together to offer inclusive concurrent enrollment programs for students with disabilities as defined in section 1 of chapter 71B of the General Law ages 18-22; provided, that the grant program will be limited to said students who are considered to have severe disabilities and have been unable to achieve the competency determination necessary to pass the Massachusetts comprehensive assessment system (MCAS) exam; provided further, that said students with disabilities shall be offered enrollment in credit and noncredit courses that include nondisabled students, including enrollment in noncredit courses and credit bearing courses in audit status for students who may not meet course prerequisites and requirements, and that the partnering school districts will provide supports, services and accommodations necessary to facilitate a student's enrollment; provided further, that the department, in consultation with the department of higher education shall develop guidelines to ensure that the grant program promotes civic engagement and mentoring of faculty in state institutions of higher education, and supports college success, work success, participation in student life of the college community, and provision of a free appropriate public education in the least restrictive environment.

Source: The Official Web site of the Commonwealth of Massachusetts-Executive Office of Education FY2009 Budget Summary http://www.mass.gov/bb/gaa/fy2009/app_09/act_09/h70619600.htm

---

MODELS OF SYSTEMS CHANGE

As indicated in Chapter 5, there are some significant challenges faced by IHEs that want to support access of students with ID but also wish to maintain their level of rigor and standards of achievement. How do they balance the needs of all students? This question is already being asked at the college level as IHEs try to come to terms with a far broader definition of "diversity."

In a publication titled *Toward a Model of Inclusive Excellence and Change in Postsecondary Institutions,* Williams, Berger, and McClendon (2005) address this very topic. This paper, one of three commissioned by the Association of American Colleges and Universities, describes a model for assisting colleges and universities in expanding the diversity of their organizations at every level by integrating diversity into other quality initiatives. It is clear from this model that the blueprint for change has already been drafted. *Inclusive excellence* is a term coined by those who support change in the higher education community. It is doubtful that when these three reports were commissioned, the authors extended their definition of diversity to include students with disabilities in general; but if they did, they most likely were not intending to include students with ID. Yet the challenges faced by other groups who want diversity to be recognized as a merit to be cultivated and expanded are the same as those faced by advocates seeking to promote the inclusion of students with ID in higher education and all other aspects of adult life. There is also a growing movement across professional and disability advocacy organizations for the inclusion of individuals with disabilities in the definition of diversity, which would therefore broaden the definition of diversity (Knapp, 2007). For example, the Office of Disability and Employment Policy of the Department of Labor (2008) defines *diversity* as

> Involving the creation of an open, supportive, and responsive organization in which diversity is acknowledged and valued. Diversity is defined as all of the ways in which we differ. Some of these dimensions are race, gender, age, language, physical characteristics, disability, religion, sexual orientation, and other differences irrelevant to one's capacity to perform a job.

Moving systemic change forward will first require acknowledgment of the context from which this movement stems and then redefining key elements. The impetus for creating postsecondary options for students with ID has stemmed predominantly from the special education community and is most often spearheaded by parents. Many of the parents, teachers, and administrators who have supported students with ID, as well as the students themselves, have decided that the next step for these students should include the choice of PSE. These people are the creators and implementers of the majority of postsecondary options that currently exist. Less commonly, but happening more frequently than in the past, IHEs are initiating services for students with ID in the postsecondary setting. Often these IHEs have also received funding from a foundation or initiative that had, at its helm, a parent or advocate with an interest in promoting this educational option (see discussion of South Carolina in Chapter 2). But to succeed, those supporting these initiatives will have to cease viewing this as a *special education* initiative and start defining it in a manner that takes into account the perspective of the system from which change is sought. For K–12 school systems and higher education to collaborate in this change in a meaningful way, the process itself needs to provide outcomes valued by both systems while simultaneously engaging the larger adult service systems.

The outcomes sought by advocates of PSE options for students with ID are similar, in fact almost identical, to the outcomes sought by other groups looking to expand and institutionalize diversity in colleges and universities. Because of their convergent agendas, it is imperative that these two movements be connected and the methods used to seek those outcomes be aligned with current change initiatives in higher education.

Clayton-Pederson and Musil (2005, p. 8) write:

> One frequently can identify educational innovations, but rarely can one detect structures that link them. Accordingly, the impact of these innovations is isolated rather than pervasive. And with so many individual diversity initiatives springing up like daffodils in springtime, people long for coherence, cohesion, and collaboration. They also want to figure out how to "get it right" as they move through this astounding transition to an inclusive academy that strives for diversity and excellence.

It is incumbent upon those of us who seek to "get it right" when expanding postsecondary opportunities to students with ID to make the connection to movements that already have an infrastructure and momentum for establishing change. However, establishing partnerships with those who are also seeking change is not as easy as it might seem. First, it is necessary to articulate what is being proposed and establish that it is viable. The proposal must also be shown to align with and, more importantly, further the mission of prospective partners.

The Making Excellence Inclusive initiative of the Association of American Colleges and Universities is intended to help "institutions establish diversity as a core component in achieving desired student learning outcomes and put diversity and inclusion efforts at the center of their decision making." But how would expanding the definition of *diverse population* (currently defined as low-income, first-generation students and students of color) to include students with ID affect the institution's mission? Does it strengthen or weaken the arguments as it sees them? In their report, Williams et al. (2005) indicate that even within the current higher education system, those colleges who seek to promote access and diversity through open-door policies are seen as "lesser than" by those colleges and universities who choose not to implement such policies. This internal conflict of prejudgment based upon traditional expectations of what college "should be" makes the context for advocating additional partnerships that much more difficult. If an organization on the "inside" such as the Association of American Colleges and Universities, which represents the higher education community, suggests that higher education needs to be more inclusive, this suggestion is likely to be seen as a tolerable self-assessment and may encourage the members of that community to consider the need for change. However, if an "outsider" such as the special education or disability community makes this same suggestion, the higher education community is likely to find it intrusive and an attempt to change the essence of higher education. We must be cognizant of this "outsider" dynamic as we attempt to build a bridge connecting the potential for increased access to higher education for students with ID to the existing higher education diversity initiative.

While those seeking to expand access to PSE for students with ID may desire some changes from institutes of higher education, they are not suggesting that the current standards of higher education be replaced with a system reminiscent of the individualized education program (IEP) in secondary school. But those in the higher education community may initially take that viewpoint. Williams et al. (2005, p. 19) state:

> The perceived conflict between inclusion and excellence is asserted with no evidence, based on a dominant, industrial model of organizational values that defines excellence in terms of student inputs without consideration of value-added organizational processes. This narrow notion of excellence limits both the expansion of student educational opportunities and the transformation of educational environments.

This internal conflict between maintaining the status quo and expanding diversity initiatives will absolutely affect both the partnership with initiatives directly and the ability of IHEs to respond to direct requests.

When school systems, parents, agencies, and faculty make requests to increase access and support of students with ID in PSE, these requests should be expressed in terms of existing and established initiatives related to diversity on campus and the IHE's mission statement. This strategy promotes the initiative within a cultural context that is valued by the existing power structure and may be conducive to promoting acceptance and eventually growth of the initiative.

Representatives in Positions of Decision Making

In some cases, not only are external forces driving diversity changes in IHEs; internal forces are also at play. Staff, instructors, advisors, professors, and others in more administrative positions who personify some element of the diversity profile (race, gender, sexual orientation) are likely not only to advocate for, but also to demonstrate the outcomes of, such initiatives. Yet this also provides a conundrum for the PSE initiative for students with ID. Those seeking to address racial diversity may hope that an African American professor or dean would participate and be open to discussions of the importance of diversity on campus. But before one can seek to partner with an advocate on campus, there must actually be an advocate on campus. It is unlikely that there could be that primary level of representation for the community of students with ID. Instead those seeking access and support in higher education for students with ID will need to seek individuals who have a secondary connection to ID: the mothers, fathers, sisters, uncles, cousins, neighbors, and friends of individuals with ID. These allies are a bit more difficult to identify. And even when they are identified, it is still not a fait accompli that they will see the benefits of supporting increased access to PSE. But when these connections can be made, and a person in a decision-making position in higher education decides that students with ID should and will be included, change is more likely to occur and be sustained. This perspective is articulated by Dr. Elizabeth Blumberg, Dean of Students, Massachusetts Bay Community College:

> Isn't the essence of true education about all of us having the opportunity to learn? We all come to the academic arena with different stories. Some of us are men, some women, some white, some Latina, some gay, lesbian, straight, some very young, some very old. . . . and in the end, this is where the true learning occurs, between us. In addition, some of us learn very quickly, some less so. For some of us, memorizing all of the names and dates of history is a success, and for some of us, writing a great sentence in a college essay is a success.

We learn at our own paces, in our own ways, in our own styles. This is true education. At MassBay, including students with intellectual disabilities means that they have the opportunity to learn, to be with students their own age, and to experience college. Our program is housed in the Office of Student Development. This is purposeful. We all have the right and should have the opportunity to develop—personally, emotionally and academically. Diversity, in the true meaning of diversity, means that people of different walks of life have the opportunity to learn and grow together. And in the end, we all do learn and grow. This is a win-win dynamic for the entire community.

Transition Legislation

It is likely that this increased focus on PSE access for students with ID will eventually affect the education legislation that addresses transition. The current regulations that support IDEA require teachers to create and implement a plan for students who will be continuing on to higher education. But these plans are seldom if ever written for students who have ID, as so few students with this label are expected to attend PSE institutions (Wagner, Newman, Cameto, Garza, & Levine, 2005). While the use of IDEA funds to support students in college settings is not specifically addressed in the body of IDEA, the issue is addressed in the preamble, which includes a summary of the comments received, the Department's response to the comments, and an explanation of any changes made to the regulations that differ from the proposed regulations (US Department of Education, 2008).

From the Preamble to the Individuals with Disabilities Education Act (IDEA) Final Regulations

> Page 46668
> *Comment:* A few commenters recommended that the regulations clarify that schools can use funds provided under Part B of the Act to support children in transitional programs on college campuses and in community-based settings.
> *Discussion:* We do not believe that the clarification requested by the commenters is necessary to add to the regulations because, as with all special education and related services, it is up to each child's IEP Team to determine the special education and related services that are needed to meet each child's unique needs in order for the child to receive FAPE. Therefore, if a child's IEP Team determines that a child's needs can best be met through participation in transitional programs on college campuses or in community-based settings, and includes such services on the child's IEP, funds provided under Part B of the Act may be used for this purpose.

While it is not clear the weight these comments have when it comes to implementing such college-based transition services, the difficulty that many parents of students with ID have faced in seeking just such experiences demonstrates that this part of the regulations is not well known or sufficiently implemented. As more services become available and options continue to expand, students with ID and their families will be more likely to seek access to a PSE experience. This increased demand, coupled with the new language present in the HEOA, will undoubtedly lead to significant changes in federal and state IEP standards, transition services, and partnerships on a local level.

What will the next generation of students with ID be seeking from PSE? Will students be interested in achieving a credential or certificate? Will there be an increased demand for residential or dorm experiences? Both scenarios are likely. Many programs that did not offer dorm living to their students have put that option on their wish list, in addition to access to dorms for summer programs and holidays, and some have looked for permanent access to dorm living. Others, such as the LifeLink PSU program at Penn State University, the Mason Life Program at George Mason University, and the UCLA Pathways program, have created residential options that include both living in dorms and residing in a house on or near campus. The College Living Experience (http://www.cleinc.net) provides students with the chance to live independently near certain colleges by providing a fee-based support system. These services meet the needs of some students, but they are limited to those who can afford them, as financial aid is not currently available. As PSE options for students with ID begin to achieve some permanence, providing a full college experience could become more of a challenge. Though many of these programs are small, providing residential experiences for 10 to 12 students with ID may prove difficult. In fact, it can prove difficult for one student. Micah's story (see Sidebar 10.3) provides a snapshot of things to come: how to merge the status quo of access with the impending desire for learning from a new constituency of college life. Micah's story demonstrates that progress and growth are not always achieved by getting what you want.

Expanding Choices for Transition Services

Secondary special education services will also be affected in the future by this movement. Parents and students who are informed early on about the possibility of a college experience during the final transition years (ages 18–21) or after high school will be approaching the transition process and all it entails in a whole new way. Parents and, it is hoped, students will be seeking information about what experiences and skills will be needed to achieve success in a postsecondary environment. Teachers, transition coordinators, paraeducators, and adult service providers and agencies will need to be given information about such options so that they too can provide potential future students with the skills they need to successfully access PSE opportunities.

As PSE options become more prevalent, it behooves professionals in the field to gather consistent data about students who are referred to PSE, the level of preparation that they arrive with, and, most importantly, their outcomes. Clearly, there are lessons to be learned not only about what should come next, but also about what should happen before these students transition to the postsecondary environment and how they can be better prepared. What do they need to know? How much job exposure or training should they have been provided with between the ages of 14 and 18? The 4 to 8 years they spend in high school should provide a foundation of skills that empower students to hit the ground running in PSE. But all too often, staff in PSE settings report that these students are ill-prepared even for the basics of job placement or college course access. These students do not possess the self-determination skills that are so necessary for all students to succeed in college. They are unsure of their disabilities, have never had to advocate for needed supports, and are generally accustomed to having others make most, if not all, of their academic and employment decisions.

As more promising practices are tested and become available, it may be that college representatives will become contributors to the IEP transition team. Certainly, collaborations that involve dual enrollment, disability supports, and adult service agencies will begin to reflect the added option of supporting students with ID in postsecondary environments.

Sidebar 10.3: Detours, Not Dead Ends: Micah's Dream to Live in a Dorm

Following an hour and a half bus ride, Micah arrived home late one evening after attending an evening college course at Oakland University. He was exhausted from the long ride, but enthusiastic over his newest realization.

"If I was living in the dorm now, I wouldn't have to take two buses home. After my class, I'd just walk across the campus to my dorm. I'd be home right away and there would be other kids to hang out with." He beamed as he realized more advantages awaited him. "Then in the morning, I could sleep in, eat breakfast in the cafeteria, and walk to class." He paused and confidently concluded, "I like that idea, Mom; that's what I want to do. I want to live in the dorm."

Thus began our next new adventure of opening more doors while politely changing the collegiate system. Micah, our 23-year-old son with cognitive impairments, is part of the new wave of adults with intellectual disabilities who are attending college courses and experiencing campus life as fully included students and citizens. His experience as a college student occurs at Oakland University in Rochester, Michigan, with the support of the Options Program.

Being a college student over the past few years has expanded Micah's knowledge of what's possible and what options exist for him. During his first years as a commuting student, Micah felt little urge to live anyplace but home. He hardly knew what a dorm was and couldn't imagine not sleeping in his own bedroom. If asked, he would adamantly say, "One day I want to live with my friends, but not *now*!"

Learning About Choices

However, the more he hung out with his college friends, the more he learned about campus life. He watched them walk back to the dorms. He listened to their stories of limitless ice cream every night in the cafeteria, with no parents looking over their shoulders. He began to understand that if he lived in a dorm he'd be surrounded by young people his age—again, no parents. During a tour of the dorm and while visiting friends, he saw the layout of the rooms, the location of the beds, the computers on the desks, and how to get to the cafeteria and lounge.

His emerging discoveries reminded me that giving people choices (*Do you want to live at home or in the dorm?*) is not enough. Micah had to be exposed to the possibilities before he could make authentic choices. He needed time and real-life experiences to imagine a different life for himself. By living the life of a college student, new opportunities naturally emerged over time.

But as any family who has a child with a disability knows, making a choice does not automatically make dreams come true. You have to proceed with confidence *and* expect the unexpected. A lot of hard work has gone into making Micah's dream to live with his college friends in a dorm match the policies of the university. Unfortunately, his happy ending of living on campus has not materialized yet, but his dream is moving forward.

Micah's first hopes took shape when he received an e-mail from the University Housing Department informing him that his dorm application was accepted. He was given the move-in date of January 6, 2008. He immediately asked a friend for help to complete the next phase of paperwork. He "borrowed" the $100 deposit from us and then proudly delivered it with his paperwork to the housing office. Later that night, he e-mailed his sister, Emma, using his voice-to-text technology. Emma already had one semester of dorm living under her belt. "I'm next, Emma," he wrote. "You have to buy me a new poster for my dorm room, like I bought you one."

We marked "Micah's Moving Date" on the calendar and prepared as best we could for this new and enormous change in our lives. His confidence and excitement grew with each box he packed.

The Detours

A few weeks later, an unexpected early morning e-mail brought the message that blocked him from achieving his dream and sent him on a detour. It said that because of some "overlooked university policy," he did not qualify to live in the dorm.

"I'm going on a hunger strike on campus," Micah's dad responded immediately. We were all deeply disappointed. We knew how important it was for Micah to move into the dorm. He had worked toward this dream for more than 3 years. It was in his bones, and he was ready.

It happened that Micah had scheduled his annual person-centered planning (PCP) meeting for the next day. This meeting is designed to help him identify his goals and supports for the upcoming year. Micah arranged the meeting to include about 15 people, including several college friends, the Associate Dean of Education, some professionals on his PCP team, and the Director of the Student Activities Center where Micah volunteers. They met in a small room in the university center with five large pizzas. He welcomed everyone and used his prepared notes to guide him.

Micah shared his accomplishments during the year, which included raising the most money for St. Jude Hospital and joining Alpha Phi Omega, the service coed fraternity. He then asked each person to offer a quick story of what they see as his achievements and his strengths. As Micah's world gradually expands beyond ours, it helps to hear how he is perceived and what roles he takes in his community. We heard about the contributions he is making in his student organizations, how his friends value his great sense of humor, and how he responsibly shows up at his volunteer job ready to work. Those vignettes are critical in helping us, as parents who let go a bit more each day. The observations from Micah's community let us know if he is finding his place and how others relate with him. We can see what natural supports are in place and what gaps might occur, both now and down the road.

We were grateful when the director of the student activities center shared that Micah needed more challenges at his volunteer job. Here was someone who had great expectations for him and wanted to see him enhance his skills. As parents, we felt less alone in our pursuit of high standards for Micah. The team was able to creatively solve problems and identify a few other tasks that Micah could learn. One student volunteered to coach Micah with these tasks.

(continued)

You Gotta Have Friends

As always, his friends—some of whom had known Micah for only a couple of months—proved to be the most important resources and problem solvers. Over the years we have learned that any planning meeting should not be dominated in numbers or ideas by well-meaning professionals, who often are removed from Micah's everyday world and less likely to make authentic connections or identify real-life solutions.

When we discussed the dorm issue, it was easy to see everyone's frustration. Rather than sink into doom and despair, several students (some hired by Micah as personal assistants and some buddies from campus) asked what they could do to convince the university that their decision was dead wrong. One student decided to write a letter to the university president, asking him to immediately reverse the decision. The other students joined the chorus. Inspired, Micah said he would collect the letters and recruit other students to join in the writing campaign. The sparks of hope were igniting and unifying the group.

During the meeting, I asked Micah if he'd be interested in staying overnight once a week with a friend who lived in student housing. I didn't know if Micah would want to do this or if a friend would come forward, but I felt compelled to find alternative ways to help Micah achieve his dream. I knew that one night a week wasn't the same as living in the dorm full time, but it might be a small step, a detour toward his dream. Micah said, "Absolutely yes," which was immediately followed by one of his fraternity friends offering the place. "Micah, you can stay with me. You've been at our apartment before, so you know the scene. What's the best night?"

As if remembering his first realization about the benefits of dorm living, Micah said, "Tuesday night I have a late class, so I can just walk over to your apartment in student housing. Tuesday's the night!"

"No, you don't have to walk home, Micah," his friend offered. "It'll be dark. I can pick you up after your class." Now I knew why this student's nickname was "Buddha." In less than 30 minutes, several interim strategies were identified—all by Micah and his friends. Once again, I witnessed his community—the "village" working.

Learning What Advocacy Looks Like in Real Life

In addition to staying over once a week in student housing with a friend, Micah became actively involved in appealing the decision barring him and other students who have cognitive disabilities from living in the dorm. He met on his own with the Vice President of Student Affairs to discuss her decision and to review the so-called policy that denies him the opportunity to live in the dorm. Micah prepared for this meeting by talking with university faculty and students to discuss the content and the best approach to take with her. He was not deterred, even after she indicated that the decision would not be changed. He then presented himself at the Oakland University Board of Trustees meeting, asking them to review and appeal the administrator's decision. At the meeting, he said, "I can be more active on campus if I live in the dorm. I pay tuition for my classes . . . I want to be like all regular college students. . . . It will help me learn to live more independently. . . . Everyone should be able to have a full education, and the chance to live in [campus residence] is part of that education."

The Student Community Gets Involved

The student campus has backed Micah. He has collected over 1,000 signatures on petitions from students saying he should have the right to live in the dorm. The staff editorial of *The Oakland Post*, the student newspaper, endorsed Micah's appeal to live in the university residence halls. Micah has reached out to Michigan Protection and Advocacy, members of the State Board of Education, several public officials, and numerous disability activists and student organizations. He is learning the importance of working with others and being persistent. In addition, he has deepened his understanding of what it means to be discriminated against, as well as what it takes to fight discrimination. He knows that he is not alone and that fighting against discrimination is always the right thing to do, even if you don't win the battle. He said, "If the university does not let me live in the dorm, it is their loss."

Lessons We Are Learning as Micah Enters Adulthood

In some ways, they are many of the same lessons that we've been practicing and relearning, and practicing and relearning throughout the first two decades of his life.

- *Our primary goal, especially as Micah moves into adulthood, is to support and strengthen his <u>interdependence</u>.* Let's face it—no one is truly independent, and in fact that is not what I desire for myself, my children, my neighborhood, or my world. Our success as a people depends on our ability to build community and connections.
- *To have dreams you must have real-life experiences.* Micah had to be a college student attending classes and navigating the campus before he could dream of dorm living.
- *Circles of support must invite, value, and engage peers.* The professionals and parents have to learn to "sit on their mouths" (Roman, 2003) and allow Micah's real community to find solutions and offer supports. This may require some expert facilitation and nudging to keep the conversation going, but it doesn't imply dominating the discussion.
- *Remember that a person's confidence is strengthened when his or her abilities are publicly recognized and expectations start high, and then reach higher.* When Micah heard that his friends were going to write letters to the university president, he was inspired to self-advocate and seek out other students to write letters. He is actively joining in the campaign for equal housing! And he was taking on leadership skills he hadn't tried before.
- *Never stop inviting and asking for help and ideas from a wide variety of perspectives.* I had no idea that someone would come forth with an invitation to have Micah stay overnight on a weekly basis, but because he took the risk and asked, the door opened and stayed opened! Buddha came forth, and now Micah stays every Tuesday with him. He loves his Tuesday nights with his college friends.

(continued)

- *Paid supports can make genuine connections that expand the circle of support.* There's a perception in the disability field that paid supports are "bad" and natural supports are "good." In reality, all supports can be instrumental in creating and nurturing authentic experiences and connections. Micah had many of his college buddies at the PCP meeting in part because one student he hired, an active student leader, had introduced Micah to many people and organizations.

- *Relationships must be intentional and strategic.* Many people without disabilities have the ability to make connections wherever they go with very little effort. But for many people with disabilities, relationships must be fostered over time and may have to start with very intentional, almost artificial, mechanisms, such as Best Buddies, lunch groups, and peer tutoring. But rich and authentic relationships can develop out of these intentional relationship-building strategies. Micah has experienced this over and over—his social calendar is very full!

- *Parents can move from the role of caregiver to that of coach or mentor when others in the community provide practical support, encouragement, and resources.* Until others show up, parents can't sit down.

- *Our children really do learn by example.* Over the years, Micah has watched us regularly ask for help from others (though it wasn't easy to do!). We learned to reach out to others, invite them into Micah's circle, and provide them with concrete, practical suggestions for supporting Micah and his dreams. Micah watched and learned about self-advocacy from his family and from many other mentors. He now sends e-mails, makes phone calls, and invites others to hang out with him.

- *Serve food at all settings! This needs no explanation.*

The Journey Continues

At this moment in time, there is no happily-ever-after ending of eating ice cream and living in the dorm. Micah, his family, and his circle are working to change the recent decision against Micah living in the dorm. Meetings are planned and strategies are being devised. Through it all, Micah knows that he is not alone. He is a genuine part of a community that cares about him and supports him. Nor is it a one-way deal. Micah too gets involved with his friends' dreams as well. Currently he is campaigning vigorously for one of his friends who is running for president of student government.

Micah has learned a lot from this experience—both disappointments and validation. He has learned what discrimination feels like, but he has also learned how to advocate and engage others to support his dream, and to never give up. His efforts took him on a path to Buddha, even if for only one night a week. Maybe that's true enlightenment!

Janice Fialka is Micah's mother. She is also a social worker, national speaker, author, and advocate. To read more of her publications and learn about her talks, visit www.danceofpartnership.com or e-mail her at ruaw@aol.com.

(This sidebar is from Fialka, J. *Detours, Not Dead Ends: Micah's Dream to Live in a Dorm.* In *Connections*, a publication of TASH, May/June 2008, pp. 25–27; reprinted by permission.)

As we move toward these changes, it will be important to determine priorities and what can be accomplished within the context of PSE. All of the skills outlined in Chapter 7 as goals of such experiences remain pertinent. However, if we also desire systems change, we will need to provide additional documentation about the promise and potential of PSE for students with ID.

Clearly there is a historical disconnect between K–12 education and higher education when it comes to standards of practice, documentation of disabilities, accommodations, and support. It is imperative that this disconnect be remedied, because it has the potential to derail the progress made on behalf of students with ID in PSE. There are options currently available, and most likely more in the planning stages, for separate life skills, independent living programs, or transition programs based on college campuses that will provide access to instruction and support related to independence and employment. These programs focus on important skills and can lead to good outcomes for students and their families. However, they are not about postsecondary access or higher education. They are not about teaching students how to navigate adult learning options, and they cannot be seen as the only option for students with ID. It will be important not to replicate some of the mistakes we have made in the past in the name of "special" education and we must be mindful of the struggles faced by those creating integrated services in adult systems, especially competitive employment. Few would argue that more segregated programs and services should be created in our K–12 education system or in the adult service systems. Legislation, policy, and practice have evolved consistently toward supporting people with disabilities in integrated living, working, and learning environments. Yet as we approach this new learning environment of higher education, it would be all too easy to revert to a separate system for students with ID. However, the more inclusive the PSE option is, and the more natural supports that are available, the greater the likelihood that students will learn the skills being taught in the actual environment in which they will use the skill.

Overall, PSE for students with ID is about accessing new learning opportunities that ideally will enhance students' employment and career outcomes, provide them with a foundation to develop needed life skills in natural environments, simply give them personal enrichment, and teach them to take advantage of further learning opportunities as their life unfolds. We espouse the need for lifelong learning over and over again. Yet without providing students with ID access to experiences that allow them to develop the skills necessary to access lifelong learning, we are stating support for an empty promise.

Clearly articulating the anticipated outcomes of a PSE experience is critical to helping those who are not familiar with students with ID to understand what is to be achieved. Just allowing students with ID on a college campus might evoke, "Sure, that's nice that they do that," from the average outsider. However, the staff, instructors, and professors at the college must be provided with consistent information about the purpose and outcome of these experiences to gain not only their understanding but also their support. Support from IHE personnel will be essential to the future success of students with ID in PSE, just as it is for other students. As evidence is amassed to convey that purpose, we will find a greater level of acceptance, support, and connection to that mission. We must partner with those who have the power to set the agenda. As Williams et al. (2005, p.16) suggest for those seeking greater diversity,

With regard to the transformational change needed to make excellence inclusive, proponents must address political realities in meaningful and strategic ways, identifying sources of formal and informal power and working to align them in support of these efforts. Sources of formal power include boards of trustees, administrators, and other positions of authority, but care needs to be taken to also consider informal sources of power based on seniority, race and gender, charisma, ability to bring in external resources, and other factors.

Systemic change requires a multilayered approach and thus the support not only of college leaders, but also of professors, instructors, staff, students, and all others who make college what it is. They will require different approaches, different perspectives to help them to see not only what is of value in the process for students with ID, but also what is in it for themselves. The following illustrates how things changed for one professor.

During a presentation to the Steering Governance Committee at Mass Bay Community College, many faculty posed questions about how the inclusion of students with ID worked in practice. One faculty member, who had experience with a student with an intellectual disability spoke up: "When I first met Taylor and had him and his coach in class, I was apprehensive. As the semester moved on, I was continually impressed. His attendance was perfect, he worked hard to complete every assignment. In the final group presentations to the class, I began to realize, working with him made the whole class a better place. . . . He asked questions that some students were afraid to ask and caused us all to reflect on what it means to work as a community."

There is an organic quality to the proposition of supporting students in PSE that seems to grow of its own accord when approached in a certain way. We talk about partnerships and agreements and memoranda of understanding, but what we are really asking for is a chance for students with ID to experience what others who go to college experience: a time to redefine themselves in society, seek learning that is self-directed, have the opportunity to succeed and fail, and use both experiences to learn about what they want to do in the future. The indicators of quality at the college level are in the eye of the beholder. Students with ID who participate will have many different experiences and their own level of knowledge about themselves—what they like or don't like, what they want to do with their time, who they like to spend time with, and how they see their future. This time of growth is one that most college students take for granted. And it is one that most students with ID, until quite recently, have never been given the choice of participating in.

Implications for Students

Students with ID have the most to gain from accessing PSE experiences; however, their voice is often unheard when it comes to advocating for this experience. Students are often unaware of the planning, negotiating, and difficulties faced by those trying to create access. Students also too often indicate a level of satisfaction with their current services because they do not have anything with which to compare them.

As the possibility of accessing PSE becomes more widely accepted and available, students with ID will need to become more aware of the rewards and responsibilities associated with gaining access to a PSE. They will need to rise to expectations associated with adult living and the code of conduct of the IHE that they are attending. These students cannot be expected to be the only catalysts for change. Students need to do their best and then take these experiences with them as they move on to their adult lives, as is expected of any other student. It would be easy to say that those who have paved the way should visit high schools, tell people about their experience, and motivate other students to try, but this should not be the role of these students unless they desire it. Most students who have gone to college typically do not visit their high school to talk to others about it unless they are at a reunion. That was someone else's job.

Given the right supports and expectations, students with ID should retain the abilities that they cultivated in PSE and use them across all aspects of their lives. Students should continue to access adult learning opportunities whenever the need or interest arises.

Implications for Research and Practice

One reported benefit of supporting students with ID on IHE campuses is that their presence on campus provides faculty and graduate students with additional research and applied practice opportunities. However, this particular "benefit" requires careful consideration of how students with ID, families, and instructional staff are approached to participate in such experiences. Not only must we ensure that human subject protections are in place, but as we approach various stakeholder groups to participate in such research, we must also maintain a high level of respect and appreciation for their participation. We must avoid using groups of students with ID on campus as convenient samples that can be used as needed to fill voids in either research or practicum placements, mentoring, or volunteering experiences for typical college students.

The reciprocity that was mentioned as so vital to the initial negotiations to create access and services in PSE initiatives for students with ID is also essential when we address research. The experiences of students with ID in all of the PSE models mentioned in this book are rife with opportunities for college faculty and students looking to conduct single-subject research, implement and analyze qualitative designs, or ascertain various levels of participation and outcomes via quantitative measures. But it cannot be assumed that because students with ID and/or the programs serving them are on campus that they are fair game to be used to meet the research needs of an individual or the university. Institutional Review Boards (IRBs) that review research proposals that involve human subjects, must ensure that students with ID are not coerced in any way or made to feel awkward, uncomfortable, or more labeled. If college is the first place that students with ID have been able to cast themselves in a new and less stigmatizing light, we need to ensure that our research agenda is supportive of these students' goal of seeking to redefine themselves.

There are currently a number of doctoral students working on topics related to PSE for students with ID as their dissertation topics. This bodes well, as this will likely foster a number of quality research articles and broaden the research agenda in this area. In some cases such research can lead to new learning opportunities for students with ID. A recent dissertation, *Inclusion In Postsecondary Education: Phenomenological Study On Identifying And Addressing Barriers To Inclusion Of Individuals With Significant Disabilities At A Four-Year Liberal Arts College* conducted by Dedra Hafner (2008), detailed the process of creating an inclusive program for students with ID on the campus of Edgewood College. In addition, the Association of University Centers on Disabilities (AUCD), as part of the new Administration on Developmental Disabilities National Consortium initiative, is going to work with the national network of UCEDDs to support their trainees who are conducting research in this area.

Finally, the Individuals with Disabilities Education Improvement Act of 2004 (PL 108-446) requires school districts to assist students with disabilities in transition planning by including their postschool goals in education, employment, and community living in their IEP/individualized transition plan and that those goals guide the development of the goals and objects on the student's IEP (Indicator 13). Indicator 14 requires school districts to collect postschool outcome data on all students with disabilities 1 year after they leave school. Indicators 13 and 14 in State Performance plans for school districts and related personnel could have positive implications, because PSE for students with ID can lead to more student-directed transition planning and yield better student outcomes.

SUMMARY

This is an incredibly exciting time in education for all students, family members, and professionals, as the next frontier for students with ID is being addressed and the field is figuring out how to create access to a PSE for a student population that has been, for the most part, excluded from this choice. As indicated throughout this book and this chapter, many disciplines are challenged with creating greater access to and support in PSE for under- and unserved student populations, including students with ID. As the national research and training and technical assistance projects unfold, related legislation is implemented (HEOA, 2008), and new laws are reauthorized, it will be important to have an eye to the future. The following are recommendations to keep in mind, but they should not limit our future vision; they are offered only as areas to consider as this movement moves forward:

- Develop a certificate or credential that students receive upon completion of a PSE option—Align with existing certificates of occupational proficiency.
- Establish criteria for payback of student loans—Consider waiving payback of student loan if students are competitively employed. Model it on the waiver of scholarship/stipend for educators who stay in the profession.
- Research effectiveness of other models, such as Gear Up, which starts working with students in middle school.
- Create access for students with ID to ensure their participation in commencement ceremonies at IHEs.
- Create policies and practices that promote greater access to integrated housing on and off campus, including participation in fraternities and sororities.
- Give students with ID the option of transferring credits to another IHE.

- Create access to integrated study abroad.
- Assist students in the development of social networks, including dating, safe lifestyles, risk taking, and so on.
- Create access to participation in student government.
- Ensure access to participation in religious offerings (e.g., Newman Centers, Hillel).
- Ensure alumni status and related activities.

Creating access to PSE for individuals with ID is a win-win situation for all involved. Students' self-esteem skyrockets, and they learn skills needed to be valued members of their local community. Overall, the attitudes of faculty, secondary and postsecondary professionals, family members, students, and employers can be transformed. The IHE community becomes more understanding and accepting of individual differences of everyone in the community, embracing a definition of diversity that includes all. Supporting students with ID to access PSE is not just about delivering services in a particular environment; more importantly, it is about the type of community that can be more universally designed. It is about making learning, in all forms, available and accessible to those who desire it.

The information in this book provides various perspectives on the foundations of creating PSE experiences for students with ID, reviews existing research, relates the experiences of key participants and stakeholders, and shares some of the lessons we have learned as we have sought to implement and improve access to such experiences. However, there is so much more that we have yet to discover. It is likely that some readers will find the answers to their questions herein, while others may say, "But what about. . . .??"

It is our hope that this book is the first of many to come on the topic of postsecondary education options for student with ID. There is so much potential for others to contribute to our current knowledge base about this developing realm of practices. The world of PSE provides a nexus for so many areas of study—transition, self-determination, employment, higher education, general, and special education. As the bridges between these lines of inquiry and practice become stronger and more frequently traveled, our ability to see where they might lead will become clearer. We must strive not merely to find the right answer, but to find *lots* of right answers, and to keep questioning how we can make these experiences better, more meaningful, and ultimately connect them to the positive outcomes sought by all. We encourage everyone to continue to ask the question, "But what about . . . ?" The future can only profit from our continued commitment to question the status quo.

REFERENCES

Briel, L., & Getzel, E.E. (2009). Postsecondary options for students with autism. In P. Wehman, M. Datlow Smith, & C. Schall (Eds). *Autism and the transition to adulthood: success beyond the classroom* (pp. 189-206). Baltimore: Paul H. Brookes.

Clayton-Pederson, A., & Musil, C. (2005). *Making excellence inclusive: Preparing students and campuses for an era of greater expectations.* Introduction to the series. Washington, DC: Association of American Colleges and Universities.

Hafner, D. (2008). *Inclusion in postsecondary education: Phenomenological study on identifying and addressing barriers to inclusion of individuals with significant disabilities at a four-year liberal arts college.* Doctoral Dissertation retrieved February 27, 2009, from http://innovationsnow.net/ InclusionResearch.html

Higher Education Opportunity Act of 2008, Pub. L. No. 110-315, § 122 STAT. 3078 (2008).

Individuals with Disabilities Education Improvement Act of 2004, PL 108-446, 20 U.S.C. §§ 1400 *et seq.*

Knapp, S. (2007). *Practical suggestions for academic unions.* Albany, NY: United University Professions. Disability Rights and Concerns Committee. Retrieved June 20, 2008, from United University Professions web site: http://www.uuphost.org/committees/disability/ uup_ada.html

Lanterman Developmental Disabilities Services Act, California Welfare and Institutions Code §§ 4500 et seq. (1969).

Rehabilitation Act of 1973, PL 93-112, 29 U.S.C. §§ 701 *et seq.*

Roman, C.P. (2003). "It's not always easy to sit on your mouth" *Social Work with Groups, 25* (1/2), 61–64.

U.S. Department of Education. (2008, November). The Negotiated Rulemaking Process for Title IV Regulations: Frequently Asked Questions. Retrieved November 15, 2008, from http://www.ed.gov/policy/highered/reg/hearulemaking/hea08/neg-reg-faq.html

U.S. Department of Labor, Office of Disability Policy. (2008, November). Diversity and Disabilities. Retrieved November 12, 2008, from http://www.dol.gov/odep/pubs/ek96/ diverse.htm

Wagner, M., Newman, L., Cameto, R., Garza, N., & Levine, P. (2005). *After high school: A first look at the postschool experiences of youth with disabilities.* A Report from the National Longitudinal Transition Study-2 (NLTS2). Menlo Park, CA: SRI International.

Welkowitz, L., & Baker, L., (2005). *Supporting college students with Asperger's syndrome.* Mahwah, NJ: Lawrence Erlbaum Associates.

Williams, D.A., Berger, J.B., & McClendon, S.A. (2005). *Toward a model of inclusive excellence and change in postsecondary institutions.* Washington, DC: Association of American Colleges and Universities.

Workforce Investment Act of 1998, PL 105-220, 29 U.S.C. §§ 2801 *et seq.*

Index

Tables and figures are indicated by *t* or *f*, respectively.